THE QUEEN'S CORSAIR

THE QUEEN'S CORSAIR

Drake's journey of circumnavigation
1577-1580

by

ALEXANDER McKEE

SOUVENIR PRESS

Printed in Great Britain by
Ebenezer Baylis and Son Ltd,
The Trinity Press, Worcester, and London

CONTENTS

Foreword   7

PART ONE

1   *'Famous and Rich Discoveries'*   15
The Genesis of a Venture: 1573–7

2   *'A Beastlike People'*   29
From Plymouth to the Cape Verdes:
15 November 1577–1 February 1578

3   *'Thou Art Not the General's Friend'*   42
From the 'Burning Isle' to the Coast of Brazil:
2 February–6 April 1578

4   *'An Enemy to the Voyage'*   58
From the River of Silver to the Gibbets of St Julian:
6 April–20 June 1578

5   *A Battle with Giants*   73
Port St Julian: 20–30 June 1578

6   *'Lo! Here is an End to Traitors!'*   83
The Trial of Thomas Doughty:
Port St Julian: 30 June–2 July 1578

7   *'Island of Blood'*   95
Port St Julian: 2 July–17 August 1578

8   *'The Uttermost Cape'*   106
The Strait of Magellan to 57° South:
20 August–1 November 1578

9   *Eaten Alive*   122
On the Coast of Chile:
1 November 1578–19 January 1579

10   *'A General Dislike of the Voyage'*   136
The Return of the *Elizabeth* to Brazil:
October 1578–February 1579

PART TWO

11 '*Too Late by Two Hours!*'   145
The Balance of Forces – Tarapaca to Lima:
4–15 February 1579

12 '*Frenchmen! Frenchmen!*'   160
The Attack at Lima and Spanish Counter-Measures:
February 1579

13 *The Hanging of the Halfbreed Boy*   172
From Callao to Cape San Francisco:
16 February–1 March 1579

14 '*Strike Sail!*'   182
San Juan de Anton and his Treasure Ship:
1–18 March 1579

15 '*The Way that Half-Dead Men Act*'   198
Pursuit from Peru: 28 February–13 April 1579
Precautions at Cartagena: April–May 1579

16 *The Last Prizes*   213
Costa Rica to Nicaragua: 18 March–6 April 1579

17 *The 'Atrocity' at Guatalco*   230
Mexico: 13–17 April 1579

18 '*By Fair or Foul Means*'   247
In New Spain and Peru: April–July 1579

PART THREE

19 *A New England*   265
The Pacific and 'Nova Albion': 17 April–25 July 1579

20 *The Shoals of Celebes*   275
The Pacific: 25 July–30 September 1579
The Islands: 30 September 1579–26 March 1580
Africa: 21 May–24 July 1580
Plymouth: 26 September 1580

21 '*Master Thief of the Unknown World*'   288
Homecoming and its Aftermath: 1580–1662

Sources   307

Index   313

FOREWORD

AN Englishman living in an English house built in the 1920s
might find little difference if he had to move into an equivalent home constructed in the sixteenth century, although perhaps the poor indoor lighting might be tiresome on winter evenings.
It would be the world outside which would take getting used to.

The bulk of the population lived in the countryside, not in
towns. There were not many of them – only about three and a half
million in England and Wales, or about one person for every ten
there are today. Only a tiny part of Ireland around Dublin was
under English control and Scotland was a small hostile kingdom,
allied with France.

With thirteen million people, France was immensely more
populous. Because of her geographical position she was the traditional rival of England; for centuries the two nations had raided
each other across the Channel. Towards the end of Henry VIII's
reign, France had sent a great armada of 235 ships and some
thirty thousand men to invade England; thousands had got ashore
briefly, in five different places.

To counter France, England usually allied herself with Spain
or Germany, or both. Indeed, Henry VIII's first Queen was
Spanish, while his daughter Mary was to marry a Spanish prince,
Philip II. But slowly the power balance changed. France became
weakened by civil and religious divisions. Spain, having expelled
the last of the Moors from Granada by 1492, in the process of
becoming a united kingdom of some six and a half million souls,
had in the same year sent Columbus westwards across the Atlantic
in search of a short sea route to Japan, China and the Spice Islands.

The economic basis for the project was a demand to reopen the
high-priced luxury goods trade with the Far East which had
been interrupted by the expansion of Islam and the capture of

7

Constantinople in 1453. The known, mainly overland route having been blocked by the Turks, the only alternative was to send ships out into the unknown. The most important of the commodities concerned were Chinese silks, spices and gold. Spices were prized because winter food was so unpalatable; and gold, of course, was currency.

The Portuguese had spent the best part of a century working their way past Cape Bojador and down the African continent, setting up bases further and further south. By 1442, having occupied the Azores, Madeira and the Cape Verde Islands, they were bringing back African gold to pump into their financial system. But it was not until 1487 that Díaz actually rounded Africa and another ten years after that before a Portuguese ship reached India. The pioneers consistently met adverse winds which could cause fatal delays to vessels capable of carrying only restricted supplies of food and water. They triumphed only when they had dared and understood the wind system of the South Atlantic, which required them to sail almost to the as-yet-undiscovered coast of South America before turning south-east towards the tip of Africa. For a sailing ship, the shortest route between two points is often much the longest way round, geographically.

Officially, Brazil was not sighted by the Portuguese until 1500, shortly after Columbus had discovered Cuba (believing it to be Japan), but it is likely that its presence was at least suspected some years before that.

To avoid an open clash between the rival Iberian sea powers, the far-sighted Pope Alexander VI had proposed a scheme to divide the world into two spheres of influence, one Spanish, one Portuguese. As Alexander was a Spanish Borgia with obligations to the Spanish Crown, the Portuguese refused to accept his proposals in detail. The Treaty of Tordesillas, negotiated in 1494, gave Portugal a larger land area in The Americas which included Brazil, shortly to be discovered.

The world was now divided by an apparently simple north–south line around the globe. Everything to the east belonged to Portugal, everything to the west was Spain's. Navigators could place the Atlantic line with fair precision, but as no one knew how wide the world was, the way the line ran on the far side of the globe was strictly hypothetical. Did the Spice Islands belong to Spain or to Portugal? That would be the question.

The other maritime powers – the Netherlands, France, England – came almost nowhere. In theory, they were left out. In practice, the Iberians would be too busy to challenge probes in the far north. So the English and the Dutch both tried for routes going around the top of the globe – the North-East Passage and the North-West Passage.

Their reasoning can be appreciated only by studying a globe or a specialised map. The popular modern map projection, while depicting the Tropics with tolerable accuracy, badly distorts the far north. We now know that the North-West Passage around Canada is not a commercial proposition even yet, but that the North-East Passage around Russia certainly exists for a nation deploying nuclear-powered icebreakers. In the sixteenth century, both these routes were dead ends, but the have-not powers, late and left out, had no alternatives – unless, of course, there was a southern route around the world. Most of the geographers maintained that there was not – that a vast southern continent barred the way. No one had been there to find out, but the experts were adamant. The name they gave it, misleading for moderns, was *terra australis incognita*, by which they meant undiscovered lands to the south. In fact, it was a combination of Australia, Antarctica, and Imagination.

Not unnaturally, the pioneering sea powers actively discouraged outsiders and freeloaders such as the English from entering the territories they had won, even on peaceful missions. For instance, in 1527, when Spain and England were allies and Henry VIII had a Spanish queen, a large English warship which entered Santo Domingo in Hispaniola for provisions was fired on and forced to leave. The captain had a rather unlikely story that he had been engaged on a voyage of northern exploration, and not all the local Spaniards wanted to see him driven off; but the Caribbean was a Spanish preserve and the authorities were merely carrying out their orders.

Later on, when the Spanish colonists had killed off most of the local available labour, they were prepared to buy slaves illegally from the English, and businessmen like Hawkins and Drake were forward in supplying them. In 1568 this risky and unpleasant trade was to bring on a really large-scale clash between an English and a Spanish fleet.

By now Ferdinand Magellan, a Portuguese in the employ of Spain, had proved what many had suspected; that Columbus had been sadly mistaken. By discovering a southern route and then circumnavigating the globe in 1519–22 this Spanish-backed fleet had shown that the world was far larger than Columbus had proclaimed; that the Atlantic was a small place compared to the vastness of the Pacific – indeed, fatally large for the crews, most of whom died there. Magellan's venture was the greatest journey of exploration ever made, not merely up to that time, but ever since. It is possible that it never will be surpassed.

Columbus had been proved wrong in his calculations, but he had not failed. His principal objective had been wealth, particularly in the form of gold and other precious metals. When the Spaniards burst into Mexico and Peru they did indeed find gold in plenty, and then, in 1545 at Potosí and in 1548 in Mexico, vast deposits of silver were located. These riches, the raw material of currency, fuelled an expansionist and aggressive Spanish foreign policy which enabled Spain to become an influential and dominant power. They paid her army holding down the Netherlands and fighting the Dutch rebels, uncomfortably close to London and the Thames; and in 1580 they allowed her the force to easily overrun Portugal and thus combine in one kingdom the seaborne empires of both east and west.

It was in the interests of the smaller powers such as England to trim this over-mighty empire somewhat, preferably short of an open, all-out conflict. This was the tightrope which England's statesmen cautiously walked during much of Elizabeth's reign; until 1588, when Spanish power proved not to be so mighty after all.

The undeclared diplomatic conflict was compounded by the religious hatreds then dividing Europe into the forces of Reform and Counter-Reform; and also by Spanish arrogance, which the English much resented, being themselves not entirely free of this sin. And in the eyes of many Englishman, there was no difference between the Spanish state and the Catholic church.

In fact, some of the most spirited criticisms of Spanish colonial policy came from the church and were published in Spain. For instance, Fray Alonso de Espinosa, condemning the way in which the Spaniards had early on taken over the Canary Islands as an advanced base in their maritime rivalry with Portugal, wrote:

'It is an acknowledged fact, both as regards divine and human right, that the wars waged by the Spaniards against the natives of these islands, as well as against the Indians in the western regions [i.e., the Caribbean and South America], were unjust and without any reason to support them. For the natives had not taken the lands of Christians, nor had they gone beyond their own frontier to molest or invade their neighbours. If it is said that the Spaniards brought the Gospel, this should have been done by admonition and preaching, not by drum and banner; by persuasion, not by force.'

And he saw how, in a lost battle at Tenerife, 'God saw fit to chastise the haughtiness and pride of the Spaniards, exceeding that of all other nations.' Nevertheless, his work was published in Seville in 1594.

When Hernán Cortés, the future conqueror of Mexico, arrived in Hispaniola in 1504 and was offered land, he replied indignantly: 'But I came to get gold, not to till the soil like a peasant.' One could indeed become rich for life in a few years, but only by surviving against deadly odds and enduring hardships far beyond the normal. A desire for fame as well as wealth undoubtedly drove many of the explorers and conquerors: and something more, difficult to define.

The Portuguese poet Luis de Camões, who himself took part in mid-sixteenth-century voyages, imagined the scene at Lisbon in 1497 when Vasco de Gama set out for the Cape.

'The mariners are torn both ways; they want to go but are still tied to the land. A son hears his mother calling, another man is implored by his wife. Friends and neighbours say they are throwing themselves away. If it's fame they want, that's a myth. If it's glory they need, battle with the Moors nearer home will more easily supply it; and wealth, too, if they take a Moorish city. They are wasting their lives. They are needed at home. But, says Camões, the sailors' resolution only falters at that moment when finally the lines are cast off from the quay, the ship moves out, and the fluttering hands of dear ones wave goodbye for the last time. Then, they are blind with grief. It doesn't last. By nightfall the hills and bays of home are sunk down beneath the horizon and only the future beckons.'

So must they all have felt, Portuguese, Spaniard, Fleming, Englishman.

PART ONE

Chapter 1

'FAMOUS AND RICH DISCOVERIES'

The Genesis of a Venture:
1573–7

FOR four days they had trudged upwards through the tree belt. Underneath it was as pleasantly cool as England in summer. So close were the trunks, so thick their branches, that only a few rays of the tropical sun could penetrate.

There were eighteen Englishmen and twenty-six local Cimarrons in the main party. The latter were former slaves of the Spaniards who had escaped; most were negroes, brought from Africa to replace native workforces which had died off under Spanish rule. A mile ahead of them, four more Cimarrons were silently breaking branches to blaze a trail. A guard of Cimarrons marched both before and behind the English, now and then cautioning them to move with extreme care and quiet. This was not so easy for men armed and, some of them, armoured in the European fashion, although the natives were carrying most of the loads.

What sustained the English as they struggled up the Cordilleras was the promise of a great tree at about the halfway point of their march across the isthmus which separated the Caribbean from the Pacific. From the top of this tree, the natives had said, a man might have a sight simultaneously of both seas: the Northern Sea across which they had just sailed from England, and the Southern Sea of legend, where no Englishman had been.

By about ten o'clock in the morning of the fourth marching day, they had clambered to the summit of a great ridge, aligned almost east–west along the mountainous spine of the isthmus between Nombre de Dios and Panama. There was evidence of permanent or transitory occupation. Strongly built native houses and a noticeable clearing of all the tall trees – and they were impressively high – which would obscure the view from the monster timber they were to ascend. The trunk of this tree had been carefully prepared

15

at some previous time by the cutting of steps in its trunk, so that the ascent was routine.

The Cimarron chief called Pedro took Captain Drake by the hand to help him up, for he still suffered from the leg wound and loss of blood he had suffered in the night assault on Nombre de Dios six months before. At the top of the tree, amazingly far above the ground, a bower had been constructed which was larger than the main fighting top of any great ship, for it would take a dozen men with ease. And, best of all, they had a fine day for it. A stiff breeze, little felt at ground level, had dispersed the cloud base which, like the brim of a man's hat, so often spanned out from the wooded heights of the mountain.

It was true! Quite plain to the north was a blue line. The shallow, translucent coralline waters between the islands, where the Atlantic ended. The Caribbean. And south! There was indeed a greenish line on the horizon. The great South Sea beyond Panama, the enormous deeps of Magellan's *Mar Pacifico*. And somewhere beyond that, many months' journey beyond, must loom the Spice Islands and Cathay.

That was certainly a prospect to please a merchant, always supposing that any would think to pursue it in person. But nearer to hand the Spanish explorers were known to have found mountains, more or less, of silver; and much mercury and gold. All of which had eventually to be shipped from the far-off ports of Chile and Peru and Mexico to the warehouses of Panama. And on the whole of that thousand miles and more of Pacific coast the trading ships of Spain might expect to meet with no foes more menacing than a handful of natives in dugout canoes. No Englishman or Frenchman or Hollander had dared to enter that sea. The Spaniards did not bother even to mount their guns, and if they carried any at all, stowed them below on the ballast so that their ships would be more weatherly in a blow.

Their carelessness was founded on the rigours of the only known entry point from the west, the still-secret Strait of Magellan. It lay somewhere far south in the regions of biting cold, of adverse and terrible winds, of continually unfavourable currents in uncharted channels. Guarded above all by the twin deterrents of time and distance.

Many corsairs had followed where Columbus had led across the Atlantic, themselves included. But crossing the Atlantic was as a sail from Deptford to the Isle of Dogs, compared to the enormity of the long haul south towards the Antarctic and the unknown. Only a carefully prepared, long-provisioned and costly expedition would stand the least chance of survival, let alone success. No corsair captain could mount such an enterprise unaided. And if there were merchants ready to risk their capital, a word in high places could suffice to check them, for even a straightforward trading or exploratory voyage into that sea would be government business.

The burly little man gazing out over the slopes of the Cordilleras towards the green line of ocean on the horizon offered up a prayer, brief but sincere, that he survive their present hazardous enterprise with profit and in due time be given leave to be the first man to sail an English ship upon that far-off, forbidden sea.

It might be as well to recruit here and now. To strike the spark at least. He called up his men in groups to see the spectacle of the two oceans, knowing how they would talk of it once back in England, and with a few words pointed their minds in the desired direction. With his chief partner, John Oxenham, he took even greater care. Here was a hard man, a Devonian feared and respected; grave and careful. And a captain himself, fully able to grasp the audacity of the plan and judge of its enormous difficulties.

Magellan had made his voyage during the years 1519–22 and now it was 1573, and still no other seaman had made another such venture. No wonder! For only one ship of Magellan's fleet ever returned to Spain and in it only eighteen men, the great Magellan himself not among them. Nor was it the natural forces alone which had decimated that expedition, but the strife between groups and between this man and that man. Mutiny, division and murder had flowered in that expedition all round the globe. Indeed, the same poison had been at work within the body of other great enterprises of exploration, including those of Columbus.

As the seamen clambered up into the bower and cried out delightedly, especially at their first glimpse of that legendary South Sea, Drake pointed to the possibilities. It took time for them to grasp that their leader was not talking about the immediate and desperate tomorrow, their impending raid on the guarded royal treasure road from Panama; but of a far distant day, when an English ship would sail that sea. All the great world names of exploration and navigation had been foreigners in the service of either Spain or Portugal. It was hard to think of themselves, untutored village lads, as likely material for similar ventures.

But their captain thought so, and he convinced even Oxenham, that grave, slow-spoken Devonian. In a thick local burr, Oxenham at last declared that nothing would stop him from entering that South Sea, except that Francis Drake himself would beat him from their company.

It was in cheerful mood that they scrambled to earth and ate their mid-day meal. Two days later they were getting occasional distant glimpses of Panama from this or that vantage point on their march. One day after that they could make out actual ships anchored in the roadstead.

By 19 September 1577, having tediously worked downriver from London between the low-lying banks of the Thames, the two ships had left the estuary behind them and were steering for the North Foreland. Summer was just gone. Within the sea was an increasing cold. At nights now, the chill which came off the sibilant dark water could be felt as a physical force. Those who could found excuses to visit the galley, to warm themselves at the only fire allowed on board. The days were drawing in, too, and lanterns and candles were lit early. By now, even the new men and boys could handle most of the ropes and other gear in almost complete darkness.

The largest of the two ships was the *Elizabeth*, of eighty tons burden, soundly built and brand new. She was commanded by John Winter, who was to be appointed vice-admiral and second-in-command of the whole expedition, when all five ships were to be joined at Plymouth shortly. Her sailing master was William Markham, subordinate to Winter who had military as well as naval responsibilities. Indeed, he came from a different world altogether, with two relatives on the Navy Board, George Winter and the Lord High Admiral himself, Sir William Winter. Both of them were backing this voyage from their own private fortunes, as were other prominent persons in the realm. Building, fitting out, storing and crewing the ships had been costly, and perhaps they hoped that with William as vice-admiral their interests might be properly considered.

The second vessel hardly ranked as a ship. She was merely a pinnace of perhaps twelve or fifteen tons burden called variously the *Benedict*, the *Bark Benedict*, or the *Christopher*. Eventually, the latter name was to stick. The *Christopher*, then, was so small that she carried only a few swivels, quick-firing man-killers of the type the Spanish called a *verso*, whereas the *Elizabeth* had proper carriage guns of cast iron, a dozen or so of them. Experience had shown, however, that for a small fleet operating in strange waters far from home, a shallow-draught armed launch which could move fast under oars regardless of what the wind was doing was not merely useful; it was vital.

Proof of her role was the character of her commander. He was the legendary Tom Moone, carpenter of the old *Swann*, Master Drake's ruthless, Spaniard-hating crony on the golden voyage to Nombre de Dios of 1572–3. One of those who had climbed that great tree astride the spine of the isthmus, who had seen both oceans, and then gone on to the assault on the mule train and the treasure it carried – and eventually helped carry it back to Plymouth. Every man who had come back from that voyage had become rich.

Moone now commanded a pinnace, Drake a fleet. They were going up in the world. Success had made it easier to gain important sponsors for potentially rich voyages and subsequently to entice experienced mariners into the crews. Also, alas, it had raised envy and opposition in some quarters and a fever for emulation in others. John Oxenham, for instance, had not followed Drake after all; but had hatched a plan of his own for plundering Panama by rowing up the rivers in boats, marching overland, and then building more boats on the Pacific coast. It was Master Drake's old plan, writ larger. Oxenham had sailed in 1575, two years before, and no word had come from him or of him since.

And there were others, haughtier, who thought Master Drake a good and useful man in his place, which was handling ropes and driving crude mariners to their work and generally organising the voyage; but as to what should happen at the end of it, that was a matter best decided by gentlemen trained to arms from birth.

After all, the affair at Nombre de Dios had been a failure, hadn't it, in spite of all the fanfares? Master Drake had got himself shot and then he and his rabble had been beaten out of the town by the Spanish rag, tag, and bobtail, no real soldiers there at all; and without the treasure, for the silver was too heavy to carry and the gold and the jewels, if ever there were any, were never discovered in the chaos.

As for those attacks on the treasure convoys coming on mule-back

overland from Panama . . . well, Master Drake had succeeded in
the end, it was true, but after how many bunglings? Look at the
time he laid that ambush . . . and up comes the leading Spaniard
on a horse, scouting for trouble well in advance of the mule train
as any soldier in his right mind would expect. And then up from
cover gets a silly English sailor, blind drunk and waving a bottle of
raw aqua vitae at the Spanish cavalier and his page. One might
just as well have put up a large sign inscribed: 'Take Warning –
Master Francis Drake Lying in Ambush Here'. If the truth was
known, probably it was the native Cimarrons who showed those
amateurs how to really ambush a mule train.

Perhaps that was harsh, for he had learned his business under
Hawkins, who fought very well from a deck but hadn't the slightest
of military skills otherwise, as he had so amply proved in that
disgraceful business at San Juan de Ulloa in 1568, all of ten years
back. The key to the whole position had been control of the land
battery which commanded the harbour. Hawkins had held it and
then let it be taken from him as easily as if from a child. He had
lost his own flagship (the property of Her Majesty the Queen) and
finally his command had disintegrated. He himself had got home
in a smaller ship after terrible privations had further decimated
the survivors of the battle.

A sinister footnote had been the arrival home, before his chief, of
the youthful Drake in an even smaller ship called the *Judith*. It
was said that Hawkins, who seldom complained, had commented
bitterly that he had been deserted in the extremity of danger, both
from the Spaniards in the port if they stayed and from the weather
outside which threatened to wreck them on the reefs if they fled.
Drake had got clear of the harbour, before the worst of the weather
had arrived, without waiting for Hawkins to extricate himself in the
somewhat larger *Minion*. And Hawkins, apparently, had not spoken
to him since.

However, one could put another interpretation on the matter.
Hawkins was notoriously careful. So cautious and slow was he,
it could be said, that another man's meat would be eaten before
Hawkins's had even browned on the spit. Master Drake, self-willed
and peremptory even then, may not have cared to be shackled to
so leaden-footed a commander, who had just led them to monumental disaster. What seemed to Hawkins like desertion may have
appeared to Drake to be but a swift extrication from another man's

shambles. There was no doubt, Francis Drake did not work well in harness. Latterly he had not needed to, for his successes had made him independent of the whole Hawkins family.

Now Winter had a rendezvous with Drake at Plymouth, where preparations for the great voyage were thought to be well advanced. So he drove the *Elizabeth* hard to make the most of the tricky tidal patterns, the two-knot ebb from the estuary which if caught at the right time can carry a ship into the four-knot run towards the Straits of Dover. Delays in the Straits were almost inevitable, because of the tides, and unfavourable winds would probably mean a slow passage down Channel past the white chalk cliffs of Kent, Sussex and Wight; and on to the west past Studland, Portland and Start. In their way, these uncertainties were the comfortingly familiar pattern of an English coasting voyage. Soon they would be going to regions for which no tide tables had been computed and where all the winds would be unexpected.

But when the *Elizabeth* and the *Christopher* reached Devon, Winter found that he had troubled himself for nothing. The three ships being made ready in Plymouth were mostly unrigged, unballasted and unvictualled. The greater part of the work on them had still to be done. The largest was the *Pelican*, of 120 tons burden. Built in the French fashion, she had seven gunports on each side and mounted eighteen guns in all, including those at bow and stern. She was to be Master Drake's flagship, with Thomas Cuttill as her sailing master. Like the *Elizabeth*, she was really a small warship, and so tonnage estimates based on cargo capacity were no good guide to her size and varied in fact between 100 and 150 tons. She looked to be about eighty or ninety feet long overall with a beam of about eighteen feet.

The other two ships fitting out at Plymouth were the *Marigold*, a bark of thirty tons burden provided by one of the expedition's illustrious backers, Sir Christopher Hatton, with John Thomas as captain and Nicholas Anthony as sailing master; and the flyboat *Swan*, a fifty-ton merchantman which was the fleet supply ship. John Chester, who commanded her, was not a Crown officer or soldier. These two vessels carried only five or six small cast-iron guns apiece. Not generally known was that the little fleet had four prefabricated pinnaces stored aboard in their component parts but easily assembled when the need arose.

The total complement of the expedition was 164 men and boys, mostly mariners, but some soldiers and a few merchants. They had signed agreements to make a commercial voyage in these ships to Alexandria, in the domain of the Grand Turk, from whom a licence to trade had been obtained by the sponsors. But already, while the *Elizabeth* and the *Christopher* were still on their way from the Thames to Plymouth, rumours had been picked up by Spanish spies to the effect that the voyage was not at all what it purported to be, a peaceful trading venture to the distant end of the Mediterranean.

Antonio de Guaras, Spanish agent in London, warned his government that Drake, the notorious pirate, was preparing to sail for Scotland, to capture by bribery the prince of that country. And that, although this was his real intention, the English were putting out a plausible cover story to suggest instead another voyage to the Caribbean and the West Indies. Captain Bingham and other well-known military men had been asked to embark, it was said, and had been astonished to find that they were expected to serve as subordinates to such a man as Drake, a sailor and a commoner.

Even in the fleet – in the London ships at any rate – Drake was not everywhere accepted as overall leader. John Cooke, who had come round from the Thames in the *Elizabeth* under John Winter, understood that the command was to be exercised by no less than three 'equal companions and friendly gentlemen'. They were the corsair captain Francis Drake; the well-connected Winter; and Thomas Doughty, a lawyer and soldier on the fringes of the Court, who was also an old companion-in-arms of Drake, with whom he had served recently during the bloody troubles in Ireland.

Divided command was not unusual in amphibious operations, its justification being the apparently logical distinction between the sea commander who in effect ferried the soldiers to their destination and the land forces commander who was responsible for operations ashore. Such a division could put severe strains on any friendship, particularly when the naval commander also had a reputation as a successful soldier, but was inferior socially to the appointed military leader. To go a fatal step further and divide a command three ways would be to invite dissension when, as was the case, one of the three was the originator of the whole scheme and might easily come to feel himself slighted and his command thereby made unsure and ineffective.

No such folly was intended by the backers of the expedition.

whose draft plan names Francis Drake as overall commander of the voyage with sole authority to take the vital decisions. This document, being secret, could not affect the groundswell of inspired whispering which suggested that Thomas Doughty, the military commander, was at least the equal, and perhaps more than the equal, of the commoner captain Francis Drake.

The Spanish intelligence was correct at least in this, that the gentlemen officers were not happy at serving under a sailor. But they were led wildly astray as to the destination of the little force. It was not meant to go north for Scotland, masked by a cover story of being yet another intended Indies raid of the notorious pirate Drake. The actual English cover story was to get the crews to sign on for a voyage to Alexandria, but probably not all the sailors believed this a likely objective for their corsair captain and they may have conjectured that the Caribbean was more likely than the Mediterranean. Perhaps the Spanish agent picked up authentic English mariners' guesswork and judged it suspect. Indeed, the beauty of the English scheme was that, regardless of whether they intended to sail east of west, their initial course must be south as far as Africa. The winds, the currents and their own limited storage space dictated it. There would be no clue as to their real destination until they had been many weeks out of Plymouth.

That destination, known to only a few, was the great South Sea by way of the Strait of Magellan. The objective, as summarised by Winter, was 'for discovery and other causes of trade of merchandises necessary and requisite'. Truly, it would be a great, historic voyage. They were all familiar with the feat of Magellan, the greatest journey ever made by man on earth, impossible to surpass. After nearly sixty years, no one had even matched it. To follow just a portion of that route was a privilege. Most sailors were mere coasters, sailing from headland to headland all their lives; most landsmen rarely ventured more than a few miles from the village or town in which they were born. The 164 who were setting forth with Drake were to venture into the unknown.

Those who returned might have made their fortunes. This was a voyage of exploration, of commercial reconnaissance. The decline of England's great export trade in wool had led to a surplus of ships and sailors. It seemed sensible to employ some of them in searching out new trading possibilities. Both the east and west coasts of South America offered thousands of miles of territory which, although of interest to either Portugal or Spain, were not actually in Portuguese or Spanish possession, unless one took seriously an outdated papal edict which divided the world between Portugal and Spain. The mariners of France, Holland and England had long since demonstrated its irrelevance.

Drake was ordered to spend five months exploring the Atlantic and Pacific coasts of South America from Magellan's Strait up to 30° North. He was to search particularly for sovereign native kingdoms with which a trade for light but valuable commodities such as spices, drugs and dyes might be arranged. Because of the present political difficulties of the overland Asian spice route and the hardly lesser dangers of the sea route pioneered by the Portuguese round South Africa into the Indian Ocean, these commodities were all ridiculously overpriced. But spices had to be obtained at almost any price; the winter meat supplies of Europe depended on them. The merchants who backed the expedition and had their representatives with it were very conscious of this trading background to the voyage.

However, other interests, not necessarily incompatible, were also involved, as they had been with Magellan's similar venture. The businessmen were essentially thinking in the short term: a quick killing in pepper, the immediate employment of laid-up shipping. The strategists thought more of the damage and the confusion that a Drake-led expedition was likely to produce in areas vital to Spain's military effort in Europe. The stream of gold and silver from the New World was transmuted into ranks of soldiers fighting under the Spanish flag. Interrupt the flow of precious metals and the result must be disaffection and even insurrection; the unpaid soldiers might mutiny. Less than 200 men in the South Sea might immobilise, perhaps even disperse, a force of 20,000 soldiers in Europe. If Drake went too far, he could always be disowned; but it would be best not to do so (unless, of course, he failed or was captured). That Spain was vulnerable would be an interesting lesson for the Spanish Court to learn.

Among the venture's supporters was a third group of men. In comparison to the merchants and the military, they seemed exotic indeed. For they were many things: scholars and scientists; cartographers and cosmographers; practical mathematicians and visionary imperialists; alchemists and, one might almost say, sorcerers. The principal among them was 'Doctor' John Dee, a Welshman who owned at Mortlake the greatest library in England, a powerhouse of information and of speculation. For the past twenty-five years his advice had been sought concerning ocean voyages of exploration intended by one route or another to reach the riches of the East. He was a confidant of the Queen and also of Sir Christopher Hatton, the new Court favourite.

Dee's vision was of a British trading empire overseas pioneered by men like Drake, Frobisher, Willoughby, Lok, Gilbert, who would find the routes to Ophir, Cathay and the Spice Islands; and then large capacious vessels would follow the tracks of the explorers, making commercial voyages with substantial cargoes at intervals of one or two years, much as the Spaniards already did with the yearly sailing of the Manila galleon across the South Sea from the Philippines to Mexico. Naturally, the survey ships of the pioneers who were to 'prove' the routes had to be small and handy; so small in fact that they could not carry enough stores for any long voyage, but must 'top up' with water and food while actually exploring unknown lands and seas. Their commanders must be men of daring and resource. The captains of the carracks and galleons which followed after might be of more sober stamp; nor need they be anything like so expert in the art of navigation. It was an art still, in spite of the efforts of men like Dee to turn it into science.

A ship's position north or south of the Equator – its latitude, or, as many preferred to say, its 'height' above or below the Equator – this could be calculated by observing the sun or the stars with certain new instruments which worked even when the observation platform was the rolling, pitching deck of a small ship. In turn, this was only possible because for thousands of years men had been systematically studying the heavens, and data were available from which sky maps or tables could be predicted. So a mariner would know roughly where he was on a north–south line, provided of course that the sun or the stars were not obscured by fog or cloud.

When it came to sailing east or west, however, matters were more difficult. For a start, no one knew the size of the globe, although calculations had been made by astrologers, astronomers and geographers for thousands of years. True, wise men had divided model globes into such-and-such a number of degrees, to help make up a neat grid pattern, but no man knew for sure what distance a degree represented on the actual surface of the earth. Columbus, the most brilliant navigator of the previous century, to the end of his life believed that he had explored the fringes of Japan or China, never realising that his actual discoveries were many thousands of miles short of his intended destination.

Even if distances and courses were known beforehand, the position of a ship at any given time was uncertain, being based only on deduced reckoning. Columbus had been uncannily accurate often enough, but generally the navigator guessed rather than calculated, for no accurate timer existed. The best clock mechanisms were unreliable, particularly in salt sea air; the old-fashioned hourglass was simpler and some preferred it. For short distances one might not go so very wrong, but sailing many thousands of miles around a sphere was a different matter; it involved frequent changes of course, the so-called Great Circle navigation taught by Dee and others.

Dee had been writing on the subject for a quarter of a century, but he had been particularly busy in 1576 and 1577, when much of this material was published. An early work which he had dedicated to the cause of the 'British Impire' was one of those now published for the first time. Dee's titles were scholarly and factual; the volume he completed in 1576, for instance, was published as *Queen Elizabeth & her Arithmeticall Tables Gabernatick: for Navigation by the Paradoxall Compass and Navigation in Great Circles*. The Welsh doctor was a scholar scientist who wrote for a purpose; not merely to be read, but to be read widely and have the results of his industry put to use by practical men. His latest composition, penned in haste during the spring and summer of 1577, was titled *The Great Volume of Famous and Rich Discoveries*. This was a frankly propagandist piece, with a half-concealed reference to the Drake expedition as 'A worthy attempt at Discovery, faithfully intended by a true Brytish Subject'. It was also a résumé of the evidence for the potential of the vast areas of unexplored lands and seas and of the possible routes which still had to be tested.

The thinking of the world's geographers was determined by a philosophy: that the globe was more land than sea and that the known vast areas of land in the north must be balanced by equally large but unknown lands to the south. The Strait of Magellan was a mere ditch separating South America from the conjectural great southern continent often referred to as Terra Australis. There might be a better, that is shorter, way into the South Sea than by the

Strait of Magellan. There was the possible North-East Passage around Russia; and the more probable North-West Passage around North America, which was at that moment being actively explored by Frobisher. Whether or not they could get into the South Sea by this route depended upon whether or not Asia was joined to America. Dee believed, with many others, that these continents were not joined, but rather separated by a theoretical stretch of water which was generally called the Straits of Anian.

There was only one way to find out, and that was to try to sail right round America, not necessarily by means of a single expedition in a single voyage. Several fleets, from the south as well as from the north, might be employed. Frobisher, Hall, Gilbert hammering their way through the northern ice in repeated voyages; Drake approaching the problem from the south, although Dee was aware that both Spanish fleets and overland marching expeditions, launched from bases actually on the American continent, had failed in such enterprises.

Some six months before Drake sailed, Dee wrote: 'Of how great importance then to you is that attempt which is by a British Subject presently intended to God's glory, the benefit of all Christendom, and the honour and profit of this realm chiefly'; and also, he added, 'to the contentment of those noble minds who wished merely to understand the earth that God had given them'.

Dee did not underrate the difficulties faced by the expedition's unnamed leader,

'who hath secretly offered up to God and his natural Soverayne and Country the employing of all his skill and talent, and the patient enduring of the great toyle of his body, to that place being the very ends of the world from us to be reckoned, to accomplish that discovery which of so many and so valiant captains BY LAND AND SEA hath been so oft attempted in vain. The consequence of which exploit is greater than is yet to any Christian State credible.'

Only in a private letter to the poet-courtier Edward Dyer, did Dee commit to paper what he really meant. That many important persons hoped that Queen Elizabeth might become:

'the Chief Commander, and in manner Imperial Governor, of all Christian Kings, princes and States; and chiefly of those, part of whose Territories did in any place admit of good landing from the sea; or whose subjects, with ship or goods, did or must pass and use, any of her Majesties appropriate and peculiar seas.'

This conception, which was Dee's and for which he coined the phrase 'British Impire', to many seemed daring in the extreme. Perhaps the world looked smaller when seen on a map in a study at Mortlake.

Even more strange appeared the Welsh doctor's utter faith in the secret leader of the expedition. If 'so many and so valiant captains' had made their attempts in vain, when the object of discovery was comparatively so close to them, how could a 'British Subject' even think to succeed, when he had first to go to 'the very ends of the world'?

Chapter 2

'A BEASTLIKE PEOPLE'

From Plymouth to the Cape Verdes:
15 November 1577–1 February 1578

ON 15 November 1577 the five ships of the Drake expedition sailed from Plymouth without fuss and set course for Gibraltar, that towering Spanish rock guarding the entrance to the Mediterranean. All was in accordance with the cover story, for the crews had signed agreements with their captain to receive wages in respect of a commercial voyage to Alexandria, under one or other of the complicated arrangements possible under the old maritime laws of Rhodes and Oléron, updated by more recent judgements such as the case of the Inquisition of Queenborow of 1375.

The medieval scheme of mutual obligation and dependence, whereby a sailor could have a part-share in the cargo, or even in the ship itself, and there was really little difference between the crew and their captain save age and experience, was tending to give way to a more authoritarian outlook. For great ocean voyages, the captain could be no ordinary mortal: he must be seaman, soldier, geographer, navigator, mathematician and leader of men. The latter above all, for mariners were still notoriously self-confident and unruly. In King Harry's time a battleship had capsized and sunk because too many of her crew had believed that they could handle the ship as well as the captain and better than any of their mates, and so refused to take orders from anybody. Drake was shortly going to have to explain to men of similarly independent mind that they had been signed on under false pretences. Instead of the mild Mediterranean, they were headed for the icy and almost unknown Straits of Magellan with winter already upon them.

They had been at sea only a day when the wind turned contrary and then began to freshen. Drake did not persevere. He abandoned the voyage for the moment and on the morning of the 16th took his ships into the shelter of Falmouth harbour. Very shortly afterwards amazing scenes were enacted. The sheltered haven was torn by sheets of wind which screamed and cracked between the hills and turned the enclosed waters seething white. For a time it seemed as if Drake's fleet was to be destroyed in an English anchorage, before ever it had a chance to dare the distant tempests. Drake's own ship, the *Pelican*, began to drag her anchors, driving slowly towards destruction. Drake ordered the mainmast cut away. Once that had gone overboard the wind pressure on the vessel was much lessened, and she held her own. But the little bark *Marigold*, thirty tons, was picked up helplessly by the waves and driven across the harbour until she grounded in the shallows. The pounding damaged her hull severely, but not as badly as it would have if her mainmast also had not gone over the side.

John Cooke, serving in Winter's *Elizabeth*, thought that it had been 'so terrible a tempest as no man then living had ever seen the like', and that they had been lucky not to have lost all their ships as total wrecks. There was so much damage to repair that the entire expedition had to return to its starting point, Plymouth, for the work to be done. It was a bad beginning. The decision to turn back and seek safety in Falmouth had clearly been the right one, but invited mockery from those who had not experienced that tempest at sea. Nor did it look very well for Drake's flagship to have got into trouble while Winter's vessel and the storeship had escaped accident.

While in Plymouth rumours spread of a quarrel having developed between Drake on the one hand and James Lydye on the other regarding the stowage in the hold of the victuals and other stores. For so long and varied a voyage, these were of critical importance. There was beer and wine in cask, better than water. There was beef and pork; also fish, never popular; and rice, for bulk. There was cheese, honey, vinegar, salt, and the inevitable 'biscuit'. The healthy appetites of English mariners were famous. The food was good, but although stored in the chill of the holds below the waterline, for how long would the meat be edible? The problems of diet and health generally loomed as large in a sea captain's mind as the hazards of the great oceans themselves; crew losses on long voyages could be appalling, and the reasons were not completely understood yet. Almost the only remedy the surgeons had was aqua vitae.

Reserves of woollen and linen clothing were held in store as well as shoes, hats and caps. Other 'issue' items included platters, tankards, dishes and bowls for use at table, as well as wood and coal for the galley fire, and candles and lanterns for lighting. The ships had to be reparable from their own resources, so the list of carpenter's stores was long: spare sails and ropes on the one hand; pitch, tar and rosin for the hulls on the other. There was a host of small items such as twine and needles and the nets and hooks the mariners would use for fishing during the voyage. Less desirable marine creatures would be attracted to the ships, particularly in the Tropics, and every vessel had been sheathed below the waterline with extra layers of outer planks which, when worm-eaten, could be taken off and replaced by new ones. Tools included scoops, shovels, mattocks, hatchets and crowbars; and of course there were nails and spikes of various sizes. There was also rough lead and sheet lead; the former for casting shot for the small ordnance and handguns, the latter for repairing hull damage, whether from enemy fire or submerged rocks.

The guns, ammunition and warlike stores were another category with which the fleet was well provided, but particularly the *Pelican* and the *Elizabeth* which, when all their guns were brought up and mounted, were virtually pocket warships. All this took up so much space that there was little room for trade goods other than trinkets designed as gifts or sweeteners for any important lords whose countries they might wish to reconnoitre.

In what way James Lydye (or Stydye) had erred in storing the ships was not clear. John Cooke of the *Elizabeth* thought he had not; that the man had taken great pains to stack the victuals so that they would keep fresh as long as possible and had placed everything so that those items which would be required early in the voyage were easy to get at. Cooke thought Drake a tyrant for peremptorily dismissing the man regardless of his professional skills and the hard work he had put in; it seemed unfair that he was not to be allowed to come with them.

It was told elsewhere that Thomas Doughty had an even higher opinion of James Lydye and had gone as far as to say in private conversations that the man was essential to the success of the voyage. These talks, which had taken place in the garden of Mr Hawkins's house in Plymouth and also on board the *Pelican*, cast considerable doubt on both the primacy of Drake as regards the voyage and his right to dismiss Lydye at all.

What Doughty confided to others was that Drake was merely his protégé. When the corsair had embarrassed the Lord Admiral and the rest of the Council by the success of his last raiding voyage to the Indies in 1572-3, Doughty had introduced him to the Earl of Essex as a first step in obtaining Crown employment in Ireland, where he would be out of the public eye for a while. It was in Ireland, according to Doughty, that the present voyage was first projected by himself and by Master Drake, thinking to do it from their own resources, Doughty to put in a thousand pounds. But when, back in London, Master Drake approached him at the Temple for the money, Doughty had learned better, and was sure that the undertaking now required the approval of the Queen and her Council as being a matter of State. So he went to Mr Secretary Walsingham and to Mr Hatton, and they went to Her Majesty the Queen, who liked the plan and commanded Captain Drake to be sent for. She had given Doughty and Drake jointly a commission as far-reaching as any ever sealed in England, which however provided that Drake was unable to act by himself alone; he must have the assent of Thomas Doughty to everything.

But here, in the matter of James Lydye, Drake had dismissed a man although Doughty actually opposed this action. So who was master of the fleet?

As soon as they were out of sight of land and steering apparently for Gibraltar, Drake gave out the rendezvous for this first part of the voyage. If the fleet became separated, the ships should meet off the island of Mogador. A buzz of rumour and conjecture began! Mogador was on the Atlantic coast of Morocco, nearly 500 miles south of Gibraltar and the entrance to the Mediterranean. So where were they heading really?

The knowing ones were confirmed in their opinion that Drake all along intended another reckless raid in the Caribbean, that wonderful, transparent Northern Sea. From Mogador, if one sailed south-west off the desert coast of Africa, one came after some hundreds of miles to the Canaries, the Fortunate Isles. Drake knew Tenerife well, from his earlier slaving voyages with John Hawkins. Columbus himself had often called at Gomera, a few miles away over the long Atlantic swells, to top up with food, wine and water before running with the trade winds and the Canary current for the Indies. The Spaniards had conquered the islands after desperate fighting with the mysterious Guanches who lived there, precisely because of their vital importance as a staging post on the outward route across the Atlantic to the New World. Sceptics muttered that it was many years since the Spaniards on Gomera or in Santa Cruz de Tenerife had willingly provisioned English ships.

But if not the Canaries (and a clash with the Spaniards), then where? The Portuguese held the Azores, as the first of their staging posts down the west coast of Africa on their own private route round the Cape and into the Indian Ocean, which led at length to the Spice Islands. They also occupied the Cape Verde Islands, further south, which served them both for their eastern route round Africa and also their western route across the northern ocean to Brazil. These monopolies had long been sanctioned by the Pope in order to avoid animosity between Spain and Portugal, but rivalry there still was; and both these favoured nations would oppose with armed force any interlopers from England, France or Holland. The soldiers whom Doughty commanded had not been shipped aboard purely for ceremonial purposes; they might well have to fight in earnest.

After such a tumultuous beginning the voyage from northern latitudes towards the Tropics seemed particularly smooth and uneventful, the winds always favourable, the only accident being the loss overboard of a boy seaman from the *Christopher* in the Bay of Portugal. On the morning of Christmas Day 1577 the little fleet, all five ships sailing in company, sighted the coast of Africa at Cape Cantin, a landmark near the port of Sophia in Barbary. Already the winds were warmer and the sea more blue than green. But their welcome from the port was odd. Two ships came swiftly out of harbour at once, as if the British fleet had been expected, and then, after inspecting them, as suddenly turned away and made for port again. Apparently the English had been mistaken for another fleet due to arrive shortly. Whatever fleet that was, it could hardly be friendly.

Drake sailed on and later that day they sighted a small island lying a mile or so out from the coast at Mogador. Anchoring in deep water, he sent a boat to sound inshore between the island and the mainland of Africa. The boat's crew reported finding a good natural harbour dangerous of entry at one side but giving safe depths of five or six fathoms on the other. The fleet then entered and set up a temporary base on the island where they could safely assemble and launch one of the prefabricated pinnaces.

In their stay on the island, during the last week of the old year,

B

1577, John Cooke noted a significant change. Drake was no longer just a corsair captain. Now he styled himself 'General' of the fleet and had to be so addressed.

It was here also that word spread of their real destination; that they were bound for the Strait of Magellan and the great South Sea beyond. However obliquely or discreetly its orders were worded, an English fleet was now to challenge both the Spanish and the Portuguese monopolies.

However, they had hardly anchored before Moors appeared on the mainland requesting a parley. Drake sent off a boat to bring on board two of the leaders, leaving one English seaman behind as a hostage. The Moroccan chiefs were invited to a banquet at which it was noted that, notwithstanding the tenets of their religion, they were very fond of wine. They also knew what seafaring men wanted, offering to trade for English merchandise supplies of fresh provisions. They promised camel-loads of sheep and chickens, sugar, figs and dates within a day. Drake sent them away with gifts of clothing and a javelin, and the English sailor was returned by the Moors in exchange.

When next morning a caravan of some thirty laden camels was seen approaching a creek which led down to the sea, the sailors were overjoyed at the thought of some brisk bargaining, first come, first served. Weaponless, they willingly manned the boat Drake ordered sent ashore and rowed into the creek where, unseen, Moorish soldiers crouched among the rocks and reeds. One of the mariners, John Fry, had picked up a smattering of Arabic from previous merchant voyages, and this made him so bold that he leapt ashore before the boat had grounded. In an instant, he was surrounded by armed Moors and a dagger placed at his chest. As the sailors in the boat frantically backed off, quite helpless to intervene and fearful of capture themselves, they could see Fry being forced on to the back of a horse and ridden off into the interior, presumably for questioning.

Drake mustered an armed landing party and sent them off in the newly assembled pinnace, but although they marched a short way into the interior, their quest was hopeless. The Moors simply kept their distance; they would neither fight nor talk. Drake gave up the attempt to recover Fry and on 31 December took his fleet out of the anchorage and headed along the coast for Cape Blanc, the White Cape, a notable landmark on the West African shore.

Had he waited only a few days, Drake would have seen John Fry again, for the Moors sent him back once they had got what they wanted, which was information, not trade. Civil war was about to break out between two rival Moroccans, one party expecting aid from the Portuguese, the other hoping to prevent it. They had thought Drake's ships to be perhaps the forerunners of a Portuguese fleet, or at least to have news of it. Once Fry had been able to make their king understand that the fleet was English and bound for the Straits, his status changed. He was laden with gifts intended for Drake and escorted back to the anchorage. Fry was grief-stricken when he found that his comrades had gone, but the Moroccan king's protestations of friendship were real enough and not long afterwards the sailor was sent home in an English merchant ship. He brought the last first-hand news of Drake which was to reach England for a long time.

Bad weather and contrary winds had plagued the little fleet as it coasted southwards along the shores of the desert. Occasionally, mountains could be seen inland, but the coast was generally low and featureless, the sand appearing white in the heat. It was a week before they sighted the landmark of Cape de Guerre, off which three small Spanish boats of a type the English called 'canters' were fishing. Their presence was not unexpected and their catches would be welcome on board ships with thousands of empty sea miles in front of them. Nevertheless, when Drake ordered Winter to capture them, using the newly assembled pinnace, the Vice-Admiral was careful to log the fact that Francis Drake had 'caused' him to go into the pinnace for this purpose. The three small prizes accompanied the fleet for the next few days, while other captures were made.

Off Rio del Oro it was Vice-Admiral Winter with the new pinnace who took a small Portuguese vessel of the type the English called a 'caravel'; off Cape Barbas it was the turn of Captain Thomas in the thirty-ton bark *Marigold* to snap up another caravel; and then before them like a wall reared up the silhouette of Cape Blanco, the White Cape, brooding over the sandy shallows which teemed with marine life. In season, this was one of the richest fishing grounds then known, the bay behind it forming a natural anchorage for fishing boats and even small ships. As Drake's vessel rounded the headland into the bay they found a small craft which had been deserted by all but two of her crew, apparently too stupid to conceive that they might be in danger. They were not harmed, but this ship also was taken for its contents, and carried five leagues up the bay where the English fleet came to anchor.

Apart from provisioning, Drake had business to transact on shore, which would take him four days. He landed a party of soldiers under Thomas Doughty, who set them to drill. Again and again they practised the standard formations and how to move from one to the other rapidly and smoothly. John Cooke was impressed by Doughty's thoroughness and care, judging him a good soldier. Drake may have intended the display of disciplined cohesion to impress the natives with whom he wished to deal and to prevent a repetition of the abduction of John Fry or worse.

'There is not to be found in all those parts of the world a more beastlike people, in manners as in religion,' noted Francis Fletcher, the fleet chaplain, shocked at the way the natives flocked out of their dens at dawn to go down on their knees and bow to the disc of the sun as it rose above the desert horizon. 'And yet I prefer them before the Papists in their religion', he felt impelled to add. For they were ignorant people who knew no better, unlike 'the Pope and his malignant synagogues of Satan, who profess themselves to be the only spouse of Christ, and to have the keys of all knowledge and power of life and death, of heaven and hell . . .'

These poor pagans, it was said, customarily traded gold, ambergris, musk and slaves for water, which was precious here. Fletcher saw that this was true, noting the terrible condition of one female Moor whom the natives tried to sell to Drake; she had a tiny baby at the breast and no milk of her own to give it. In this sort of merchandise Drake would not deal, noted Fletcher, and 'the circumstances whereof considered, our general would receive nothing from them for water, but freely gave it them that came to him'. Winter was to be critical of the failure to replenish water stocks, but opportunities were limited on the coasts of the Sahara. Even the captured fishing boats, he was to report, afforded only a meagre addition to their food supplies.

Once their catches had been taken into the English ships, most of the fishing boats were given back to their owners. There were two exceptions. One of the Spanish canters was retained permanently with the fleet, her owner being given in exchange the fifteen-ton pinnace commanded by Tom Moone, usually called the *Bark Benedict*, but sometimes the *Christopher*. This Spanish boat hereafter became known as the *Christopher*, taking the name of the craft for which she had been exchanged. The new *Christopher* was twice the tonnage of the old, however. One of the Portuguese caravels was retained for the moment but was to be returned to its owner when the fleet reached the Cape Verde Islands, the last possible watering place before venturing out across the South Atlantic towards Brazil.

The stay in the anchorage, the last they might be able to occupy for months, was also used to thoroughly wash down and trim the ships. In the Tropics particularly, the filth that accumulated at the bottom of the hold, among the stones or shingle used as ballast, was a prime cause of disease and the spoiling of stores. A quick cleansing could be made by pumping in sea water and then pumping it out again, but if at all possible, it was far better to remove the ballast temporarily and give the ceiling planks underneath a thorough scrub. With their ballast removed, the ships would be at the mercy of the weather or of an enemy, and therefore the sites where such work could be done in safety were few and far between. The great bay behind Cape Blanco contained within its sweep a number of smaller bays or coves which were secluded and defensible; indeed the whole area was too shallow for any large warship to venture in.

That they were well within the Tropics was plain to everyone now. It was not merely a matter of the heat or the desert shores or the height of the sun at mid-day. The night sky marked the greatest change. For many, the new stars were a novelty. For the navigators, they were vital. The main grouping was four stars in the form of a cross, these four being known as the Crosiers or guards of the South Pole. A ship's position along an imaginary north south line – a line of latitude – could be calculated with fair accuracy provided these stars could be seen. As depicted on a globe, north was 'up' and south was 'down', so in the mariners' jargon latitude was called 'height'. There were many navigators in the fleet and invariably, in their logs or diaries, they were recording the 'height' the fleet had reached. On the other hand, its position along any imaginary east–west line – a layman might call it the 'width', but technically it was known as longitude – was hard to calculate, being more a matter of art than science, due to the lack of accurate data. After all, it was only recently that even an approximate idea of the size of the globe had been established; Columbus had been ludicrously in error and Magellan and his men had nearly died in discovering the fault. Much of the information derived from that later voyage was still kept secret by the Spaniards, so that other navigators had to deal more with rumours than with facts in planning their voyages.

On 21 January the fleet left the little bay five leagues within the Cape which had been their shelter while the ships were cleansed and fresh provisions obtained. For a week, they steered a south-westerly course which took them out from the coast of Africa into the deep ocean, with miles of water beneath their keels. The current was with them and the wind also was continually astern, so that the ships ran forward easily without labouring, as if it were a holiday. Some of the secrets of the ocean circulation of winds and waters were becoming more widely known; not just the most direct course from A to B, but the *best* course, the one which made an ally of the elements or avoided hazards.

This south-westerly run had been pioneered by the Portuguese in the previous century, when they were proving an African – as opposed to an American – route to the Spice Islands. It avoided a most dangerous stretch of the desert coast of West Africa as well as making the best of the prevailing winds and currents; but it was more difficult navigationally, because its target was the Cape Verde Islands, lying far out in the ocean wastes. The navigationally easy way would be to keep the African shore in sight all the time (accepting the dangers of that), until one reached the known 'height' of the Cape Verdes. Then one would turn and sail westwards out into the ocean, keeping the 'height' constant. No matter how vague one's knowledge of the distance the ship had sailed each day, sooner or later the desired islands must appear.

Drake, however, knew these waters from earlier voyages he had made as a subordinate of John Hawkins, and confidently headed out south-west. If the fleet was to water at all now, it must be at the Cape Verdes. There was no land between those islands and South America; there were areas of fickle winds to be crossed. where ships might be becalmed for weeks, and if they did not refill the water casks they might all die of thirst. But because the Cape Verdes marked almost precisely the halfway point between Portugal and Brazil, the Portuguese had colonised and fortified them more than a hundred years before, and might be expected to resist any breach of their monopoly, let alone a landing by heretics.

When, on 27 January, the first of the islands was sighted, a plan of attack embodying the vital element of surprise had been prepared by Thomas Doughty and Vice-Admiral John Winter. It was based on information obtained from the captured Portuguese fishermen who were to be released once they had reached the Cape Verdes. The fleet coasted past Bonavista and under cover of night anchored close inshore to the next island, called Maio, or Mayo. Doughty and Winter disembarked with seventy men and began the tense and anxious business of a night march into hostile territory. The principal town of the island, they had been told, lay about three miles inland. Long before dawn the storming party was in position, resting silently. No sound came from the shadowed buildings in front.

At first light the reason became plain. Although there were a great many houses in the town and also a chapel, all were desolate and ruined. The inhabitants had gone and the wells and springs, they found, had been stopped up. As far as the English could grasp, the damage had been done by what Francis Fletcher, the chaplain, called 'pirates and hyaenas of the sea' who were raiding the Portuguese trade routes in revenge for wrongs done to them in the past. Although the English were prepared to trade for water, they found it impossible even to talk to the local people. Many of the inland valleys through which they marched were clearly inhabited, with low cottages set among vineyards and groves of fig-trees, but their owners had abandoned them at the approach of the soldiers.

The landing party were reduced to the status of impotent but amazed sightseers. A number, including Cliffe, Cooke and Fletcher, wrote detailed descriptions in their diaries of the peculiar but prolific plant life of the island. There were two exotic fruits which few Europeans had ever seen, the *nux Indica*, or coconut, which held a pleasant and nourishing liquid; and the smaller *plantains*, or banana trees, whose fruit grew in clusters. Incredibly, on one and the same banana tree could be seen both green fruit and ripe fruit. Then, on the seashore, salt collected naturally in great heaps like snowdrifts, without any intervention by man such as was necessary on the English coast. What impressed Fletcher above all was the fact that, although in Europe it was the depth of winter, here in the Tropics all the trees were green.

It annoyed him immensely that many learned bookmen back home in England would not believe him if he described this. 'Feather-bedded milksopps,' he called them, 'boasting of their deep judgement in cosmography at a smith's forge, hammering out a globe, to make a childish bray amongst simple people'. Such theorists 'do laugh and mock and say it is a lie to report such things of God's great and marvellous works; and to confirm their blind error and ignorance, their own new-forged globe must be showed, whether it be so or no . . . they will lie and cogg, yea with brazen faces slander the truth believed by them which have seen such wonderful works of God.'

It was an oddity of human nature that cosmographers who could not bear to depict an empty ocean but must fill it pell mell with non-existent islands and mythical sea monsters should wax merry with mockery at a plain description of a banana plant. Fletcher was to have opportunity for further reflections on this theme in the months ahead, when confronted with many strange and indeed downright unlikely creatures.

Mayo held only known beasts, such as the herds of goats so wild that none could be captured or killed; although the English had been told that the Portuguese had hidden stocks of dried goat meat on the island. There was water, very good water, in many places; but always too far from the track and the ships for the casks to be filled with it. After a few days of much exertion with nothing achieved, Drake became impatient and ordered Doughty and Winter to bring the soldiers back to the ships. On 30 January they weighed anchor and under cover of darkness ran over to the next island, Santiago, ten leagues distant.

Next morning, sailing close to the shore, they could see, according to Fletcher, that 'the inhabitants were too superstitious, according to the Pope's anti-Christian traditions; for upon every cape and small headland they had set up a cross, on most of which were engraved an evil-faced picture of Christ.' Fletcher led a party in throwing down one of these crosses, an act which gave offence to some of the crew. This island was the centre of Portuguese power, much reduced by revolts of the original inhabitants and the negro slaves. Fletcher presumed that the Portuguese had provoked the uprising by the cruelty of their rule. 'Under the heavens,' he wrote, 'there is not a people that exceed them and the Spaniards in murdering and insatiable shedding of blood, whether Infidels or Christians, men, women, and children, where they can overcome by sword or policy.'

Drake's fleet passed three towns sited by the shore, all of them fortified. Of the first two, the guns of the one remained silent while the guns of the other opened up with a few ranging shots. There was the abrupt rising whistle of the approaching ball, the shriek and spurt of spray as it struck the sea short of the ships, followed by the distant anticlimactic thud of the discharge. From an English ship a single gun replied, the hull vibrating with the shock, the gunsmoke momentarily wreathing the decks and blowing out of her ports.

The third town was St James, the capital, fortified with a castle and a blockhouse. Two strange ships were sighted just outside the harbour, the nearest seemingly rather larger than Drake's flagship, the *Pelican*. Immediately he sent a pinnace away to go out to these vessels and bring them to the English fleet. The ship closest to the harbour swiftly ran for the protection of the shore guns, but the other had further to go and was soon being closed by the pinnace.

Vivid yellow flashes sparkled on the walls of the castle ashore and the gunsmoke billowed up. Again came the rising whistle and shriek of approaching round shot, the heavy projectile crashing into the water between the pinnace and the more distant ship, covering its escape. The nearer vessel, however, had no chance and the pinnace swiftly ran alongside, the English boarders leaping for the sides.

Technically, this was piracy. But then, even to trade peaccably for goat flesh or drinking water with the inhabitants of Mayo would have been illegal. Although Portugal was a smaller power than England, there might yet be unpleasant repercussions. Vice-Admiral Winter was careful to log the fact that the action had been initiated by Francis Drake.

Chapter 3

'THOU ART NOT THE GENERAL'S FRIEND'

From the 'Burning Isle' to the Coast of Brazil:
2 February–6 April 1578

THE captain of the Portuguese ship was a small, dark-complexioned man in his late fifties, with a long beard not yet streaked with white. Nuño da Silva had been at sea for half a century and not merely in coasters. His first voyage, at the age of eight years, had been to Brazil, accompanying his uncle, Adan Fernandez, the ship's navigator. Alvaro Joanez, his father, was also a seaman and away from home for long periods, so the boy had been brought up mainly by Joan, his mother, until he reached the age of eight. By the time his uncle died, Nuño was twenty and had made many voyages between Portugal and Brazil in the King's ships. His uncle had taught him well, and his early start had been an advantage too. From seaman he had risen to pilot, and then to ship captain and navigator combined.

Now he was master of his own ship, the *Santa Maria* of 150 tons, sailing between his home town of Oporto and Brazil. This particular voyage had begun in November 1577, with La Palma in the Canary Islands as the first stop. Here he loaded his cargo of 150 casks of wine before heading for the Cape Verde Islands, the final staging post for a Portuguese, where he had intended to top up with fish, fuel and water. He was about to enter Santiago harbour when he sighted seven ships to windward. For many years, Nuño da Silva's life had been routine. Now he was to be a witness, a vital participant even, in incredible events; to be ruined by corsairs and racked by the Inquisition.

When the English pinnace ran alongside the Portuguese merchantman, and armed men leapt for the projecting chain plates, and so up the standing rigging and on to her main deck, da Silva promptly surrendered. He considered that he had no choice. By his estimation the English *capitana* or flagship, Drake's *Pelican*, was of about 220 tons according to the Portuguese method of calculating ship

42

capacity. Winter's smaller vessel, the eighty-ton *Elizabeth*, was the same size as the *Santa Maria*, rated at 150 tons, which was in fact her cargo capacity in wine casks. The thirty-ton *Marigold* da Silva estimated to be of fifty Portuguese tons. Nor was it a matter only of size and of numbers, but of armament.

It was a very expensive armament too, as da Silva plainly saw when he was taken out of his own ship and brought into Drake's flagship. She carried eighteen guns, thirteen of gleaming bronze, the remainder of cast iron. Her hull had been pierced for seven gun-ports per side, the other four guns being mounted as bow and stern chasers. Quite apart from this impressive ordnance were the ammunition stocks which gave those guns a wide range of capabilities, together with the arms and armour available for the crew. That this was a warship fitted out for a long cruise, da Silva had no doubt.

On the other hand, she was not a new ship, nor, da Silva judged, was she English. Her lines seemed to him to be French. She was well built, planked inside and out, and with good masts and sound rigging. The high stern was a useful feature if she had to run before the wind, pursued by mountainous seas; she was unlikely to be overwhelmed in such conditions, unlike a lower built ship, and da Silva thought that she was capable of making several voyages to Brazil without having to go into dockyard hands.

Much more interesting than the ship, da Silva found, was the man who commanded her and the little fleet. Short, thick-set, very strong, with a ruddy face and a fine countenance fringed by a full, golden beard, Francis Drake appeared to be in his late thirties. He spoke a little Spanish, but initially da Silva's information came from a negro named Diego, who spoke both Spanish and English, and had been captured at sea off Nombre de Dios some seven or eight years ago. He explained that the Captain-General's slight limp was due to an arquebus ball, a souvenir of the Indies which he had carried around with him ever since that night at Nombre de Dios.

His captor, then, had earned a little local fame and besides, like da Silva himself, came of a seafaring family. For many years he had been a companion of the noted John Hawkins, to whom he was supposed to be related. What particularly impressed the Portuguese captain were the surprising social divisions – or lack of them – on board this foreign flagship. Birth appeared to have nothing to do with rank. Drake included among the chosen few who ate at his table the captain, the pilot and even the doctor, but not his young brother Thomas, who served as a seaman like any ordinary member of the crew. Thomas Drake, a lad of twenty-two, resembled his brother in build – short, broad-shouldered, sturdy, and a good seaman – but had a fair complexion and a scanty beard. No boy of gentle birth would put his hand to a rope in such a situation, and so it followed that Francis Drake, the Captain-General, must be a self-made man.

With the captured *Santa Maria* in company, the English fleet sailed on southward past Fuego, the Island of Fire. Like those other staging posts for the great ocean voyages, the Azores and the Canaries, the Cape Verdes also were volcanic. Fuego was awe-inspiringly active, the towering central crater emitting first smoke so dense that it seemed to turn day into night, then flames so fierce that they turned night into noon. Then came a hail of pumice stones which floated thickly on the surface of the sea, and lastly an eruption of heavy black cinders which rolled down the mountain-side with a great noise. The display far exceeded that of Etna, judged Francis Fletcher, who had seen the Italian volcano in eruption. Fuego he thought to be one of the wonders of the world, a rare and fearful spectacle, teaching men the great incomprehensible power of God.

Two leagues beyond Fuego they came to Brava, the Brave Island, so called because it was the greenest of all the Cape Verdes. Yet it was inhabited, they found, only by a hermit. Many sweetwater streams ran into the sea here, but collecting the water in cask was not easily done except by sending boats. So steep-to was the coast here that even close in the least depth they found was 120 fathoms, or more than 700 feet of water, an impossible depth for anchoring any of the ships. They were not able to re-water completely, indeed one at least of the ships received no water at all.

It was this fact which decided the fate of the Portuguese prize, Nuño da Silva's *Santa Maria*. She was laden with Madeira and Canary wines, with clothes of wool, linen, silk and velvet, and many other commodities. 'She was the life of our voyage,' declared Fletcher, 'the neck whereof otherwise had been broken for the shortness of our provisions.'

Vice-Admiral John Winter was to declare that the capture and spoiling of the Portuguese ship was contrary to his will, but that he dared not oppose Drake for fear of his life. Nevertheless, many

items from the *Santa Maria* were to find their way into the hold of
Winter's *Elizabeth*. Everything useful, from spare sails to chests of
fishhooks, combs, knives and scissors, was taken; and the English
crews were grateful, for Drake had told them already that they faced
a long voyage of two years or more.

John Cooke, one of Winter's men, watching the rummaging going
on in the captured merchantman, worried about the fate of her
unfortunate captain and crew. In the event, he misjudged Drake:

'But our General showed himself not so rigorous as every man
thought he would. Neither did he hurt or pain the poor men of
their bodies (though he a little pinched them by the purse), nor
did he yet altogether disfurnish them of principal necessaries,
for after retaining with him the pilot, he gave to the rest of the
Portuguese his pinnace, with a butt of wine and some victuals
and their wearing clothes, and so let them go. But I think their
whole stock rested in our hands'.

The pinnace was the prefabricated vessel which Drake had had
assembled at Mogador for scouting, sounding and boarding. In
return, the *Santa Maria* joined the English fleet, and in effect
Drake had gained a fully laden supply ship to augment the stores
of the fifty-ton flyboat *Swan*. He put into the prize as captain his
friend Thomas Doughty and as one of the seamen his young
brother, Thomas Drake. The vessel's name was anglicised as the
Mary.

Nuño da Silva, the ship's former captain and pilot, was another
sort of prize altogether. Once they reached Brazil, his knowledge
and charts of that coast might be at least as vital to the success of
the English voyage as the cargo which they had taken from him
already. For the ocean crossing, however, the Portuguese was
returned to his own vessel, where he would be of use to Thomas
Doughty in running the ship with its new crew of twenty-eight
Englishmen.

Doughty was given the command because his birth entitled him
to it, although by training and education he was better fitted for the
field or the law courts than for a mariner. But he assumed that his
rank in society and his stake in the voyage entitled him to much else
besides, including the right to look over Drake's shoulder, perhaps
even to take over from him if he fell ill or died. From some of the
talk now going round the fleet, one might guess that he even half

looked forward to that eventuality, judging himself the more capable as a captain-general.

For his part Francis Drake, who lacked long education in higher command and was but self-made, violently resented any attempt to curb or oversee him. He was told that Doughty was claiming to be the prime mover in this enterprise, the real power behind the scenes and one of its principal shareholders, having paid out £1,500. Mockingly, it was reported, Doughty had remarked that this was but a venture for impoverished gentlemen.

Such a cut could hurt. The Drakes were indeed the poor relations of the Hawkins family, much come down in the world. His grandparents, John and Margery Drake, had been well thought of in the parish of Tavistock in Devon during the reign of the first Tudor, Henry VII. That was before the religious upheavals of the sixteenth century, which had spread from the Continent to England in the time of Henry VIII. His father, Edmund Drake, had been a strongly incautious supporter of Protestant ideas, and although Francis had been born in Tavistock parish in the closing years of Great Harry's rule, he did not long remain there. During the brief kingship of the sickly Edward VI there was a Catholic uprising in the West and the whole Drake family had to flee for the safety of the strong walls of Plymouth Castle and its Crown garrison.

After the rising had been put down the Drakes made their way, almost as refugees in their own country, to the south-east coast, where Edmund found a home for them all in a ship-hulk lying in the Medway near the naval base of Chatham. For many years Edmund Drake and his wife had been reduced to poverty, with twelve children to bring up. Later, when Elizabeth was crowned, Edmund became vicar of Upchurch in Kent. Meanwhile, Francis had left their 'home' in the hulk to go to sea with the master of a small merchantman employed in the coasting and cross-Channel trade. When her elderly owner died, he had bequeathed the vessel to the still very young Francis Drake, who had used it to turn the family fortunes upwards once more. But he had never forgotten the poverty and disgrace which had overtaken his family when he was still a boy, nor the cause of it.

The fleet left on its great ocean crossing on 2 February, but before that the first violent quarrel had occurred between Drake and Doughty over a reported case of pilfering in the Portuguese prize. Vice-Admiral Winter, whose ship was partly restocked from the

Santa Maria's stores and cargo, nevertheless penned a damning official note: 'Francis Drake, in the *Pelican*, took a very plentiful prize of wine and bread, with other necessaries, which with good order would have done good to his company, but the discommodities that it bred through disorder, I leave for brevity'.

John Cooke, serving in Winter's ship, noted many details of the 'disorder', for which however he blamed the Captain-General's young brother, Thomas. According to Cooke, Francis Drake had made a swift inspection of the prize and her cargo and then entrusted the safe keeping of it all to Thomas Doughty, for there were many tempting items aboard. He told Doughty that if there was any breach of discipline then the matter should be reported to him, no matter who the offender was. But, wrote Cooke:

> 'It thus chanced that Master Drake had a brother (not the wisest man in Christendom) who he put into this said prize, as also divers others. This Thomas Drake, as one more greedy of praise than covetous of honesty or credit, offered himself the first and only man to break the General his brother's commandment, for he, contrary to this straight prohibition, did not only break open a chest, but did dive suddenly into the same. Master Doughty knew not how to discharge himself against the General but by revealing it unto him. Yet first Master Doughty called Thomas Drake unto him and showed him his great folly.'

According to Cooke, Tom Drake admitted that he had been wrong to break open the chest and asked Doughty not to tell the Captain-General; and Doughty replied that he could not keep quiet about it, but would put his case in as good a light as possible. Drake's reaction, when he next came aboard the prize and heard of the matter, was explosively violent:

> 'The General, immediately falling into some rages, not without some great oaths, seemed to wonder what Thomas Doughty should mean by touching his brother, and did assure himself that Master Doughty had some further meaning in this, that he meant to shoot at his credit, and he would not, nor could not ("by God's life," as he swore) suffer it. From this time forth, grudges did seem to grow between them from day to day . . . '

Francis Fletcher, who was in the *Pelican*, told quite a different story, in which the man accused of pilfering was Doughty. He 'was charged and accused by John Brewer, Edward Bright, and some others of their friends, to have purloined some things of great value, and therefore was not to be put in trust any longer, lest he rob the voyage and deprive the company of their hope'. John Brewer was the trumpeter of the *Pelican*, now put into the prize, while Edward Bright was the ship's carpenter of the flagship, the man responsible for the watertightness of the hull.

According to Fletcher, Drake himself 'speedily went on board the prize to examine the matter'. He found that one of the Portuguese, in the hope of favour, had given Doughty some small gifts out of his chest. These consisted merely of

'certain pairs of Portuguese gloves, some few pieces of money of a strange coin, and a small ring all of them being not worth the speaking of; not purloined, but openly given him, and received in the sight of all men.'

That is, a trivial matter, but, as captain, Doughty should not have set this sort of example. This story does not really contradict Cooke; probably both are true, being charge and countercharge. Cooke was a member of the Doughty faction and unlikely to record anything derogatory against him. Fletcher seems reasonably unbiased and his version rings true, especially in its mention of an anti-Doughty faction in which John Brewer and Edward Bright were noisily prominent.

Both Fletcher and Cooke agree as to what Drake did. He removed Doughty from his post as captain of the prize, and put him into the *Pelican* as temporary captain of the flagship. He appointed his young brother, Thomas Drake, as captain of the prize but remained in her until after the Portuguese prisoners had been sent off in the pinnace, so was himself effectively in charge of the *Mary* during this time.

After that, Fletcher and Cooke part again, but not in any contradictory way; both stories are very likely to be true. Cooke showed tyranny on Drake's part against the Doughty faction:

'But it so fell out that of Master Doughty's part great submission must be made, not only of himself, but by friends. In consideration whereof, Master Leonard Vicary, a gentleman, and Master Doughty's very friend, gave greatly to persuade with the General for and in the behalf of Master Doughty, and praying him to be good unto him, which in the end he yielded unto, and to the outward show forgave and seemed to forget all that had passed, and with this he let him rest still in the *Pelican*, thought by the company to have the authority of Captain from Drake.'

Nevertheless, wrote Cooke, Drake 'daily sought matter against Master Doughty, seeking at every man's hand what they could invey against him'.

This appears to be inexplicable, a contradiction within the space of a paragraph, unless Cooke had omitted some incident from his narrative. Fletcher supplied the missing evidence:

'In the meantime, Thomas Doughty, being aboard the Admiral [i.e., the flagship *Pelican*], was thought to be too preremptory and exceeded his authority, taking upon him too great a command; by reason whereof, such as had him in dislike took advantage against him to complain the second time . . . '

When that happened, it was to be John Brewer, once more, who challenged Doughty.

Fletcher, the chaplain, would later testify that there existed a conspiracy to set one ship against another and to carry away the *Pelican* from Drake's grasp. He had asked Doughty to warn Drake, but Doughty had refused, saying that he himself would be thought the chief conspirator. And when Fletcher had replied that he personally would inform Drake, then Doughty had earnestly asked him not to, because Drake would immediately suspect Doughty of being behind it. From this source, there was also testimony regarding frequent secret conferences aboard the *Pelican* between Doughty and a close friend, Thomas Cuttill, the ship's master, as if the pair were plotting. Doughty had been overheard to promise Cuttill immunity from official reprisal if Cuttill would assist him in some way.

Even the Portuguese captain, Nuño da Silva, who did not speak English but remained in the *Santa Maria* with Drake (who spoke some Spanish), grasped the fact that the Captain-General suspected that an uprising of the fleet against him was being contemplated by 'a very noble gentleman'. While Fletcher's evidence was to be to an English drumhead court martial, da Silva's testimony was to be made to a Spanish inquisition, surely a neutral body in this matter, although not without the means to apply pressure.

Such suspicion, enmity and resentment, embittering the leadership, turning it inwards to rend itself, might have imperilled the success of any voyage. On a venture of great hazard, the cost could be total ruin. Even some of those committed to one faction or the other saw plainly how unwise the conflict was. It may be that Drake's action in making Doughty captain of his own flagship was a last short-lived attempt to patch up the quarrel and forge some sort of working relationship with his noble colleague.

Ahead of them now stretched sixty-three days without sight of land, three weeks of that time spent drifting becalmed in the doldrums. It was nothing to da Silva, but it was new to the Englishmen. For the greater part of the time they were in the *torrida zona*, the Tropics, the burning belt girdling the earth for $23\frac{1}{2}°$ either side of the Equator. From a reading of the classical authors of antiquity, such as Aristotle and Pythagoras, pointed out Francis Fletcher, one would expect the Tropics to be without moisture and therefore uninhabitable, whereas it proved an earthly paradise, both by sea and by land. They were all enjoying the warmth, so luxurious, while far behind them England was iron-bound in winter. For the mariners it was holiday; there was virtually nothing to do. The ships simply ran southward with miles of water under their keels and the minimum of attention required except when a brief tempest or thunderstorm blew up. But these were always quickly over and soon after, such was the heat, everything would be dry again. The miseries of damp and cold were far behind and far ahead of them; for the moment, they were privileged beyond most men.

At least, that was how Fletcher regarded this time in their lives. He filled page after page with lengthy descriptions of the multitude of life that surrounded the ships, both in the seas beneath and in the air above, as they lay becalmed near the Equator. And he added a few untutored sketches, perhaps as evidence, fearing to be mocked when at last he returned to England and the seats of learning. The bonito and the dolphin fish, extremely good to eat, he thought might be accepted. But who would believe him, should he proclaim that fish could fly? 'And because I have made mention of flying fishes, which to the most part of men may seem an absurd thing, and as our green-headed carpers say, a lie, I have thought good here to set down the true report of them to the greater glory of that God which made them.' Fletcher drew the moral from the abundance of excellent if uncommon food with which they were surrounded and noted how even the tempests served their purpose, in that hardly a day went by, for the first three weeks, without a brief rainstorm to augment their still sparse supplies of drinking water.

John Cooke saw the same scenes but read them differently. He called this the 'mean season'. It seems he was a member of the English crew put into the *Santa Maria* and now serving directly under Drake. He wrote how:

> 'We drew towards the Line, where we were becalmed the space of three weeks, but yet subject to divers great storms, terrible lightning and the thunder; and here we had great store of fish, as dolphins and bonitos and other great and mighty fishes. We also found here flying fishes in great abundance, which by the sharp and eager chasing of the dolphins and bonitos, and, as it were to avoid a great bird that seemed to watch to prey on her above the water, did divers times fall into our ships, where she could not rise again.'

As Fletcher described it at greater length, the fleet was followed a thousand miles from land by birds as large as eagles, which perched on the masts, spars and rigging, even on the rails; and were easily captured or knocked on the head for food. Da Silva told the Englishmen, what they could hardly believe, that these birds slept on the wing; first rising to a great height and then soaring with stiff, unmoving pinions. As easily captured were the fish, and they were food for kings, if eaten fresh; but if stored, turned poisonous. And some, like the flying fish, delivered themselves up to the men, showering down on the decks. Mostly, these were used as bait on lines trolled out astern for the bigger game fish.

One peculiarity, Fletcher noted, was the welcome absence of a type of small life, namely the lice which had plagued them since England. Being winter and at sea, it had been hard to get a good wash and change of clothes; and thus the lice had multiplied at a great rate from Plymouth to the Cape Verdes. But the 'burning zone' near the Equator put paid to them; the men flourished in the heat but the lice dropped off and died. Soon the ship was clean and there was no more itching and scratching; the loathsome pests were gone.

In what John Cooke called 'this mean season', the ships idly drifting through the burning, windless days along the Line, the ill feeling between Drake and Doughty sparked into the first public clash. Cooke was unsure whether Drake had planned the incident from the start, or if it was an accident. The dialogue he was able to quote he had from one of the two prime participants, John Brewer, Drake's trumpeter, who was then with Drake in the Portuguese prize.

One day Brewer rowed over to the *Pelican*, now commanded by Doughty, to visit some old companions among the crew. He was offered refreshment, but Doughty butted in in a mocking way and apparently laid hands on him or incited some of the crew to do so. Whereupon Brewer 'began to swear wounds and blood to the company to let him loose' and shouted at them:

'They are not all the General's friends that be here!'

He then turned from the crew and spoke to Doughty directly:

'God's wounds, Doughty, what dost thou mean to use this familiarity with me, considering thou art not the General's friend?'

At first, Doughty protested his innocence:

'What, fellow John, what moves you to this and to use these words to me, that am as good and sure a friend to my good General as any in this fleet, and I defy him that shall say the contrary?'

Then he added a sentence which makes it seem that Brewer might have drawn a weapon to defend himself:

'But is the matter thus, why yet, fellow John, I pray thee let me live until I come into England.'

Brewer at once got into his boat and went back to the prize, where he spoke to Drake, very briefly. Then the boat was rowed over to the *Pelican* once more. When it finally returned, all could see that the passenger this time was Doughty. Drake had been holding a religious service, sitting down at a table, but he got up and went to the bulwark; and at that moment Doughty reached out for the ship's side in order to come aboard. A roar from Drake checked him:

'Stay there, Thomas Doughty, for I must send you to another place!'

He ordered the mariners to row Doughty over to the fleet store-ship, the fifty-ton flyboat *Swan*, commanded by John Chester. Doughty protested, asking to be allowed to speak to Drake, but was refused; and when he raised his voice, Drake turned away.

It was in a fair fury that Doughty arrived at the side of the small storeship. And it was with surprise and puzzlement that he was received aboard. John Saracold, a member of the *Swan*'s crew, heard him rage that he came to them as a prisoner, suspected of sorcery and a traitor to the General; but that he would prove his innocence in England before his betters could even accuse him; that the law would serve him, to their great shame. To the captain, John Chester, he said that he considered him an enemy and would never forgive him for it; that he had friends who had worked for him and would continue to do so; and that he had a promise to be given command of another and much better ship. But a prisoner he remained, although only under open arrest, free to talk.

Meanwhile, Drake had gone back to his flagship, the *Pelican*, taking Nuño da Silva with him and leaving his young brother, Tom Drake, in command of the *Santa Maria*. The fleet kept well together in spite of darkness and storms, but once the *Santa Maria* became separated from the rest. Although it was only for one day that she was missing, out of the two months it took to cross the great ocean, it was a worrying time because she carried the bulk of the wine and the water. Cooke noted that although Doughty was now absent in the flyboat:

> 'our General never ceased to invey against him, terming him a conjuror and witch, and, at any time when we had any foul weather, he would say that Thomas Doughty was the occasioner thereof, and would say that it came out of Tom Doughty's cap-case, and would avouch the same with great oaths; which he at no time scanted, they cost him so little.'

For his part, Doughty never ceased to make propaganda for himself in the flyboat. Firstly, by stressing how important he was to the voyage, how it was through his influence and activity in London that they had got the backing for it and that he had a financial stake in it and was of equal rank in it to Drake. Secondly, by denigrating Drake's past in various ways; stressing that Drake had to flee out of sight to Ireland after his West Indies voyage, and that it was Doughty, the gentleman and man of influence, who had set him on the road to preferment with the Earl of Essex, and had been his equal both in England and abroad in Ireland. And thirdly, several times, the hint that he knew certain secrets about Francis Drake which he would never divulge, but if he did divulge them, Drake would be both sorry and ashamed.

Fourthly, Thomas Doughty claimed that both he and his brother, John Doughty, possessed supernatural powers, that they could conjure up the devil in the shape of a bear, a lion, or a man in armour; and that they had good knowledge of poisons. If anyone believed any of this, they might well be intimidated. There was also, it was reported, straightforward bribery, such as a promise to Henry Spindelay, gunner of the *Swan*, that Doughty would lend him £40 when they got back to England, which was near to a year's wages for an ordinary soldier or sailor.

There was a further strand to Doughty's talk which was very dangerous; it came later in the voyage. Four men were to recall that Doughty had told John Chester, captain of the flyboat, that the ship's master seemed to have taken away his authority from him, but if Mr Chester would accept his, Doughty's orders, then he would be given his authority again and he would put the sword into his hands to rule as he thought good; and Doughty would make the ship's company ready to cut one another's throats. This was the same Mr Chester whom he had previously sworn never to forgive. Chester was one of those who were to recall this conversation.

John Cooke heard, from two or three witnesses, that there had been much more to it than that. 'A sort of bad and envious people, sailors and suchlike' had set out to make life in the flyboat hard for 'Master Thomas Doughty and some other gentlemen'. The ship's master pointedly would not eat with Doughty and his gentlemen friends, but left to sit at table with the sailors, where, Cooke was told, the food was better and more plentiful; whereas Doughty and his friends began to complain of hunger at the captain's table, and Doughty hinted that Chester ought to do something about it.

'I marvel, Master Chester, that you will take it at the Master's hands to be thus used, considering you were appointed to command here by the General . . . '

As that did not produce the desired effect, Doughty got up and sought out the shipmaster, to whom he read the same lesson in management and discipline.

'You do use too much partiality,' he pointed out, 'considering the extremity that for want of victuals we are like to fall into. It is against all reason that you and your mates should be so plentifully fed while others are on the point of starvation.'

There may have been a slight pause while the master digested this, then, according to Cooke's informants, he 'began hereat to storm' at the gentleman. 'Such rascals as you should be glad to eat the thole-pins if I tell you to!' he shouted.

Doughty was not amused, particularly as he was one of the expedition's backers. He took care to make the master aware of the fact that he had a cash stake in the venture. 'Reason will have it that I should be used as other men,' he pointed out, 'considering my adventure.'

'Thou an adventure here?' bellowed the master. 'I will not give a point for thee nor thy adventure, and if thou comest home to enjoy any adventure, I'll be hanged!'

After that, for a minute or two, the sequence of events was too quick to follow. They got very heated, had 'further words' and, heard Cooke, 'a blow or two has passed between them'. The master finished up by saying that Doughty could think himself fortunate if Drake did not get to hear of this.

Doughty then turned to John Chester, captain of the flyboat, and according to Cooke's informants, said: 'Master Chester, let us not be thus used at these knaves' hands. Lose nothing of that authority that the General has committed unto you. If you will, we will put the sword again into your hands, and you shall have the government.'

It is hard for men to recall exact words and phrases, unless they are very important or striking in themselves, but both Drake's witnesses and Cooke's informants were to be in basic agreement as to what Doughty said; and it was very clever. A lawyer himself, he could pretend to be standing up for Drake's authority in supporting the appointed captain, the gentleman John Chester, against the shipmaster, who was a mere sailor, even if a senior one. In Cooke's view, the Master was a member of a clique of 'bad and envious people, sailors and suchlike'. What was unspoken was the fact that Drake was a sailor too, a commoner like the rest; and maybe as quarrelsome, headstrong and unruly as mariners usually were, being men very independent and hard to govern. And, of course, the duty of gentlemen was to govern, by right of breeding and upbringing and because of their long, expensive and superior education. It was a valid, understandable division.

In the flyboat, one day after dinner, when the talk had veered uncomfortably towards the real topic underlying all this – who is to command us? – someone spoke his thoughts aloud and asked, what should be done if there be those among us who are traitors to the General or enemies of our voyage? Without pausing, John Saracold blurted out:

'Deal with them as Magellan did. Hang them up to be an example to the rest!'

That brought in Doughty at once. Swiftly, he interjected:

'Nay, soft! His authority is none such as Magellan's was; for I know his story as well as he himself doth. And as for hanging, it is for dogs and not for men.'

The cabin must have gone very quiet. All knew how frequently the most deadly disputes had broken out on the great voyages of exploration, under the stress of fear, hardship and danger; and of how, all too often, they had been settled. Sometimes the divisive factors had been present at the project's initiation. How many could be sure that the Queen and all of her ministers were of one mind as regards the objects of their own voyage? Magellan's backers had certainly been divided even on basic aims. One party had ordered exploration and conquest, the other sought merely a better, faster route for the spice trade. Some of the ship captains had been Spanish and controlled by the merchants, the others Portuguese and answering to the King – an unhappy combination. Again, there had been the difference between the gentlemen and the mariners: the gentleman captain had brought with him no less than eight personal servants, to wait on him, not to work the ship. From Tenerife onwards, three of the captains who were Spanish and gentle born had attempted to take over the command; and it was many months and thousands of miles later before the matter had been at last resolved. Mendoza and Quesada slain, then their corpses drawn, quartered and hung up as a dread warning; Cartagena and the preacher Sanchez de Reina marooned by the ghastly gibbets and never heard of again.

Whether or not Magellan had held power of life or death was unsure, despite what Doughty said; but most certainly he had acted as if he had. Now perhaps Doughty was right when he told them that Drake had not been granted such powers. But they were thousands of miles from home and were voyaging on many thousands of miles further. In no way was it possible to appeal to the Queen or request a ruling from the Lord Admiral of England.

On 5 April 1578, noted Edward Cliffe, they became aware of a scent which was quite different to that of the sea winds. It was a sweet smell, the smell of a strange continent. Next day, 6 April, they sounded at noon and got thirty-two fathoms, less than 200 feet of water after months on blue ocean many miles deep; and shortly

after the depth had shallowed to twenty-eight fathoms. At three that
afternoon a land mass was sighted – a low-lying coastline with
mountains looming distantly far inland. The latitude of the sighting,
according to the navigators, was $31\frac{1}{2}°$ south of the Equator.

No doubt da Silva had told Drake, if he did not already know,
that the coast of Brazil was dangerous to approach, a shallow shelf
stretching as much as seventy miles out to sea. Keeping a great
distance from the land, the little fleet turned and ran south-south-
west, parallel to the continent of South America, and continued on
that course for a week.

Chapter 4

'AN ENEMY TO THE VOYAGE'

From the River of Silver to the Gibbets of St Julian:
6 April–20 June 1578

THERE are slight discrepancies of dates and positions when different narratives are compared. Naturally, the Spanish interrogation records are inexact on these matters because they were of no importance by the time, when, long afterwards, the witness had come into their hands. Consequently, the Captain-General's cousin, John Drake, who was a lad of fourteen or fifteen at the time of this voyage, but was captured on the Fenton expedition in 1582 and was to be closely questioned regarding the armament and ammunition of Drake's fleet, was allowed to go his own way regarding dates.

Similarly, Nuño da Silva, who was to be interrogated many times and often gave dates differing from each other by a week or more, was not pressed even on discrepancies, although minutely examined regarding the personality and ability of the Captain-General and hardly less so on the capabilities of the ships for fighting. Apparently it was not thought worthwhile to check the dates he gave with the entries in his logbook, which he took with him into captivity.

As regards their first sight of the New World, the trio in the vice-flagship *Elizabeth* were unanimous. John Winter, John Cooke and Edward Cliffe all wrote that they first saw land on 6 April. Cliffe even specified the time, three in the afternoon, after 'smelling' land the previous day, 5 April. Both Winter and Cliffe mentioned the latitude, which they gave as $31\frac{1}{2}°$.

Interestingly, all reports emanating from the flagship, the *Pelican*, gave the date as 5 April, one day earlier than those from the *Elizabeth*. Similar slight discrepancies of a day or so occurred later on, and may suggest sometimes that the ships concerned had become separated and made their landfalls at different times.

Estimates of latitude also varied, although this is not surprising, the instruments used being not very exact and accurate observations

58

anyway being dependent on visibility. Francis Fletcher noted $31\frac{1}{2}°$, the same as the two observations from the *Elizabeth*, but Nuño da Silva, who may actually have taken a sight himself, entered 30° in his log. A narrative printed some years after by the Hakluyt publishing house gave 33°. Unfortunately, the prime evidence, Drake's own personal and elaborate log, although it survived the voyage, disappeared afterwards.

In broad terms, however, it is clear that the fleet steered a course slowly converging with the coast, so that the land was sighted well down the continent to the south of the main Portuguese strongholds in Brazil. This kept them clear of trouble and avoided also any accusation that they had infringed territorial rights. Drake had given out, on leaving the Cape Verdes, that the fleet rendezvous in case of separation would be in the estuary of the Plate, the River of Silver. There they would rest, re-water, scrape the hulls, and wait for stragglers.

On 7 April, the day after the Brazilian coast was first sighted, there blew up from the south a violent tropical thunderstorm with drenching rain so intense that from no ship could any of the others be seen. The storm was driving them onshore into the rocky, dangerous shallows but fortunately lasted only three hours. When it had died away and the heaped seas began to flatten out, they could only count five ships instead of six. The canter, the captured forty-ton fishing vessel which they had exchanged for the *Bark Benedict* and had renamed the *Christopher*, was missing; whether wrecked, sinking or simply blown out of sight beyond the horizon, they could not tell.

Fletcher, who was responsible for two narratives, one more detailed than the other, wrote in the latter:* 'If the Portugal pilot had not been appointed of God to do us good, we had perished without remembrance.' Da Silva, he said, was now in Drake's flagship the *Pelican*, and knowing this coast was able to get them out of danger. The story he had was that the natives had conjured up the winds by throwing sand in the air and praying to devils, who promptly turned the sand into a blinding storm as black as night in Egypt. They did this, apparently, because they had mistaken the English for the Portuguese, who oppressed them. Many of their huge ships of war had been cast away for this reason, Fletcher

* Probably the original; the shorter seems to have been 'expurgated' by a member of the Drake family.

was told. One way or another, it was certainly a dangerous coast
for ships, more hazardous to the great carracks the Portuguese
employed for trade and war than to the small ships of exploration
such as Drake was using.

On 14 April, everyone agreed, the five vessels of the fleet reached
the wide estuary of the River Plate, famous as a place where a
stream of fresh water could be found in the sea. They passed Cape
Saint Mary and coasting on for another six or seven leagues –
twenty miles or so – they came to anchor in a bay under another
cape. Drake called it Cape Joy because, on the second day they
were anchored here, the lost *Christopher* found them. This was no
accident. It arose from Drake's appointing a rendezvous and
insisting that, as they approached the Plate, the ships should keep
within sight of the shore.

Fletcher, who was in the flagship with Drake and da Silva, was
well placed to discover the principles on which Drake planned:
'To keep our whole fleet (as near as possibly we could) together;
to get fresh water, which is of continual use; and to refresh our
men, wearied with long toils at sea, as often as we should find any
opportunity of effecting the same.' They sound simple enough,
but the crew wastage on long voyages was often well above 50 per
cent. It was vital to keep everyone healthy, although easier enun-
ciated than performed.

On 16 April, after the canter had rejoined, all six ships moved
twelve leagues farther up the estuary to where a long, rocky island
just offshore presented a solid barrier to the dangerous southerly
winds. They rode here in calm water until 20 April and killed for
food some of the seals which had a home on the rocks. Fresh meat
was always welcome. However, Fletcher found a medical use for
seal oil. 'It is a present help for outward inflamations in any members,
whereof divers of our men had good experience by my directions
to their great comfort.' He was also something of a herbalist, and
noted the presence of a strange and poisonous plant.

They spent approximately two weeks in the Plate estuary, moving
from anchorage to anchorage, making expeditions ashore, and
generally recuperating after the long ocean voyage and in preparation for the ordeals ahead; for, southward of the Plate, it was now
turning into winter. On 27 April, having already crossed to the
south side of the estuary, the fleet stood out to sea to continue the
the voyage. That night the flyboat *Swan*, in which Doughty was,

parted company, so that the fleet was reduced to five ships again. According to John Cooke, this was the occasion for Drake to fulminate against Doughty, saying that any bad weather they had must have come out of Tom Doughty's capcase, that he was a conjuror and a witch. Although Cooke seems not to have been a first-hand witness, no doubt Drake did say something like this; but it was far from being the whole truth.

Fletcher, who was with him in the *Pelican*, and recording events quite independently, noted that the incident, the second of its kind, impelled him to a policy decision:

> 'Our flyboat, the *Swan*, lost company of us: whereupon, though our General doubted not of her happy coming forward again to the rest of the fleet, yet because it was grievous to have such often losses, and that it was his duty, as much as in him lay, to prevent all inconveniences that might grow – he determined to diminish the number of his ships, thereby to draw his men into less room, that both the fewer ships might the better keep company, and that they might also be the better appointed with new and fresh supplies of provision and men, one to ease the burden of another; especially for that he saw the coast (it drawing now toward winter here) to be subject to many and grievous storms. And therefore he continued on his course, to find a convenient harbour for that use; searching all that coast from 36 to 47 degrees (as diligently as contrary winds and sundry storms would permit), and yet found none for the purpose. And in the meantine, May 8, by another storm the canter also was once more severed from us.'

According to Fletcher there were seventeen leagues to a degree, so the distance was about 500 miles.

On 10 May, according to both Winter and da Silva, the fleet, now reduced to four ships, anchored in a rocky bay in 47° under a headland which Drake dubbed Cape Hope. Before taking the ships further in, it was necessary to make a reconnaissance by boat to sound out the hazards. The witnesses do not agree as to whether this was done on 12 or 13 May, but all reported that Drake in person went in this boat. Fletcher explicitly stated that it was a matter of policy that he did so:

> 'Our General, especially in matters of moment, was never wont to rely on other men's care, howsoever trusty or skilful they might be; but always contemning danger, and refusing no toil,

he was wont himself to be one, whosoever was a second, at every turn, where courage, skill, or industry was to be employed; neither would he at this time entrust the discovery of these dangers to another's pains, but rather to his own experience in searching out and sounding them.'

Reading between those lines, it seems as if Drake either did not yet know the capabilities of everyone in the fleet, or did not trust them; the one would follow from the other.

'A boat being hoisted forth,' wrote Fletcher, 'himself with others, the next morning, May 13, rowed into the bay.' This boat was not from the *Pelican* but from Winter's vice-flagship the *Elizabeth*, so Winter may well have taken Drake's decision to go in it personally and control the reconnaissance as a slight on his own capabilities or, what was virtually the same thing, the competence of his crew. As the boat closed the shore, a native appeared, seemingly friendly, singing and dancing to the beat of a rattle which he had in his hand and was shaking musically; apparently he was very glad to see them. The English looked at him curiously, for there were tales of giants, over seven feet tall, living in the interior; they had earlier found footprints which indicated men of extraordinary size.

'But there was suddenly so great an alteration in the weather, into a thick and misty fog, together with an extreme storm and tempest, that our General, being now three leagues from his ship, thought it better to return,' wrote Fletcher. As the ships were lying off the entrance to the bay, some nine miles away, those in the boat soon lost sight of the fleet and those in the ships soon after lost sight of the boat, which also was being rapidly blown away from them by the force of the wind. To make matters really critical, the storm had sprung up from the south-east, so that the ships were on a lee shore. They dared not go into the bay because it was rocky and dangerous; they could not run seaward for safety because that meant abandoning Drake and the boat; and if they stayed at anchor, the anchors might drag or the wind shift in direction slightly so as to pin them against the shore, embayed without chance of escape.

Winter recorded that his decision was to remain with the vice-flagship at anchor and attempt to ride out the storm where they were. If the *Elizabeth* ran seaward for safety, all the other ships would necessarily follow her lead and Drake would be lost. On the other hand, he was risking the whole fleet by this action. He says that he ordered the thirty-ton bark *Marigold* commanded by John Thomas, who was Christopher Hatton's man, alone to weigh anchor and go into the bay in search of the boat. Fletcher wrote as if Captain Thomas himself had made the decision:

'Yet the fog thickened so mightily, that the sight of the ships was bereft them, and if Captain Thomas (upon the abundance of his love and service to his General) had not adventured with his ship to enter that bay in this perplexity . . . where the winds were more tolerable and the air clearer, we had sustained some great loss, or our General had been further endangered.'

Winter had given him up for dead. 'The *Marigold*, by great chance, as they say, found him; which was a great joy to all the company, for they all judged them that were in the boat lost men.'

A few hours before the gale blew up, the missing canter, the *Christopher*, had found the fleet again, so that they were now five ships strong, lacking only the flyboat *Swan* with Doughty aboard to make their numbers complete. This state of affairs did not outlast the storm, for Tom Drake, now commanding da Silva's old ship the *Santa Maria*, was unable to ride it out and had to run seaward for safety. The other ships, although they did not actually run out to sea, remained well offshore. Only the *Marigold*, with the boat of the *Elizabeth* and Drake himself, remained inside the bay.

The wind blew up overnight and although it had died down by the morning of 14 May, there was no sign of the ships which had been riding outside. Consequently Drake went ashore to build a signal fire as a marker for them. Fletcher says they saw no natives on this occasion, but only the special huts in which they prepared ostriches for eating, or dried them for the winter. When the *Pelican*, *Elizabeth* and *Christopher* appeared, there remained missing the *Santa Maria*, which could not be far away, and the flyboat *Swan* which no one had seen for some time. As this bay was not convenient for watering or the gathering of wood, the *Marigold* went out on 15 May to join the others and the fleet slowly coasted southwards looking for a better anchorage, which they found on 17 May, remaining there more than two weeks. They were to call this Seal Bay, from the number of seals which they killed there and salted down; it was no great distance from the rocky bay.

Thus Fletcher's chronology. Da Silva's dates differ occasionally by a day or two, but the only significant entry is for 13 May (which is Fletcher's 14 May, the day Drake went ashore), for the Portuguese wrote: 'Went ashore, and the Indians took the captain's cap.' The incident of Drake's cap appears in many narratives, mostly after 18 May in a paragraph beginning, usually, 'Meanwhile . . .' This is because the writers normally divide their narratives into Sailing Matters for a given period followed by Matters Ashore or Interesting Observations upon the countryside, which is convenient and logical, if chronologically imprecise. Anyway, all except da Silva appear to place the incident near Seal Bay, after Drake had carried out his search on 18 May.

Two ships were still missing. For three weeks they had had no news of the flyboat *Swan* with Doughty aboard, which had parted company during the night of 27 April; she could be anywhere. The captured *Santa Maria* commanded by Tom Drake had not been missing for anything like as long, having parted company during the night of 14 May. If she had survived, she was likely to be close. In these two storeships were the bulk of their supplies. so there was no possibility of wintering here without them, let alone carrying the voyage to a successful conclusion.

Drake ordered a double sweep. While Winter in the vice-flagship *Elizabeth* would go south in case the ships had overshot the Bay of Seals, he himself would take the *Pelican* north. The northward sweep was immediately successful, the long-lost flyboat *Swan* being sighted by Drake on the very first day, 18 May. Winter went out again on the following day, to look for the *Santa Maria*, but returned unsuccessful.

Drake now began to carry out his policy of reducing the number of ships in the fleet, starting with the fifty-ton *Swan*. She was to be run up on the shore at Seal Bay after her cargo had been removed. Then her ironwork and other gear was to be salvaged, and finally the hull was to be broken up for firewood, a vital necessity during the bitter months ahead. But first, during the removal of much of her cargo, she was brought to lie alongside the *Pelican*, and so Thomas Doughty returned to the flagship.

While this activity went on aboard the ships, shore parties explored inland and made friendly contact with the natives. The longest and by far the most detailed accounts of them were written by Fletcher; the shortest was by John Winter, so short indeed as to be seriously misleading. He wrote:

'Here I saw first this people which they call Giants, which indeed be not at all, though being afar off, for the greatness of their voice a man would think them so. Here six or seven of us went to see them, being a mile from us, because we would make true report of them, what people they are. The which we came nearer to them seemed rather to be Devils than men.'

A casual remark by one of Winter's men, John Cooke, explained the 'Devils' aspect. The natives, he wrote, were largely unclothed, but painted their bodies in bright colours, and 'some had on their heads the similitude of horns'. Another of Winter's men, Edward Cliffe, described an aspect of their meeting which the Vice-Admiral failed to mention. 'They afterward approached nearer to our men, shewing themselves very pleasant, insomuch as Mr Winter danced with them. They were exceedingly delighted with the sound of the trumpet, and viols.'

Fletcher's much longer narrative makes all this quite comprehensible. The natives, he says, were much given to music and dancing; they wore musical rattles around their waists:

'. . . which no sooner begin to make a noise but they begin to dance, and the more they stir their stumps the greater noise or sound they give and the more their spirits are ravished with melody, insomuch that they dance like madmen . . . They did admire at our still music, but the sound of the trumpet, noise of the drum, and especially the blow of the gun was terrible to them.'

On trumpets, therefore, Fletcher and Cliffe did not agree as to the natives' reaction; but perhaps they met different natives at different times. While Cliffe described them as being of 'mean stature', Fletcher unequivocally wrote:

'For as the men in height and greatness are so extraordinary that they hold no comparison with any of the sons of men this day in the world, so the women are answerable to them in stature and proportion every way; and as the men never cut their hair, so the women are ever shorn, or rather shaven, with a razor of flint stone, whereof they make all their edged tools and cut one of them with another.'

On their military capabilities, however, there was complete agreement between on the one hand Fletcher, who no doubt went

c

ashore with parties from the *Pelican*, and on the other Cliffe and Cooke who may have gone separately with men from Winter's *Elizabeth*. 'They were very agile people, and quick, and seemed not to be ignorant in the feats of war, as by their order in ranging their few men might appear,' wrote Cooke. 'Their munition is only bow and arrows,' wrote Fletcher. 'The string of their bows is slack and never bent, wherewith they give a deadly blow and send an arrow with wonderful force.'

Fletcher, the preacher, naturally took an interest in their religion, which he stated was the worship of a Devil-God called Settaboth. The native priest wore two small horns on his head and carried two broad black feathers. The sun and the moon played a part in their devotions. What seemed (from a distance) to be horns worn by ordinary men were in fact ostrich feathers used to keep their very long hair in place. The way they painted their bodies was most extraordinary:

'Some wash their faces with sulphur. Some paint their bodies black, leaving only their necks behind and before white, much like our damsels that wear their squares, their necks and breasts naked. Some paint one shoulder black, another white; and their sides and legs interchangeably, with the same colours, one still contrary to the other. The black part hath upon it white Moons, and the white part black Suns, being the marks and characters of their gods, as before noted.'

Edward Cliffe confirmed this custom, although briefly, and added:

'They be much given to mirth and jollity, and are very sly, and ready to steal any thing that comes within their reach. For one of them snatched our General's cap from his head (as he stooped) being of scarlet with a golden band. Yet he would suffer no man to hurt any of them.'

The cap was probably of silk, for ceremonial wear. According to Fletcher, the native put it on his own head and was delighted. According to John Drake, the General's cousin, the Indian ran away and when an Englishman raised an arquebus to fire at him, Drake commanded him 'not to kill a man for a cap,' but to beat him instead if they could catch him. When the Indians realised that they had given offence, testified John Drake later (to his

Spanish inquisitors), one of them cut himself with an arrowhead until the blood ran, to show he was sorry. Fletcher (who was writing for an English audience) described exactly the same action by the native, but gave a rather more involved interpretation of its meaning. As the English and the locals could converse only by means of signs, there is no certainty as to who is right.

Another native, however, who showed himself just as familiar as the remover of the cap, made the mistake of trying to join a party of Englishmen who were standing around drinking their morning glass of strong Canary wine. He snatched a glass and tried to drink it, but, wrote Fletcher:

'it came not to his lips when it took him by the nose, and so suddenly entered into his head, that he was so drunk, or at the least so overcome with spirit of the wine, that he fell flat upon his buttock, not able to stand any longer, so that his company began to startle as if we had slain the man . . .'

The native then tried to drink the wine while sitting down (he had not spilled it all during his collapse); and by sniffing and sucking, succeeded. 'From which time he took such liking for wine, that having learned the word, he every morning would come down the mountains with a mighty cry of "Wine! Wine! Wine!" till he came to our tent, never ceasing till he had his draught . . .'

The natives ate their food raw, including seal or sea-lion meat (the Spaniards called the creatures sea-wolves), and, as far as Fletcher could see, had no boats or canoes, so that the islands in the bay held massed colonies of undisturbed seabirds which made good eating for the Englishmen. The paint the natives so carefully daubed on their bodies was, he thought, done as a form of protection against the cold, for they wore no clothes apart from a scrap of fur thrown round their shoulders when they sat down or lay down, instead of moving around. They had 'clean, comely and strong bodies', he observed; and as the women as well as the men went undressed, it must have been a sore trial to the young mariners.

Fletcher perhaps hints at some relationship when, having recounted how they had in their fortnight's stay collected a good stock of provisions, some 200 seals as well as the birds, he wrote his farewell: 'We were ready, being the sons of God, to leave the daughters of men.'

Almost their final act was to burn by the island where they lay what still remained of the flyboat *Swan* in order to salvage the ironwork used in her construction.

While the two ships had lain alongside each other, the stores from the doomed *Swan* being loaded into the *Pelican*, Doughty had been moved back to the flagship, which he had once commanded and where he had friends, including Thomas Cuttill, the master. According to Fletcher, who was reasonably unbiased, his removal originally had been due to the fact that he was 'thought to be too peremptory and had exceeded his authority, taking upon him too great a command.' John Cooke, who passionately favoured Doughty, but whose meanings are not always clear, wrote that:

'Master Doughty, delivered out of this flyboat, remained as yet in the *Pelican*. But yet upon some unkind speeches, as in saying that the worst word that came out of his mouth was to be believed as much as his oath, whereupon the General did not only strike him, but commanded him to be bound to the mast.'

John Chester, commander of the flyboat, whom he had tried to subvert earlier, carried out the binding, according to Cooke, who added some innuendoes against Chester which are not now easy to comprehend.

Shortly afterwards Doughty was forced into the captured canter, the *Christopher*, protesting vehemently, according to Cooke:

'Here was Master Thomas Doughty put into the canter, although greatly against his will, for he said he knew them to be there that sought his life, as, namely, the master of the flyboat [John Chester], and some other desperate and unhonest people.'

But Drake answered that he would go whether he wanted to or not, and if Doughty resisted, he would have him lifted out of the flagship and into the flyboat with the tackle as if he was a bit of cargo, and Drake ordered the tackle to be lowered ready for this task. Unwilling to face such indignity, Doughty went quietly. 'Thus aboard the canter he went, and his brother John Doughty with him.'

Cooke did not see the final act in Seal Bay, but wrote down what he was told by a credible witness.. The ships were about to weigh anchor and the very last company was about to leave from the shore, when a row broke out between Drake and Thomas Cuttill, master of the *Pelican*. What they said to each other, Cooke did not know, but he was told that Cuttill 'departed in great fury' from the little island, splashing through the shallow water between it and the mainland with his firearm slung round his neck to keep it dry. Then he turned round and shouted out his defiance of Drake over the water:

'Well, my masters, I am heavily borne here, because I will not accuse this gentleman [Doughty] of that as I take God to witness I know not by him, and therefore I take you all to witness whatsoever becomes of me, I never knew anything by him but to be the General's friend, and rather than I will bide this hard contenance at the General's hands I will yield myself into Cannibals' hands, and so I pray you all to pray for me.'

All the men returned aboard their ships, making no attempt to persuade Cuttill to come with them. When he was alone, Cuttill fired a shot in the air, to summon the friendly natives to him, but without result. 'Our General taking it that it had been for a boat sent his boat ashore, and the company by entreaty brought him aboard,' wrote Cooke. 'And so we departed this harbour, not forgetting we had watered and made new provision of victuals.' But the feeling among the crews was not happy; there was too much dissension.

Reduced to four ships, with the prize missing and the flyboat burnt, the little fleet left Seal Bay on 3 June; and shortly afterwards, in bad weather with Doughty aboard, the canter went missing again and they were reduced to three. Once more, according to Cooke, Drake pretended to blame Doughty. 'Our General always thought or at least would so give out, when he saw any foul weather, that Thomas Doughty was occasion thereof.' Still, it was getting slightly monotonous, first the flyboat and then the canter, and what may have been intended as a joke, that Doughty brought ill luck, could have collected a gloss of belief after all. But this separation must certainly have stiffened Drake's resolution to reduce the number of his ships and so make it easier for the fleet to keep together. When the *Christopher* was found again after a search, a few days later, Drake determined to dispose of her at once. They had all been blown back up the coast towards that rocky bay where Drake had nearly lost his life in the boat when the storm blew up.

They anchored her on 12 June, taking the cargo and gear out

of the canter, and also making trips ashore to contact the natives.
By 14 June they had finished and the fisher boat was abandoned;
or, as Cliffe put it, they 'let her float in the sea.' And once again
a home had to be found for Thomas Doughty, for Drake did not
want to go near him, and yet he feared the man would use his
influence to the full if he was not watched by those he could trust.
The best solution he could find to an intractable problem was to
hand him into the custody of Vice-Admiral Winter in the *Elizabeth*,
hedged with such restrictions as he could think of. Winter recorded:
'Here he put Mr Thomas Doughty aboard the *Elizabeth*, and his
brother, commanding them upon pain of death neither to write
nor read but in English: that he would hold him as an enemy to
the voyage any that had conference with him.' This prohibition
on language made clear what sort of person he most wanted to keep
from communicating – an educated gentleman who might have
the gift of Greek or Hebrew, as Thomas Doughty did, which would
give them an almost unbreakable code for letters or speech.

These orders appear most carefully thought out and are therefore
evidence that Drake believed in the existence of a conspiracy
against him, led by Thomas Doughty, and thought that it might
spread, particularly among the gentlemen. Most certainly there
did exist an anti-Drake faction, which regarded mariners as 'bad
and envious people' with dishonest motives and felt honestly
intimidated and afraid under Drake's rule. John Cooke complained
of 'Master Doughty's woes, which did daily increase through this
tyranical government, and although most, and especially such as
were honest, did lament his case, yet durst they not to be known
thereof but to their assured friends'.

Although Cooke often wrote vaguely when reporting at second
hand what he had been told by others, he proved an excellent
first-hand witness when, after the empty *Christopher* had been
abandoned, Drake made a speech to the crew of the ship Cooke
was serving in before sending the Doughty brothers over to it for
close custody:

'Master Drake himself came aboard the *Elizabeth* and calling
all the company together told them that he was to send thither
a very bad couple of men, the which he did not know how to
carry along with him this voyage and go through there withall,
as namely, qd. he,

"Thomas Doughty who is a conjuror, a seditious fellow and a very bad and lewd fellow and one that I have made that reckoning of as of my least hand, and his brother the young Doughty, a witch, a poisoner, and such a one as the world can judge of; I can not tell from whence he came, but from the devil, I think."

And so warning the company that none should speak to them nor use any conference with them; if they did he would hold them as his enemies, aye, and enemies to the voyage; and he willed that great care should be taken that they should neither write nor read. And then he declared what wealth the worst boy in the fleet should get by this voyage, and how the worst boy should never need to go again to sea, but should be able to live in England with a right good gentleman, for qd. he,

"You shall see that we will have gold come as plentiful as this wood unto the ships, and when I have made my voyage I will stay four days for you, my masters, to take the spoil."

With divers other like invectives against him, he departed, and shortly after he sent the said Thomas Doughty and his brother aboard the *Elizabeth*, commanding them as they would answer it with their lives not to set pen to paper nor yet to read but what every man might understand and see. And soon their entertainment there was accordingly, for men durst not speak to him (although willingly perhaps they would).'

If Drake promised gold in the future for any who would faithfully follow him, so did Doughty to those who would make his present conditions more comfortable. Wrote Cooke:

'And as his fare was with the simplest in the ship, so was his lodgings agreeable unto the same. But he having agreed with the boatswain of the ship for a cabin room, which stood, God knows, in an uncomfortable place, yet he must pay three pounds for the same in England.'

The boatswain was found out, lost his office, and came under 'heavy displeasure'.

On 14 June the fleet stood out from the bay and sailed south again, reduced to the *Pelican*, the *Elizabeth* and the *Marigold*. Two pocket warships and a thirty-ton bark. The flyboat *Swan* had been burnt, the canter *Christopher* abandoned; the *Santa Maria*, the

Portuguese prize captained by Tom Drake, was still missing. They had not seen her for a whole month now.

Drake kept on southward until almost at the Strait of Magellan, his route into the great South Sea, but anchored in a small bay to hold a conference. The advice he was given, according to Fletcher, was that it would go hard with the *Santa Maria* if she attempted the Straits alone, and equally the fleet needed her; it would be best to sail back to the northwards and try to find the ship and their friends again.

Next morning, 18 June, they put out to sea and sailed back towards the Equator. On the evening of the second day, 19 June, when within a few leagues of a natural harbour, Port St Julian, they sighted the *Santa Maria* labouring southwards alone for the Strait of Magellan. She was in a bad way, in poor condition to attempt the most critical stage of a testing voyage. This fact was to have strange consequences.

Fletcher recorded the decision:

'And forasmuch as the ship was far out of order, and very leaky, by reason of the extremity of weather which she had endured, before her losing company as well as in her absence, our General thought good to bear into Port St Julian with his fleet, because it was so nigh at hand, and so convenient a place; and intending there to refresh his wearied men, and cherish them which had in their absence tasted such bitterness of discomfort, besides the want of many things which they sustained. Thus the next day, 20 June, we entered Port St Julian, which standeth in 49 deg. 30 min., and hath on the south side of the harbour picked rocks like towers . . .'

The preacher gave directions as to how to recognise Port St Julian and how to enter safely. What he did not point out was the painful truth that this haven was almost certainly bound to be the watershed of this voyage as of Magellan's, the point beyond which any expedition was irrevocably committed to attempting to pass through into the great south sea.

And so they entered. *Pelican*, 100 tons, *Elizabeth*, eighty tons, *Marigold*, thirty tons, and the battered *Mary* (ex-*Santa Maria*), 150 (Portuguese) tons.

Chapter 5

A BATTLE WITH GIANTS

Port St Julian:
20–30 June 1578

THE entrance to the harbour faced north-east and proved to be a narrow bottleneck obstructed by sandbanks, but opening out into a useful stretch of protected water. It was desolate, snow-swept and bitterly cold, for summer in this part of the world last only from January to March. There was some argument among the crews as to whether or not this was really the infamous Puerto San Julián, the barren harbour found and so called by Magellan. Those with access to charts said that it was, from the latitude. John Drake was later to tell his Spanish captors that they had a Magellan map (supposedly secret) which proved the identity of the place.

Drake was fond of acquiring charts, by purchase or otherwise. Da Silva was to testify that 'on capturing vessels the first things that he seized were the navigation charts, the astrolabes, compasses and needles'. From da Silva himself Drake had taken:

'his navigational chart (which did not include more of the Indies than the Rio de la Plata and the Cape of Good Hope); his astrolabe, his commissariat book, his chart of the coast of Brazil . . . What is more, after taking the chart, which was in the Portuguese language, he had it translated into English, and, as he navigated along the coast of Brazil, he went on verifying it, from 24 degrees, to which the Portuguese charts reach, until the town called San Vicente. In point of fact Francis Drake wrote down all he had learnt concerning the routes of the Portuguese . . . as well as the ports and land and sea forces of the Portuguese Indies.'

On one of the English charts this place was named Abra de Islas, but, said da Silva, they all called it 'Port St Julian'. That it was indeed so, they shortly discovered.

According to da Silva, they chose for their anchorage a small,
low sandy island two leagues inside the harbour and only a short
distance from the mainland of Patagonia. This would make an excellent shore base, safe from any attack by natives. That there were
natives about, they could see, by the many distant fires. Then, on
the mainland close by the sea, opposite their island, they came
across something so strange that at first they could hardly believe
in its implications. Fletcher wrote:

> 'For our men found a gibbet, fallen down, made of a spruce mast,
> with men's bones underneath it, which they conjectured to be the
> same gibbet which Magellan commanded to be erected, in the
> year 1520, for the execution of John Cartagena, the Bishop of
> Burgos's cousin, who by the king's order was joined with
> Magellan in commission, and made his vice-admiral.'

They were astonished that timber in the open could last so long
in such perfect condition, for the gibbet was found 'sound and
whole', although it must have been there for more than half a
century. Fletcher speculated that this might be because it was made
of a fir-wood. It was in such good condition (he wrote in his un-
expurgated narrative) that a gruesome trade in 'souvenirs' sprang
up. Out of the wood of the gibbet 'our cooper made tankards or
cans for such as the company as would drink in them, whereof for
my own part I had no great liking . . . '

Almost certainly, the gibbet and the human bones were relics of
Magellan's stay in the harbour from March to August of 1520,
fifty-eight years before. But Fletcher was wrong in thinking that
Juan de Cartagena, captain of the *San Antonio*, had been gibbeted,
although he must have died there. Cartagena was one of three
Spanish captains who tried to take over the fleet and kill Magellan.
One of them, Mendoza, captain of the *Victoria*, was assassinated
during Magellan's countercoup; another, Gaspar de Quesada,
captain of the *Concepción*, was beheaded. The corpses of these two
men were ritually disembowelled, then cut into four pieces, and
these 'quarters' hung up on gibbets as an object lesson to the
defeated mutineers that Magellan was master of the fleet. What
Drake's men had found must have been part of either Mendoza or
de Quesada.

However, there must have been three other bodies from the
Magellan expedition lying somewhere about Port St Julian, for

two of the conspirators, Juan de Cartagena himself and the lay priest Sanchez de Reinea, were marooned. What neither Fletcher nor anyone else in the English fleet at first realised, apparently, was that an ordinary soldier had been killed in a clash with the local 'giants'. Wanting to take two giants back home with him as proof, Magellan had carried out a deception in which two unsuspecting giants were shackled by the legs. But the trick went wrong, a giant was wounded, a European soldier was killed, and the whole tribe of 'giants' turned into enemeis of all Europeans (as they could not distinguish between nations, let alone expeditions). Cartagena and the priest would have been at the mercy of the giants as soon as their ammunition ran out.

On 22 June 1578 Drake took a boat ashore with half a dozen friends, looking for water and generally exploring. With him were Thomas Drake, his brother, John Thomas, captain of the *Marigold*, Robert Winterhey, a gentleman, a Dutchman called Oliver who was master gunner of the *Pelican*, John Brewer, the trumpeter, and Thomas Hood, or Flood. They went armed. Some wore swords and shields, but Oliver had a handgun (a fowling-piece with a scatter-charge of hailshot), while Winterhey carried one of the deadly longbows which combined long range with a high rate of fire. In effect, it was an officers' patrol, and John Cooke was probably not far wrong in judging them overconfident. He was certainly right in saying one should never underrate an enemy, no matter how weak. However, they probably went ashore relaxed, not expecting to meet anyone, let alone an enemy, for in a thousand miles' journeying along this continent they had yet to meet with hostility from natives towards a landing party. But there is always a first time.

Patagonia was named after the giants who, according to Magellan and his chronicler, Pigafetta, inhabited the country. The word came from *patagón* (big-foot) because the first giant met by his expedition wore llama-hide buskins stuffed with straw on his feet. But Magellan had been in Puerto San Julián two months before he even saw one. Drake met three shortly after going ashore. They were all young, one being only a boy and unarmed, but the other two had conventional bows and arrows. The English made friends in the usual way, by showing trinkets and manufactured articles, which the natives eagerly accepted, as all natives had done before. Admittedly, none had been so huge as this trio; they really were monster-men.

However, what interested them much more than the trinkets was the longbow, with its great length and strong drawing technique. They were amazed when Winterhey loosed an arrow for them and they saw the distance to which it went. In turn, they tried their own bows. The first shots fell ludicrously short, so they walked forward to where the shafts had fallen, picked them up, and fired again from there. And still the shots fell short – although, this time, only just! How could so small a man send an arrow such a long way? More than twice the distance they could manage!

Everything was friendly until, wrote Fletcher:

> 'suddenly there came two other giants (old and grim weatherbeaten villains) to their company, to whom our men offering the like kindness as they had to the others, they found them nothing so tractable as they did the rest, yet being without all suspicion of any treachery to come.'

The veterans sent away the naive youngsters (clearly suspecting another Magellan trick to capture live 'specimens'), with what seemed to be, to the puzzled English, angry words. And according to John Drake, the chief of the old giants 'kept beating a small dog he carried so that it should bite Captain Francis'. But still the English had no apprehension, for were there not six of them to two of the natives? And although the two natives had bows, the English matched them with one longbow and one handgun, plus the cutting weapons, the swords and a block-bill. Then a slight mischance changed everything and tilted the delicate balance of force. Winterhey draw the string back with his gloved hand towards his ear, preparatory to loosing a shaft that with a pull of 100 lbs behind it would go better than 200 yards . . . when the string broke.

The two veteran giants saw only one weapon which they recognised as a weapon – the bow. And that single bow was now broken. The invaders were defenceless. But they would not be for long, for Winterhey had taken out another bowstring and was busy restringing the weapon.

A giant stepped forward, charging his bow, and clapped an arrow into Winterhey which penetrated the English archer's lungs.

Oliver, the master gunner, raised the fowling piece to his shoulder and took steady aim at the giant. But the touchhole was damp with the drizzling rain of Port St Julian, and the gun would not fire. Oliver half-lowered the caliver to clear the touchhole. Then, wrote

Fletcher, 'the giant again shot at him and struck him in the breast, and through the heart and out at the back through a rib, quarter of a yard at least, and immediately died'.

Two Englishmen down, one dead and one dying, with arrows sticking out of them. The rest with cutting weapons only and some with shields, but not all. And none able to close the distance to the giants without for a certainty having an arrow clapped into him.

Drake was very swift-thinking. He got the survivors ducking and weaving, then called out for the men with shields to go in front, those without to hide behind them. They were to collect arrows with the shields, to break arrows which missed, and to make the giants loose all their arrows, after which they would be defenceless.

Arrow after arrow hissed through the air, but in a short time one giant had but one arrow left, doubtful at whom to loose it. Drake then picked up the caliver where the dead gunner, Oliver, had dropped it. 'The General then took the fowling piece in hand, and priming it anew, made a shot at him that first began the quarrel, and striking him in the paunch with hail shot, sent his guts abroad.' Struck by a burst of scattershot, the giant was disembowelled, his intestines bursting out of his body in an obscene tide. He screamed 'with great torment; it seemed by his cry, which was so hideous and horrible a roar, as if ten bulls had joined together in roaring'.

His companions turned and ran, as did a number of fresh arrivals who had appeared among the trees. Drake's party retired quickly too, for the gentleman-archer Winterhey was still alive, with an arrow in his lung. They carried him down to the boat and out to the ship, but he died two days later. In their haste to get him treatment, they had abandoned the body of Oliver, and when they finally recovered the body, for burial in the same grave with Winterhey, they found that the giants had thrust an English arrow as deep into one eye as they could, and had removed one shoe, one stocking, and his cap. It seemed as if the giants were as curious about the strangers as the Europeans were about them. After this, the English had no trouble from them, whereas they had most effectively harassed Magellan for months.

The word 'giant' has too many implications and might be thought to indicate a man twelve feet or even twenty feet high. Of course, this was nonsense, the English found. Fletcher wrote that although:

'Magellan was not altogether deceived in naming them Giants,
for they generally differ from the common sort of men, both in
stature, bigness, and strength of body, as also in the hideousness
of their voice; but yet they are nothing so monstrous or giantlike
as they were reported, there being some Englishmen as tall as
the highest of any that we could see. The name *Pentagones, Five
cubits*, viz., 7 foot and a half, describing the full height (if not
somewhat more) of the highest of them. But this is certain, that
the Spanish cruelties there used, have made them more monstrous
in mind and manners, than they are in body, and more inhospitable to deal with any strangers that shall come hereafter.'

These were the first casualties the fleet had suffered, apart from
the boy sailor lost overboard soon after they left England. And that
had been an accident. This was not. This had the brutal violence
of war, and so with full military honours the two men had been
buried.

'This bloody tragedy being ended, another more grievous ensued,'
wrote Fletcher in his original narrative:

'I call it more grievous, because it was among ourselves begun,
contrived and ended. For now Thomas Doughty, our country-
man, is called in question, not by giants, but by Christians, even
ourselves. The original of dislike against him you may read in
the story of the Islands of Cape Verde, at his taking the
Portuguese prize, by whom he was accused, and for what. But
now more dangerous matter and of greater weight is laid to his
charge, and that by the same persons, namely, for words spoken
by him to them, being in England, in the General's garden in
Plymouth, long before our departure thence . . . '

Such charges had a chill sound, when spoken at Puerto San Julián
by the raw graves of Winterhey and Oliver, by the unburied
mouldering remains of part of a human being which might have
been one of Magellan's captains similarly arraigned so long ago.

It is hard to write impartially from partial narratives, but not
impossible when the witnesses make clear their stand, as John
Cooke does, for instance. Here Drake, wrote Cooke:

'spewed out against Thomas Doughty all his venom, here he
ended all his conceived hatred, not by courtesy or friendly
reconcilement, but by most tyranical blood spilling, for he [Drake]

was never quiet while he [Doughty] lived, which in wisdom and honest government as far passed him as he in tyranny excelled all men.'

Precisely because he felt so passionately, Cooke made or preserved a detailed record of the trial, of the dialogue, of the speeches. But also because he felt so deeply, he became quite unable to depict Drake in anything but a luridly unfavourable light.

In Cooke's narrative of the tragic episode with the giants, there is only condemnation of Drake for being careless. There is no mention of the fact that he extricated the party from a difficult position by quick thinking and accurate shooting, although Fletcher says so. Similarly, when Cooke describes the first clash between Drake and Doughty at the Cape Verdes, all we are told is that Doughty reported Tom Drake for breaking open a chest in the Portuguese prize. In Fletcher we hear that there was a charge the other way round – that it was Doughty who was accused of pilfering, not by Drake but by John Brewer and Edward Bright, two men who were now making much more serious allegations against him.

Fletcher was not a partisan in his original narrative, which was probably something of an occasional diary. He may even have modelled it on Pigafetta's chronicle of his voyage with Magellan (and later, El Cano, after Magellan's death). There are the same 'set-piece' traveller's descriptions of the natives and the local flora and fauna. He may even at times be arguing with Pigafetta, for he is swift to pounce on Spanish inaccuracies, and equally swift to trounce armchair scholars who never dare to verify their facts. But his reactions to what was about to happen again at Port St Julian show that he did not side with Drake in this matter, whereas generally Fletcher merely tells us what happened, not what we ought to think about it (unless the subject is religion).

Fletcher's manuscript was headed: 'The first part of the second voiage about the world, attempted, continued, and happily accomplished within the tyme of three years, by M. ffrancis Drake, at her highness command, and his company, written and faithfully layed downe by Ffrancis Ffletcher, Minister of Christ and Preacher of the Gospell, adventurer and traveller in the same voyage.'* This narrative, 'the first part', takes the story only as far as November, 1578; if a second part was written, it did not survive. The Manuscript, or

* British Museum. Sloane MS No. 61.

a copy of it, came into the hands of a nephew of Drake who used it to glorify the family name. Certain parts were rewritten, others omitted, some new material was inserted, and the whole published in 1628 as a book 'carefully collected out of the Notes of Master Francis Fletcher, Preacher in this employment, and diuers others his followers in the same'; this takes the story to 1580. Although largely based on Fletcher, and many times using the words of Fletcher, yet in fact it is really Drake speaking through his family. And this is just as well, to counter-balance the bias of John Cooke, who indeed often reproduces Drake's words so vividly that we seem almost to have a picture of the man haranguing the crew. But not always do we have all Drake's point of view or his full meaning, because Cooke so burns with hate that he cannot allow himself to grant the 'tyrant' any realistic, comprehensible motive.

Fletcher's original narrative began: 'This bloody tragedy being ended, another more grievous ensued.' The second version starts:

'To this evil, thus received at the hands of infidels, there grew another mischief, wrought and contrived closely amongst ourselves; as great, yea, far greater, and of far more grievous consequence than the former, but it was by God's providence detected and prevented in time, which else had extended itself, not only to the violent shedding of innocent blood by murdering our General, and such others as were most firm and faithful to him, but also the final overthrow of the whole action intended, and to divers other most dangerous effects.'

That there was a Doughty faction we know, so there are only two real queries: how far did they intend to go? and if they took over, what would they do with the fleet – sail on or go back? These had been the issues in 1520 between Magellan and some of his captains, one of whom did manage to desert successfully.

That Francis Drake's viewpoint was shared to some extent is indicated by a ragbag of evidence which is all that remains. John Drake, under interrogation twice by the Spaniards, twice told the same story about Doughty: 'He wished to mutiny with the men' and: 'He was inciting the men to mutiny.' Under interrogation by different Spaniards in a different place and at a different time, Nuño da Silva stated that Drake had a 'suspicion that a very noble gentleman intended to rise against him with the other ships, and kill him'.

A document written by a Portuguese compatriot of da Silva by the name of Lope Vaz was captured by the English later and proved to be an account of this voyage by Drake; regarding the Doughty affair, it stated that this arose 'because he would have returned home'. Similar testimony was given by a Spanish nobleman, de Zarate, who was captured by Drake later. Reporting to his superiors the gist of a conversation with Drake, he was able to quote Drake's version of Doughty's words:

'We have been a long while in this strait and you have placed all of us, who follow or serve you, in danger of death. It would therefore be prudent for you to give order that we return to the North Sea, where we have the certainty of capturing prizes, and that we give up seeking to make new discoveries. You see how fraught with difficulties these are.'

Da Silva was to remark that they only had two days of good weather while on the coast of South America, because they had come at the wrong season for sailing in the southern latitudes. That, and not 'Tom Doughty's capcase', was the real reason for the appalling series of storms they had had to survive. In those circumstances, there always was the temptation to take the easy way out; to go back to England or to go to the Spice Islands by a known route, round Africa. A failure of resolution at the top at this critical moment could imperil the whole voyage.

De Zarate added that Drake had not spoken ill of Thomas Doughty, instead he had spoken much good of him, but said that he had had no alternative but to act as he did because this was what the Queen's service demanded. 'He showed me the commissions that he had received from her and carried', added the Spaniard. To go onward or to go back was more than a technical difference of opinion; Drake had been ordered to go on by the Queen herself, and the Queen was England. In effect, it was for their country that they go into the great South Sea and not falter short of the entrance to it.

There was more still. Drake's rages against Doughty, as reported by John Cooke, make sense if it was true, or even if Drake only thought it was true, that little by little Doughty was scheming to take over the command of the fleet, aided by the rest of the gentlemen; and that he had almost succeeded. In a part of Fletcher which is surely Drake, the heart of the matter is made clear. Drake:

'at length perceiving that his lenience and favours did little good, in that the heat of ambition was not yet allayed, nor could be quenched, it seemed, but by blood; and that the manifold practices grew daily more and more, even to extremities; he thought it high time to call these practices into question, before it were too late to call any question of them into hearing.'

In short, it appeared to Drake that Doughty was utterly obsessed with obtaining power; that he never could be happy without it; and that, left alive, he never would stop intriguing until he got it. If left alive. Even if he could be stopped, there would be constant friction, the expedition would be rent between the two of them, and must surely fail. Many men's lives might be lost if Doughty lived.

The possession of ambition is not a capital offence. Nor are interminable attempts, little by little, to usurp command, besides being difficult to prove. To allege the 'overthrow' of the voyage would be better, but a case could be made for giving up. To invite really severe penalties, the authority of the state would have to be questioned; the Queen and her ministers would have to be involved. The offence would have to be treason.

Chapter 6

'LO! HERE IS AN END TO TRAITORS!'

The Trial of Thomas Doughty:
Port St Julian: 30 June–2 July 1578

THE trial of Thomas Doughty was held ashore on the island, where all the crews of the fleet were assembled, on 30 June 1578. They numbered now about 160 men and boys. Forty of the most senior were to be empanelled as a jury shortly after the proceedings began. The Drake version of the opening of the trial and the charges made (found in Fletcher) state that he began by enumerating the many good points which he found in Thomas Doughty; what great friends they had been; and in how high a regard Doughty was held among important people in England.

Drake introduced the evidence against Doughty, which was in the form of written testimony by various persons in the fleet warning him of what Doughty had been saying and doing all the way from Plymouth to Port St Julian. Generally, these things had been observed 'not so much by himself [Drake] as by his good friends; not only at sea, but even at Plymouth; not bare words, but writings; not writings alone, but actions, tending to the overthrow of the service in hand, and making away of his person.'

This story, particularly where it refers to the initial praise of Doughty, is more or less what Drake personally was to tell de Zarate a few months later, and as the Spaniard's report on Drake and the Doughty affair went firstly to his own superior, the Viceroy of New Spain, and then into the appropriate Spanish archives to be preserved, this document* does give an informal view of the formal prosecution case beyond any possibility of later tampering or rethinking.

Some of the prosecution documents† still exist, because they went into the English archives and were preserved. They are affidavits signed by one or more witnesses certifying that they heard

* *Archivo General de Indias*, Patronato, E.1, C.5, L.2–21, No. 19.
† *Harleian* MS, 6221, fol. 9, vid. ante, p. 62.

Thomas Doughty say this or that, and without doubt they are some of the documents referred to by Drake as printed in Fletcher. They tend to show Doughty as conspiring and claiming to have higher friends at Court than Drake and to be co-director of the venture (e.g.: 'Our captain was not to do anything without the assent of the said Thomas Doughty'). A few signed by Drake. Others were attested to be by Francis Fletcher, John Saracold, John Chester, Emanuel Watkins and Gregory Cary. A few accusations were made by no fewer than twenty-nine witnesses, including the Vice-Admiral, John Winter, and Nicolas Anthony, master of the *Marigold*.

The mass signatures were to a different class of accusation – for instance: 'That the said Thomas Doughty was not to be charged with the least paring of a nail, and that the Captain knew it well; but that he dissembled to please a sort of cogging and lying knaves which are about him.' In the context of what Drake was to say later, this appears to be a claim that the gentlemen, of whom Doughty was the leader, could not be ordered or even expected to take any part in the hard manual work inseparable from life in a small sailing ship. And of course it contained another unflattering reference to the men around Drake ('cogging and lying knaves'), which is believable because Cooke had independently dubbed them 'bad and envious people, sailors and suchlike'. Little wonder so many mariners signed the document, if indeed Doughty had said something similar. Obviously matters were on the boil and Cooke, in defending Doughty with such intemperance, proves the prosecution case here.

Similar mass signatures were attached to an allegation that Doughty made threats against people who opposed him and his faction: 'That whosoever did speak against him here, he ... in their mouths when the said Thomas Doughty came to England.' One of the twenty-nine men who signed was Leonard Vicary, a gentleman said by Cooke to be a great friend of Doughty's, a man who had interceded for him with Drake.

By contrast, the most serious allegation of all, that Doughty had been heard uttering treasonable speeches in Plymouth, on board the *Pelican* and elsewhere, was to be backed only by a single accuser – Edward Bright, ship's carpenter. That came later.

The Drake version of the trial, as given in Fletcher, seems unnaturally smooth and glossy, with Doughty easily admitting his guilt in the face of overwhelming written proofs. The real affair was rough and gritty, with Doughty, the trained lawyer, fighting every inch of the way, according to John Cooke. Biased or not, Cooke was there and he describes how the whole company were brought ashore to a prepared place and Drake sat himself down with John Thomas, captain of the *Marigold*, close beside him. Thomas was carrying bundles of rolled up documents containing the written evidence to be read out. While he was sorting them, Doughty was brought in 'more like a prisoner than a gentleman of honest conversation,' complained Cooke. Drake did not wait for Captain Thomas to arrange all the rolls of paper before starting proceedings. He addressed the prisoner:

'Thomas Doughty, you have here sought by divers means, in as much as you may, to discredit me, to the great hinderance and overthrow of this voyage, besides other great matters wherewith I have to charge you withall, the which if you can clear yourself of, you and I shall be very good friends, where to the contrary you have deserved death.'

Doughty answered: 'It shall never be proved that I merited any villainy towards you.'

'By whom will you be tried?' asked Drake, meaning who from among those present.

'Why, good General, let me live to come into my country, and I will there be tried by Her Majesty's laws.'

Drake beat that point down: 'Nay, Thomas Doughty, I will here empanell a Jury on you to enquire further of these matters that I have to charge you with all.'

'Why, General, I hope you will see your commission be good,' said Doughty.

Drake snapped back: 'I warrant you my commission is good enough!'

'I pray you let us then see it,' insisted Doughty. 'It is necessary that it should be here shewed.'

'Well, you shall not see it,' replied Drake. Turning to the company he exclaimed: 'But well, my masters, this fellow is full of prating!'

Doughty probably here made an indignant rush at him, for the transcript shows Drake continuing:

'Bind me his arms, for I will be safe of my life! My masters, you that be my good friends, Thomas Hood, Gregory, you there, my masters, bind him!'

Doughty's arms were tied behind him while Drake belaboured

him with 'divers furious words', saying he thought him to be the
man who had poisoned Lord Essex (the Queen's General in
Ireland). Doughty, undismayed, told Drake to his face that it was
he who had first brought Drake to the notice of Lord Essex when
they were in Ireland.

'Thou!' shouted Drake. 'Thou bring me to my Lord! Lo, my
masters, see how he goeth about to discredit me. This fellow with
my Lord was never of any estimation, I think he never came about
him; for I that was daily with my Lord never saw him there above
once, and that was long after my entertainment with my Lord.'

At this point a forty-man jury was formed to try the case, with
the Vice-Admiral, John Winter, as foreman of it. Captain John
Thomas than read out to them the written evidence, much of
which has survived, He may have rather rushed through the
documents, or perhaps his words were part blown away by the
wind, for Cooke insinuated that the reading was carried out in
such a manner as to prevent anyone memorising any part of them.
Nevertheless, he was able to recall that they all appeared to consist
of words of unkindness written in rage, 'all of which Doughty did
not greatly deny . . .' This brings Cooke's testimony close enough
to the Drake official view as narrated in Fletcher. The single
exception, and a most significant one, was the evidence of Edward
Bright, ship's carpenter of the *Pelican*. Doughty strenuously
combated Bright's written evidence (which has survived). According to Cooke, Bright introduced his own written evidence, which was
to be read out by Captain John Thomas, by saying to the prisoner:

'Nay, Doughty, we have other matter for you yet that will a
little nearer touch you, it will, I swear, bite you at the quick!'

'I pray thee, Ned Bright,' said Doughty mockingly, 'charge me
with nothing but truth, and spare me not.'

Thomas then read out Bright's long written statement, coming
to the part where Doughty was alleged to have said, back in Drake's
own garden at Plymouth, that 'their whole Council could be
corrupted with money; yea the Queen's Majesty herself'. In spite
of his not being able to hear very well, John Cooke's version is
identical in meaning to the actual written statement, but uses
slightly fewer words. When that bit was read out, Cooke noted
that Bright held up a finger and said:

'How like you this here, syrra?'

'Why, Ned Bright, what should move thee thus to belie me?

Thou knowest that such familiarity was never between me and thee, but it may be I said, if we brought home gold we should be the better welcome, but yet that is more than I do remember.'

Cooke said that they then discussed what was known of the voyage in government circles. Bright's written evidence, quoting what he was told by Doughty, alleges that in the beginning, Doughty and Drake together planned the present voyage; then Doughty:

'considering this voyage was more meat for a Prince than a Subject, went to Mr Secretary Walsingham and to Mr Hatton, and they broke it to the Queen's Majesty, who had good liking of it, and caused our Captain to be sent for and commanded this voyage to go forwards; and joined the said Thomas Doughty and our Captain together and gave them as large a commission as ever went out of England, and that the whole adventure had passed under the hand and seal of the said Thomas Doughty, which was no small matter . . . And that our Captain was not to do anything without the assent of the said Thomas Doughty.'

In going over this disputed ground, something new and unexpected cropped up. Doughty mentioned that Burghley, the Lord Treasurer, had a 'plot' (or draft plan) of the voyage. Burghley was the senior statesman of the discreet faction at Court which did not believe in giving aid to foreign Protestants or troubling Spain overseas, whereas his rival, Sir Francis Walsingham, did; and so too did Hatton. If Burghley had been told of Drake's voyage, he might have had it stopped, as other voyages had been recently, out of fear of giving offence to a state more powerful than England. Consequently, when Doughty casually mentioned that the Lord Treasurer had a 'plot' of their venture, he touched on sensitive nerves.

Drake burst out: 'No! he hath not!'

Doughty insisted that Burghley knew.

'How?' snapped Drake.

'He had it from me,' replied Doughty.

Drake's shocked surprise turned to a feeling of triumph. 'Lo, my masters!' he cried, 'what this fellow hath done! God will have his treacheries all known! For her Majesty gave me special commandment that of all men my Lord Treasurer should not know it. But, see, his own mouth hath betrayed him.'

Doughty, it seemed, knew he was beaten. He asked: 'If you will permit me to live and to answer these objections in England, I will set my hand to what is here written, or to anything else you will set down.'

Drake replied: 'Well, once let these men find whether you be guilty in this or no, and then we will further talk of the matter.'

Drake then gave the documents of indictment to Winter, as foreman of the jury, and they were all sworn to bring in a true verdict.

Leonard Vicary, Doughty's great friend, here stood up for him (although he had signed several documents of indictment), saying: 'General, this is not law, nor agreeable to justice that you offer.'

'I have not to do with you crafty lawyers, neither care I for the law,' said Drake, 'but I know what I will do.'

Vicary, who was also a member of the jury, objected: 'I know not how we may answer his life.'

'Well, Master Vicary, you shall not have to do with his life, let me alone with that. You are but to see whether he be guilty in these articles that here is objected against him or no.'

'Then there is, I trust, no matter of death?'

'No, no, Master Vicary,' said Drake.

Cooke recorded that the jury found the prosecution case proved without doubt in all respects except one. 'So with this the Jury went together,' he wrote, 'finding all to be true, without any doubt or stop made, but only to that article that Edward Bright had objected against him.' Reading all the narratives, including Fletcher's original, it seems probable that they did not believe Bright; that they thought the accusation against the Queen and her Council said to have been made by Doughty in Drake's garden at Plymouth was a fabrication. Further, as Cooke put it:

'It did argue small honesty in a man to conceal such a matter if it had been spoken in England, and to utter it in that place where will was law and reason put to exile; an honest subject would not have concealed such a matter. But to be brief, answer was made that Bright was a very honest man, and so the verdict being given in, it was told to the General that there was doubt made of Bright's honesty.'

Later, Drake was to find this point rather difficult to explain, but at the time he swept it aside peremptorily with: 'Why, I dare swear that what Ned Bright hath said is very true.' And that was that. Doughty had been found guilty on all charges now, including this, the fatal one. The jury having judged, Drake had to pronounce sentence. But how much power did he really have? Did he have a commission from Elizabeth, and if so, did it grant him powers of execution?

According to that part of Fletcher which probably reflects Drake's view, the jury, having discussed the matter with men from both factions, judged that: 'He had deserved death: And that it stood, by no means with their safety, to let him live: And therefore, they remitted the manner thereof, with the rest of the circumstances, to the General.' That is, that Drake was responding to popular demand rather than leading it.

Cooke on the other hand shows him making a great play of proving his authority and powers, taking a large bundle of documents with him and leading everyone (except the two Doughty's) down to the water's side where, shuffling through the letters, he looks up and exclaims, theatrically:

'God's will, I have left in my cabin that I should especially have had . . .'

Just 'as if he had forgotten his Commission,' wrote Cooke, 'but whether he forgot his commission or no he much forgot himself, to sit without showing his commission if he had any; but truly I think it should have been showed to the uttermost if he had had it.' Drake then riffled through the letters, displaying first this one and then that one, saying this was from Hankens to Essex and that from Essex to Hankens and these from Essex to Walsingham, all commending Drake; and this was from Hatton to himself, asking him to accept his two followers, Captain John Thomas and John Brewer, the trumpeter; and finally he read out the words of a document showing that the Queen had adventured a thousand crowns on the voyage. Cooke did not believe in these documents, not being given the opportunity to examine them; but if they were accepted, they would certainly tend to impress people with Drake's importance to the voyage. The fact that Drake and not, say, Doughty, possessed the key document from the Queen showing her share in the project, would demonstrate that he, and not Doughty, was the officially accredited leader.

In spite of Cooke's suspicions, these documents must have been genuine, because there was nothing to stop almost anyone from asking to examine all or any of them; to have forged the bill of adventure from the Queen would have been a particularly perilous proceeding. Indeed, the very fact that Drake forgot the document he most wanted to have, presumably his commission from the Queen, leads one to think that the papers he did show were not only genuine but read exactly as he said they did; whereas, although he seems to have had a commission, the powers it granted him may well have fallen short of executing a high-ranking colleague. He therefore could not risk a demand to examine it, and the best way out of that was to 'forget' to bring it, Or it is just possible that in the very great tension preceding the trial Drake did genuinely overlook this one paper among so many, particularly when they were all stored in rolls, like charts, the written sides innermost.

After flourishing the documentary proof of his primacy, Drake (according to Cooke) summed up with a bias towards death.

'My masters, you may see whether this fellow hath sought my discredit or no, and what should be here meant but the very overthrow of the voyage, as first by taking away of my good name. and altogether discrediting me, and then my life. Which I being bereaved of, what then will you do? You will be fain one to drink another's blood, and so to return again unto your country. You will never be able to find the way thither. And now, my masters, consider what a great voyage we are like to make. The like was never made out of England! By the same, the worst in this fleet shall become a gentleman. And if this voyage go not forward, which I cannot see how possibly it should if this man live, what a reproach it will be, not only unto our own country but especially unto us, the very simplest here may consider of. Therefore, my masters, they that think this man worthy to die let them with me hold up their hands, and they that think him not worthy to die hold down their hands.'

These quotations may well be from notes taken officially or unofficially at the time; but it was in his own words that Cooke described the show of hands: '. . . divers that enveyed his former felicity held up their hands, some others again for fear of his severity sticked not to lift their hands although against their hearts, but some again lifted up their hands and very hearts unto the Lord to deliver us of this tyranous and cruel tyrant . . .'

Drake led them all back to where the Doughtys were still standing and told Thomas Doughty that the jury had voted for death. According to one Fletcher narrative, Drake then asked Doughty: 'Whether he would take to be executed on this Island? Or to be set a land on the main. Or return into England, there to answer his deed before the Lords of her Majesty's Council!' Cooke agrees that this was the subject of the ensuing discussion, but gives what, once more, may well be verbatim dialogue jotted down by a clerk.

Drake told Doughty: 'If any man can between now and the next morrow devise any ways that may save your life, I will hear it. And I wish you yourself to devise some way for your own safeguard.'

'Well, General,' said Doughty, 'seeing it is come to this pass that I see you would have me made away, I pray you carry me with you to Peru and there set me ashore.'

'No, truly, Master Doughty, I cannot answer it to her Majesty if I should do so,' replied Drake. 'But how say you, Thomas Doughty, if any man will warrant me to be safe from your hands and will undertake to keep you, sure you shall see what I will say unto you.'

Doughty then turned to John Winter, the Vice-Admiral and foreman of the jury:

'Master Winter, will you be so good as to undertake this for me?'

Winter agreed to take Doughty into the *Elizabeth* and to make sure that he would be unable to attempt Drake's life. Cooke says this and Winter confirms it. Cooke then says that Drake paused a little before replying:

'Lo then, my masters, we must thus do! We must nail him close under the hatches and return home again without making any voyage. If you will do so, say your minds?'

This was greeted with a cry of 'God forbid, good General!' from many of the men.

Cooke described this faction as 'a company of desperate bankrupts that could not live in their country without the spoil of that as others had gotten by the sweat of their brows'. No doubt these were 'the sort of bad and envious people, sailors and suchlike' whom he had identified previously as enemies of Doughty. In this case, he wrote, their urgings were superfluous, 'for there was no need to spur a willing horse'. Drake at once told Doughty that he could have one day in which to prepare for death, in which time he should set all his affairs in order. Then, rising, he said that he would pray to God to put into his head some way of doing him good. Cooke commented cynically: 'But he had so often sworn that he would hang him, that I think at this present he meant to do him little good.'

Doughty spent that night and most of the next day, 1 July, in

prayer, although he took a little time then to divide up his possessions and give them to his friends. July the 2nd was the day fixed
for the execution. On this day also Francis Fletcher, as fleet chaplain,
held a service of communion which was attended both by the condemned man and by Drake. Fletcher was in a privileged position,
for if Doughty was going to confess, he would now do so privately,
with only Fletcher between him and his God. Doughty denied the
fatal charge, the accusation made by Ned Bright that in Drake's
garden at Plymouth he had said the Queen's Council and even the
Queen herself could be corrupted and made to look the other way,
if the proceeds of the voyage were great enough. Fletcher was utterly
convinced that this part of the evidence at least was a fabrication.
Doughty had said no such thing. Ned Bright was a perjured
unholy liar.

The tension was terribly highly charged, for Drake himself, with
Doughty, went up to take communion; they went up almost side-
by-side, to kneel before God at an English altar not far short of
the Strait of Magellan and an entry into an ocean where no Englishman had ever been and where every man would be their enemy.

Doughty, wrote Cooke, went up with a more cheerful countenance
than he had ever shown in life, accepting death and so contemptuous
of it; his features as steady and firm as if he walked up merely to
deliver a message to some nobleman. And accepting Drake's offer
to walk beside him with cool contempt, never once addressing
the Captain-General as a superior, by his rank, but only as a man
and a colleague.

In the Drake family version, supposedly Fletcher's, the story is
the same but the meaning is different:

> 'The General himself communicated at this Sacred ordinance,
> with this condemned penitent gentleman, who showed great
> tokens of contrite and repentent heart, as who was more deeply
> displeased with his own act than any man else. And after this
> holy repast they dined, also at the same table together, as cheer-
> fully in sobriety, as ever in their lives they had done aforetime;
> each cheering up the other, and taking their leave, by drinking
> each to other, as if some journey only had been in mind.'

Between the sacrament and the banquet, according to Cooke,
there occurred a conversation which is partly confirmed by the
Drake/Fletcher version where, however, after Doughty has con-

fessed his 'sin', he requests 'that he might not die other than a
gentleman's death'. Undoubtedly, he said this. His previously
reported comment, in the flyboat *Swan*, that hanging was 'for dogs
and not for men' rings most true. Drake, having got his way, could
now afford to be magnanimous, even friendly, and, says Cooke:

'Master Drake withal offered him to make choice of his own
death, as if he would, and for that he said he was a gentleman
he should but lose his head; the which kind of death was most
agreeable to his mind, in as much as he needs die. And truly I
heard say that Master Drake offered him if he would, that he
should be shotten to death with a piece, and that he himself
would do that exploit and so he should die at the hands of a
gentleman.'

This was perhaps the 'good' deed that Drake had mentioned to
Doughty; not so small a favour, when the hideous butchery of
Magellan's defeated captains in this same place is remembered.
Such contemptuous treatment of their carcases was nothing extraordinary, either in England or in Spain. Indeed, it had deliberate
purpose; the overawing of any support for the dead men and the defeated cause by dishonouring their corpses.

A quick death by shooting, or a ceremonial end under the axe,
was a boon, something to be grateful for, especially when there
was no dishonour. Drake was to be punctilious about that, praising
Doughty to the skies, once he was removed from out of his path.
While they dined together for the last time, the place of execution
was being made ready and the men who were digging the grave
found their spades ringing on stone, for under the earth were the two
parts of a great, broken grindstone, a relic, perhaps, of Magellan's
five-month stay in this very place. It would make, they thought,
an excellent headstone for the new victim.

No doubt the macabre waiting stretched everyone's nerves.
Doughty said abruptly to Drake that he was ready as soon as he
was, but he would like a private word or two first. They got up and
walked off together. But it was more than a word or two they spoke
to each other, for they were still talking fifteen minutes later.
Then Drake signalled, and the soldiers fell in around Doughty
with their bills and staves for the death march to the appointed
and prepared ground.

Once there, Doughty knelt. John Cooke described how:

'He first prayed for the Queen's Majesty of England, his sovereign lady and mistress; he then prayed to God for the happy success of this voyage; and prayed to God to turn it to the profit of his country; he remembered also there his good friends, and especially Sir William Winter, praying Master John Winter to commend him to that good knight, all which he did with so cheerful a countenance as if he had gone to some great prepared banquet, the which I sure think that he was fully resolved that God had provided for him.'

The Drake/Fletcher account agrees, saying: 'yet he had a care, and that excelling all other cares, to die a Christian man, that whatsoever did become of his clay body, he might yet remain assured of an eternal inheritance in a far better life.'

Finally, according to Cooke, he turned to Drake and said: 'Now, truly, I may say, as did Sir Thomas More, that he that cuts off my head shall have little honesty, my neck is so short.'

Doughty then looked around all the assembled ship's companies, and asked them all to forgive him, but particularly those who had fallen into official displeasure for his sake. And he named Thomas Cuttill, former master of the *Pelican*, and Hugh Smith, and said there were many others.

Smith spoke up and begged Doughty to say in front of the General whether they had had any talk together that might be taken to the prejudice or detriment of Drake.

Doughty answered: 'At my death I say, that neither I nor any other man ever practised any treachery towards the General with you, neither did I myself ever think villainous thoughts against him. I pray you, good General, be good unto Hugh Smith and forgive him for my sake.'

Drake said: 'Well, Smith, for Master Doughty's sake, and at his request, I forgive thee, but by the life of God, I was determined to have nailed thy ears to the pillory and to have cut them off; but become an honest man hereafter.'

Wrote Cooke: 'So then Master Doughty embracing the General, naming him his good Captain, bade him farewell, and so bidding the whole company farewell, he laid his head to the block . . .'

With his own hands, he bared his neck; signalled. The axe fell.

Swiftly, Drake stepped forward, seized by the hair the bleeding head, raised it high.

'Lo, this is an end to traitors,' he said.

Chapter 7

'ISLAND OF BLOOD'

Port St Julian:
2 July–17 August 1578

FRANCIS FLETCHER stood by the grave. It was hard digging in the frozen ground. Better to raise a monument than to carve deeply into the earth. The corpse was lightly covered, the severed head laid by the bloody neck. At that end one part of the great grinding stone was set upright; and the other part placed at the feet, also upright. In the middle, between the stones, to deter the wild creatures from digging up the poor body, they laid small stones and turfs; and for any who might come there hereafter they engraved on the broken grinding stones the names of those buried there, for this was Magellan's graveyard too, and the dates of their deaths, and the name of the English general, Francis Drake, and all this in Latin, that men of all nations who should come after them might understand.

Afterwards, brooding upon these events, Fletcher was convinced that he had assisted at a murderous injustice. Ned Bright's accusation was false:

'He utterly denied it upon his salvation at the hour of communicating the Sacrament of the Body and Blood of Christ, and at the hour and moment of his death, affirming that he was innocent of such things whereof he was accused, judged, and suffered death for. Of whom I must needs testify the truth, for the good things of God I found in him in the time we were conversant, and especially in the time of his afflictions and trouble, till he yielded up his Spirit to God, I doubt not to immortality . . . For his qualities, in a man of his time they were rare, and his gift very excellent for his age, a sweet orator, a pregnant philosopher, a good gift for the Greek tongue, and a reasonable taste of Hebrew; a sufficient secretary to a noble personage of great place, and in Ireland an approved soldier, and not behind many in the study of the law for his time . . . '

That part of Fletcher which is really Drake did not disagree, mentioning 'the worthy manner of his death', which 'fully blotted out whatever stain his fault might seem to bring upon him; he left unto our fleet a lamentable example of a goodly gentleman, who in seeking advancement unfit for him, cast away himself . . . '

Fletcher continued to brood on the injustice of Doughty's last hours, which he had spent:

'reading, meditating to himself, conferring with others, instructing of the ignorant, as if he had been a minister of Christ, wherein he profited so much, that long before his death he seemed to be mortified and to be ravished with the desire of God's kingdom; yea to be dissolved and to be with Christ, in whose death so many virtues were cut off, as drops of blood were shed; who, being dead, was buried near the sepulchre of those which went before him, upon whose graves I set up a stone, whereon I engraved their names, the day of their burial, the month and the year, for a monument to them, which shall fall with that place in time to come. Those things, with drops of blood from the hearts of some, thus ended, we went about our other businesses and necessary affairs.'

Drake intended the death of Doughty to settle not only who was to command but to smooth over the differences and ill-feelings which plagued the venture. After the execution, before the crews had dispersed to their ships, he had warned that if anyone now should offend so much as an eighth part of what Doughty had done, he would die for it. He swore by the love of God and the blessed sacrament he had that day received, that if any man in the fleet whatsoever should strike another a blow, then he should lose that hand. Almost certainly he had no firm intention of carrying out these noisy threats, recorded by Cooke. But in the circumstances it would have been a brave man who challenged him; that is, if he was of the Doughty faction.

Cooke describes how, on the day following the execution of his brother, John Doughty was walking, solitary and alone, reliving the terrible events of yesterday and weighing his own chances of suffering a like fate, when he was accosted by Edward Bright, the chief instrument of his brother's death, looking for trouble.

'God's wounds, thou villain, what knowest thou by my wife!' snarled Bright, striking out at John Doughty with a large ruler, one of the tools of a ship's carpenter's trade.

Doughty parried the blow with his arm, breaking the ruler, and appealing to his assailant: 'Why, Ned Bright, thou seest what case I am in, I pray thee let me alone.'

But Bright was so furious that he thrust the jagged end of the broken ruler into Doughty's face with such force that the splinters entered an inch into the flesh (according to Cooke, who thought Bright was deliberately forcing a quarrel so as to kill the other Doughty). The injured man then went to Drake to complain of Bright's assault on him, but Drake, in spite of what he had said the day before about brawling, passed it off with:

'Why, John Doughty, Ned Bright will lie open to your revenge in England, for I dare say thy brother did belie her when he said that she had an ill name in Cambridge.'

Cooke's reaction was to launch into a denunciation of Drake, for not chopping off Ned Bright's hand; to dub him dishonest; and declare: 'Then might a blind man have seen the ruin of the voyage even at hand, for how can God prosper that government where no justice is, but either extreme tyranny or favorable partiality!' However, it is possible that John Doughty, in his rage against Bright, had in fact made use of some story told him by his brother concerning the morals of Mrs Bright. Denigration was rather a forte of the Doughty faction and, it must be admitted, Cooke himself was not behind in this field. No doubt the men he dubbed 'a company of desperate bankrupts' might not have been too pleased had they got to hear of it, particularly as the crime alleged against them appears to be poverty, or at least the guilt inherent in anyone who was not so rich as Thomas Doughty and able to stand a substantial stake in the voyage. An equally cutting but equally ill-based slur on Mrs Bright might perhaps have created genuine resentment, Bright being a responsible officer in the flagship.

The execution of Doughty cannot have had the hoped-for effect. Drake commanded that there should be a communion service for the whole fleet the following Sunday, at which all old quarrels should be forgiven and forgotten and every man confess himself to Master Fletcher. Cooke would not do this, wrongly imagining that Fletcher was Drake's man entirely, and in his narrative questioned ironically whether in fact Fletcher's God was the same as that commonly worshipped in England. The sneer was quite misplaced, for Fletcher was at least as grieved as Cooke, indeed he was probably the more deeply affected of the two by the execution. For refusing to confess,

D

however, it seems that Cooke was put in close arrest ashore for a fortnight, dressed in little more than doublet and hose, and refused his cloak. It was very cold, the diet was not healthy and many men were falling sick, he wrote. He thought Drake was trying to kill him off from exposure and was most bitter. He could have studied with profit the fate of Magellan's mutineers, loaded down with chains and yet forced to work half in half out of the bitter cold water on the ships' hulls for months, not weeks.

On 11 August, once again every man of the fleet was ordered ashore. A tent had been set up with one side open, so that the three sides acted as a sounding board. Drake entered, then called for Vice-Admiral Winter to sit on one side of him and Captain John Thomas on the other. Then his manservant laid before him a large manuscript book, presumably the elaborate fair copy of his log (which has been lost). Francis Fletcher offered to preach the sermon, naturally, but Drake declined, saying: 'Nay, soft, Master Fletcher, I must preach this day myself, although I have small skill in preaching.' Then, raising his voice: 'Well, be all the company here, yea or not?'

The answer came that everyone was accounted for and all were there. Drake then ordered the crowd to regroup by ship's companies, and with a good deal of shuffling, this was done. Clearly, something very important was to be said. Drake began: 'My masters, I am a very bad orator, for my bringing up hath not been in learning, but what so I shall here speak, let any man take good notice of what I shall say, and let him write it down, for I will speak nothing but I will answer it in England, yea and before her Majesty, and I have it here already set down.' Apparently, it was already entered in the log, but Fletcher wrote that his own version had 'the effect of and very near the words' of Drake's set speech:

'Thus it is, my masters, that we are very far from our country and friends, we are compassed in on every side with our enemies, wherefore we are not to make small reckoning of a man, for we can not have a man if we would give for him ten thousand pounds. Wherefore we must have these mutinies and discords that are grown amongst us redressed, for by the love of God it doth even take my wits from me to think on it; here is such controversy between the sailors and the gentlemen, and such stomacking between the gentlemen and sailors, that it doth even make me mad to hear it. But, my masters, I must have it left, for I must have the gentlemen to haul and draw with the mariner, and the mariner with the gentlemen. What, let us show ourselves all to be of a company, and let us not give occasion to the enemy to rejoice at our decay and overthrow. I would know him that would refuse to set his hand to a rope, but I know there is not any such here; and as gentlemen are very necessary for government's sake in the voyage, so have I shipped them for that, and to some further intent, and yet though I know sailors to be the most envious people of the world, and so unruly without government, yet may I not be without them.'

This was a clever and powerful call to unity, which Drake reinforced with a sly offer which every man must refuse:

'If there be any here willing to return home let me understand of them, and here is the *Marigold*, a ship that I can very well spare. I will furnish her to such as will return with the most credit I can give them, either to my letters or any way else. But let them take heed that they go homeward, for if I find them in my way I will surely sink them. Therefore you shall have time to consider hereof until tomorrow, for by my troth I must needs be plain with you. I have taken that in hand that I know not in the world how to go through withall. It passeth my capacity. It hath even bereaved me of my wits to think on it.'

That frank confession did not deter them. On the contrary, none voted to return, all wanted to go with him. 'Well, then, my masters, come you all forth with your good wills or no?' asked Drake.

They shouted out that they all came of their own free wills.

'At whose hands, my masters, look you to receive your wages?'

'At yours,' they answered.

'Then how say you, will you take wages or stand to my courtesy?'

'At your courtesy,' they replied. And some added: 'For we know not what wages to ask.' Of course they all hoped to do better than mere wages; they hoped to make their fortunes. They were being asked to follow a corsair captain of, literally, golden reputation. Having demonstrated that he had mass support, Drake then took a line which surprised all and shocked some. First, he commanded the steward of the vice-flagship *Elizabeth* to hand over the key of the cabin. Then, turning to Vice-Admiral Winter; he said:

Master Winter, I do here discharge you of your captainship of the *Elizabeth.*'

Turning to the other senior officers in succession, he said: 'I discharge you, John Thomas, of your captainship of the *Marigold*; and you, Thomas Hood, of your mastership in the *Pelican*; and you, William Markham, of the *Elizabeth*; and you, Nicolas Anthony, of the *Marigold*; and, to be brief, I do here discharge every officer of all offices whatsoever.'

The two captains, Winter and Thomas, both asked Drake why he should displace them; and Drake replied with a question: could they give him any reason why he should not do so? He then called for silence and an end to discussion of this matter, for:

'You see here the great disorders that we are here entered into, and although some have already received condign punishment as by death, who, I take God to witness, as you all know, was to me as my other hand. Yet you see, over and besides the rest, his own mouth did betray his treacherous dealing, and see how trusting in the singularity of his own wit, over reach himself at unawares. But see what God would have done, for her Majesty commanded that of all men my Lord Treasurer should have no knowledge of this voyage – and see that his own mouth declared that he hath given him a plot thereof. But truly, my masters, and as I am a gentleman, there shall be no more die. I will lay my hand on no more, although there be here that have deserved as much as he . . . '

Drake then said that a man named Worrall represented a case worse than Doughty's. Worrall humbled himself on his knees and Drake said: 'Well, well, Worrall, you and I shall talk well enough of this matter hereafter.' The next name he mentioned was that of John Audley, and he said he would talk with him alone after dinner. What apparently irritated Drake about these two was that they were spreading what they claimed to be the real story of the origins of the voyage and the objects of it, without in fact really knowing anything. With the critical risks of the venture still ahead of them, in and beyond the Strait of Magellan, Drake thought it vital that all should be quite clear as to what they were about and for whom they were being asked to risk their lives:

'Here is some again, my masters, not knowing how else to discredit me, say and affirm that I was set forth on this voyage by Master Hatton, some by Sir William Winter, and some by Master Hawkins; but this is a company of idle heads that have nothing else to talk of. But, my masters, I must tell you I do honour them as my very good friends, but to say that they were the setters forth of this voyage, or that it was by their means, I tell you it was nothing so, but indeed thus it was . . . My Lord of Essex wrote in my commendations unto Secretary Walsingham more than I was worthy, but belike I had deserved somewhat at his hands, and he thought me in his letters to be a fit man to serve against the Spaniards, for my practice and experience that I had in that trade. Whereupon indeed Secretary Walsingham did come to confer with him, and declared unto him that for her Majesty had received divers injuries of the King of Spain, for the which she desired to have some revenge. And withall he showed me a plot, willing me to set my hand, and to note down where I thought the King of Spain might most be annoyed. I told him some part of my mind, but refused to set my hand to anything, affirming that her Majesty was mortal, and that if it should please God to take her Majesty away, it might be that some prince might reign that might be in league with the King of Spain, and then will mine own hand be a witness against myself . . . '

Drake then explained how, soon after, Mister Secretary Walsingham (a political opponent of the Lord Treasurer, Burghley) sent for him one evening; and next day he was presented to the Queen. Elizabeth had said to him: 'Drake, so it is I would gladly be revenged on the King of Spain, for divers injuries that I have received.' She told him that he was the only man in her realm capable of carrying out this venture, that she had 'craved his advice'; and he had told her 'of the small good that was to be done in Spain, but the only way was to annoy him by his Indies'.

Although they were unaware of Palace business, his listeners would have been greatly impressed by Drake's direct contact with royalty. From their own experience, many would have realised the strategic and economic importance of the Indies trade. Without it, the Spaniards would not be able to field such large armies in Europe, with which they were able to threaten England and her allies. Enough of them had been to the Indies, to see for themselves how rich were the Spanish possessions and at the same time, how vulnerable.

To stress the royal nature of the task entrusted to him, Drake again produced documents for people to see.

'He shewed forth a bill of her Majesty's adventure of 1000 crowns which he said at sometime before that her Majesty did give him towards his charge, he showed also a bill of Master Hatton's adventure, and divers letters of credit, but he never let them come out of his own hands. He said also that her Majesty did swear by her crown that if any within her realm did give the King of Spain hereof to understand (as she suspected but two) they should lose their heads therefore.'

If true, this was highly confidential information: that the Queen thought there might be at least one leak, possibly two, from Court level. Drake may have been trying to make clear to all why it had been so wrong of Doughty to have told Lord Burghley the secrets of the venture, because he might have passed on the news, wittingly or unwittingly, to one or more persons under suspicion (or even used the information himself for legitimate purposes of state); the permutations are endless. But the implications were not: if, one way or another, the Spaniards knew in advance that an English fleet of stated force was on its way into the Pacific, they could move in time to meet it with a greater force. There was absolutely no answer to that, no hope of reinforcement from England if anything went wrong. As Drake had pointed out earlier, out here every English life was precious because irreplaceable.

In this manner, Drake worked up to the climax of his appeal:

'And now, my masters, let us consider what we have done. We have now set together by the ears three mighty princes, as first her Majesty, the Kings of Spain and Portugal, and if this voyage should not have good success, we should not only be a scorning or a reproachful scoffing stock unto our enemies, but also a great blot to our whole country forever. And what triumph would it be to Spain and Portugal! And the like would never again be attempted.'

He then restored to their offices all the captains and shipmasters and others whom he had earlier required to lay down their powers to him. It had been a gesture, one more gambit in the battle to assert his authority over his crews (who were causing him more trouble than the Spaniards were likely to do). He concluded by satisfying them all that their wages would be paid, even if he had to sell his last shirt.

'For I have good reason to promise and am best able to perform it, for I have some what of mine own in England, and besides that I have as much adventure in this voyage as three of the best whatsoever. And if it so be that I never come home, yet will her Majestie pay every man his wages, whom indeed you and we all come to serve, and for to say you come to serve me I will not give you thanks, for it is only her Majesty that you serve and this voyage is only her setting forth.'

Drake reiterated that he wished all men to be friends and on this note closed the meeting.

They had been in the harbour nearly two months now and were to leave in less than a week. For some time, most of them had been living in tents ashore, because the ships were being 'trimmed'. This involved grounding the vessel at high water, moving ballast and guns to one side, so that she heeled over, and then, from low water to about mid-tide, the exotic marine growth on the underbody of one side could be scraped off – hard and stinking work this! Once off, a protective coat of some ill-smelling tarry composition would be put on in the hope of discouraging marine beasties, particularly those strange worms with hard heads like drills which could bore long tunnels in planks and frames. When one side of a ship had been so treated, the interior weights were moved again, so that she heeled over the opposite way. And, of course, during the moving of the ballast, opportunity was taken to cleanse the hold of filth. There was no shortage of rough, disgusting work. And now that Doughty was gone, no one could shirk his share of the toil.

There was additional work in transhipping the cargo, stores and gear of the *Mary* (ex-*Santa Maria*, the Portuguese prize) to the three English vessels, for she too was to be scrapped and abandoned in pursuit of Drake's aim of reducing his fleet to manageable numbers, so that even in the foulest weather they might not lose each other for long. Her planking was useful either for sheathing the other ships or for firewood, and finally all that was left of Nuño da Silva's vessel was but the keel and the ribs, a still-articulated skeleton on the beach of 'Blood Island', as Fletcher called it.

Vice-Admiral Winter's *Elizabeth* received many useful stores from the *Mary*: spare sails, clothing, cloths and furs, oil and wine.

Winter in due course was to protest that he took all this aboard against his will, because Drake told him to, and without an inventory being made. Drake certainly did go aboard the *Elizabeth* at this time, and according to John Cooke:

> 'swore very vehemently, I know not upon what occasion, that he would hang to the number of thirty in the fleet, and again charge Worrall that his case was worse than Doughty's, and that by God's wounds he had deserved to be hanged. "Master Winter," quoth he, "where is your man Ulysses? By God's life if he were my man I would cut off his ears; yea, by God's wounds I would hang him." '

By now, even Master John Cooke was beginning to suspect that Francis Drake was more often bark than bite, unless sorely provoked, and entered a note to the effect that he was not sure that Drake truly meant all he was saying.

17 August 1578 was a Sunday and before the fleet weighed anchor at noon, Francis Fletcher held a last communion service at Port St Julian. The English psalms rang out for the last time across the icy harbour and over the frozen Patagonian wastes; over the skeleton ship and the skeleton crosses. In the narrative ascribed to Fletcher, but which is usually Drake's own view (or that of his relative who published it), the place was named the island of 'true justice and judgement'. But in Fletcher's original manuscript the preacher had written: 'At our departure we named the island the Island of Blood, in respect of us and Magellan.'

There was a further clash of testimony between Francis Fletcher in the *Pelican* and John Cooke in the *Elizabeth*, regarding the instrument of the slaying, Edward Bright. Cooke, hating Drake above Bright, recorded that the Captain-General got into a rage with Bright two weeks after the trial and put him out of the *Pelican*, where he was ship's carpenter, and into the *Marigold*, because Drake feared for his safety when Bright was about. Fletcher, however, hating Bright rather than Drake, wrote that the carpenter was 'newly placed captain' of the bark *Marigold*. Although the position of ship's carpenter was important, for this man was responsible for the integrity of the hull, the transfer might be thought to smack of promotion, perhaps for services rendered. And Fletcher, being in the same ship as Bright, perhaps had better opportunity of learning the truth. In any event, this move was to prove fatal to Edward Bright.

On 20 August, three days after their sailing from Port St Julian, the little fleet sighted a landmark which the pilots said was only four leagues off the entrance to the legendary Strait of Magellan. Fletcher wrote that the headland was:

'called by the Spaniards *Capo Virgin Maria*, with high and steep grey cliffs, full of black stars, against which the sea beating, shewing as it were the spoutings of whales . . . At this cape, our General caused his fleet, in homage to our sovereign lady the Queen's majesty, to strike their top-sails upon the bunt, as a token of his willing and glad mind, to show his dutiful obedience to her highness, whom he acknowledged to have full interest and right in that new discovery. And withall, in remembrance of his honorable friend and favorer, Sir Christopher Hatton, he changed the name of the ship which himself went in from the *Pelican* to be called the *Golden Hind*.'

A golden hind was part of the crest of the Hattons. Fletcher's original, uncensored narrative contains no extra insight here and John Cooke did not think the renaming of the flagship worthy of remark. Nor was the claim to original discovery any more than a gesture, for the Spaniards had been here long before them. Surely this was all an attempt at a fresh start, to wash their hands clean of all quarrels and bloodshed. That was now in the past. It was over.

And so they entered the fabulous Strait. *Golden Hind*, 100 tons, Captain-General Francis Drake; *Elizabeth*, eighty tons, Vice-Admiral John Winter; bark *Marigold*, thirty tons, Captain John Thomas (or ex-carpenter Ned Bright?). Now truly, if his luck held only a short time more, Drake would sail in an English ship upon the Pacific, that great Southern Sea that rolled endlessly upon the lands where half the silver and gold of the world was mined.

Chapter 8

'THE UTTERMOST CAPE'

The Strait of Magellan to 57° South:
20 August–1 November 1578

O N 20 August 1578 Drake's three ships were off the entrance
to the Strait but it was not until the 23rd that they were able
to enter, whereupon the great snow-stained mountains on
either hand seemed to close in upon them, rising tier upon tier into
the clouds. The Strait was never less than a mile broad, but nevertheless the thick woods upon the coast seemed to be so near that
an arquebus shot would carry the distance. Sudden tremendous
gusts of wind would come screaming down the slopes from some
hidden gap high up inside the cloud layer, threatening to lay the
ships on their beam ends. At certain states of the tide, eddies would
begin to swirl in the lee of headlands and form whirlpools. At
night, the red glow of fires waxing and waning ashore showed that
even this desolate cold land was inhabited.

The place had a bad name. So far as was known, it was twenty
years since anyone – and then he had been a Spaniard – had so
much as attempted to pass through. There was even a popular
poem – in Spanish, naturally – which postulated that the Strait
might have been blocked, rock-stopped, choked by some upheaval
of nature since Magellan's time, thus explaining why no one could
emulate his feat.

Patagonia was indeed volcanic, but no new upheaved island was
necessary to make a passage of the Strait difficult. It had never been
anything like, say, the Straits of Dover. In length it was more like
the entire English Channel, exceeding 330 nautical miles. They were
exceedingly dangerous and difficult miles, for the area was not a
straight channel but a maze of water and land. How to tell the
most direct line from the dead ends was quite a problem in
itself. And there were dire rumours that the current flowed only
one way, and that continuously, so that once through, there was no
coming back; at least, not by that route. Which meant that one

would have to circumnavigate the world just in order to return home.

Magellan had taken thirty-seven days to pass through in 1520 and one of his captains, Gomez, had liked the prospect so little that he had turned back for Spain while actually in the Strait. The next fleet, led by de Loaysia, took seven weeks for the passage in 1526; and similarly, one captain had deserted with his ship rather than risk going on to the Pacific. Losses from sickness in this fleet had been even heavier than in Magellan's ships. The 1535 expedition of de Alcazaba Sotomayor met with annihilation: first the crew forced him to turn back, then they mutinied and killed him, then the mutiny was put down and the surviving rebels hanged or marooned. A single ship of the Camargo expedition got through in 1540 and eventually reached a Spanish port on the west coast of South America. This was regarded as such a tremendous feat that the vessel was hauled out of the water at Callao, the port of Lima in Peru, to be kept for all time as a kind of monument cum museum. Her mainmast was taken out and set up as a flagstaff in front of the viceregal palace at Lima.

Some half a dozen expeditions had been recorded as attempting the passage with a total of about seventeen ships. A dozen of these vessels had been lost, mainly near the eastern entrance to the Strait. Only one ship, the *Victoria* from Magellan's fleet, ever returned to its home port (but without Magellan); and more than three quarters of the sailors who set out never came home.

The Spaniards had also begun to attempt the Straits from the other direction, with ships built on the Pacific coast of South America; these had no great success either. The last successful passage was made from this direction in 1558 by Ladrillero, who then returned by the same route. But now twenty years had passed and it was 1578. Spaniards had made little enough use of Magellan's great discovery; it was to be seen what the English could do.

In the eastern entrance, where so many Spanish ships of exploration had been wrecked, the English found the tales of a one-way current to be false. There was a perfectly ordinary ebb and flow with a rise and fall of some five fathoms; big tides of thirty feet and more, like the Bristol Channel. A very narrow pass separated this entrance bay from a series of interior bays.

On 24 August, the wind having died away, they anchored in a

bay by three islands. Drake proceeded to give them English names (they already had Spanish ones); he called the largest one Elizabeth Island, the next Bartholomew Island (because it was Bartholomew's Day), and the third St George's Island, for England's patron saint. They stayed here two days, going ashore to replenish their fuel wood and fresh water.

These islands were teeming with a type of subaquatic flightless bird which Magellan met and called geese, but which the Welsh called penguins. Edward Cliffe wrote:

'We victualled ourselves with a kind of fowl whose flesh is not far unlike a fat goose in England; they have no wings, but short pinions, which serve their turn in swimming. Their colour is somewhat black, mixed with white spots under their belly and about their neck. They walk so upright, that a far off man would take them to be like children. If any man approach anything near them, they run into holes in the ground.'

To get them out, the men fixed hooks to the ends of staves; and when hauled out, hit them on the head. Cliffe wrote, feelingly, that it was impossible to handle them otherwise, 'for they bite so cruelly with their crooked bills'. According to Fletcher, they killed three thousand in one day; Winter gave no figures, but said sufficient of them to feed 140 men for seven weeks.

They also made a gruesome discovery. 'In the Island of St George,' wrote Fletcher, 'we found the body of a man, so long dead before that his bones would not hold together, being moved out of the place whereon they lay.' Perhaps he was not a native, but some unfortunate explorer who had come before them, a Spaniard wrecked or marooned.

The English had expected the famous Strait to be a distinct and definite waterway, like a canal, between two continents. To the north the Indies, that part of the American continent which was known; and to the south a vast continent stretching right round the world and known as *terra australis incognita*. This continent existed only in theory, as a balance to the land masses further north, but informed world opinion so favoured the theory that it was already taken for fact. Fletcher, who was never afraid of fighting scholars, was sure they were wrong long before the fleet emerged into the Pacific: 'In passing along we plainly discovered that same *terra australis*, left or set down to be *terra incognita* before we came there, to be no Continent (and therefore no Strait), but broken islands and large passages amongst them . . . ' That was blunt and brutal enough, but the learned men who had never seen the Strait of Magellan were to be unshaken by Fletcher's attack.

The fleet had a 'hard passage', wrote Fletcher:

' . . . and for divers causes. First, the mountains being very high, and some reaching into the frozen region, did every one send out their several winds; sometimes behind us, to send us on our way; sometimes on the starboard side, to drive us to the larboard, and so the contrary; sometimes right against us, to drive us farther back in an hour than we could recover again in many; but of all others this was the worst, thus sometime two or three of these winds would come together, and meet as it were in one body, whose forces being become one, did so violently fall into the sea, whirling, or as the Spaniard saith, with a *tornado*, that they would pierce into the very bowels of the sea, and make it swell upwards on every side; the hollowness they made in the water, and the winds breaking out again, did take the swelling banks so raised into the air, and being dispersed abroad, it ran down again a mighty rain. Besides this, the sea is so deep in all this passage, that upon life and death there is no coming to anchor. Neither may I omit the grisly sight of the cold and frozen mountains rearing their heads, yea, the greatest parts of their bodies, into the cold and frozen region, where the power of the reflection of the sun never reacheth to dissolve the ice and snow . . . '

An oared vessel, independent of the wind for motive power, might well have been endangered here, let alone small sailing ships which, being compelled to carry sail, could be cast to destruction by the sudden 'williwaws' and tornadoes, either overthrown or driven ashore. Fletcher, probably for security reasons, gave no hint at all of what Drake's solutions were to these problems; but da Silva, being forced to tell by his Spanish captors, was to show Drake carrying out a policy which made the passage of the notorious Straits appear an easy matter. He told his interrogators:

'They passed along without any let or hindrance either of wind or weather. And because the high land on both sides lay covered with snow, and that all the Strait is fair and clear, they held their course a harquebus-shot in length from off the North side, having nine and ten fathoms depth, with good ground, where (if need require) a man may anchor . . . '

The Spaniards suspected that it was Nuño da Silva himself who piloted Drake through, a deadly accusation which the Portuguese captain was strongly to deny.

Whoever made the decisions, they were the right ones; Drake's passage of the Straits was going at unprecedented speed. Other decisions, of at least equal importance, concerned the critical subject of crew health. As well as continually finding fresh food and water, stops were also made to obtain plants and herbs to add to the diet. This apparently barren place was particularly rich in them because, according to Fletcher, groves of trees at the shoresides were so bowed down by the weight of the snow and the rain upon them that their trunks and branches were so closely crushed together:

'that no art or labour of man can make closer and sweeter arbours than they be; under the which, the ground being defended from cold, is engendered such temperate heat, that the herbs may seem always to be green and to flourish as it were in our summer. Amongst the other simples we had in this place (many being to me very strange and unknown) were naturally growing, without industry of man, Time, Marjerom, Alexander's scurvy grass, as seamen call it (scirby grass), and divers others well known to us, all whereof were more excellent in their natures than we find them in our gardens. And for other strange plants they were so gummy and full of fatness, that touching them the fat and the gum would stick to our hands, being so pleasant that it yielded a most comfortable smell to our senses, whereby we received great help, both in our diet and physick, to the great relief of the limbs of our men.'

Ordinary shipboard diet was plainly deficient, showing itself in a disease of the gums and a loosening of the teeth. This cure by the 'scurvy grass' and other herbs was not nearly as well known as it might have been, either at this time or later. Often it made the difference between a healthy crew and a dying one.

The ships had been working their way through the Strait for two weeks when, on 4 September, having anchored by an island, the English made contact with the natives. Throughout their journey they had been aware that the north shores at least were inhabited, from the continual camp fires they saw burning. The place was well named Tierra del Fuego – 'land of fires'. Now, five natives came out to them in canoes from an encampment ashore, bringing an offering of seal meat.

What astonished the English most of all, as it had amazed the Spaniards before them, was that the natives wore no clothes. The English sailors and soldiers had put on every scrap of clothing they possessed, to keep out the piercing winds, the driving rain, the bitter sleet and snow, and still they shivered in the wind. Yet here was a land, wrote Fletcher:

> 'frequented by a comely and harmless people, but naked, men, women, and children, whom we could not perceive to have either set place or dwelling, or any ordinary means of living, as tillage, breeding of cattle, but wanderers from place to place, and from island to island, staying in a place so long as it would naturally yield them provision to live without labour . . . They build little cottages of poles and bowes, like arbours in our gardens in England, wherein they themselves for the time lodge and keep their household stuff.'

Fletcher was curious enough to make an inventory of the contents of one dwelling, seemingly that of a rich chief: 1 pail for water, 2 cups for drinking, 2 boxes of paints for the person, 2 wooden spits, 1 pair of racks, 2 hatchets, 1 knife, and '1 fair floor of earth for a bed to lay upon without any clothes'. All these possessions were left behind when the people moved camp, because in due course, when the game had recovered, they would return to the site for fresh hunting and collecting. These artefacts were not made of the materials to which Europeans were accustomed. Their pails, cups and boxes were not constructed of wood in the English fashion but of the bark of trees only, sewn with gut. Their hatchets and knives were not hammered or cast from metal, but were made of mussel shells. These were no ordinary mussels but huge shellfish more than a foot long which, once the brittle part had been broken off, 'they grind them by great labour to a fine edge and very sharp, and as it seemeth, very durable.'

The people, both men and women, 'are gentle and familiar to strangers, and paint their bodies with forms and divers colours; the men making red circles about their eyes and red strokes upon their foreheads for the most part, and the women wear chains of white shells upon their arms, and some about their necks, whereof they seem to be very proud.' The parallel with European male finery, flaunting and colourful, matched by the less gaudy attire of the women bedecked with meaningless geegaws, was very obvious.

The native family boats, however, evoked unqualified praise:

'Being made of large bark instead of other timber, they are most artificial and are of most fine proportion, with a stern and foreship standing semicircularwise, and well becometh the vessel; with these boats, they travel from place to place among the islands, carrying every man his family. In all our travels in any nation, we found not the like boats at any time for form and fine proportion, in the sight and use whereof princes might seem to be delighted.'

The boats, like the buckets, were stitched, but with thongs made probably from sealskin.

All the logs and diaries mentioned 6 September 1578. Cliffe was brief but exact: 'We passed by *Cape Deseado* into the South Sea the 6 of September.' *Cabo Deseado*, the westernmost headland of Desolation Island, apparently got its name of Cape Desire because effectively it marked the western end of the Straits on the south side, thought to be the unknown Australian continent. Magellan had taken five weeks, de Loaysa had taken seven weeks. Drake had done it in a little over two weeks – sixteen days, to be precise. No wonder the Spaniards suspected that he had been piloted through; but how could da Silva, a Portuguese, know the navigation of the Strait better than the Spaniards?

On the other hand, the time for the passage was wrong. Magellan had struggled through the Strait but once out on to the great South Sea he had met such wonderful weather that he called it *Mar Pacifico*, the Pacific Ocean. It was anything but that when Drake led his ships out. The Captain-General had intended to set up ashore at this western exit an engraved metal plaque commemorating the feat and dedicating it to Her Majesty, Queen Elizabeth. Drake had had the plaque prepared and inscribed in advance, and had intended to go ashore with all his men and have Fletcher hold a service, but there was no anchoring now, the wind was rising and howling; all might soon be in deadly danger, for the western exit of the Strait is a ships' graveyard of halftide rocks.

The rendezvous was at 30° south, on the coast of Peru beyond

Valparaiso – the latitude also, more or less, of the southern tip of Africa. Anyone who imagined that Drake's real purpose was to explore that theoretical southern continent, *terra australis incognita*, sometimes called 'Beach', had mistaken their man: and no doubt mistaken the Queen also (although Lord Burghley might have approved, a diplomatic gaffe being impractical down in those southern wastes). But that, like it or not, was where the little English fleet was driven, 'spooming' south-east under bare poles, not a rag of canvas aloft.

Gale after gale came roaring out of the north-west with a violence unimaginable, the waves heaving themselves up so high as to hide the masts of one ship from another, the foaming crests being blown off in solid sheets like snowdrifts; it was hard to tell which was water and which was air. No fires could be lit, no hot food had. The upper decks streamed water, the deckheads dripped it. Every space in the ship was damp; sodden the bedding, wet and shivering the men. But over all was the fear of death; while the storm, hoarse and remorseless, raged unchecked about them, hurling the ships' hulls like toys, 'like a ball in a racket', as Fletcher put it, each man clinging on, every second of every hour of every day; at night, wedged to snatch sleep. Day after day and night after night the screaming winds stormed about their ears and drove them south, south, south. 'Yea, such was the extremity of the tempest,' wrote Fletcher, 'that it appeared to us as if God had pronounced a sentence, not to stay his hand, nor to withdraw his judgement, till he had buried our bodies, and our ships also, in the bottomless depth of the raging sea.'

There was darkness at noon. So low were the clouds, so thick the air with sea spray torn from the tumultuous waves, that midday was like last light. No sun, no moon, no stars. 'Palpable darkness by the space of 56 days,' wrote Fletcher, 'without the sight of sun, moon, or stars, the moon only excepted, which we see in eclipse the space of a quarter of an hour or thereabouts.' That eclipse was on 15 September, we know. But men lost count of time. Hours ceased to matter, then days; finally, weeks ceased to have significance. The storm took on the nature of eternity. There never had been anything else but this helpless flight southwards, 'spooming' down the slopes of waves higher than houses. There never would be anything else until the roaring of the waters on the rocks heralded the coming of the unknown southern continent, the last lee shore. Da Silva ceased to make daily entries in his log. Way back on 7 September, the day after they had emerged from the Straits into the Pacific Ocean, he had written: 'The wind came from the prow, we going south-east with a strong north-west wind.' After that the entries ceased, summed up by a single line written afterwards: 'All this month we went along in this manner.' Southwards. Yet there was one entry, before the end of the month. It was for 28 September: 'We lost the *Maragota*.' Da Silva probably only heard about it, afterwards. Fletcher was a witness.

In his original manuscript he wrote:

'The storm being so outragious and furious, the bark *Marigold*, wherein Edward Bright, one of the accusers of Thomas Doughty, was captain, with 28 souls, were swallowed up with the horrible and unmerciful waves, or rather mountains of the sea, which chanced in the second watch of the night, wherein myself and John Brewer, our trumpeter, being on watch, did hear their fearful cries, when the hand of God came upon them.'

Opposite the name of Edward Bright, in the margin of his manuscript, Fletcher scribbled: 'Marked judgement against a false witness.'

John Thomas, Hatton's man, whom Doughty had endeavoured to influence, unsuccessfully, went down with her. John Brewer, who had also been a factor in Doughty's downfall, ironically was on watch in the *Golden Hind* with Fletcher when the little thirty-ton craft was overwhelmed and sank forever into the black water. Now there were only two ships in the fleet, and about 130 men. Fletcher thought the storm was God's judgement upon them for their treatment of Doughty. But what did Drake think? His was the ultimate responsibility, even if he did not live to bear the blame. He had been oppressed by his task and its overpowering difficulties at Port St Julian; but in the Straits of Magellan, with Doughty dead and himself with no rival left to debate the command, he had been overconfident, exuberant; while only halfway through he ordered an enormous, strange tree to be cut down and put into the hold as ballast and as proof, to be presented to Her Majesty, that her Captain-General had beaten the perils of the Straits. And indeed he had made an incredibly swift passage. But was it at the wrong time of the year? Should he have wintered at Port St Julian? And if he had, would the men have had the heart to come on through the

Straits after such a delay in such a fatal place? All speculation and quite hopeless. Decisions had had to be made. If he had decided wrongly, he would die for it; and so would they all.

They were all too harassed by the tempest, stunned, chilled, exhausted, turned into automatons, damp stumbling zombies, to deeply ponder the implications of their driven path so far south. Had the grave and scholarly cosmographers been correct in their reasoned arguments regarding the balance of land masses, then it followed inescapably that Drake's ships were now several hundred miles from the nearest water, aground in the heart of *terra australis incognita*. Would to God they were! But they saw no land at all, mere heaving wastes of water, for a month, until 7 October. According to Fletcher, it was thought they had during this month gone as far south as 57° or a little more. The Strait of Magellan, supposedly flanked by this unknown southern continent, was in 52°. But there was no southern continent! Only unknown southern water. The Strait of Magellan was an irrelevance!

They had been driven back, driven northward again, when on 7 October land was sighted for the first time in four weeks. Before, they had been in open sea, hundreds of fathoms deep, and clear of the complications of high mountains. Now, in the shallows, in the troughs of the gigantic waves, black-maned reefs appeared. Fletcher wrote:

'Every mountain sent down upon us their several intolerable winds, with that horror that they made the bottom of the sea to be dry land, sending us headlong upon the tops of the mountains and swelling waves of the sea, over the rocks, the sight whereof at our going in was as fearful as death itself. At the last, in this miserable state we were driven as through the eye of a needle into a great and large bay, by a most narrow passage of rocks, where coming to anchor within small time (being night) we had like entertainment from the hills as we had before from the mountains, with greater and more dangerous violence. Our cables brake, our ankers came home, our ships were separated, and our spirits fainted as with the last gasp unto death, and though the Lord set both our ships from perishing, and spared our limbs, yet we in the Admiral were fully persuaded the Vice-Admiral was perished; and the Vice-Admiral had the same opinion of us (as since it hath been confessed).'

Vice-Admiral John Winter, writing in the *Elizabeth*, recorded that on the morning of 7 October they had a glimpse or two of land and that later, although they could now see nothing for the fog and the storm, they were so close they heard the wash of the sea upon the shore. 'After this Mr Drake came to an anchor in a deep, dangerous bay,' wrote Winter. 'He lost his cable and anchor, willing us to haul out, which was as much as we could do, and having hauled out we both lay ahaul, Mr Drake being to the south-east of us, a league astern.' An unwary reader, perusing Winter's reports, might many times fancy that Drake, an indifferent mariner, had carelessly got himself into trouble and had to be extricated by the immaculate Winter. We wonder that Drake had managed to survive this long and fear for him should he be parted from his second-in-command. Winter intended to make sure that no one should take that eventuality to be his fault, and wrote:

'A little before night I called the Master into my cabin, showing him the *Pelican* astern, which we could see but now and then, by reason of the fog and outrageous weather, and willed him to have a great regard for the keeping of company that night.'

Next morning, 8 October, there was no sign of the flagship from Winter's *Elizabeth*, but Winter covered himself in his report by blaming the master. When, that same morning, those in the *Golden Hind* saw no sign of the vice-flagship, the worst was assumed. That is, some thought that she had been lost, others that she had deserted. Fletcher's authorised narrative, published later with hindsight, stated:

'With a sorry sail we entered a harbour: where hoping to enjoy some freedom and ease till the storm was ended, we received within a few hours after our coming to anchor so deadly a stroke and hard entertainment, that our Admiral left not only an anchor behind her, through the violence and fury of the flaws, but in departing thence, also lost the company and sight of our Vice-Admiral, the *Elizabeth*, partly through the negligence of those that had the charge of her, partly through a kind of desire that some in her had, to be out of these troubles and to be at home again . . . '

This was the Drake view, and it ran in the family, for young John Drake, under interrogation much later, told the same story to his Spanish captors: 'The second ship said she did not want to follow the General and turned about and re-entered the Strait and was seen no more.' There was indeed a powerful faction on board the *Elizabeth* which favoured turning back and abandoning the whole venture. The decision had not yet been made, for it was weighty and could cost Winter his head. An honest factor in it would be the state of health of this ship's crew; many were ill with the scurvy, a sickness which brings debilitation and depression.

For nearly a week more the storm continued to drive them south and without sight of land until about midnight on 13 October. Next day the *Golden Hind* anchored three leagues off shore in $54\frac{1}{2}°$, according to da Silva. For some days they threaded their way among islands, landing on one of them for water. The loss of the little *Marigold*, the 'handmaiden' of the fleet, was now particularly felt. With her shallow draught she could have reconnoitred these dangerous and unknown coasts – literally unknown, not just to them, but to all the world, for they were far south of the discoveries made by Magellan and those few who succeeded in following him. In the stead of the lost bark, Drake appointed the ship's pinnace, a five-ton boat with eight oars, and into her he put eight men, led by Peter Carder.

Carder was a Cornishman. There were a number of other West Countrymen with him, including Richard Joyner of Plymouth, Paschie Gidie of Salt Ash, and two men who were servants of John Hawkins; there were a couple of Londoners, Richard Burnish and William Pitcher, and a Dutch trumpeter called Arthur. They were all shortly to be launched on one of the most terrible open-boat journeys of all time, for as Carder later testified:

'This company was commanded to wait upon the ship for all necessary uses, but not having passed one day's victuals in us nor any card nor compass, saving only the benefit of eight oars, in the night time by foul weather suddenly arising we lost the sight of our ship, and though our ship sought us and we them for a fortnight together, yet could we never meet together again.'

It was to be nine years before Carder saw England again and by then his adventures had been such that he was given an audience with the Queen, who talked to him for an hour. One of the questions she asked was about Thomas Doughty's execution.

On 18 October the *Golden Hind*, now quite alone, anchored among islands which partly protected her from the storm, and lay there until the 23rd. Fletcher reported that the men were sick and that once again greenstuff made them better:

'Finding divers good and wholesome herbs, together with fresh water, our men, which before were weak and much impaired in their health, began to receive good comfort, especially by the drinking of one herb (not unlike that which we commonly call Pennyleaf), which purging with great facility, afforded great help and refreshing to our wearied and sickly bodies.'

John Drake added further detail, stating that:

'They took in water and wood and found many herbs which they cooked, to eat. Captain Francis having heard that one of these herbs was medicinal, had much juice squeezed from its leaves and gave this, in wine, to the sick. For nearly all were ill with swollen legs and gums; from which illness all recovered excepting two who afterwards died.'

This sickness was certainly scurvy.

There was to be no respite. They had got ashore at all only with difficulty, had met natives (very similar to those encountered before in the Straits), with whom they had bartered; they had collected the greenstuff (perhaps on the advice of the natives), and then another terrible blast came driving yet more monstrous seas down upon them. This time they lost not merely an anchor but most of the cable as well, for they had to cut and run. The little ship, the only survivor of the fleet so far as they knew, was whirled helplessly south, pitching and rolling in confused seas that battered their high stern first on one quarter and then on the other. Then they saw land, and the sea fell calm. Drake maintained, according to Fletcher, that it was God's will that had sent them so far south to their great discovery (which, however, no scholar would subsequently admit).

The dying away of the wind just in time, so that they could approach the land in safety, was followed in the calm by an event so uncanny that it was Fletcher now who saw the hand of God in it. In his original and private narrative, he wrote:

'But before our going to land, we had a strange and sudden accident, for John Brewer, our trumpeter, standing upon the poop sounding his trumpet, being now as great a calm as it had been a storm, without any wind to move or shake a silken thread, most strangely a rope was so tossed and violently hurled against his body that it cast his body over into the sea, with that strength that ten men with all their powers could not have done more to a block of his weight, for by estimation his body lighting the water, was eight times his length distant from the direct point below to the place where he fell, where labouring mightily for life (the boat being not ready) many ropes were cast round about him and some upon him, but he could not catch hold of any one at all to help himself, till he called one by name to cast one to him, which no sooner was done, but he received it, and was saved at the last pinch, or, as it were, at the end of all hope.'

Just one of those days, one might think, when the impossible jostles the incredible; but there must be a mundane reason, if only one could see it.

Of course, once in the water, the unfortunate Brewer must have been shocked almost unconscious with the icy chill. Whose name did he call out at last – Fletcher's? Fletcher does not say, but in the margin of his private manuscript he scribbled an even more personal note: 'His judgement worth noting.' He meant God's, of course, on John Brewer for his part in the death of Doughty. Brewer was not beyond saving at last, unlike poor Ned Bright who went down in the night with the *Marigold*. Had Brewer then told the truth, as he saw it, and thus avoided Fletcher's total condemnation?

In Fletcher's original, the place at which they had now arrived, and where they landed and stayed for some four days, was the 'uttmost island' further south than 55°. In his published narrative, he calls it the 'uttermost cape' in nearly 56°. John Drake told his Spanish captors that it was in 56°. Da Silva, in his log, noted it as 57°, and that it was yet another island. Edward Cliffe, in the *Elizabeth*, claimed that this ship also had been driven, like Drake's to 57° South. The Strait of Magellan wanders from 52° to 53°, so assuming approximately 56° for Drake, he had been driven by the winds hundreds of miles farther south than any man had gone before – and had seen there no great southern continent but only open sea. So 'the way lay open for shipping in that height without let or stay, being the main sea', commented Fletcher in the original. In the published version, he wrote similarly:

'The uttermost cape or headland of all these islands, stands near in 56 degrees, without which there is no mainland nor island to be seen to the Southwards, but that the Atlantic Ocean and the South Sea, meet in a most large and free scope'.

That disposed, he thought, of the 'dream through many ages', that the south side of Magellan's Strait was an unknown great continent 'wherein many strange monsters lived'. In both versions he berated the scholars for believing tall tales without proof and then spreading the lies, but had no ill words for Magellan. The original is more temperate than the published narrative and reads:

'It was ever uncertain, from the first discovery of that passage by the Spaniards, and could not be determined by Magellan himself, that that land was a continent, but left it under the name of *Terra Incognita*; and what others afore or since have written or said of it are but guesses and imaginations, seeing he himself could determine nothing: and that from his time there was no other trial made of it until now we have by manifest evidence put it out of doubt to be no continent or mainland, but broken islands, severed by many passages and compassed about with the sea on every side, and therefore no strait.'

Fletcher was then forced to fall upon one of the 'light' proofs put forward by the cosmographers, 'namely, there runneth such a current between the land of America and this *Terra Australis*, (caused, say they) by the continent, that it carrieth ships headlong through to the South Sea, but admitteth no return back again . . . ' This idea Fletcher considered 'frivolous'. He thought it should be made known to the world 'that there is neither continent, current, nor strait, as idly it hath been surmised and foolishly defended'. That is, if you defined a strait as a sea passage between two continents. In his published account, Fletcher gave up hope of being believed and merely advised the scholars to suspend judgement until they had either seen for themselves at first hand or consulted other travellers who had actually been there.

What he and the rest of the ship's company were seeing was the visible disproof of virtually all contemporary world maps, charts and globes. This critical discovery was theirs. After following for so long where Spanish and Portuguese pioneers had led, at last the English and the Welsh had come to the forefront. This at least the sick and weary men knew they had achieved. As they went ashore, it was like a conquest.

Fletcher had brought with him a bag containing tools for engraving on stone. Carrying it, he made hurriedly for the southernmost cliff of the island which, he calculated, was by three parts of a degree more southerly than any of the other islands. Here he found a large stone and set it upon end as a monument. Then he got to work with chisel and hammer, engraving 'Her Majesty's name, her kingdom, the year of Christ, and the day of the month'.

Sir Richard Hawkins was later to relate that Drake himself had entered into the spirit of the thing. Lying down flat on the clifftop, he had stretched out his arms southward over empty space, so that, indisputably, he had gone by that much further south than anyone in his company. In more serious mood he claimed the islands for the Tudor Crown, giving them all the name of the Elizabethides.

The empty wastes of sea, surging endlessly around the world, were the spectacle that held them all, however. The water seemed to stretch away southwards to infinity, as if there was nothing but ocean between them and the bleak Pole.

In a few more days, their stay on the southernmost island was finished. A strong and favourable wind blew for the coast of Peru. They had collected a great deal of fruit from this island, black berries which Fletcher described as 'currants' and the men called 'raisins'. Hoisting sail on 28 October, they sighted two more islands on the 30th. So many birds crowded there, that Fletcher said they resembled 'storehouses' of food for both the *Golden Hind* and the *Elizabeth*, if she should still be afloat. They stayed two days collecting these provisions, and then on 1 November 1578 stood out once again to the north-west. Their objective was latitude 30 degrees on the coast of Peru, the agreed rendezvous for the fleet, should the ships become separated.

There was only the *Elizabeth* to look for, the second largest ship of the original fleet of five vessels. Of the five, only one had actually sunk, the thirty-ton *Marigold*, overwhelmed by the storms and taken down into the depths with all her crew. They would be a horror now, bloated, or half-devoured, many fathoms deep. However, if the *Elizabeth* had not shared her fate, or had not gone home to England, then she should meet them at the rendezvous, a welcome reinforcement for their entry thereafter into Spain's dominions in the Pacific.

Chapter 9

EATEN ALIVE

On the Coast of Chile:
1 November 1578–19 January 1579

BETWEEN the 1st and the 25th of November 1578, the *Golden Hind* covered more than one thousand miles and had risen past the height of 40° up the globe and was not far from the rendezvous in 30°. Very early, they discovered that the Spanish maps and charts were wrong in showing the coast of South America to trend north-west, for on steering that course initially, they found themselves moving away from the land. The true lie of the coastline was rather to the north-east, by their calculations.

There were many ways in which a navigator could err, even if his own observations and calculations were correct; the data he was forced to use might be inaccurate or insufficient, his instruments inadequate. If he did not know the right variations to apply to the lying compass needle, which pointed usually to magnetic north and hardly ever to true north, then all he could determine was the direction of the magnetic pole from where he was, given that iron objects close to the compass, such as cargo, armament, ballast, bolts, anchors and so on, did not cause it to deviate by a substantial amount. Provided therefore that he knew where the true pole lay in relation to the magnetic pole in that year, that he knew the amount of error caused by local deviation, and also that he knew approximately his own position on the globe to start with, then the navigator might use a compass to find true north. But he could still be wrong if the ship changed course, for then the relative positions of the compass needle and the metals in the ship would change also. The *Golden Hind* had in fact changed course to northerly, which is also a difficult course to steer, as the needle seems to 'stick' and then moves suddenly well past the desired bearing.

Fletcher had no sympathy with the difficulties of Spanish map-makers, indeed he thought they were wrong because they had not been there themselves to make the survey. Sternly, he wrote: 'Therefore the setters forth of such descriptions are not to be trusted, much less honored, in their false and fraudulent conjectures which they use, not in this alone, but in divers other points of no small importance.'

In the *Golden Hind* herself there were often differences in the results obtained by individual navigators. For instance, at that 'utmost island' to the south, where probably it had been possible to make observations from a steady platform, ashore, Fletcher had given the latitude as somewhere between 55 and 56°, while da Silva had made it 57°. The difference there was important, for it was an unknown island whose 'height' was being taken.

On 25 November they sighted the island of Mocha. This was a large place, about the size of the Isle of Wight, and like it, lying close to the mainland. But not so close as to be dangerous, for here the mainland was Spanish – a low coastal plain backed by the towering mountain chain of the Andes. Fletcher (probably consulting the ship's official log) gave its latitude as about 37°, whereas the Portuguese navigator da Silva entered 39° in his own personal log. The direction of disagreement was just as it had been at the 'utmost island' in the south. As later surveys were to give the height of Mocha as being between the 37° and 39° variously calculated in the *Golden Hind*, it is likely thay they obtained a similar 'bracket' for the latitude of Drake's important southerly discovery.

Drake, with a picked company of fighting men, was rowed ashore on Mocha in the ship's boat, and met a most friendly reception. The bartering went rapidly and much in favour of the English, who were delighted to obtain so cheap the prime foodstuffs they were offered – fat mutton, chickens and a maize commonly called Guinea wheat. In sign language, the English mimed their need for drinking water and by signs also the natives answered – 'In the morning – at the rising of the sun – gladly.' Fletcher wrote:

'That night our mutton and hens was to us so sweet, that we longed for day that we might have more such bargains at their hands, yea every man desired to be a South Sea merchant. But the Captain, the time being come, made such choices as he thought fit for the action, who together with joy set forwards to land, as well appointed almost, but that they had neither bows nor other

shot, as they were in Port Julian when they met with the Giants,
when they slew two of our men. Being well armed with sword
and targets, they feared no perils, nor maybe no doubt but to
have as kind entertainment now as the night before, and that
infidels were faithful as Christians.'

The chosen men who got down into the ship's boat with Francis
Drake were his trumpeter, John Brewer, John Marten, Thomas
Flood, Tom Brewer, 'great' Neil the Dane (a gunner), 'little' Neil
the Fleming, John Gripe, John Mariner, Gregory Rayment, and
Diego the black Moor who was Drake's native interpreter. The oiled
steel blades, firm in the scabbards at their waists, and the small
shields or 'targets' they wore on their arms, made them confident;
they were anyway confident men, or they would have been at home
in England and not on the far side of South America.

Now, as they rowed for the shore, they were thinking of the
bargains they would make once the business of filling the two
watercasks was completed. The creek they were directed into by
the natives was narrow and fringed by walls of tall Indian reeds.
At the far end were some of the natives, apparently waiting to
welcome and guide them to the springs. Tom Brewer and Tom
Flood jumped out as the boat grounded and ran ashore, taking the
boat rope with them and hauling the boat further in, for naturally
it had lifted off again after the release of their weights. That done,
they threw down the rope for a moment. And that seemed to be
the signal.

One Indian picked up the rope at once and hauled hard on it,
so that the boat could not back off, but was held fast aground. A
moment later, the rest of the 'welcome' party seized Brewer and
Flood before they had chance to draw swords, and rushed them
inland away from the landing place. Simultaneously, the silent
reeds on either side of the creek came to life. According to the
lowest English estimate, the ambush party numbered a hundred
men. They were armed either with bows firing stone-tipped reed
shafts or they flung darts of cane tipped with sharp iron or bone.
Before, they had been completely silent and invisible. Now they
shot or threw a multitude of missiles at the eight men left in the boat.
They were so close that they could plant the shafts almost where
they liked. The English shields did little to protect their wearers,
for the hail of venom came from all directions; their swords were

almost useless, for they were all penned awkwardly close together in the swaying boat.

Every man was hit at least twice; some were struck by eight or ten arrows or darts; one man was a porcupine, with twenty-one shafts sticking in him, quivering. Some were hit in the head or face, as Francis Drake was; others were pierced through the throat, or in the chest, the belly, the back. All must have been massacred within minutes had not 'one of the simplest of the company' severed with his sword the boat rope and some of the less severely wounded taken up the remaining oars and struggled to back off down the creek, pursued by a flight of arrows 'so thick as gnats in the sun'.

Fletcher, watching from the deck of the *Golden Hind*, was shaken by the appearance of the returning boat, which he knew had contained ten men and now seemed half-empty; its sides held so many arrows that they were virtually touching each other. 'A man might by the sight of the boat afar off judge what was the state of their bodies which were in it; who coming on shipboard, the horror of their bloody state wounded the hearts of all men to behold them.' Drake had been hit twice, a messy wound in the head and a nearly fatal arrow which had struck him full face, going in under his right eye close by the nose. The wounds were extremely painful, 'the extremity and crazy state of the hurt men' demanding immediate medical attention. There was none to be had. The chief surgeon was already dead and the second surgeon was in the Vice-Flagship, the *Elizabeth*, which was supposed to rendezvous with them near this locality but was in fact on the other side of the continent, going home with a favourable wind.

The medical section was reduced to one boy, a lad who was formerly the menial assistant to the chief surgeon; he had plenty of goodwill but no skill at all. He could not possibly deal with eight wounded men, some seriously injured or dying, all of them in agony. The whole crew of the *Golden Hind* came to his help, to share what medical or surgical knowledge they had, and in fact only two men died, the gunner, 'great' Neil the Dane, and Drake's native interpreter, Diego. Fletcher gave the credit for this equally to God on the one hand and the ship's company on the other. John Drake, however, stated that most of the arrow wounds were not deep.

Two immediate crises had come upon the ship. First, there were eight tormented men with arrows or arrowheads in their bodies, the extrication of which required the experience of skilled surgeons, to probe the wounds for the embedded heads of jagged iron, stone or bone. As there were no surgeons, the task would have to be done by the unskilled, with wine perhaps to numb the mind a little beforehand.

Secondly, there was the fate of the two men taken by the natives and still ashore, Tom Brewer and Tom Flood. The boat was manned with a fresh crew and sent towards the shore to see if help could be given them. When it came within view of the landing place, the task could be seen to be impossible. A crowd of natives, two thousand at the least, they thought, had gathered together; and they were armed with bows, darts, spears, pikes and shields, most of the weapons being decorated with pure silver, 'which in the light of the sun made a wonderful show and glittering.' What they were doing was revolting and obscene.

They had Brewer and Flood bound and helpless on the ground; and while the mass of natives danced exultantly, the two Englishmen were being slowly scraped and cut to pieces with knives, and the slivers of flesh from the living limbs devoured on the spot by the dancers. Hand-in-hand, they danced and sang while the torturers worked upon their screaming victims.

Wrote Fletcher:

'Our men were in their execution and torments . . . The tormentors, working with knives upon their bodies, cut the flesh away by gubbets, and cast it up in the air. The which, falling down, the people catched in their dancing, and like dogs devoured in most monstrous and unnatural manner, even most horrible to nature, and thus continued till they had picked their bones, life yet remaining in them.'

The rage and hatred of the boat's crew was beyond belief. This time they were armed with guns; they raised them and fired a volley into the crowd of natives and then, reloading, another. But the second volley had little effect, for as soon as the muzzles of the guns were levelled at them, the Indians dropped flat on the ground and offered no target at all. And when the shot had gone whining uselessly overhead, they jumped to their feet again and recommenced the dance around the bloodied screaming hulks of what had been men, so tenaciously, so intensely that it seemed they loved the ghastly spectacle as much as life itself.

The boat's crew came back, having been but helpless spectators, and raging for the great guns to be brought up out of the hold, where they had lain so long on the ballast, in order that whole batteries of ordnance might pound the native multitudes with great shot, dice shot and hail shot. In their turn, the natives should be helpless against their punishment and torment.

It was not to be. It was Drake himself who stopped it, according to Fletcher's original, uncensored manuscript. 'We might have taken a revenge upon them at pleasure with great shot out of our ship, but the General would not for special causes consent to it,' he wrote. His reasons were basically the same as those which had dictated his policy after the attack on himself and his landing party by the Giants at Port St Julian. The natives, he understood, had been badly treated by the Spaniards, and had retreated to this island as a refuge. And although he had given strict orders to his landing party to speak English only, so that there should be less risk of a mistake, nevertheless he had since learnt that the sign language to ask for water had not after all been confined merely to signs. One man had used the word *aqua*, which was the very word the Spaniards employed for water. Of course the natives could be mown down by the heavy guns at long range, without risk to any Englishman, and they would have had their revenge. But to what purpose? The poor Indians, having, not without some reason, mistaken them for Spaniards, had bestowed upon them, as Fletcher put it, 'a Spaniard's reward'. That afternoon, 26 November, they up-anchored and sailed in search of a quiet, convenient place where the wounded men might have ease and peace to recover, as well as some delicacies perhaps for their sick diet.

26 November 1578 marked also the end of Fletcher's original manuscript which he compiled (obviously from notes) after he returned home. He had intended to write a second part to describe the rest of the voyage, but if he did so, then the manuscript has been either mislaid or destroyed: it has not come down to us. The remaining story from Fletcher's point of view is the edited version, the censored or published document. This is less emotional and more bland, more an 'official' story. For instance, this version omits much regarding the tragedy of 26 November, especially the torture of Brewer and Flood and the sufferings of the wounded.

As most, if not all, of these men must have had relatives still living, this censorship was not without its point.

At the same time we gain a witness, with an overlap of one day. There is preserved a short narrative of the voyage,* beginning with the anchoring at Mocha on 25 November. We do not know who the author was, except that he served in the *Golden Hind* and was strong on factual detail of the sort Fletcher all too often does not bother about; for instance, he gives the names of all ten men who went in the ship's boat on the fatal day, and he tells us who was killed and who died of wounds. Fletcher gives no names, except that of Drake, and his figures differ slightly: eleven men instead of ten, one only died of wounds instead of two. As the anonymous author can quote all the names, one tends to prefer his version, perhaps wrongly. He is certainly to be preferred on military matters, where the precision of his narrative makes a welcome change from Fletcher's woolly handling of sequential affairs. On the other hand he does not bare his heart and express his deepest feelings, whereas Fletcher's strength (in his original narrative) was that he treated a blank sheet of paper like the confessional, utterly private between him and his God.

Within a short period of time, less than two weeks, a third type of documentation was to appear. The English were entering Spanish-controlled territory, where the bureaucracy was bound to record the encounter, often in that uninhibited and carefree way which is entirely Spanish. One class of documentation on the Spanish side held no hint of levity however – the inquisitions of suspected heretics. Although generally the English seemed to bear no grudges against the Spaniards as such, they detested their cruel colonial system and showed real hatred for the Spanish church; there was a vengeful spirit in some of them that sought only an opportunity of expression.

On 30 November they sighted what Fletcher called Philips Bay in 32° or thereabouts, anchored and sent a boat ashore in search of fresh water and delicacies for the wounded. Apart from 'huge herds of wild buffes', they saw nothing. However, on their return they came across an Indian fishing in the bay from a reed-straw canoe, and brought him and his strange craft back to the *Golden Hind*. Fletcher describes him as:

* Harleian MS No. 280, folio 23.

'A comely personage, and of a goodly stature; his apparel was a white garment, reaching scarcely to his knees; his arms and legs were naked; his hair upon his head very long; without a beard, as all Indians for the most part are. He seemed very gentle, of mild and humble nature, being very tractable to learn the use of every thing, and most grateful for such things as our General bestowed upon him. In him we might see a most lively pattern of the harmless disposition of that people, and how grievous a thing it is that they should by any means be so abused as all those are, whom the Spaniards have any command or power over.'

Drake had been most successful with his native diplomacy during previous expeditions, even organising a local revolt. Thus far, in this expedition, his record was either indifferent or disastrous; no achievements to speak of and two bloody setbacks, where he had lost men unnecessarily. On this occasion he seemed to have regained his old skill. Through this single native in the canoe he was put in touch with a small group and so handled negotiations that the chief himself offered to come with Drake and pilot him to a harbour where fresh water and choice wines and foods might be obtained. The chief, whose name was Felipe, spoke some Spanish, and so Drake was able to converse with him directly. The harbour also was Spanish – Valparaiso, the port for Santiago. The newly discovered mines of Valdivia, producing some of the finest gold in the Indies, were not far off.

They had in fact overshot Valparaiso by some six leagues, according to Felipe. The bay they had explored was known to the Spaniards as Quintero. Drake had no objection to lingering in this area, for it was not far from the appointed rendezvous with the *Elizabeth* and the *Marigold*; that is, 30° South or, alternatively, a prominent cape in 32½°. The *Marigold*, they knew, was at the bottom of the deep and terrible seas south of Magellan's Strait, but if they turned back they might still meet the *Elizabeth* coming north to join them. So Drake went south again, looking for this harbour in which, according to Felipe, a large Spanish ship was lying at anchor. On 5 December he found it.

She was in fact a famous ship, having served as the *Capitana*, or flagship, of the great explorer Pedro Sarmiento de Gamboa, who in 1567 had been flag captain of the Mendana expedition which had discovered the Solomon Islands in the Pacific. Sarmiento, who

E

was born in Galicia in 1532 and had twice been in trouble with the
Holy Inquisition, was now at Lima, further up the coast; but he
was very shortly to report on what happened to his old flagship,
as well as the other vessels. The English referred to her as the
Grand Captain, because of her fame, and Fletcher went so far as
to mention that she was named the *Captain of Moriall, or the Grand
Captain of the South, Admiral to the Islands of Solomon*. This was
pure confusion, *Admiral* being the Spanish term for vice-flagship,
Captain the word for flagship; and of course King Solomon had
nothing whatsoever to do with the cannibal islanders of the Pacific.

John Drake estimated her as being of 120 tons, presumably
English tons, or about the same size as the *Golden Hind*. Had this
been a Spanish measurement, she would have been smaller. The
Golden Hind came in boldly, like any merchant ship, and dropped
anchor close in to the beach of Anton Gonzalez; her great guns
were still below as ballast and her ports were all unarmed. There
was nothing to indicate that she was a heavily-manned warship
with close to eighty men aboard, nor that she was English. As a
freighter, the *Grand Captain* carried the smallest crew possible,
for reasons of economy; only eleven men – eight Spaniards and
three negroes. Seeing what appeared to be another Spanish merchantman come in to join them, they beat on a drum to signal
'welcome' and brought up a great butt of Chile wine with which
to entertain their visitors.

A skiff put off from the new arrival, packed with men – eighteen
of them, 'arquebusiers, archers and men with shields', according
to Sarmiento's information. Drake was not with them, remaining
behind in his flagship, probably because his wound was not yet
healed. Tom Moone, his former boatswain and captain of the
Bark Benedict of this expedition originally, appears to have been
in command of the *Golden Hind*'s boat. He was a pockmarked,
aggressive little man who hated Spaniards and clearly believed
in shock tactics.

La Capitana was owned by the Licentiate Torres but her master
and pilot on this occasion was Hernando Lamero. John the Greek,
a seaman from the Aegean, was her boatswain. The English swarmed
on to the deck of the unsuspecting Spaniard and as Lamero, her
master, stepped forward to welcome those he assumed to be fellow
countrymen, Tom Moone smashed him in the face with his fist,
shouting '*Abasso Pirra!*'"

'Go down, dog!' he roared, and with the arquebusiers and archers at his heels, drove them all down below and slammed the hatches on them. All, that is, except one. This man ran the length of the deck to the stern and leapt overboard. Then he swam for the shore and gave warning to the townsfolk of Santiago, and this took him no time at all, for the town possessed only about eight or nine buildings.

According to both Sarmiento and the *Golden Hind*'s anonymous witness, their first objective was a warehouse, which the English broke open in the hope of loot. Sarmiento says they found no gold, only wine, flour, salt pork, lard and suet; 'Anon' mentions only the wine, but Fletcher says they found the various items of food they needed for the wounded and sick. Neither Sarmiento nor Fletcher mention anything other than the warehouse; but 'Anon' recorded that the inhabitants having fled, the English 'rifled their houses'. Also that Drake:

'found there a chapel, which he rifled and took from thence a chalice of silver and two cruets of silver . . . and the altar cloth, all which he took away with him and brought them on board, and gave all the spoil of that chapel to Mr Fletcher, his preacher, and then he set all the men of the Spanish ship on shore, saving one John Grego, a Greek born, whom he took with him to be his pilot to bring him into the haven of Lima.'

The Spanish authorities were to bring formal charges against Drake, that, among other things, he 'did rob the vestments of the churches and broke down the bells and broke up the King's Storehouse besides a great many other insolences . . .'

Having plundered both Church and State ashore, a careful search was made of the captured Spanish ship. She had been about to set sail for Peru with a cargo of timber and Chilean wine – no less than 1,770 jars of wine. This was very welcome, but there were other discoveries to take the breath away. She held no less than four 'forcers', or strongboxes for treasure. Three had rounded lids and were of black leather reinforced with iron bands. They were full of the finest Valdivian gold. It took careful probing to locate the fourth treasure chest, which had a low, flat cover and was totally invisible at first, having been hidden in a huge chest of meal placed innocuously under the steering compartment. It did not require a suspicious mind to see that this must be 'unregistered'

gold which the owner had had no intention of declaring to the
Spanish customs authorities, who would deduct one fifth of the
value as a tax for the Crown. Fletcher alone mentioned a further
item, 'a great cross of gold beset with emeralds, on which was
nailed a god of the same metal.'

'Anon' gives an estimate of the amount of gold – '400 weight'.
Sarmiento gave the value as being 24,000 pesos. The official
complaint was for the loss of '200,000 pesos of fine gold, registered
and unregistered.'

The *Grand Captain* and her boat were useful prizes and Drake
brought them along when he sailed on 8 December, putting two
dozen of his own men into Sarmiento's old ship, keeping John the
Greek and using the vessel's charts for the voyage from Chile to
Peru. The two ship's boats were used for scouting and sounding
ahead of the *Golden Hind* and *La Capitana*, really a task for a
pinnace which could set a fair amount of sail as well as carry
numerous oarsmen and enough soldiers to perform port and beach
reconnaissance without too much risk. It was high time to assemble
another of the prefabricated pinnaces. Next day, Drake put the helpful
native 'Felipe' ashore at Quintero, six leagues north of Valparaiso,
not too far from his home. For a week more they sailed cautiously
up the coast, looking for a watering place and not finding it.

On 18 December they sighted a likely spot and anchored in a
safe six fathoms close to shore. Sarmiento identifies the port as
La Herradura, near Coquimbo (which Fletcher calls Cyppo). Next
day a party of fourteen men were sent ashore to secure water and
food, while a sentry was placed in the crow's nest of the *Golden
Hind*. They had been ashore all morning and had got hold of two
pigs and some water when an arquebus shot was heard from inland.
Drake came out of his cabin in time to see a Spanish force attempt
to destroy his landing party. Fletcher estimated the enemy to
consist of a hundred Spanish horsemen, all well-mounted, followed
by about two hundred Indians, 'running as dogs at their heels, all
naked, and in most miserable bondage'. Sarmiento said there were
between fifty and sixty Spanish horsemen, and was probably right:
sixty enemy horsemen could look like a hundred, unless one counted
carefully. The Spaniard did not bother to say how many Indians
there were, but the combined force outnumbered Drake's fourteen
men many times over, apart from being fleeter, so they should
have ridden down the English and annihilated them.

However, the Spaniards were much too noisy in their approach. The landing party were able to run back to the beach in time and then splash out through the shallows to a half-tide rock, behind which they hid, while Drake sent a boat in from the ship to pick them up. The leader of the landing party, Richard Minivy, was the last to wade out to the rock, but he would not take cover behind it. Instead, from the Spanish side of the rock he took aim with his arquebus and fired. The ball missed, but instead of retiring behind cover to reload, Minivy drew his sword, apparently anxious to take on the whole Spanish party. He did not last very long, being shot through the head by a Spaniard.

Although by the least count the Spaniards and their Indian auxiliaries outnumbered the English by ten to one, they contented themselves with a fire-fight, which only wasted powder and shot. Hidden behind the rock, the landing party waited in safety until the ship's boat came in and took them off. Then came a macabre incident. The Spaniards sent their Indians to wade out to the rock in front of which Minivy's body still lay, and to drag it ashore. The English were forced to watch them mutilating this brave man's corpse. It 'was there manfully by the Spaniards beheaded, the right hand cut off, the heart plucked out; all which they carried away in our sight, and for the rest of his carcase they caused the Indians to shoot it full of arrows, made but the same day, of green wood, and so left it to be devoured of the beasts and the fowls,' testified Fletcher.

They could not leave their comrade like that, and as soon as the Spaniards had gone Drake went ashore himself with a second landing party, 'and buried his man's body without a head, and so made sail to depart, and at his departure the Spaniards came to the sea side with a flag of truce, but Drake would trust none of them, and set sail', wrote the anonymous narrator. Fletcher ascribed the Spaniards' behaviour to fear of being murdered by their Indian 'allies'. Hence the carrying off of Minivy's head on a pike and allowing only fresh-cut green wood for arrows. It was high time to mount the heavy ordnance as well as assemble a new pinnace.

They carried on northward for a few days more, anchoring on 21 December off the Islas de Pajaros (Bird Islands) where they collected some of the birds for their food. Next day, 22 December, just in time for Christmas, they found a suitable bay, Bahia Salada, where they were to remain for four weeks, spied on but not attacked by the Spaniards, except for a few stray arquebus shots. They began to assemble the pinnace and to make sails for her; and no doubt *La Capitana* supplied many useful items for this craft as well as replacements for the *Golden Hind*'s losses, especially cables and anchors. Christmas Day passed, but the great feast they celebrated was that of New Year's Day 1579. A few days later they were busy caulking the completed pinnace and cutting out the topsails ashore, presumably having marked them out on the beach. The 7th of January was a day of alarms, with six Indian spies discovered during the morning and a party of Spaniards coming close under cover of night and firing off a couple of arquebus shots. But 8 January was fine and sunny and da Silva was able to take a sight of the sun. He made their latitude to be just over 29°. Fletcher, however, recorded 27° 55' (i.e., just under 28°).

On the afternoon of Friday, 9 January, the pinnace was launched and ready for fitting out. A small bronze gun, a muzzle-loader, was placed in the bow. At nightfall on 10 January Drake, with sixteen men, embarked in the pinnace and set off southward towards the appointed rendezvous with the *Elizabeth*. When they came back, unsuccessful, on the evening of the 12th, the main party had already got the guns up from the hold of the *Golden Hind*, where they had been lying with the ballast, and no doubt used their weight for heeling the ship first on one side and then on the other, during the careening process. They would soon be in tropical seas again, where shipworm flourishes in the warm water, so after the ship's bottom had been cleaned of all trailing and encrusting growth, the planks were smeared with a noxious mixture of grease, brimstone and tar. They still had plenty of tar; in fact, they dumped six pipes of it to make house room for jars of wine. During this careening process, which took five days, the *Golden Hind* almost suffered fatal injury by capsizing; it was only prevented because Drake had rigged safety tackle to the mainmast.

By 19 January, all was ready again. Most of the wounded had been able to rest and recover, with some delicacies to eat and fresh water and wine to drink. The underwater body of the hull was armed against the teredo and other shipworms, which in a matter of months in tropical waters can turn timber planks into sieves, massively tunnelled, the tunnels lined with a white calcareous substance made by the creatures, which may exceed a foot in length and are really a species of shellfish. The decks were armed too, with eighteen guns of cast bronze or cast iron. Their purpose was rather to overawe than to destroy, to induce instant surrender, which besides being swifter is more profitable than battle. And ahead of them now, for scouting and raiding purposes, they would have the sixteen-man pinnace with its forward-firing bronze gun. As they sailed out, the two English vessels were accompanied for the moment by *La Capitana*, well known to the Spaniards on that coast as one of their own more notable vessels.

Chapter 10

'A GENERAL DISLIKE OF THE VOYAGE'

The Return of the *Elizabeth* to Brazil:
October 1578–February 1579

No one in the *Golden Hind* had seen Vice-Admiral John Winter's eighty-ton *Elizabeth* since the night of 7 October the previous year. Blown south of the Straits of Magellan for a month by high winds raising tremendous seas, they had found dubious shelter in a dangerous anchorage as darkness was falling. Before retiring to his cabin, Winter had told the master to be careful not to part company with the *Pelican* (as he still called her), which could be made out now and then about a league astern of them.

There is a conflict of evidence between the two witnesses who left brief reports – Winter himself in an official document dated 2 June 1579, a fateful day for him, when he had to account for his actions; and Edward Cliffe in what appears to be a private history, brief, factual and as far as may be, unbiased. John Cooke merely comments that it was Winter, being vice-admiral, who had to take the perilous responsibility for final decision. The fate of Doughty was in their minds and the tensions which had preceded the trial were still high. Almost the only test which may be applied is to see how the two witnesses recount that affair, of which we know a good deal from many sources.

Edward Cliffe wrote:

> 'The last of June Master Thomas Doughty was brought to his answer, was accused, and convicted of certain articles, and by Master Drake condemned. He was beheaded the 2 of July, 1578, whose body was buried in the said Island, near to them which were slain.'

Accurate and careful, he does not betray which side he was on.

John Winter was wary, but in stressing his offer, rejected by Drake, to keep Doughty safe in the *Elizabeth* as an alternative to execution, makes it seem he was on Doughty's side. He says nothing untrue, even quoting Drake's reply, 'that if he should suffer him to live, he could not answer it to Her Majesty when he came into England; with other speeches which I let pass for shortness.'

So we have the two men telling the truth, one in much more balanced, historical fashion than the other, for Winter's report was addressed to his influential official relatives, Sir William Winter of the Navy Board and George Winter, and was intended as a means of propagating his version of events in case anyone else might have a different story, as Cliffe did, for what was soon to take place.

There was no doubt that on the morning of 8 October they were in great danger, penned in against a coastline fringed with broken and sunken rocks by unfavourable winds. Winter thought they would have 'doubtless perished, if God had not given us a clear of a sudden, by the which we escaped the danger, and made the Straits'. The blame for thus losing sight of Drake's flagship he placed on the ship's master, the first of five accusations against that man. The same day, at night, they reached the entrance to the Strait of Magellan and anchored there. According to Winter, the master had urged that they should instead go inside the Straits to the place where Drake had last watered. Winter had refused, on the grounds that from the mouth of the Straits he would be able to see Drake's ship if she came in, and that in turn Drake would see the signal fires which Winter ordered to be kept burning. Winter wrote:

'The 10th day of October I went ashore, and landed on a high mountain, being the highest in all the Straits, in the top whereof I engraved her Majesty's name, and we praised God together for the great danger we had escaped. Here we found stones which were full of glistening sparkles like gold; the like sparkles we saw in the sand, whereby we conceived some hope that there should be some kind of metal. From this harbour we were driven with loss of an anchor, and had like to have lost ship, and all through the Master's unskilfullness. From this place I brought the ship to a very good harbour, contrary to the Master's and the Mate's goodwill, where we spent 22 days, and looked still for Mr Drake, and for a change of wind.'

Edward Cliffe had nothing to say about Winter's reported differences with the master or the mate, but everything else he confirmed:

'After, we went into a sound, where we stayed for the space of three weeks, and named it *the port of Health*; for the most part of our men being very sick with long watching, wet, cold, and evil diet, did here (God be thanked) wonderfully recover their health in short space. Here we had very great mussels (some being twenty inches long) very pleasant meat, and many of them full of seed-pearls.'

It was the change of diet which was important and Winter also may have known that in some as yet unidentified way, there was a deficiency in the normal rations, even when the quality was good (which, after a long passage through the Tropics, it was unlikely to be).

Cliffe's next sentence was the critical one: 'We came out of this harbour the first of November, giving over our voyage by Master Winter's compulsion (full sore against the mariners' minds).' According to Cliffe, Winter told them that he despaired both of having favourable winds for a passage up the west coast of South America to Peru and also for the safety of Drake and the flagship. In brief, there was no hope of making the appointed rendezvous with Drake in about 30° and Drake was probably lost anyway, the flagship no longer afloat but gone like the *Marigold* in deep water or cast away on the rocks, such as those from which they themselves had so narrowly escaped.

1 November 1578 was also the significant date for Drake himself and the crew of the *Golden Hind*, then far to the south in unknown, undiscovered waters, exploring the 'uttermost island'. On 31 October they brought back the last of the birds and seals they were collecting for food, according to da Silva's log, and on the first day of November set sail. For twenty-five days they had strong and mostly favourable winds for the northward run past the entrance to the Straits of Magellan and up the coast of Chile to 39° latitude. Drake did not go inside the Straits to look for Winter but kept on for the appointed rendezvous. No one could blame him or his ship's company for not wishing to be caught again near this place by southward-driving storms.

According to Winter himself, 1 November was also a decisive day, for he then left the sound just inside the entrance to the Straits and sailed back for three days to the Island of Geese. He would now have no chance of seeing Drake pass northward; if the *Golden Hind* was still afloat, that is. This decision did mark the abandonment of the voyage, but Winter's account of it utterly contradicts not only the logic of the move but Edward Cliffe's narrative: all roles are reversed, although the arguments used are the same in both versions. 'And now,' wrote Winter, 'being out of hope almost of a wind, and of his [Drake's] safety, except he should be to the leewards of us, persuaded with my Master and some of my company for the Moluccas. And to confirm my reports of the same voyage, I read to them Magellan's voyage, which they seemed to like well of.' As Magellan's men were reduced to eating their own sails and rigging during their desperate struggle across the unsuspected vastness of the Pacific towards the Spice Islands, this seems a rather strange reaction on the part of Winter's crew (unless Winter was really arguing, not for a return to England, but a passage to the Moluccas by the Portuguese route, round the southern tip of Africa).

The *Elizabeth* spent three or four days collecting provisions at the Island of Geese, but it was not until 8 November, according to Winter, that the final decision for a return was made. But whereas Cliffe reported that Winter had used 'compulsion' to make the men give up the voyage, and that it was 'full sore against the mariners' minds', Winter, while indeed describing angry scenes, again completely reversed the roles:

'The 8th day, calling my whole company together, I made my determination generally known, which was for the east parts of the world, using what persuasion I could. And protested unto them upon the Bible that Master Drake told me that he would go thither when I was last aboard him. But all was in vain, for the Master did utterly dislike of it, saying that he would fling himself overboard rather than consent to any such voyage to be steered, through which speeches and secret promises used by him, he caused a general dislike of the voyage. Sometimes he wished himself whipped at a cart's tail in Rochester. He said Master Drake hired him for Alexandria, but if he had known that this had been the Alexandria, he would have been hanged in England rather than have come in this voyage.'

There seems no way of reconciling the testimonies of Winter and of Cliffe on this crucial point (knowing that normally both were truthful men), but perhaps Doughty's friend John Cooke does give us an answer in the final sentence of a long narrative:

'The last of September we lost the *Marigold*, and the 8th of

October we lost the General and put ourselves to harbour in the Straits, where we rested, harboured until the 1st of November, and then for our return I think our Captain, Master Winter, will answer, who took the peril on him.'

If Winter had admitted that he, the Vice-Admiral, had been in favour of abandoning the voyage contrary both to the wishes of the Queen and the orders of the Captain-General, it was easy to imagine him sharing Doughty's fate. But to say that he believed the Captain-General was dead, that the winds were consistently against him, and that the ship's master (and by implication others) refused to go into the South Sea, would be a defence difficult to breach. And who can blame a man for wanting to live? In almost the last sentence of his letter, Winter wrote: 'Many other causes there be which did cause a general dislike of the voyage.' And this, of course, was true. The Doughty faction was strong in the *Elizabeth*, John Cooke being an example of their thinking. But it was only a faction. It was a divided and defeated ship which threaded its way back through the Straits of Magellan, out into the Atlantic and up past the sinister cliffs of Port St Julian where Doughty's body lay, and also the corpses of Robert Winterhey and Oliver the gunner, killed by Giants, and of Magellan's men too . . .

By some ironic chance, both ships now were going north. The *Golden Hind* on the Pacific coast of South America, the *Elizabeth* on the Atlantic coast. And, almost exactly, they kept in step. At the end of November 1578, the *Elizabeth* was back in the estuary of the River Plate, in about 35° latitude. And at the same time the *Golden Hind* was going north from Mocha towards Santiago in about 35° also. South lay the gold mines of Valdivia, north the silver mines of Potosí. And in the *Golden Hind* now there was no division, no factions any more; a light-hearted, almost schoolboy spirit pervaded the ship's company as they closed in on the fabulous treasure coasts of Chile and Peru.

The activities in both ships were also much the same. Both Drake and Winter decided to assemble a pinnace. The *Elizabeth* lay for two weeks off an island in the estuary of the Plate, while the pre-fabricated pieces were put together. They had only seals for company, the island swarmed with them. Some were sixteen feet long and they were not at all afraid of men. When the men lay down to sleep at night in their camp ashore, the seals joined them, and

would not move over 'unless mortal blows forced them to yield', as
Cliffe put it. This episode took place during the first half of December 1578. Drake decided to assemble his pinnace and found a
suitable site near Coquimbo in about 30°, the rendezvous latitude,
on 22 December, a week later than the man for whom he was waiting
on the other side of South America. Building the *Golden Hind*'s
pinnace took from the 23rd of December to the 9th of January, and
on the 10th she made her maiden voyage of four days, cruising
southward to look for the *Elizabeth* approaching the rendezvous.

Drake left in his flagship for the north on 19 January 1579. The
Elizabeth was now drawing away slightly. On 20 January she was
in 24°, near the Tropic of Capricorn, when she was separated from
the newly-built pinnace by bad weather. Neither the pinnace nor
the eight men in it were ever seen again, a melancholy echo of the
fate of the *Golden Hind*'s pinnace commanded by Peter Carder.
Shortly after, the *Elizabeth* herself was in dire trouble with a strong
onshore current; first she lost an anchor by the cable breaking, then
while weighing the second anchor the capstan ran away. That is,
the capstan pulled the men, not the men the capstan, from the
heavy sea that was now causing the ship to pitch and roll in violent
jerks. This was one of those situations where Winter was often
primly righteous at other people's expense, sometimes Drake's;
now it was happening to him, and with much more serious consequences. The ship's motion 'threw the men from the [capstan]
bars, and brake out the brains of one man: one other had his leg
broken, and divers others were sore hurt', recorded Cliffe.

Coming on top of the loss of the eight-man crew put into the
pinnace, the strength of the ship's company was much reduced;
later on, Winter was to lose two more men by desertion, together
with his ship's boat, in which they rowed off to join the Portuguese in
Brazil. In the meantime, the *Elizabeth* had watered at an island near
a place called Tanay and while pretending to negotiate with the
local Portuguese, Winter managed to barter with the natives, giving
them linen cloth, combs, knives and other trifles for food and fruit.
The meat they got consisted of two small oxen, a young hog and
some hens. Cliffe listed also the category: 'pome-cytrons, lemons,
oranges, and other fruits of the country'. It seems as though Drake
and Winter guessed at the cure for the dietary deficiency which
caused scurvy, long before any specific mention was recorded or
proofs offered. Fresh meat, vegetables and fruit – but particularly

lemons and oranges – were later established to be the remedy.

A pinnace crew under Peter Carder had lost touch with the *Golden Hind* one stormy night in October. From Drake's point of view, therefore, there were two vessels missing – the *Elizabeth* and his own pinnace. They might have joined together, but in any case Winter's vice-flagship at least might be expected to try to make the rendezvous. Failing that, she might seek shelter in some harbour or bay further north, the nearest being the port of Arica, according to Drake's information. The coast south of that appeared to be completely inhospitable.

According to Sarmiento, there was in fact a port there, that of Copiapo, but the English lookouts failed to see the entrance and so the *Golden Hind* sailed past unaware. On 22 January they anchored in the lee of a small island and were approached by four Camanchaca Indians in canoes. Hoping that they might guide him to fresh water, Drake turned on the bonhomie. As Fletcher put it, 'our General made great cheer (as his manner was towards all strangers), and set his course by their direction'. The Indians led him to a source, but it was so scanty that Fletcher reckoned the amount of water they got out of it was less than the amount of wine they had poured into the Indians to make them cooperate.

They spent some days moving from place to place, fishing or bartering with the natives in an area which they believed to be called Mormorena but which Sarmiento says was really Morro Moreno. According to the Spaniard it was near here that:

> 'the Corsair sent ashore, in an Indian canoe, an Englishman who spoke several languages. While on land, this Englishman began to shout, telling those in the launch that the Indians there had seen two other English ships pass by . . . '

Two English vessels, the *Elizabeth* and a pinnace, were what Drake might expect to see; or the *Elizabeth* and a prize. If all had gone well. In fact, there was no truth in the story, which may easily have been a mistake in understanding what the Indians were really saying. Nevertheless, those phantom ships were to play a part in the calculations of both English and Spanish over the next few months.

Winter and his men had lost their chance. It was the *Golden Hind*, newly careened and with her heavy ordnance mounted at the ports, which was about to embark alone on the richest raid in the history of the world.

PART TWO

Chapter 11

'TOO LATE BY TWO HOURS!'

The Balance of Forces – Tarapaca to Lima:
4–15 February 1579

THEY were coasting past fabulous country. Throughout this province of 'Cusco', according to what Fletcher heard, the common earth, if taken up and treated, would yield 25 shillings' worth of pure silver for every one hundred pounds weight of soil. Silver is, of course, a more common metal than gold and although the ground also contained valuable deposits of iron, copper and nitrates, it was the great silver mines of Potosí, sited among the mountains they could see rising up behind the coastal plain, which supplied the annual treasure convoy to Spain with much of its valuable heavy cargo and also its name. The convoys were popularly known as the Plate Fleets; that is, the Silver Fleets. Although they carried many items apart from silver, it was the precious metals primarily which sustained the Spanish economy and its European war machine.

Twice within a day or so, Drake's raiding parties, while exploring for water, managed to surprise and capture unwary merchants returning from the Potosí mines. Early in February, at Tarapaca, they found their victim literally asleep, and beside him thirteen bars of silver to the total worth of about 4,000 Spanish ducats. Shortly after, having entered the Pisagua River behind a canoe paddled by an Indian guide, they landed and waylaid a Spaniard accompanied by an Indian boy who was driving before him, like pack mules, eight odd-looking creatures, seemingly a cross between a sheep and a stag, and about the size of a cow, the necks being not unlike that of a camel. Fletcher learned that these beasts were the principal Spanish pack animal when alive; when dead, they provided excellent wool and meat. It was the loads they bore which interested the Englishmen, for each creature carried two leather bags, and in each bag fifty pounds weight of refined silver, the total being 800 pounds weight. Sarmiento heard that its value was equal to 3,000 Spanish

145

ducats and that the poor man was also robbed of much *charqui*, or sun-dried beef.

Fletcher adopted a jocular manner towards such thefts. In this case, he wrote that they 'could not endure to see a gentleman Spaniard turned carrier so, and therefore without intreaty we offered our services and became drovers; only his directions were not so perfect that we could keep the way he intended . . . ' One of the robbed Spaniards was a Corsican, and he was brought on board the pinnace to act as pilot for their raid on Arica, the next settlement on the coast of any size, numbering about twenty houses.

Consequently, the nature of the documentation undergoes a drastic change. We have three English witnesses only: Fletcher, 'Anon' and John Drake (under Spanish interrogation twice). They are all brief, quite lacking the deeply felt asides of the early Fletcher. Additionally, from the *Golden Hind*, we have Nuño da Silva many times. Firstly, his log. Then interrogation after interrogation, examinations, sworn depositions, the results of all sorts of questioning, some of it no doubt extremely painful. Further, his examiners may not have been familiar with the exact meanings of mariners' speech, so that what was written down may contain errors of technical fact.

We have also lost the trio from the *Elizabeth*. John Winter, anxious to absolve himself from any blame in connection with various matters; Edward Cliffe, brief and as neutral as may be; John Cooke, lengthy, passionately anti-Drake, and in so being, taking down and recording for us, almost verbatum, the man's very speech.

The burden of evidence from now on, however, is markedly Spanish, for Drake was attacking Spanish settlements, taking Spanish ships, and carrying off Spaniards as prisoners for periods of time varying from three hours to four weeks. When they were released by Drake, and had made their way back to Spanish territory, they were immediately questioned as to who this corsair was, what he did, what kind of ship he had, how he had come to be on this coast, and what his future intentions might be. These examinations complement the testimony of John Cooke, they add vivid cameos of how Drake lived on board the *Golden Hind* and what sort of man he was; and because they show him in action, professionally, some can add an extra dimension.

High-born witnesses often supplied their own written testimony in the form of reports or semi-official letters, while others were examined by the local officials and dictated statements. Of the latter, some could sign their own names, and some could not; some knew their own ages, others were vague. By no means all were Spanish-born. There were several Corsicans, a Fleming and a Portuguese, not surprisingly; but there was also a Greek and one man who may well have been an Englishman from Southampton. Some of the earlier, more informal questioning was done by Pedro Sarmiento de Gamboa, who became actively involved, almost from the start, in Spanish countermeasures, and who was to incorporate the gist of what witnesses said to him in a useful narrative of events. When placed beside the English versions, and also da Silva's evidence, a combined narrative emerges with only a few discrepancies and those of no account.

Drake dominates all the narratives from the Spanish side. His first prisoner, John the Greek, was to tell Sarmiento:

'The first thing we learnt was that the ship was English and carried seventy or eighty men, the chief of whom was named Francisco Draquez, a medium sized man, robust and a great mariner and cosmographer. It was he who some years ago robbed much silver in Chagres and Cruces. The Englishman said that they had sailed from Plymouth, England, by order of the Queen of that country.'

This was to become a familiar story to Spanish officialdom in the months that followed. Many witnesses were to testify in similar fashion. Drake had impressed them not merely as a successful corsair but as that rare being, the great mariner and navigator who was also a world geographer and explorer, and who, not surprisingly, had been sent by the highest authority of his homeland.

His situation now, however, was less impressive than it had been when he had set out with 164 men and a balanced fleet of five ships of varying types and sizes. Ignoring the *Elizabeth*, which might or might not appear to reinforce the *Golden Hind*, Drake was reduced to one ship, a prefabricated pinnace, and seventy or eighty men, of whom perhaps fifty were fit to fight. Although Spanish estimates ranged from a total of sixty crew on the one hand to a total of eighty-six on the other, the figure of fifty fighting men, the rest 'rabble', occurs nearly unanimously. The 'rabble' might include the more seriously wounded from the Indian ambush at Mocha (Drake himself was still recovering from two wounds received two months before); it certainly included the ship's boys, and probably the invaluable craftsmen and tradesmen vitally necessary for an extended voyage such as this. By virtue of their experience, these craftsmen (carpenters, smiths, coopers) were likely to be older; too old to go leaping up the sides of Spanish ships or to storm ashore through the surf from ship's boats, in torrid heat, under the weight of armour and weapons.

Now that at last he was sailing in an English ship on that great South Sea he had dreamed of for so long, Drake was reduced to commanding an assault force numbering rather less than half of an ordinary infantry company. The small Spanish coastal settlements presented no great problem individually; but he could not afford to linger long enough for the Spaniards to concentrate mounted troops against him from their towns in the interior. This infantry force was vital to his techniques for taking ships swiftly, quietly, and in good condition. He could not afford to waste it in heavy fighting ashore.

The other half of his method lay in overawing any opponent by the heavy guns of the *Golden Hind*, and if they refused to be sufficiently impressed, the actual firing of some of them so that noise, smoke and confusion would work to distract attention from the swift pinnace, filled with armed men, which would then shoot out from behind the hull which had previously masked it from view, and put its boarders on to the opponent's deck with amazing swiftness. Drake did not want casualties, on either side; he did not, above all, want a battle. He wanted the greatest plunder with the least loss. Nevertheless, the armament of his flagship was no bluff. He did not attempt to conceal it from his prisoners, nor the extent of variety of ammunition which went with it.

There is no doubt that the armament of the *Golden Hind* consisted of eighteen sizeable guns. John Drake, who served the whole voyage in her, said so. Nuño da Silva, who was in her for more than a year, said so. Some of the Spaniards who were prisoners in her said so. Other Spaniards, who gave the lesser figure of fourteen guns, also mentioned that she did not always mount all her guns; often up to four pieces of ordnance, usually of brass, were below on the ballast. This may have been because of high seas and bad weather or merely to give more space on the fighting and working decks. A single Spaniard gave the figure of twenty-two guns, and another twenty-five, but they may have been including light swivel pieces, such as bases, which fired lead shot varying between half an inch and two inches in diameter, according to the weight of the piece. Usually these were mounted fairly high up in the stern castle.

The witnesses deposed that the main battery guns were mounted four, five, or seven aside. The latter figure, which gives a total of fourteen broadside guns, probably represents the maximum, if all guns were brought up from below; da Silva was one of those who testified to this. Almost all the witnesses who go into details of disposition mention two additional heavy guns mounted low down in the poop, beside the helm; this was a traditional place for stern guns. The total now is sixteen sizeable guns as maximum. Further single witnesses refer to two guns mounted in the poop above the level of the main deck (presumably lighter guns) and to two definitely heavy guns at the prow. This gives a total of eighteen sizeable guns plus probably two lighter pieces on an upper deck; or, possibly these were alternative arrangements for no more than eighteen guns. Two of the Spanish witnesses say that four of the heavy guns were of brass, whereas da Silva puts the figure as thirteen, the rest being of cast iron. Whatever the truth here, this represents a much heavier armament than that of any Spanish opponent they were likely to meet; and might well overwhelm any shore defences also.

The ammunition included fireballs and chainshot for use against a ship's rigging. In the gunroom, or armoury, in the poop, the small arms were stored. These included arquebuses, bows and arrows, ordinary long pikes for land use and the short pikes (Morris or 'Moorish' pikes) for employment on shipboard. Additionally, there was a stock of steel helmets and body armour, steel shields and swords. There was also miniature chainshot for use with the arquebuses.

The *Golden Hind* was regarded by those who saw her or who took involuntary passage in her for a while as being well built and formidable for her size. She was not, of course, fit to take part in the close action of a major naval engagement, which demanded a ship a great deal heavier, mounting really substantial batteries of the most formidable siege ordnance, and carrying many hundreds of fighting men. Spanish estimates of her size varied between 180 and 300 tons, which probably represented what they thought she could carry if used as a cargo ship, according to Spanish weights and measures. Da Silva judged her to be 220 tons, which compares with Edward Cliffe's 120 tons and Fletcher's 100 tons, both being English

measurements, of course. A similar English measurement for a major
warship would lie in the range of 600 to 1,500 tons.

The ex-*Pelican* was a small raider well suited to an extended
voyage on which dockyard facilities would be lacking. She would be
fairly easy to careen, a vital necessity in tropical waters. Da Silva
was to depose that she had 'two sheathings, one as perfectly finished
as the other'; but there is no actual evidence from the description of
various careenings that a complete layer of hull planking was stripped
off because it was riddled with teredo. Instead, reliance seems to
have been placed on a really thick coating of a noxious chemical-
impregnated anti-fouling paint, and renewing it fairly often. The
'two sheathings' perhaps refer to the vessel having had a second
skin of planking, inboard of the frames, as well as the outer skin, a
common type of construction which because of its boxlike nature
was very strong in relation to its weight.

Da Silva told his examiners that the eighty-strong crew of Drake's
ship consisted not of Englishmen only, but also of Frenchmen,
Biscayans, Scotsmen and Flemings; and it appears that some of
these were chosen for their knowledge of and experience in the
provinces of New Spain, as the Spaniards called their possessions
north of South America (which to them was Terra Firme). That is,
the crew was partly composed of veterans, already partially
acclimatised to the torrid heat zones they were entering.

Drake himself was zealous to record the voyage in such a way that
it could be repeated by others. He carried with him, da Silva said,
three books on navigation: one in English, one in French, and
Magellan's, in what language he knew not. Also:

> 'Drake kept a book in which he entered his navigation and in
> which he delineated birds, trees and sea-lions. He is an adept at
> painting and has with him a boy, a relative of his, who is a great
> painter. When they both shut themselves up in his cabin they
> were always painting.'

The relative was his cousin, John Drake, then about fifteen years
of age. The principal subjects of their artwork were coloured recognition pictures, from seaward, of the approaches to the various bays,
anchorage, islands, ports and harbours that they passed or used,
with an indication of the 'marks' or 'transits' to be employed in
order to go safely from A to B. Anyone possessing such an illustrated
guide could not only operate more safely but could move with speed

and certainly through dangerous waters. This detailed and illustrated log was a valuable property and was in due course to be presented to the Queen.

Without a now non-existent Drake diary it is necessary to guess at the reasoning behind the moves made by the *Golden Hind*. But it is necessary to remember also that Drake was by way of being an expert on the complicated system of interlocking convoys in both oceans, linked by two overland routes across the narrow neck of land between the continents of north and south America. He had operated both ashore and afloat from the Atlantic or Caribbean side before, where the Spaniards organised convoys on three different routes for the inward voyage, joining together in one great convoy, the Plate Fleet, for the rich return to Spain. This vast collection of ships was heavily escorted by warships, the galleons of the Indian Guard. A single small galleon such as the *Golden Hind* would only court disaster if she operated in the Caribbean against the 'silver ships'.

This system had begun in about 1550, but various developments since then had added two new convoy routes, both on the Pacific side where, by intention, the *Golden Hind* now was. In about 1555 a technical discovery – how to separate silver from other minerals by means of mercury – enabled the Spaniards to make economic use of the Peruvian deposits, notably those at Potosí. At first, the mercury was obtained in Hungarian mines and brought over from Europe in the outward-bound fleets together with much else required by the Spanish colonists; later, supplies were obtained locally from the Juancavelica mine conveniently located in Peru. The result was a flow of silver and some gold by way of small harbours to the large port of Callao, which served Lima, the capital of Peru where the Spanish governor flew his standard. There each spring shipping assembled which would sail north for Panama at the end of May or early in June as the *Armadilla del Mar de Sud*, or South Sea Squadron. From Panama, these ships' cargoes would go over-land to Porto Bello for embarkation in ships of the Silver Fleet. No man living was more aware of that fact than Francis Drake.

However, since about 1560 there had been another land bridge taking the rewards of another new convoy route; that from Manila in the Philippines. This was the effective result of Spanish explora-tion in the great South Sea, because of its size the most hazardous of all oceans. The crews of the Manila Galleons brought back silks, porcelain and other luxury goods from China and Japan, but at the cost of 50 per cent losses in human life. The distances to be covered across the vast Pacific Ocean were so great that water and provisions rarely lasted. The port on the Pacific side at which these ships unloaded was Acapulco in Mexico, from where pack animals conveyed their cargoes to Veracruz on the Gulf of Mexico, looking out to Havana, the eventual rendezvous of all the cargoes of all the ships, once the annual trade fairs had taken place.

These two Pacific convoy systems, that which assembled at Callao, Lima, bound for Panama, and the Manila Galleons which would come in from the expanses of the limitless South Sea to harbour at Acapulco, were now well established and secure; the Spaniards had been running these routes for twenty years or so. They did not expect trouble and were not prepared for it. Even their largest cargo ships were armed only at the level required to beat off attack by Indian canoes. Anyway, to have fitted them with heavy ordnance, powder and shot would have seriously limited their carrying capacity, as would the provision of infantry on board. These ships with their fabulous cargoes were virtually defenceless against even a small raiding galleon, such as the *Golden Hind*, with her eighteen guns, ample ammunition, and fifty fighting men who knew how to use the accompanying pinnace to full advantage. Tremendous results might be obtained by the captain who first hit this tempting target. Not only would he, his crew, and his backers be immensely enriched, but considerable military and economic disarray would be created in the most critical area of a rival, and potentially enemy, power. It cannot therefore have been a mere afterthought or whim of the moment that took the *Golden Hind* first into all the southern ports Drake could find, which fed Lima, and then into Callao itself, and that he intended to end the whole series of raids from seaward with a descent upon Acapulco.

However, as in most operations of war, there are many factors which may not be predicted or accurately allowed for in advance, such as the wind, the weather, the workings of chance, and the actions or reactions of the enemy. All that the General can do is to make an informed appreciation of the situation, formulate a basically sound plan, make his preparations with foresight and care, and then be alert for the fortunate chance on the actual day. This latter quality is not the least.

Behind the logical appreciation that on this seaboard the smallest force might inflict the greatest damage upon the dangerous might of Spain, undoubtedly there were reasons even more compelling which were far from being causes of state. Almost at the start of the venture lay the port of Lima and in the Inquisition prison there, awaiting death at the stake, were men Drake knew; including his former lieutenant, John Oxenham. How Drake found out that his old companion was being held in Lima is not recorded, but probably he had the information from the local Spaniards he questioned. With a fleet at his back, Drake might have been able to bring significant pressure to bear on the Spanish authorities; with one ship only, the chances were smaller, but worth trying. Even if nothing could be done, it was still a defiance; a defeat for Spain, where Oxenham's capture by them had been a small victory.

And at the end of all the raids lay Acapulco, the Pacific port for Veracruz, of which the Caribbean harbour was San Juan de Ulloa, the place of treachery and defeat for John Hawkins, and of ruin for Drake, at the hands of Don Martin Enriquez, Viceroy of Mexico, eleven years ago. This high position Don Martin still held, but it was not to be for much longer.

He was loathed in England, particularly by the survivors of the Hawkins expedition. As they saw it, they had been magnanimous. Hawkins had been driven by weather and the state of his ships, particularly his flagship, Henry VIII's old German purchase, the carrack *Jesus of Lübeck*, to take shelter in this port which served the yearly Plate Fleet on the Caribbean side. Then, with tragic irony, the Silver Fleet of 1568, commanded by the Viceroy, Enriquez, arrived outside the harbour with what the English believed to be some £200,000 worth of treasure on board already. Hawkins, in possession, could have kept the Spaniards out of their own port and let them be driven ashore by the storm; if he let the armed and escorted convoy in, he was running a great risk.

So Hawkins agreed a covenant with Don Martin, and they exchanged hostages, as guarantees of peace; that they would not molest each other while both sheltered together in the same port.

The Viceroy, who may have found the English attitude presumptuous had no intention of keeping his word; the hostages he sent were 'men of straw' and he secretly prepared and suddenly launched a surprise attack, from which only Hawkins and Drake and a handful of their followers escaped. Don Martin's second-in-command, Juan de Ubilla, while critical of his superior, reported to the King:

'It was a well-fought battle, and one of the hardest in which I ever took part, although I have served Your Majesty in most of the notable fights in the Levant and in the West, from the battle of Tunis until now.'

At the moment, however, it was the first week of February 1579; the coast of Chile was behind them and they were off Peru, abreast of Potosí. On the evening of 6 February the *Golden Hind* approached the harbour of Arica, accompanied by her pinnace and the captured *La Capitana*, with a prize crew aboard. Inside the port were two ships, one belonging to Felipe Corço (Philip the Corsican), the other to Jorje Diaz. Johnny the Greek was still with Drake and may have guided him in; if so, he was sensible enough not to admit it later. The pinnace ran alongside the two ships in turn and poured armed men over their rails to take possession of them and also to get prisoners. Nicolas Jorje, a forty-two-year-old Fleming, was taken in the Corsican's ship. He deposed that Drake threatened to kill him many times, because he had not told Drake as much as he knew about another ship with a silver cargo; nevertheless, he was to be kept by the English for a month. Out of Corço's ship, he said, they 'seized thirty-five bars of silver, alloyed with white mercury, and a chest which belonged to men who had come from Potosí and contained small pieces of silver.' The anonymous narrator from the *Golden Hind* wrote, however, that there were '57 slabs of fine silver weighing about 20 pounds each . . . about the bigness of a brick bat.' Some stickler for detail in the *Golden Hind*, also anonymous, left detailed notes behind; not a narrative, just descriptive details and miscellaneous facts, jotted down mostly in the order of their occurrence. The relevant entry read: 'At Arica, the 57 slabs of silver we found lying openly upon their wares, piled one over another three bars high.' The other captured ship, as all regretfully agreed. contained no treasure at all, merely three hundred jars of wine. These were transferred out of the ship of Diaz and into the ship of Corço, which Drake intended to bring out with him when he left next day.

Meanwhile, according to Sarmiento and also to Anon, all enjoyed a noisy and exciting night, for the alarm was given ashore by the ringing of bells and the inhabitants of the village armed themselves and mounted their horses. Sarmiento learnt that the *Golden Hind* fired some of her guns at the village and that from the shore that night the Spaniards could hear trumpets being blown aboard the English ship and also the sound of musical instruments. Quite a wild party seems to have got under way, during which the ship of Jorje Diaz began to burn. As her cargo, in addition to the wine, consisted of large quantities of oil and wax, it must have been quite a blaze. In his log, da Silva wrote that the firing of this vessel was 'not by order of the Senhor' (by whom he meant Drake). Anon wrote that it was done:

> 'by one Fuller and one Tom Marcks, and so burned to the very water. There were not in these barks one person, for they mistrusting no thieves were all gone on shore. In this town of Arica were about 20 houses, which Drake would have set upon if he had company with him, but wanting [i.e. lacking] company of pirates, he departed hence.'

Possibly the whole English force was suffering from a monumental hangover, or at least were not thinking straight, for according to Sarmiento they seized three fishing boats and used one of them to get rid of guests they no longer required – three Spanish prisoners and nearly a dozen Indians. The three Spaniards made good use of of the opportunity, and instead of tamely going ashore at Arica made off up the coast towards the port of Chule, near Arequipa, to warn any ships in harbour of the approach of the corsairs.

According to Sarmiento, a very rich prize indeed lay anchored there, the ship of Bernal Bueno, which was loading for Lima a cargo which included 500 bars of Spanish royal gold. As soon as they heard the news, the people in the port gathered round and helped to unload the ship again, taking the gold inland and burying it. Drake was close behind the three Spaniards in the canoe; he had got into the pinnace which was moving along close inshore under both sail and oars, while the Golden Hind remained a league out to sea. When the pinnace came into the harbour, the English found a large crowd assembled ashore, jeering at them. Among the taunts shouted across the water were 'Go away, you thief!' and 'Too late by two hours!'

No doubt Drake did then threaten to kill Nicolas Jorje, the Fleming, for not warning him about this treasure ship. Jorje was then in the Golden Hind and he saw the pinnace come back out of the harbour of Chule, bringing Bernal Bueno's ship with her, and later heard the pinnace's crew shout out the bad news, that the ship was now empty, although clearly it had been heavily laden, they presumed with silver. In Nuño da Silva's log the pilot wrote: 'By two hours we missed taking 500 bars of silver.' Sarmiento heard that it was 500 bars of gold, and presumably his information was better. Another Spanish source, the claim for damages, referred to 'wedges' instead of bars. But, gold or silver, wedges or bars, what eventually became plain was that a warning message had been allowed to reach Chule ahead of them, and that this sort of thing must not happen again.

Therefore the prizes, which slowed them, must be got rid of. Some parts of their cargoes were transhipped to the *Golden Hind*, then their sails were set, their helms lashed, and they were allowed to drive seaward with no man on board. In this way, three ships were cast off into the South Sea – the 120-ton *La Capitana* taken at Santiago, Felipe Corço's ship taken at Arica, and Bernal Bueno's sixty-ton ship taken at Chule. These vessels could not be used now either to pursue the English or to give warning of their coming, but with luck one or two might still be recovered by their owners. It would have been easy to have burnt or scuttled them, as would be the case in all-out war, but Drake was behaving with studied moderation towards private individuals. Possibly he had orders to do so (in anticipation of ambassadorial protests in due course), but on the other hand he had disposed of one of his own ships in this fashion. Within the next few days, however, Drake was to show unmistakably that he was not acting as a commerce-destroyer; the damage he caused was selective and limited. Even this must have gone hard with at least one man on board, or 'Anon' would not have written that the only reason why Drake did not plunder the houses at Arica was that he lacked a crew of pirates.

While Drake's men were dispersed among the prizes, Nicolas Jorje the Fleming had had no opportunity to estimate their strength accurately. With the fleet once more reduced to the *Golden Hind* and her pinnace, an actual count was possible, although he had to do it surreptitiously; and he made their numbers to be either seventy-one or seventy-two, rather than the vague seventy to eighty given by most of the witnesses. And while those witnesses in the main judged the fighting men to be about fifty in number, Jorje gave the low figure of 'only thirty men who are fit for warfare'. Sarmiento was shortly to show how three hundred fighting men could be quickly assembled at Lima, outnumbering Drake's comparable force by ten to one, if Jorje was correct, six to one if the other witnesses were right. This factor must have been in the forefront of Drake's calculations. He could not afford to get mixed up in fighting ashore, nor could he risk running aground or even losing a mast. Any one of those things would mean probable annihilation. If they could, the Spaniards would wipe them out, although it was just possible that they might spare the few youngsters among the crew.

The two English vessels spread out into their usual hunting formation, the pinnace (often with Drake aboard) sailing in the shallows and close enough to shore to be able to make out the figures of men on the land, if there should be any, while the *Golden Hind* stayed a league or more, perhaps three miles, out to sea. This way, they covered a wide front and appeared to have nothing to do with each other, and the larger vessel was too far out for any watcher on shore to discern her surprising armament; also it was safer, as the pinnace drew only a foot or two of water whereas the *Golden Hind*, fully laden, might draw a dozen feet or more. What form of discreet signalling they employed, we do not know.

On 15 February, off Quilca, they sighted three Spanish coasters steering south, two inshore and one far out. The English were now within seven or eight leagues of Lima, so it would have been foolish to risk giving the alarm by attacking the pair of inshore vessels. But they did very badly need information, up-to-date intelligence on Spanish shipping movements. Drake decided to capture unobtrusively the detached offshore craft, which proved to be a bark owned by Francisco de Truxillo of Lima and bound for the local port of Valle. Her captain, Gaspar Martin, a Portuguese, was known to Nicolas Jorje. Jorje was not present when this man was questioned by Drake, but deposed later that Drake had told him of the valuable information he had had from Gaspar Martin. This may have been an attempt by Jorje to avoid any suspicion falling on himself, for clearly Drake had squeezed him hard.

The bark carried a cargo of linen clothes. Drake took out some of these for his own crew and also two men for questioning, one of them Gaspar Martin; then he let the ship go. Jorje's version of the information Drake obtained from Gaspar Martin was that two silver-carrying ships were shortly expected to arrive in Lima from Panama – the ships of Miguel Angel and Andres Murielo – but that a much greater prize, the vessel captained by a man called San Jaun de Anton, had left Lima northward bound only a few days previously. Her destination was the Spanish Main via Panama and some intermediate ports where she was to load flour in addition to the great treasure she carried. Da Silva referred to her as the *Nao Rica* – the 'Fat Freighter' or rich merchantman. Her real name was *Nuestra Señora de la Concepción*, although Spanish seamen generally called her by a crude functional nickname which the English understood to be Cacafuego. This news introduced an additional note of urgency.

The prisoners of the last few days provided additional information of a quite different sort – they were a window on the world of which Drake and his men had heard nothing for more than a year. There was no word of their comrades in the *Elizabeth* or of Peter Carder in the pinnace, noted Fletcher, but:

'We heard report of some things that had befallen in and near Europe since our departure thence; in particular of the death of some great personages, as the king of Portugal, and both the kings of Morocco and Fez, dead all three in one day at one battle; the death of the king of France and the Pope of Rome, whose abominations, as they are in part cut off from some Christian kingdoms, where his shame is manifest, so do his vassals and accursed instruments labour by all means possible to repair that loss, by spreading the same the further in these parts, where his devilish illusions and damnable deceivings are not known . . . It's true that in all the parts of America, where the Spaniards have any government, the poisonous infection of Popery hath spread itself . . . '

Specifically, Fletcher accused the Roman Church of encouraging 'not only whoredom, but the filthiness of Sodom, not to be named among Christians', because the Pope's pardons for sin were even more easily obtained in the colonies than they were in Europe. But even there, he went on, there were to be found people to protest:

'For in this city of Lima, not two months before our coming thither, there were certain persons, to the number of twelve, apprehended, examined, and condemned for the profession of the Gospel, and reproving the doctrines of men, with the filthy manners used in that city: of which twelve, six were bound to one stake and burnt, the rest remained yet in prison, to drink of the same cup within a few days.'

Probably Drake had this information from prisoners.

There were four Englishmen at that moment in the Inquisition prison at Lima: Captain John Oxenham, John Butler, Henry Butler and Thomas 'Xerores' (a cover-name, real name unknown). They were all that was left of Oxenham's expedition to the South Sea by the overland route: the remainder had been killed in battle by the military or hanged by the Civil Power. Oxenham had in fact sailed on the South Sea earlier than Drake, but in small craft only after a march across the Isthmus; nevertheless he had captured two treasure ships. Then he had lost it all during the return march, when the Spaniards had rushed his camp. Now he and his three companions were receiving special treatment: instead of summary execution as pirates, they were to be tried for heresy before they were hanged. Only Henry Butler was to survive, on account of his youth.

Lima was two leagues inland from Callao, the port which served the capital. As the *Golden Hind* sailed in that night, three hours after darkness had fallen, Drake had come to within a mere six miles of where his old companion was imprisoned; but could do nothing directly to free him.

Also in Lima that night was Pedro Sarmiento de Gambao, now serving the Viceroy of Peru, Don Francisco de Toledo, as a captain. He too had vivid memories of the cells of the Inquisition at Lima, for he had been tried there in 1565 for necromancy, found guilty, and as a penitent paraded during the auto-da-fé on 8 May that year. In 1572, he had again been tried and found guilty, but was saved by the intervention of Don Francisco, the Viceroy.

It was not until after midnight that the alarm was given in the capital, by the ringing of the church bells, the hoarse shouting of the town criers, and once by the distant thunder-peal of an English cannon shot.

Chapter 12

'FRENCHMEN! FRENCHMEN!'

The Attack at Lima and Spanish Counter-Measures:
February 1579

PILOTED probably by Gaspar Martin, and nudging the ground at one point, the *Golden Hind* made her way through the channels into Callao between ten o'clock and midnight. Both her pinnace and her skiff were in the water, and a short distance away another ship was also coming in. She was larger than the *Golden Hind*, John Drake judging her to be of 130 tons. Francis Drake ordered one of his Spanish prisoners to hail her. The answer came back that she was from Panama with a cargo of Castilian goods for Lima. In reply, Drake's prisoner was ordered to say that the *Golden Hind* was a galleon from Chile, which was perfectly correct, although her home port was at a somewhat greater distance away.

Inside the harbour were lying about thirty vessels of all types, many being of only twelve or thirteen tons, other much larger. The *Golden Hind* moved slowly through their moorings, accompanied by her pinnace and skiff, fully manned, and with a Spanish prisoner calling out on their behalf for the 'silver ship'. The reply he got was discouraging. The ship was there, but the silver had not been loaded yet; it was still in the King's warehouse ashore, guarded by the customs men. Now, instead of being too late, they were too early! So what was to be done?

As Fletcher pointed out, if Drake had intended indiscriminate revenge, he could have easily created havoc among that mass of shipping. All their sails were on land, so safe did the Spaniards think themselves. Instead, he got into the *Golden Hind*'s boat, half a dozen men with him, and began to cut the cables of the ships, directing the pinnace, carrying more than twenty men, to do the same. John Drake understood that the idea was that the offshore breeze would carry the Spanish vessels out to sea, where only Drake could get at them, and that he would then use them as a ransom for the release of John Oxenham from his Lima prison.

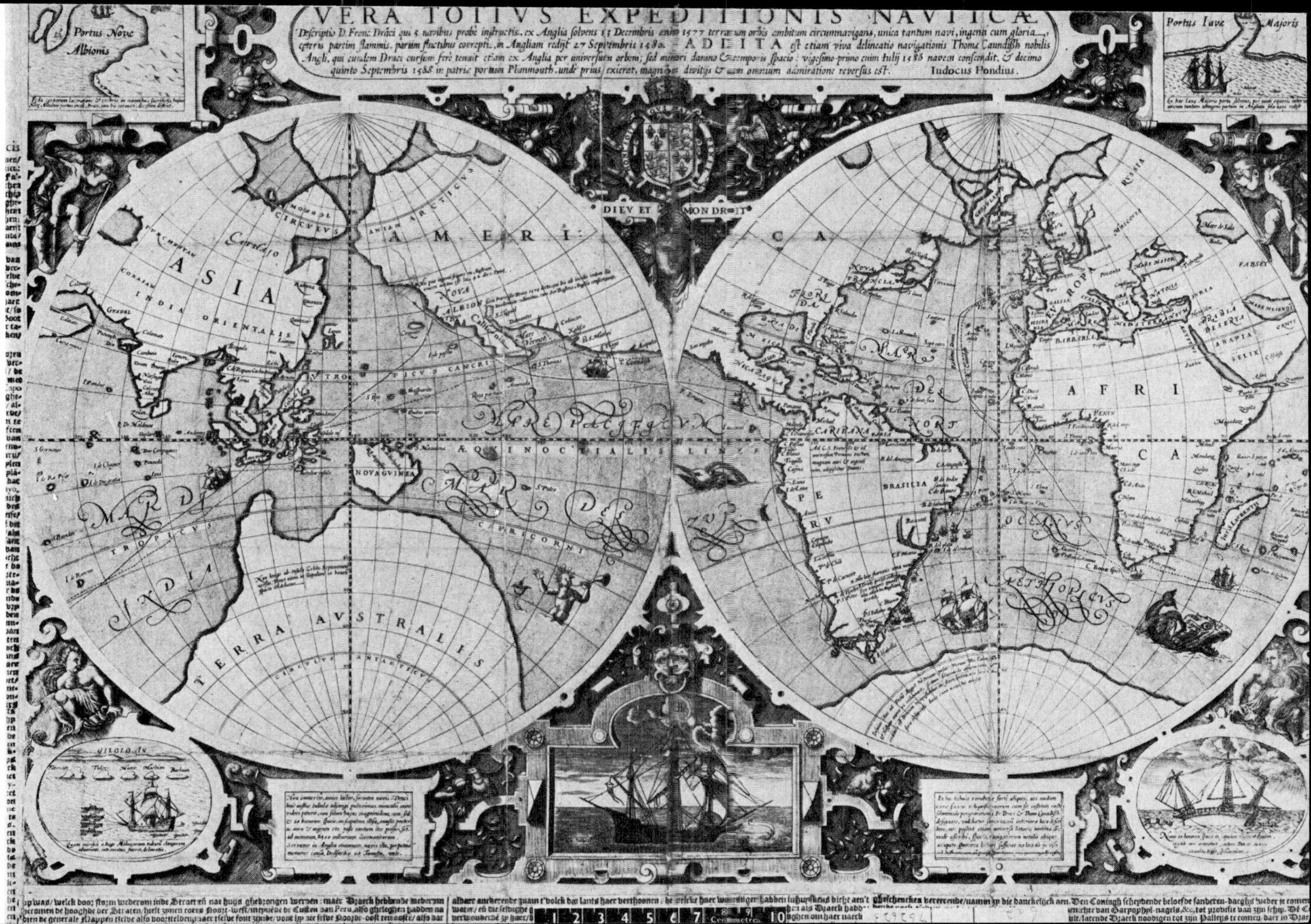

Fig. 1
WORLD MAP by Jodocus Hondius c. 1595, showing the voyages of Francis Drake (1577–80) and Thomas Cavendish (1586–88), with inset pictures of the *Golden Hind* and incidents from Drake's voyage. Hondius was in London when the *Golden Hind* was on display, so he must have known what she really looked like. (*British Library Board*).

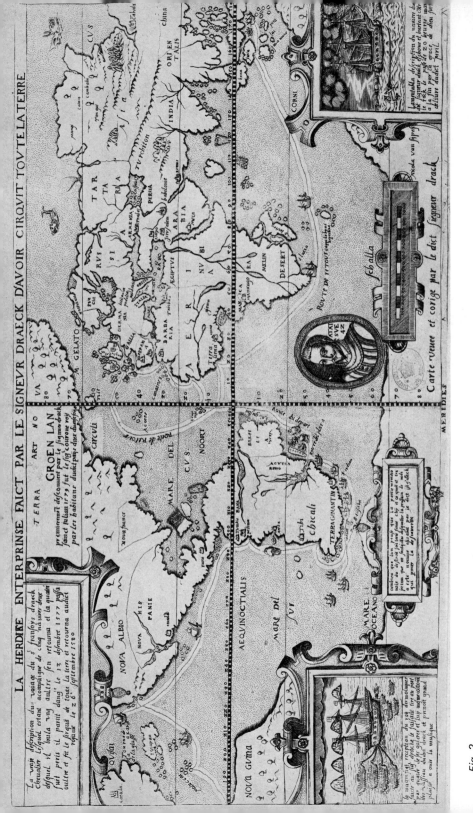

Fig. 2
WORLD MAP by Nicola van Sype c. 1581, showing the 'heroic enterprise' of Sir Francis Drake and, correctly, open sea between South America and Antarctica. This diagram ...

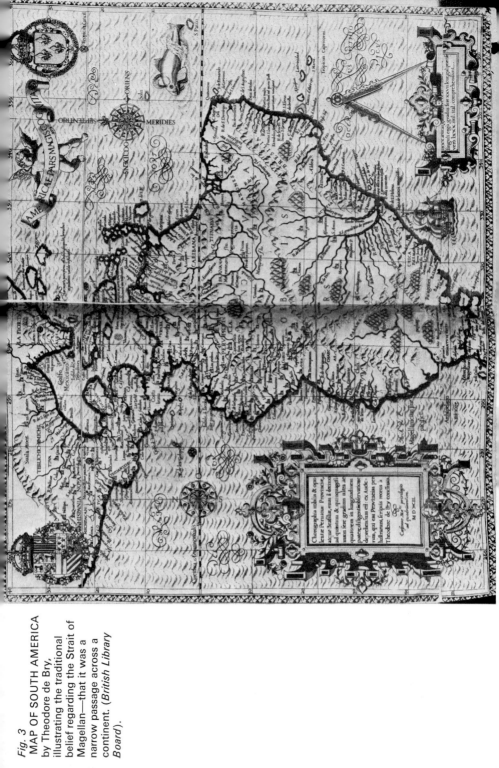

Fig. 3
MAP OF SOUTH AMERICA by Theodore de Bry, illustrating the traditional belief regarding the Strait of Magellan——that it was a narrow passage across a continent. (*British Library Board*).

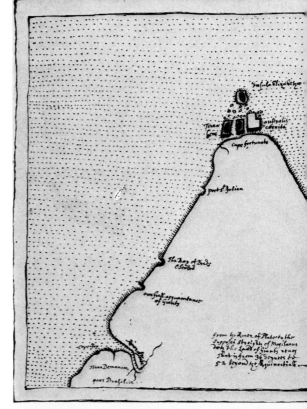

Fig. 4
Above. Part of a MAP OF BRAZIL by Theodore de Bry c. 1599, showing what an explorer might expect to meet—strange animals, a headless monster and a splendid Amazon. (*British Library Board*).

Fig. 5
Right. MAP OF SOUTH AMERICA, ascribed to Francis Fletcher, showing Elizabeth Island and a main sea passage south of a rather cursory Strait of Magellan. (*British Library Board*).

Fig. 6
SEAL BAY NATIVES IN MAY 1578, by Theodore de Bry. The people and their customs as described by Francis Fletcher—the women are unadorned and busy cooking; some of the men have painted their bodies, wear 'ostrich' feathers in their hair, use a skin of fur round the shoulders as their only item of clothing, and dance to the music of rattles. (*British Library Board*).

Fig. 7
SCENES AT SEAL BAY, 1578, by Theodore de Bry. A typical Tudor-period work where in a single picture a number of stories or themes are developed, cartoon-fashion.

In the centre we see a native snatching Drake's 'scarlet sea-capp' off his head while at lower right he is showing his prize to a friend.

At lower left the penchant for dancing on the part of male natives is depicted. Centre and upper left illustrate English arms and armour—swords, pikes, halberds and arquebuses, with breastplates and steel helmets. The 'crooks' are stands for the heavy firearms. The entire upper strip of the picture depicts Drake's fleet. On left a work party is burning the hulk of the abandoned 50-ton flyboat *Swan* to recover the ironwork.

On right are two ships with gunports—Drake's 100-ton *Pelican* and Winter's 80-ton *Elizabeth*. In the middle are two ships with uncut sides, perhaps the 30-ton pinnace *Marigold* with the 150-ton *Santa Maria* of Nuno da Silva in the background. The captured 40-ton canter *Christopher* was set adrift near Seal Bay shortly after. (*British Library Board*).

Fig. 9
A MODERN *GOLDEN HIND* AT SEA, 1975. A hypothetical reconstruction of what Drake's ship might have been like was built in England and sailed across the Atlantic to San Francisco, via the Panama Canal. This photograph by John Cadd, who went with her, well catches the atmosphere aboard a small sailing ship.

Fig. 8
A FAMOUS BATTLE PICTURE showing the taking of the Spanish treasure ship *Cacafuego* by the *Golden Hind* on 1 March 1579. The encounter actually took place at dusk, and surprise gave Drake an almost bloodless victory, San Juan de Anton being slightly wounded. (*British Library Board*).

Fig. 10
SHIP SAILING ACROSS A WORLD MAP, by Diego Ribero, 1529. The writing tells us that it was 'coming from Malucco' (the Spice Islands) and therefore it would have been built by the Spaniards in the New World. It appears to be a carrack type of vessel with high, overhanging forecastle and the capacious hull necessary for carrying cargo and a large store of provisions on long Pacific voyages. Note the very large mainsail. (*British Library Board*).

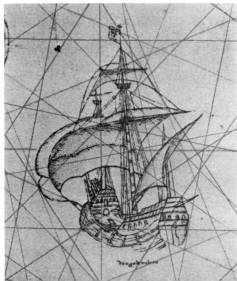

Fig. 11
THE *GOLDEN HIND* engraved by Jodocus Hondius, who probably saw the actual ship when he came to London in 1584. He shows her as a galleon with a low forecastle and beakhead. (*British Library Board*).

Fig. 12
SHIP MODEL in the Ashmolean, Oxford, which some scholars suggest is a toy for a Royal child intended to represent the *Golden Hind*. Hard evidence in the form of a builder's model or builder's plans do not exist, so some speculation is permissible, but in the Museum is a chair made from the authentic timbers of the *Golden Hind* after she was broken up in about 1662. (*Ashmolean Library*).

Fig. 13
NEW ALBION,
JUNE 1579, by
Theodore de Bry.
This is another
multiple-story strip-
cartoon. Top left are
two *Golden Hinds*
and Drake going
ashore to be greeted
by natives bearing
gifts. A little later
(left and centre)
Drake, prudently
followed by a
formed body of
troops, is greeted by
a native standard
bearer and a chief.
On right, native
customs are depicted
by showing a family
inside a dug-in tent
and an old woman
tearing at her cheeks
with her fingernails.
(*British Library
Board*).

Fig. 14
NEW ALBION, JULY 1579, by
Theodore de Bry. In the
foreground a native chief is
shown apparently offering the
crown of California to Drake.
Top are four views of the
Golden Hind, and the erection
of a post bearing an inscribed
plate to inform all whom it may
concern that Drake claims New
Albion for Queen Elizabeth. The
so-called 'plate of brass'
discovered in 1933 is almost
certainly not authentic.
(National Maritime Museum).

Fig. 15
MAP OF DRAKE'S BASE AND ANCHORAGE IN NEW ALBION, by Hondius. The modern identification of the site is hotly contested, but may well be the area known as Drake's Bay. (*British Library Board*).

Fig. 16
THE *GOLDEN HIND* IN THE SPICE ISLANDS, by Hondius. She is being towed into Ternate by the Sultan's barges as part of a welcoming procession. (*British Library Board*).

Fig. 17
ON THE ROCK NEAR CELEBES by Hondius. The *Golden Hind* is heeling over as she begins to fall sideways off the reef into deeper water. Note the jettisoned cargo and the imminent storm. (*British Library Board*).

Fig. 18
FRANCIS DRAKE. (*Trustees of the British Museum*).

However, the wind dropped away completely. Both the raider and her victims were immobilised, potentially a critical situation for the English. Drake ordered the masts of the largest Spanish ships to be cut away, but before this could be done properly, there was an embarrassing diversion. The Spanish customs service was on the alert that night. Seeing two large ships come in, they had sent out a customs launch to them. This boat first visited the ship from Panama, which announced itself as the *San Cristobal*, owned by Alonso Rodriguez Bautista Patagalana, with a complete cargo from the homeland destined for Lima. The customs officials decided that the work involved in checking so much varied freight had better wait until morning. Then they rowed over to the *Golden Hind*, to inquire what ship she was and what cargo she carried.

One of the Spanish prisoners, suitably primed, shouted out in answer to the hail from the customs launch that she was the ship of Miguel Angel from Chile.

This reply caused some surprise among the Spanish officials, for Drake's information was out of date. Miguel Angel's ship, the *Nuestra Señora de Valle*, had already arrived from Panama and was in the harbour instead of being, as Drake thought, still on her way. Suspicious, the customs officer shouted out that he was going to come aboard, and the launch manoeuvred to give him handhold on the *Golden Hind*.

In semi-darkness, without a word, the English watched the Spaniard climb up the side of their ship. The man blundered inboard on to what was in fact the main gundeck and found himself standing next to a piece of heavy ordnance that only a warship in another ocean might carry. No Spanish vessel on this sea was so armed. The menace of the disciplined silence on that gundeck was palpable. In a moment, he was gone, scrambling down the ship's side and jumping into his boat. With frantic haste, the customs launch pushed off from the hull, the official screaming 'Frenchmen! Frenchmen!'

He made such a racket that the crew of the Panama ship heard and became alarmed. French sea rovers had troubled the Caribbean coasts of New Spain so much that any pirate, almost automatically, was presumed to be a Frenchman; and they had a reputation for ruthlessness. In their haste to get clear, the crew of the *San Cristobal* did not bother with the time-consuming business of hauling in the anchor on the capstan. They simply cut the cable, abandoning an

F

expensive item of equipment, and let the ship drift with wind and tide. As both were weak, this was a futile manoeuvre. Drake had more men put into his pinnace and, oars beating the water, she cut across the harbour to the slowly drifting vessel. As she raced under the high sides of the *San Cristobal*, the English called on the Spaniards to strike. Then occurred a most extraordinary thing. This Spaniard did not surrender. Instead there was the whine of a ball and the bang of an arquebus shot, so close together that it was hard to tell one from the other, and a man in the pinnace, Thomas by name, collapsed, mortally wounded.

The English replied with a storm of arrows, the shafts clapping over the bulwarks with a whine and a howl. That made the Spaniards get their heads down while the pinnace drew away out of range. The bowmen had definitely scored one hit, even in the darkness, wounding the captain and owner, Alonso Rodriguez. Drake took the pinnace straight back to the *Golden Hind* and had a gun trained and laid on the drifting *San Cristobal*. The match was applied to the touchhole, there was a hissing as the priming powder caught, then a bellow as the gun fired and plunged backwards to the limit of the breaching ropes.

In the Panama ship it was as if a peal of thunder and lightning had simultaneously struck the vessel. The roundshot clapped in at one side of the hull, whined through between the decks and screamed out the other side, hurling wooden splinters like hail.

The crew took the hint and decamped, unwilling to ride a target for cannon fire. They got into their boats and rowed for the shore, with Drake's pinnace nosing back after them, and they were in such a hurry that one of them, a half-breed Spaniard, fell out of the boat into the water. Drake stopped to pick him up, and that gave the *San Cristobal*'s boat just enough of a lead to be uncatchable on its race to the shore.

When they arrived, they raised the alarm in Callao and soon the English heard a great shouting echo over the water. Then the bells of the church began to peal. Their stealthy raid by night had become very public.

There was still virtually no wind and the *Golden Hind* could be trapped in the harbour. Drake decided to withdraw, using the ebb tide, but he sent the pinnace to board and secure the *San Cristobal* as well. For their pains, out of all the ships, they had got only one treasure chest full of silver; it had a flat top and was covered with black leather, being about two feet long and just over ten inches deep. Yet ashore, in the King's warehouse, stored ready for loading, was the whole treasure for Panama – more than 200,000 pesos' worth of bar silver. It was now out of their reach, for already horsemen were galloping towards Lima to notify the Viceroy of Peru and bring help.

They reached Don Francisco de Toledo with the news an hour after midnight, according to Sarmiento. 'His Excellency, with great dispatch, armed himself and ordered the gentlemen and his retainers to do the same. The bells were rung to give the alarm and criers were sent from door to door to explain what had occurred and to summon all inhabitants to assemble in the public square, where His Excellency took his stand.' In armour, and carrying the Royal Standard, the Viceroy formed a rallying point for the alarmed population, ignorant of who exactly was threatening them. As pikes, arquebuses and ammunition were being distributed from the armoury, news was received that the corsairs were English. That stilled the rumours. An hour after the news had been received, some two hundred armed men, with Diego de Frias Trejo as their general, were on their way to defend Callao and the King's treasure.

At dawn, the winds were light and tricky. The *Golden Hind* was still in sight from the port, moving away slowly to the north-west in company with its prize, the *San Cristobal* from Panama. So instead of a defence, a pursuit had to be organised, in which the men of Callao with their ships could join with the troops from the capital. 'Three hundred men, more or less, thus embarked, all with a great desire to chastise the Corsair, just as though it were each man's private affair,' reported Sarmiento.

General Diego de Frias Trejo, their leader, had had some success in the land campaign against Oxenham and had captured his shipmaster, Thomas 'Xerores', while his second-in-command had taken Oxenham himself. For his flagship against Drake, the General chose the vessel of Miguel Angel, the *Nuestra Señora de Valle*. For vice-flagship, or *Almiranta*, he picked the *Nao de Muriles* of Christobal Hernandez (probably the vessel meant by the Fleming, Jorje, when he referred to the ship of Andres Muriel). Pedro de Arana was made second-in-command and also appointed Camp Master, or O.C. Troops. The wind was so fluky in the lee of an island outside the port that the *Almiranta* overtook the General's *Capitana* and then, for a bonus, picked up a stronger breeze further out.

The *Golden Hind* was not a particularly swift sailer, which was the reason Drake disposed of all the fast ships he found, to prevent effective pursuit, but in this case he had a lead of some four leagues, more than a dozen miles. The English saw what they took to be a spy vessel come out first – a small craft with both oars and sails – and then two ships of about their own size.

According to Sarmiento, the 'Corsair Francis' now realised that he was being pursued and so gave up his prize:

'Dissembling, he said to the sailors whom he had taken prisoners that he would now release them according to his previous promise. He ordered them to enter the merchant ship which he had seized and to return in her to port. He sent them to the merchant ship in the pinnace and gave order that the Englishmen who had been working that vessel were to return in the said pinnace. As these Englishmen delayed in returning, and he saw that we were in pursuit, he jumped into his skiff and went to the vessel, wrangling with his men. These all jumped into the pinnace and went to their ship in fear that they might be overtaken by the two vessels that were pursuing them. After collecting his men, the Englishman spread his top-gallant sails and took flight towards the north-west. The merchant ship, with four or five liberated sailors, returned towards the port.'

The freed men included Johnny the Greek, taken from Sarmiento's old ship at Santiago on 6 December, as well as the pair taken out of the bark off Callao the previous evening, one of whom was Gaspar Martin. The release of the *San Cristobal* with these men in her fatally delayed the pursuit, for the *Almiranta*, in the lead, made the recapture of this ship a priority. The questioning of the recovered prisoners, particularly the Greek who had been in the *Golden Hind* more than two months, gave them a fairly exact idea of what they were up against. They were told that: 'The English vessel was large and strong and carried seventy-five or eighty men and many pieces of artillery, besides many incendiary devices.'

The pursuit went on all day, the *Golden Hind* drawing away from the Spanish ships. 'At sunset she was almost out of sight, and had gained headway because our vessels were without ballast, and being crank, could not bear sail and pitched with the moving about of the men, thus navigating very slowly. Moreover, the English ship, being further out at sea, caught a stiffer breeze and sailed on the wind.' The awkward motions of the ships had a most miserable effect on the Spanish landsmen, who soon ceased to care whether or not they caught up with the corsair. Those less affected were perturbed and that night a council of war was held in the *Capitana*, with senior officers from both ships present. Like many another council of war, it decided not to fight. Sarmiento was one of them. He reported:

'It was the General's view that they should continue to follow the enemy, but many held a contrary opinion and argued that it was advisable to return to harbour, the principal reasons they gave being the defectiveness of the vessels and the fact that they carried no food whatever and not sufficient artillery and ammunition or incendiary devices to cope with the English who were many in number ... Our men would certainly be injured by the enemy's artillery, for our ships carried nothing but arquebuses to use against him. Moreover, the most imperative reason for returning seemed to be that many of the gentlemen were very seasick and were not in a condition to stand, much less to fight. Yet there were many who were capable of doing both.'

The council, as is usual in such cases, gave a splendidly aggressive reason for failing to engage: 'Finally, it was resolved to return in order to obtain reinforcements so as to sally forth again, better equipped to attack the enemy.'

On their return to Callao, General Diego de Frias Trejo had the unpleasant task of reporting to Don Francisco de Toledo, Viceroy of Peru. The Viceroy in person went down to the port and placed the senior officers and soldiers in the two ships under arrest, ordering no man to set foot ashore, on pain of death. Some were exiled, some were fined, all were censured, including Sarmiento.

The Viceroy ordered that a swift bark be sent northward to warn all ports and shipping between Callao and Panama that there was an English corsair on the coast; any treasure then at sea was to be landed and guarded ashore. A second, more effective, pursuit force was to be formed, consisting of two ships and 120 soldiers; Sarmiento was to sail in this as Sergeant-Major, third-in-command.

An extraordinary council meeting of all the senior officials of Peru was immediately convened at Callao to discuss anti-corsair measures in this crisis which was declared to be 'the most serious matter that this kingdom has ever had to consider'. Nevertheless, the country's forces would 'capture and destroy the tyrant'. Word must be sent ahead to two ships which had left Callao just before the corsair struck. They were particularly rich ships, those of Sebastian Perez and San Juan de Anton, the latter carrying 115,000 pesos in royal silver and much private silver besides. They must not forget that 'Captain Francisco' expected to be joined shortly by his two other ships, which were missing, but were to meet him either in 30° or 32½°. No firm news had yet been received regarding these vessels. The presence of three English ships could 'render it impossible to carry on trade between this kingdom of Peru, the Isthmus, and Spain, or to transport there the King's silver and that of private individuals, without incurring great risks and expense'.

After considering these questions, the council decided that they were serious enough to warrant offensive and defensive measures being financed out of the royal revenue. The principal lack on their side was ordinance; there was no local gun-making industry. Silver pesos could not produce cannon of cast bronze or iron; skill and knowledge were required. This fact, together with speculations as to the inner and ultimate meanings of the English raid, opened cell doors in the prison of the Holy Inquisition at Lima a few days later, on 20 February by the Spanish calendar. The Viceroy instructed the Holy Office to make available for questioning three of the English prisoners – Butler, Oxenham and 'Xerores'.

After taking the oath, each man was required to answer the same set questions, which began with the subject of gun-making. John Butler, the pilot of Oxenham's expedition, was:

'questioned whether he knew how to manufacture artillery, or had seen it made, or whether any of his companions knew how to do so, or to make other fireworks such as are used in the defence of towns. He answered that neither he nor his companions knew how to manufacture artillery, nor had he seen it made, but he knew very well how to make the devices which were attached to arrows, pikes and lances in order to set fire to the sails of ships and to the ships themselves. He also knew how to make "fire-wings" with nails which caught in the woodwork and set fire to vessels. And these are much used in England to defend ships and burn others.

'On being questioned, he stated that he had made them several times, and had seen them made more than a thousand times, for every ship carried them.

'On being questioned, he said that the necessary ingredients for making the said projectiles are powder, oil, pitch and sulphur; and that in order to make them very effective, camphor and spirits were added.

'Asked how these ingredients were used, he said that, after making the said mixture into a paste, some of it is put on the point of the said pike or arrow, leaving a touch-hole in which dry powder is poured. They lighted this and shot the arrows, or thrust with the pikes, on approaching near to the enemy's ship. The same paste was used with balls made of hemp, studded with nails, the points of which stuck outwards. In order to transport these, they were covered with pitch. When about to be thrown by hand they were lighted at the touch-hole.'

Most of Drake's prisoners had reported the presence on board of various incendiary weapons and appeared to rate them as something to be feared. Therefore this information was useful. Then the inquisitors turned to larger questions of English state policy:

'Questioned whether he had heard or understood, while in England, or since he left there, that Queen Elizabeth of England was entertaining or carrying out the project of fitting out a number of vessels which were to come to found settlements on the coast of the North or South Seas, he said that he had not heard or understood more about this than that a gentleman named Grenville, who is a knight, had applied to the said Queen for a licence to come and found settlements, but not in lands belonging to King Philip, for the Queen did not wish to give a licence for that, as treaties of peace had then been made. The said gentleman had asked for a licence to settle on the River Plate towards the Strait of Magellan. For this purpose he had bought four vessels, and John Oxenham who is here, in prison, had agreed to go with him. But as the Queen did not give them the licence, they sold the ships . . . The Queen had demanded that they were to give a security of thirty to forty thousand pounds that they would not touch lands belonging to King Philip, and on this account the expedition was frustrated, as aforesaid.'

To a later question, Butler answered 'that he knew that no company of armed vessels can come to the Indies without a licence from the Queen, and that it is customary for the Lord Admiral to give licences for single ships, for which he receives payment'. In Spanish law, these licences were illegal. Only Spanish ships could trade with the colonies carved out by Spain, and similarly only Portuguese ships were lawfully allowed to trade with Brazil. The line of questioning was designed to reveal the current attitude of the English Queen. If Drake was not acting purely on his own account, but held a licence, then English policy must have changed since the proposed expedition of Sir Richard Grenville (one of Drake's rivals) had been forbidden by her. Butler told the inquisitors that Drake must have royal support, for 'only a man having great power could possibly come here'.

The examiners also wanted to find out what knowledge the English had of the Straits of Magellan. Butler answered that:

> 'when he left England, there was no man in England who had passed the equinoctial line towards the south or was planning to come, although they have here the description of Magellan's navigation and of all these Indies, and they look into these matters, and discuss them.'

Without alerting Butler to the fact that an English ship had just come within six miles of his prison, the Spaniards probed gently to find out the most likely route by which Drake would return; but Butler only said that if one could pass through the Strait in the first place, he assumed one could also return that way, and if not then there was no alternative to making the round trip by the Portuguese Indies, the coast of Africa and the Canaries. Fletcher had thought that the Spaniards were telling deliberate lies with their stories of a current so strong it would prevent a return through the Strait; but here was evidence that there were Spaniards who knew so little about this continent they were trying to make their own, that they had to ask an Englishman.

It was late that night before the examination of John Butler was completed. When Captain John Oxenham and after him Thomas 'Xerores', his shipmaster, were brought in. The questions of gun-casting and the making of incendiaries were put, but only briefly answered. No, they could not make guns. No, they could not make incendiaries. If Butler knew anything about this, then 'it must be but little'.

Butler had mentioned the alarming possibility of the English wanting to establish colonies in the New World, which would give them bases dangerously close to Spanish and Portuguese possessions. The inquisitors pressed very hard on this point. First with Oxenham, who answered that:

'Four years ago an English knight named Richard Grenville, who lives at a distance of a league and a half from Plymouth, and is very rich, applied to the Queen for a licence to come to the Strait of Magellan and to pass to the South Sea, in order to search for land or some islands where to found settlements, because, in England, there are many inhabitants and but little land. The Queen gave him the licence and witness saw it. It was very large. The said Grenville bought two ships, and was about to buy two or three more, when the Queen revoked the licence, because she had learnt that beyond the Strait of Magellan there were settlements made by Spaniards, who might do them harm. The said Grenville sold the ships, after the licence had been taken from him. Previously to that, he had spoken many times with the witness, trying to persuade him, to accompany him but witness did not wish to do so. Grenville's project was to come and found a settlement on the River Plate and then pass the Strait and establish settlements wherever a good country for such could be found.'

Oxenham may have been prompted here, for the transcript goes on:

'Witness thinks that if the Queen were to give a licence to Captain Francis Drake he would certainly come and pass through the Strait, because he is a very good mariner and pilot, and there is no better one than he in England who could accomplish this. Witness thinks that the Queen will not, as long as she lives, grant the licence, but that, after the Queen's death, there will certainly be someone who will come to the Strait. The said Captain Francis had often spoken to witness saying that if the Queen would grant him the licence he would pass through the Strait of Magellan and found settlements over here in some good country.'

With a straight face, the inquisitors put the next, ironic question: 'With how many ships would it be possible for Francis Drake to come to the Strait?' They already knew, from Drake's released prisoners, that the answer was five in fact. Oxenham answered, theoretically: 'With the aid of his relatives and companions he might be able to bring two or three vessels but that, after discovering

a good country, they would be able to come with more ships.
Captain Francis discussed this with me.'

When they turned to questions concerning Drake's return route,
Oxenham became vague. He seemed to remember that some had
said it was to be by the same Strait, but others said there was a
route through another strait that passed into the North Sea – but
there was no certainty that such a passage existed and no one had
ever passed that way.

Thomas 'Xerores' was brought in, took the oath, and had the
set questions put to him. Regarding the major one – possible
English colonial intentions – he answered:

'Four years ago a gentleman named Grenville bought two vessels,
and thought of buying four more, in order to come and pass
through the Strait of Magellan and take possession of some land
where King Philip had no settlements. The Queen did not wish
him to come for fear that he might do harm in the possessions
of her brother King Philip. I understand that if the Queen
should die, many will come and pass through the Strait and found
settlements. The Queen is the cause that no one comes. England
is so full of people that there are many who wish to go to other
parts.'

Again, tongue-in-cheek, the inquisitors asked the prisoner if he
knew Drake and if he had heard it said that Drake wanted to come
to Peru through the Straits of Magellan. The shipmaster's reply
had no regard for Spanish susceptibilities:

'Yes, I knew him. I was with him on the voyage when we robbed
the mule train on the road to Nombre de Dios. I've heard it
said that if the Queen should die, Francis Drake would come,
because the Lord Admiral has a great affection for him.'

And that was that. After a very short examination indeed, the
shipmaster was conducted back to his cell in the Inquisition prison.

All three men had testified separately to the fact of a Grenville
imperial expedition which had reached an advanced stage of
planning and preparation, and then been cancelled by order of
Queen Elizabeth because it might lead to diplomatic trouble with
the King of Spain. One of the witnesses, Oxenham, could speak
from first-hand knowledge, for he had discussed the project with
Sir Richard Grenville himself and had later talked to Drake about

a similar scheme. That was hardly surprising, as they were all sea captains from Plymouth, and all in the same business of plunder or illicit trade. The logic of what they said, when taken in conjunction with the actual appearance of an English fleet in the Straits of Magellan and the arrival of the flagship on the coast of Peru, must mean that the policy of the Queen of England had hardened towards Spain. And it would seem at the least very likely that the English now intended to prospect for areas suitable for colonisation, if not to actually found a settlement.

The question of how Drake intended to return was not academic. A colony, they well knew, had to be sustained from the homeland or collapse was certain; so there had to be a route and the shorter the better. If by the Strait of Magellan, then there might ensue a race between Spain and England to be first to capture and fortify the narrows. However, there was Oxenham's mention of another strait that was supposed to pass through into the North Sea around the top of North America (the cosmographers called it the Strait of Anian and, although unproven, it was shown as though it existed on some maps, Cabot's, for instance). If such a strait was practical, the route would be very short for the English. In the long term, these seemed to be the important considerations.

In the shorter term, an accurate appreciation of Drake's return route was the only certain way of intercepting the corsair, with a sufficient force to overwhelm him. Thus began a great debate which was to last for months. The renewed pursuit from Lima, by a force consisting of two large ships carrying 120 soldiers between them, was in many ways merely a gesture. As Sarmiento, who went with it, reported: 'All the men left with a great desire to fight the enemy but with little hope of being able to overtake him, for he already had a start of fifteen days.'

As the two ships sailed northwards, accompanied by a launch for inshore work, all they met were merchant ships which complained of having been stopped and robbed by Drake two weeks before. And when the launch went into the harbours, it returned in many cases with the news that Drake had been there some fourteen days previously. In one case they found a settlement completely deserted, but with a message pinned to the door of the empty inn. It was from the landlord, telling whoever it might concern that he was fleeing for the interior because he had heard that the English were on the coast.

Chapter 13

THE HANGING OF THE HALFBREED BOY

From Callao to Cape San Francisco:
16 February–1 March 1579

F ROM February the 16th to the 20th in the morning, the
corsair group sailed north without incident along the haze-
hidden coast of Peru. The *Golden Hind* rode the Pacific swells
a league and a half out to sea, the pinnace with Drake in command
running closer inshore where the surf could be seen bursting high
on the rocks that bordered the burning desert dunes of the coastal
plain. Beyond, above the clouds, was a pale purple shadow with
irregular outlines but so vague as to make it hard to grasp that it
was a seemingly endless mountain range. On the 18th, the heat
haze must have cleared to give da Silva a good view, for he logged:
'Land very high.' He was not exaggerating. Those peaks reach
20,000 feet.

Up in the thin air of the Andes the native Incas had built their
strange cities of blocks so huge that men said only giants could
have made those walls. There were tales of unknown cities the
Spaniards had not found yet, and of the treasures of gold and
silver and jewels they held. These were real cities, it was said, not
like the Spanish settlements which were little more than villages
in European terms. Even Lima, named 'City of the Kings' by
Pizarro, who founded it in 1534, was no more than a small town
in the foothills; above the relentless heat of the coastal plain but
far below the heights where any exertion made the heart pound.
But over there, in these jagged cordilleras, was the treasure house
of the world; so much gold and silver that in native eyes the precious
metals had little value.

It was not until the 20th that they saw a ship, which on being
closed by Drake's pinnace, proved to be a bark bound for Lima
with an unexciting cargo of provisions and local wares. She had
two pilots aboard, and to them both Drake put the question: had
they seen the Silver Ship? One pilot said he had not seen her, the

172

other that he had seen her three days ago. One of them, named Domingo Martin, was taken out of the bark to be their guide into the port of Payta, further up the coast. They found a few items of silver in the cabin, including a lamp and a jug, and they took those along, too.

Da Silva testified:

'Two days after they came to the haven called Payta, where they found a ship laden with Spanish wares, which the pinnace boarded and took without any resistance. For as soon as the Spaniards perceived the Englishmen, they immediately made to land with their boat, and two of them leapt into the sea, none staying in the ship but the Master, Pilot and some Negroes. The Englishmen took the pilot, and all the bread, hens, and a hog.'

The pilot was a fifty-year-old mariner named Custodio Rodriguez, a Portuguese like da Silva. And he recognised him, or thought he did, as soon as the immediate business of capture and interrogation by Drake was over. Rodriguez deposed:

'They took from my bark sixty jars of wine, two boxes of wax and some other things. leaving all the remainder of the cargo, which consisted of wine, in the bark. Captain Francis took me with him, but did not do any harm in the port. The Corsair inquired from me how many days had passed since Sant Juan de Anton had left the port and I answered that it had been a little over two days. As the said tyrant had received word that San Juan de Anton carried much silver, he did not delay at all and with full sail made haste to overtake him.'

The captured ship was released just outside the port.

A number of Drake's prisoner's thought that Nuño da Silva was an officer of the *Golden Hind*, not understanding that he had been captured, like themselves. Nicolas Jorje, the Fleming, was to report: 'I do not know him and I was not able to ascertain his name. But he is of low stature; is darkly complexioned, has a long beard and is not very grey-haired, although aged about sixty years, rather less than more.'

Custodio Rodriguez, on the other hand, was convinced that he did know Nuño da Silva. He deposed:

'The pilot who is bringing Captain Francis is named Hernan Perez. I knew him well because he had been a pilot in this sea. He is a

Portuguese and is the man who, twenty years ago, seized much money and ran away. He had not been heard of until now. Although I am a Portuguese and knew Hernan Perez well, he would not admit his identity to me. Yet he made inquiries about certain women living in Sonsonate, where the said Portuguese pilot has a wife.'

As long as da Silva remained on the *Golden Hind*, then this allegation, right or wrong, made no difference; but if the *Golden Hind* was taken, or if Drake put da Silva ashore when his usefulness was ended, then, right or wrong, it could make all the difference in the world.

Like all the prisoners who told Drake what he wanted to know, quickly, and did not try to trick him or conceal anything, Rodriguez was well treated, with one exception: 'The Corsair made us eat meat on Friday and in Lent. This was because they were Lutherans and gave us to eat what they ate themselves.' Drake's attitude to prisoners who refused to give information, or proved uncooperative in any way, was different.

Off Parina Point, six or seven leagues north of Payta, Drake sighted a ship steering south. It was the bark of Gonzalo Alvarez, bound for Peru. No one on board knew of the presence of English vessels on the Pacific coast, testified a passenger, Gaspar de Montalvo, until Drake in his pinnace closed them.

'Sixteen of these Englishmen, well equipped with arms, came alongside of the bark in which I was in their launch which carried a piece of ordnance at the prow. The bark of Gonzalo Alvarez immediately surrendered, because those on board saw, at a distance of an arquebus shot, the ship of the Englishmen which seemed to them to contain a great number of men. I did not, however, go aboard her. I and my companions were held as prisoners for three hours and then released by the said Englishmen . . . they were making inquiries from those on board the bark whether they had met with any ship on their voyage thither.'

Nicolas Jorje, the Fleming, said that they took from this vessel a negro who claimed to have been a Cimarron in Panama. These were Drake's old allies from the days of the raids on the Panama–Porto Bello mule trains. Jorje reported that he had heard Drake 'saying that he loved them, speaking well of them and inquiring every day whether they were now peaceful. It seems to me, from what I heard him say, that Captain Francis has a very great desire to see them again.' Captain Drake had a very great desire to perplex the Spaniards as to what he was going to do next, and no doubt he laid many false trails.

However, there is no reason to disbelieve his reminiscences to Jorje, of how the Cimarrons had taken him to a clump of high trees on a headland, from which eyrie he had been able to make out the royal buildings in Panama itself. Shrewdly, Jorje remarked: 'It seemed to me that if Captain Francis had with him more men, he would attempt some raid on land like the one he already made. But because he had but few men he now acts warily . . .' This was exactly what the anonymous English witness on board the *Golden Hind* had written earlier, but with its contemptuous reference to 'pirates' added. What was uppermost in Drake's mind at the moment, however, was the 'Silver Ship', the *Nao Rica* of San Juan de Anton. Without a doubt, she could not be too far ahead now.

At the end of February they sighted a ship going the same way as themselves, towards Panama. Off Los Quiximies, between Cape Pasado and Cape San Francisco, they closed her. She proved to be a bark out of Santiago de Guayaquil, owned and piloted by Benito Diaz Bravo, a man of thirty-four, and carrying a general cargo for the Spanish crown – ropes and ship's tackle for the fleet outfitting for the Philippines; maize, salt pork, hams and other preserved foodstuffs for the same fleet and also for the soldiers of the Panama garrison out on campaign. There was, further, a registered load of gold and silver, worth about 18,000 pesos according to Bravo himself. According an English note: 'The gold in the friar's bark was all in round slabs, it was thought to be French crown gold.' The anonymous narrator in the *Golden Hind* wrote:

'This ship he rifled, and found in her about 80 pounds weight of gold, and he took out of her great quantity of ropes to store his own ship, and let her go. The owner of this ship was a friar. He found also in her a great crucifix of gold [set with] certain emeralds near as long as a man's finger.'

Bravo was kept in his own ship, but his clerk, 'a halfbreed negro boy' according to da Silva, named Francisco Jacome, was brought on board the *Golden Hind*, and also four passengers. They were all closely questioned about the 'Silver Ship' of San Juan de Anton, but had no information to give, according to Jacome. Probably as part of his interrogation technique Drake began to boast. All the ships in the South Sea were in his power, he told them. As for the silver ship, she was within fourteen leagues of this place; after taking her, he would rob all the coast of Nicaragua. And if God spared his life, he would return from England within two years with a fleet of six or seven galleons.

Drake knew perfectly well that these men would be questioned by the Spanish authorities in due course and anything he told them, provided they remembered it, would be noted in Spanish records and passed on to the appropriate place for information and action. The statement that he was going to Nicaragua, just beyond Panama, would fit very well with the hints he had given the Fleming, Nicolas Jorje, of an intent to link up again with the Cimarrons who lived in the rain-forests of nearby Panama.

Bravo, being kept in his own ship, heard none of this; but did report a curious conversation with one of his English guards. The man asked him what arms were those he saw on the flag which Bravo's ship flew from her mainmast. Bravo told him that they were the arms of his sovereign, King Philip II (who at one time had very nearly become King of England as well). The Englishman told him to lower that flag, then. But before it could be done, Drake himself butted in, saying: 'Leave the arms of King Philip where they are, for he is the best king in the world.' This may have been a diplomatic reply, hopefully intended to sweeten matters for his return to England, which was bound to create an international incident. When he sighted Plymouth again, only in a limited sense would it be the end of the voyage. Queen Elizabeth might even be dead, and a Catholic on the throne.

Benito Diaz Bravo was himself indulging in a certain amount of double-thinking. He suspected that he was being prevented from entering the *Golden Hind* (whereas his passengers and clerk had been transferred to her for questioning) because, like Custodio Rodriguez, to whom he had spoken, Bravo also knew the Portuguese criminal, Hernan Perez, who had led a rebellion at Santa Elena and escaped with a treasure in gold. That had been a long time ago, twenty years or so, but if Drake's Portuguese pilot and this Hernan Perez were the same, he would recognise him. Bravo never did get close to da Silva, so the identification rested solely on the accuracy of Custodio's memory.

Both Bravo and his clerk, Jacome, looked very closely at the powerful mounted ordnance of the *Golden Hind*, although the clerk, being on board, had the better chance to evaluate it. Both agreed that she had twelve heavy guns mounted at that time: four on each side, two in the poop firing astern and two in the prow firing ahead. Then a scheme Francis Drake had for arming Bravo's bark, an eighty-ton vessel by John Drake's reckoning, and adding it to his fleet revealed that his flagship carried at least two more heavy pieces. They both saw these guns being swayed up out of her hold and swung over to the bark. So that made a total of fourteen guns, all heavy pieces in their estimation.

The bark was a fast sailer, and this may have given Drake the idea of taking her with him temporarily as part of a wide-flung net to catch the ship of San Juan de Anton, regardless of her distance out from land. It would give his search pattern three prongs instead of two, and just when it was most required; for ahead of them lay the Gulf of Panama, where a ship might strike out across the ocean instead of hugging the humid equatorial coastline.

The *Golden Hind*'s guns were mounted in the bark and her sails tested to Drake's satisfaction. But next day he changed his mind and ordered the guns moved back again and the bark to be cast off. Probably the full-scale sailing trials had revealed that the three vessels – the two ships and the pinnace – were too thinly manned to be efficient. That was Bravo's belief. When his clerk, Jacome, was first in the *Golden Hind*, she seemed packed with professional soldiers, brimful of fighting men. But when they were taken out and distributed among three vessels, Drake's force did not look nearly so impressive. Jacome judged them to number no more than sixty or seventy at the most, and of these only fifty were fit for warfare, the remainder were 'mere rabble'.

That news also would get back to the Spanish authorities, if Drake released his prisoners; as usual, he did so, retaining only those men useful to him. On the other hand, he had no intention of allowing Bravo's bark to be used to pursue him or to keep track of his movements. Before releasing her, he had her topsails wrapped around her anchor and cast into the sea. Until she could get new canvas, the bark would be slower now than he was. But no sooner had she begun to move away from the sides of her captor than Drake's pinnace came after her and men stormed up the side, looking for Francisco Jacome, the halfbreed clerk.

What started the hunt is not recorded, but da Silva was to tell his Spanish captors during three separate interrogations that this young sailor had taken some gold and hidden it about his person; that he was accused of this, and searched, and the gold was found on him. In his three interrogations, da Silva mentioned successively 'a bar of gold', 'two bars of gold', and 'two plates of gold' as the amount he had concealed in his clothing. The basic story is the same, the discrepancies minor. John Drake was to be interrogated also and he mentioned the incident on both occasions. The first interrogation is nonsense; possibly he was too exhausted, or had been hurt too much to be coherent or even care whether he told the truth or not; or the examiner did not speak much English and just muddled it up.

John Drake's more accurate second interrogation makes sense, and does not contradict da Silva or anyone else; it merely omits the finding of the gold on Jacome as the factor which probably touched off English suspicions. According to this testimony, the twenty-one-year-old Jacome, who John Drake thought was the boatswain of the bark, had told the English that there was no more gold in her; the English had found it all. But the negro crew of the bark insisted to their captors that there was more gold. John Drake recalled that Francis Drake had then ordered Jacome to be hung by the neck to a beam and questioned further. When Jacome maintained his denial and said the negroes were lying, he was released and allowed to go back into the bark. Da Silva's reference to Drake having 'hanged a man of the ship, because he would not confess two plates of gold that he had taken, which after they found about him' was capable of misinterpretation.

The halfbreed was not 'hanged' in the full sense of the term, he was 'tactically squeezed'; that is, made to fear for his life, and had considerable pain and shock inflicted on him, so that if he was lying he was almost certain to break down. His ordeal must have been terrifying, for he certainly thought he was going to die. But he survived to be interrogated by the Spanish authorities, although in more kindly fashion.

'As I had not hidden anything whatsoever and was unable to reveal anything to them, they hanged me by the neck with a cord as though to hang me outright,' testified the clerk. 'And then they let me drop from high into the sea,' he added. 'From which they fetched me out with the launch and took me back to the ship on which I had come.' Surely, the question would have been put one last time as the halfbreed boy hung over the gunwales of the launch half-strangled, half-drowned, utterly shaken and now, unimaginably, reprieved. If he was asked, now, was there any more gold aboard, was it not likely that his reply would be the truth? Francisco Jacome's final memories of Drake and his crew were not the happy and courteous moments recalled by those many captives who cooperated.

February was a bad month for dates, all through. For instance, the date of entry into Callao was Sunday the 15th according to both da Silva's log and Fletcher's diary. The Spaniards, however, reported the event as taking place on Friday the thirteenth. This discrepancy might be explained by the fact that the traveller gains time going west. Alas, there is another disagreement at the end of the month, but it is in the opposite direction. Da Silva's log recorded Bravo's bark as being taken on 26 February, while the Spaniards had it down for the 28th, two days later. This makes it hard for the historian to collate the movements of the pursuing vessels with those of the raiders, but it would appear that they were lagging by a full fortnight, in spite of, or perhaps because of, the strict disciplinary measures taken by the Viceroy. Drake cannot have known this and no doubt the nagging thought of the ships which must be hunting him urged on his own pursuit of the 'Silver Ship'.

All sources are agreed, however, that it was on the first of March that the bark of Bravo was cast off and let drive, crippled by the loss of her topsails, and began to make her way towards Manta in the Gulf of Panama for repairs. It was on this day also that Drake began to feel that he was nearing his quarry but might easily miss it because a lookout failed to see some tiny flicker of white on the horizon.

Like many important men, or men who thought themselves important, and anyway were very rich, Francis Drake the Captain-General could wear a chain of gold round his neck on ceremonial occasions. These chains were useful also to travellers, because a link or two, as required, could always be broken off to pay a reckoning if sufficient ready money in coin was not available. Drake told his ship's company that whoever was the first man to see the 'Silver Ship' of San Juan de Anton would receive his own personal chain as a gift. That was an incentive of tremendous proportions.

It was only a few hours later, at about noon on 1 March, that the lookout in the fighting top of the mainmast hailed the deck. The keen-eyed youngster was John Drake, reporting a sail, by his estimation three leagues to seaward.

Over to starboard lay Cape San Francisco and Galera Point, the southern promontories of a great bay which only local ships would enter. That placed the unknown sail, nine miles out, as being on the direct track to Panama, the known destination of their quarry.

But as John Drake called down further observations on his sighting, it became clear that a problem had arisen. The distant vessel, although steering probably a parallel course, lay actually somewhat behind the corsair group, not ahead; and as the minutes passed, she was slowly falling still further behind.

It was necessary for the *Golden Hind* first to reduce speed and then edge in towards the other ship very gradually, making no large alterations of course which would imply a deliberate interception. Simply to reduce speed by taking in sail was no good; that would appear extremely suspicious to the far-off captain, whose ship might well be faster than Drake's and in any case had a commanding lead if it came to a stern chase.

So what was done was a sly pirate's trick, also known to most fishermen and coastal seamen in the different context of steep, heavy seas off a lee shore. They put out a drogue, not as in a gale to steady the ship and reduce the drift to windward, but to act as an unseen brake. Stringing together a row of *Botijas* – Spanish oil jars – they cast them out astern of the *Golden Hind*. The drag of the open-mouthed jars being towed in the ship's wake slowed her considerably, so that even with all sail set for the fastest possible pursuit, the *Golden Hind* began to lag until eventually the far-off sail could be seen from the deck. By that time, the pinnace was lying on the landward side, screened from view by the ship's hull. With the ports closed, there was nothing at that distance to distinguish the raider from any peaceful coaster bound for Panama from Peru or Chile.

Throughout the heat of the humid afternoon the corsair group dawdled nearer their victim. Their languid pace matched the climate, for it was only yesterday that they had crossed the Equator. Dusk or night would be the time to move in, so that darkness would shroud the concealed guns, the armed men waiting behind the bulwarks, and the pinnace with its picked crew as it came out from cover for the pounce.

Then, an hour or so before the onset of tropical night, a strange thing happened, The Spanish vessel, which was as large as they or larger, began to turn. They saw her masts change their relationship to each other as the hull swung round. So she had become suspicious, and yet they had done nothing to give themselves away! But after a minute or so it became clear that the silver ship was not turning away from them but towards them! It was as if the quarry had decided to give herself up.

What on earth was her captain thinking of?

Chapter 14

'STRIKE SAIL!'

San Juan de Anton and his Treasure Ship:
1–18 March 1579

SAN JUAN DE ANTON, owner and master of the 120-ton freighter *Nuestra Señora de la Concepción*, was thirty-five years old. Da Silva said that he spoke Spanish with the accent of Biscay, and English as well, for he had been brought up in Southampton, the main commercial port on the south coast of England. His name does anglicise exactly as St John (pronounced 'Sinjen') of Hampton (as Southampton was commonly called).

He had sailed from Callao on 22 January for Panama and had called at Guaura, Barranco and Truxillo to load gold, silver, flour and other goods. The treasure, amounting to some 400,000 pesos, belonged partly to the Spanish Crown, partly to his passengers, and partly to his crew who, as was customary at sea, had taken their own stakes in the success of the voyage.

On 1 March the freighter, or *nao*, was some way offshore between Cape San Francisco and Galera Point. At about noon another ship was sighted, close inshore, apparently steering the same course as they were. Anton assumed that she had just come out of Guayaquil, a port he had passed but not entered, and like himself was bound for Panama. He ordered his ship to be steered towards her. But it was nine o'clock that evening, and already growing dark, before the two ships were close. Then the other ship turned and, indistinct in the failing light, came up alongside the freighter.

She could be a rebel ship from Chile, thought Anton, alarmed. There was trouble in that province, he had heard. So he ran to the side to find out.

According to John Drake, who had first sighted Anton's ship from the *Golden Hind* and thus earned the gold chain, the Spaniard hailed them, asking who they were. And again, as at Callao, a Spanish prisoner had been primed to call out: 'The ship of Miguel Angel!'

Once more, that proved to be the wrong answer. A puzzled voice replied: 'You can't be! We left her empty at Callao.' Then a peremptory Spanish command: 'Strike sail in the name of the King!'

The interchange had gained the raider enough time to throw her grapnels out, so that the two ships could be hauled together bodily, while the spokesman in the *Golden Hind* continued to hold Anton's attention by calling out to him personally: 'Strike sail yourself, Master Juan de Anton, in the name of the Queen of England! Or we'll send you to the bottom!'

Disbelief, surprise, anger warred together to spur the Spaniard's indignant reply. 'What so-and-so is this that gives *me* orders to strike sail!' shouted the Spanish captain. 'Come on board and strike sail yourselves!'

A whistle shrilled out from the raider, stilling the voices.

A moment later, a trumpet pealed briefly, probably tongued by John Brewer.

Whistle and trumpet, they were the 'Preparatory' and the 'Fire!'

Flashes, dying into gouts of smoke, sparkled out from the raider's deck. At least sixty arquebusiers there, thought Anton, as the heavy leaden balls whined over his deck. Then came the howl of arrows loosed at short range, whipping overhead; a sudden shock to the nerves.

Like a ringing thunderclap, a heavy cannonshot climaxed the fire of the small arms. Loaded with chainshot, fired point-blank, it brought down in an instant the mizzenmast with its sail and lateen yard; that single strike blew them right out of the ship and over the side into the sea.

A second thunderclap and with a horrible whining howl another pair of chained projectiles screeched high overhead, just missing the mainmast.

'Strike sail!' shouted the English spokesman.

Simultaneously, the English boarded their victim from both sides.

Men from the *Golden Hind* leapt for the Spaniard's starboard bulwarks, the hulls of the two ships grinding and groaning beneath beneath them, held together in the rising, falling sea by the weight of men pulling on the grapnels. But the bulk of the boarders came over her port side, from the unexpected direction.

The pinnace had pulled out unseen from its cover behind the raider's hull, crossed over to the disengaged side of Anton's ship, and laid alongside one of the chain-plates. This was a strong wooden ledge projecting low down from the ship's side, in which were bedded the shrouds which stayed one of her forward masts. For agile men, although armed, it was a ready-made path up to her deck. Forty archers, by Anton's dazed reckoning, came swarming up this way on to the deck of his ship.

He was the only man there. All the rest had fled below or to the cabins.

The English demanded to know who was the captain and who was the pilot, but Anton, although wounded by an arrow, would not reply. They found out elsewhere, for they locked the crew and passengers in the poop cabin, under guard, but moved San Juan de Anton and his boatswain Sancho de Anton over to the raider.

They were brought before Drake, who was removing his steel helmet and coat of mail. Seeing that the captain was wounded, he embraced Anton, saying: 'Have patience, for such is the usage of war.' The Spanish captain was then put under guard in the poop cabin of the *Golden Hind*, the servants being instructed to treat him as a guest rather than as a prisoner of war.

Next morning, Drake examined his prize, which he had captured almost without bloodshed. Out of the dozen crew and passengers, San Juan de Anton, slightly wounded by an arrow, had been the only casualty of the encounter. The treasure ship had been taken entirely by shock and surprise. There had been no fighting whatever. Aided by the poor light he had made fifty fighting men seem like a hundred, so that the Spanish captain thought he faced sixty arquebusiers on one side and forty archers on the other. The Spanish crew had been overwhelmed and dispersed by fire alone: the flame, smoke and sound of an arquebus volley cracking overhead, followed by the whip and howl of an arrow storm.

The broadside cannon of the raider had been held in check and no shots whatever had been fired into the hull of the Spanish ship. Two guns only had fired a single aimed shot apiece. The first had fired one shot, chain-loaded, at the mizzenmast so as to bring it down and cripple the *nao* without really damaging her. The second gun had put a shot over the freighter, high up by the mainmast, where it could hit no one; and that shot was possibly aimed to miss. The surprised Spaniards had been defeated psychologically by the expenditure of a few shillingsworth of black powder, lead and iron.

The discipline required to do this was formidable. No one could be sure that the opponent was unarmed, harmless and incapable of retaliation. When it comes to either risking one's own life, or taking an enemy's instead, the almost universal tendency is fire first and hang the orders. But here fire had been withheld, when the opponent was of equal size and looming menacingly in the semi-darkness. The natural instinct of nervousness had been denied; as had the equal and opposite instinct of those biased the other way, who, with so much fire-power under their hands, might have been tempted to loose off aggressively. Anton was to depose that Francis Drake 'was much feared by his men. He kept guards and when he dined they sounded trumpets and clarions.' This time at least, no careless, drunken soldier had got up from cover to give away Drake's ambush before the prey was in the trap.

On the morning of 2 March, Drake had breakfast on board the prize, which most of his men now referred to by her common name, *Cacafuego* (although da Silva used the Portuguese form *Caguafogo*). At the same time, nine o'clock, Drake's own table in his own cabin was set for San Juan de Anton, with as much formality as if it had been for himself. The elaborate chivalry probably had a purpose beyond that of impressing the visitor (and perhaps his own men also) with the high standing of the Captain-General, although he did stress to all his captives from now on that he was acting for the Queen of England and had her commission for what he did. Possibly there was something else, something he wanted Anton to do for him that would require the Spaniard's continuing goodwill even after his release from captivity.

It was not until noon that Drake finished inspecting the treasure in Anton's ship. Custodio Rodriguez, captured in Payta a week previously, testified that Drake 'displayed amazement and wonder at seeing such a great amount of treasure.' He had heard him say: 'Now I believe in the riches of the South Sea!' San Juan de Anton deposed officially that the registered treasure totalled 362,000 pesos in silver bars, silver reals and gold, of which 106,000 pesos was Crown property; but that if the unregistered treasure was included, the total would certainly exceed 400,000 pesos' worth. Francis Fletcher, Drake's chaplain, could only take Anton's word for the value. What he saw were thirteen chests full of silver coins ('royals of plate'), twenty-six tons of uncoined silver, many jewels and precious stones. Custodio Rodriguez testified that five trips by the pinnace from the prize to the *Golden Hind* were required to transfer the treasure. When the transfer was completed then, quite literally, she was ballasted with silver. The English also removed some provisions, mainly bags of flour, salt pork, sugar and preserves.

The transfer took three days of calm weather, and before it began Drake moved his small fleet far out to sea, where they could be unobserved from the land. During this time Drake had leisure to talk to San Juan de Anton and also to his ship's clerk, Domingo de Lizarza, aged thirty. Both men dictated official statements within a fortnight and Anton in addition gave Pedro de Sarmiento a more uninhibited version of events.

Their assessments of the corsair's force were similar. The clerk put the *Golden Hind* at 180 tons, Anton at 200 tons, adding that she was 'covered with seaweed, greatly needs to be careened and cleaned'. (John Drake put the Spaniards' ship at 120 tons, English measurement, the same as the *Golden Hind* by his estimation.) The clerk estimated her crew as eighty men, sixty being fighters; Anton thought eighty-five men, fifty being fighters. (His own crew he gave as being six men, plus five or six passengers.)

The clerk listed the *Golden Hind*'s maindeck armament as being five guns aside, plus two in the poop (i.e., firing astern on either side of the rudder); and he added that four more guns, two of them bronze, were brought up from below at one time (presumably when the old ballast was being removed to make way for the new ballast, the twenty-six tons of silver). Anton, who spent five days in the ship, gave the higher figure of seven guns aside on the maindeck plus two large cast-iron pieces by the helm, firing astern; but in addition he mentioned another six heavy guns, two of them bronze, on the upper deck. Drake probably could have mounted this many because, apart from the eighteen sizeable guns he had in her originally, the guns of the flyboat *Swan* (five cast-iron pieces) and of the pinnace *Christopher* (some *versos* only) would have been taken out of these ships before they were destroyed or abandoned and shared among the remaining three – *Golden Hind*, *Elizabeth* and *Marigold*. Da Silva's *Santa Maria* probably mounted some armament also, which would have been removed before her destruction. All such guns, lying on the ballast, would have had to be moved out of the way temporarily during the redistribution of ballast and cargo necessary to accommodate the silver and stores of the *Nuestra Señora de la Concepción*.

On the other hand, Anton's estimate of eighty-five men as the crew of the corsair's ship was probably a dozen too many. Nicolas Jorje, who spent four weeks in the *Golden Hind* and actually tried, surreptitiously, to count them made the total either seventy-one or seventy-two. Anton put the number of officers at 'twelve gentlemen and cavaliers', one of whom he had heard (correctly) was a relative of that Captain John Hawkins who had been defeated at San Juan de Ulloa by the Viceroy of Mexico.

Drake told him that he had been present at that affair, which had cost the lives of three hundred of his comrades and caused him a personal loss of 7,000 pesos, due to the treachery of Don Martin Enriquez. 'Since that time,' he told Anton, 'you could say that the King of Spain has been looking after my money for me. But now, in my turn, I want to be the treasurer of the King's estate. The treasure in your ship which belongs to the King, I will take for myself, as recompense; the rest I will have on behalf of my Sovereign Lady, the Queen.' Even after undergoing several translations, the underlying phraseology is certainly Drake's: the element of robbery-with-a-jest is the style employed by Fletcher throughout, and probably representative of the badinage used by them all.

What was not a joke was Drake's plain statement that the English wanted to take part in the Indies trade and were quite prepared to pay King Philip his usual percentage (the 'Royal Fifth'), but if they were not given licences to trade peacefully then they would raid the silver routes. In 1494, Spain and Portugal had made a far-sighted agreement, the Treaty of Tordesillas, to divide the unknown world between them before it had been discovered; this prevented a major clash and may have been largely responsible for the remarkable pioneering achievements of these two nations. The provisions of the treaty explained, for instance, why Brazil was now Portuguese when, at the time the treaty was signed, no one knew that there was such a place because no one had been there.

The treaty had served the best interests of Spain and Portugal very well. But in 1579 a treaty signed in 1494 and excluding all European nations save Spain and Portugal from all the earth appeared presumptuous to the excluded maritime powers. First France, then England, then the Free Netherlands (once their revolt from Spain had succeeded) set out to challenge the trade monopoly.

A settlement in this field, however, would not have lessened the enmity between Lutheran and Catholic. Among the crew of the *Golden Hind* were many convinced Lutherans, according to the testimony of Spanish prisoners. Anton himself was the object of an example. He was shown a golden crucifix, set with emeralds, the figure of Christ also being in gold, which he was told was loot from the *Grand Captain of the South Sea*, the treasure ship taken at Santiago three months before. If this was God, the Englishmen demanded to know, why had He not safeguarded the ship which was carrying it? They told him that God was in Heaven, that there was nothing holy in such useless objects as this.

Anton's clerk, Domingo de Lizarza, deposed similarly to the Spanish authorities:

'The said Englishmen are Lutherans, and their deeds and speech prove them to be such. They eat meat in Lent and on Friday and do not keep the commandments of God as Christians do. They also manifest themselves as being very much against the Pope.'

The interests of Spain and of the Pope were not always one and indivisible. For that matter, Pedro Sarmiento, who had commanded the *Grand Captain of the South Sea* on the great voyage which had won her that name, had twice suffered for heresy; and twice escaped because he had powerful friends in the Spanish governmental machine.

Drake gave San Juan de Anton and those of his crew who were with him a conducted tour of the *Golden Hind*. Domingo de Lizarza was certainly one of them, being taken to the galleon a little later than Anton and the boatswain. They were shown the guns, the ammunition of all types, the pikes and arquebuses, the steel helmets and body armour in the poop. When they had seen over the whole ship and been suitably impressed, he hoped, Drake turned to Anton and in the hearing of the others gave him the message which above all others he wanted delivered to Don Francisco de Toledo, the autocratic and empire-building Viceroy of Peru.

'I well know, Master John,' he remarked, 'that the Viceroy will send for you so as to obtain information about me. Well, tell him this: he has killed enough Englishmen and he is not to kill the four who remain, for if he does kill them it will cost him more than two thousand Spaniards. They will be hanged and their heads will be thrown into the harbour of Callao.'

Anton tried to pacify Drake by pointing out that Oxenham and his three companions were still alive and it was hardly likely that the Viceroy would kill them after all this time.

Drake replied by asking Anton what he thought the Viceroy's intentions towards them might be.

Anton said: 'Oh, probably they'll be sent to Chile to serve as soldiers in a garrison engaged in the Indian wars.'

Anton told Sarmiento that this answer was well received: 'Francis rejoiced greatly on hearing this and became pacified; for he displayed much anger whenever he spoke about them.'

What Drake probably did not know was that the Inquisition as well as the Viceroy were interested in the case and that all four men were held in the Inquisition prison. In the Viceroy's eyes, they were merely pirates. In the Inquisition's, they were heretics, and doomed.

In his turn, Anton probed Drake for information. By what route did he intend to return home? It was the crucial question to which the Viceroy of Peru was then addressing himself, as well as many less important authorities. If they could divine the way by which the corsair intended to return, they might assemble superior forces across his path. Drake might have been expected to dodge answering the question when Anton put it to him, but no: he seemed enthusiastic, took Anton and Lizarza to his cabin and unrolled his maps. One was enormous, two rods long, said Anton; Drake told him that this one had been made for him in Lisbon at the cost of 800 cruzados.

The corsair then pointed out that there were four alternatives before him, according to this chart. There was the long route, via the Spice Islands, India and Africa – a complete circumnavigation of the globe at approximately its greatest width. Another option was by Norway (Anton did not explain how Drake intended to get there, but perhaps it was by sailing to the north of China). The third route was to return by the way he had come, by the Strait of Magellan. There was a fourth way, but Drake would not tell Anton what it was. Domingo de Lizarza, however, remembered another route being mentioned – the overland route by the pass of Vallano in the country of the Cimarrons who were friendly to Drake; this would mean carrying out a plan similar to that of Oxenham's, but from the reverse direction. It would mean the destruction of the *Golden Hind* and the carrying of the gold and silver overland, using the rivers part of the way, and then perhaps capturing a ship in which to make the return voyage from the other side of the Isthmus of Panama.

Without indicating which route he would take, Drake told Anton that he was thinking of returning to England very soon, perhaps within six months.

Anton replied bluntly that he wouldn't get back, even in a year's time, because he was 'in a bag'.

De Lizarza testified that Drake abruptly stopped the discussion, rolled up his map and locked it away.

When Anton outlined this conversation to Sarmiento shortly afterwards, the latter became convinced that Drake intended to return round North America by using the Strait of Anian. Presumably the chart had showed that such a strait existed, dividing North America from Asia (although no one had ever seen such a strait because no one had been that far north to find out), and probably it showed alternative routes opening out beyond – either round the unknown coasts of North China and Russia to Norway or round the unknown coast of North America to Labrador and Greenland. There was supposed to be both a North-West Passage round North America and a North-East Passage round Russia, and English expeditions to probe both routes were in active preparation. An explorer in his own right, Sarmiento probably had his own definite views on which of the two routes was the most promising. The shortest route undoubtedly was that which returned round North America – if, in fact, such a route existed. If it did, Drake might well be back in England within six months. If it did not, Drake and his crew might soon be dead in the icefields of the polar regions.

Of course, Drake knew what Anton did not – that there was yet another route round the bottom of South America. He spoke always of the Strait of Magellan; he never mentioned that there was now no need to enter the Strait at all, for there was open sea south of the broken islands. He did not tell them, because this was information they did not have. Drake discussed with his captives only those matters which were either common knowledge or the subject of speculation among mariners everywhere, and also of governments.

Drake must have agreed his stories beforehand with those likely to fall into conversation with Spaniards. For instance, Anton obtained from da Silva the story of Drake's voyage from Plymouth and on asking the specific question, was the Strait of Magellan a real strait, between mainlands, or only a route through a maze of islands? received the misleading reply that it lay between mainlands. Those who were in the *Golden Hind* for any length of time did gather details of the voyage so far, but there was no mention of the alternative route to the Strait. Nicolas Jorje, for instance, was told that they could return home only by one of two ways, noncommittally, 'by the way they had come', or the long way round across the South Sea past China.

The Spaniards knew a good deal more about the first half of this route, to the Philippines, than the English did; and anything they said was likely to be of use to Drake. At what time of the year were the right winds encountered? and at what distance out to sea? and how did the currents flow? and when was the season of storms? These were the really important questions regarding any route to be taken by sailing ships. Cosmography and great circle courses were all very well, in theory, but this was the practical information which brought ships back safely or lost them forever with all their men. No doubt Drake listened very carefully for what experienced pilots like Anton might let slip.

For his part, Anton was aware that he was likely to be fed false information by the English, at least one of whom spoke 'intelligible Spanish', apart from da Silva the Portuguese. It is possible that Anton himself may have understood English; da Silva certainly said he did. What was clear, without need of language, was the state of the *Golden Hind*'s bottom timbers. Along her waterline she trailed a luxuriant growth of green sea moss and sea weed which impeded her, and what the unseen marine borers were doing to her sheathing below that was an easy conjecture. She had to be careened, and soon. A bay or creek secure from storm and enemies was required.

A ship during the careening process was appallingly vulnerable. If Anton could find out where Drake intended to go to careen, and if he could get word back to the Spanish authorities in some way, the corsair and his crew could be overwhelmed by the ships which surely must by now be in close pursuit.

All the Spaniards were questioned by the English as to suitable careening and watering places. Anton heard Custodio Rodriguez quizzed about Cabo Blanco; he said it was a good place. Then Drake asked Anton whether the island of Lobos, beyond Payta, towards Lima, was a good port for these purposes. But, reported Anton: 'It seemed to me that this was said to put me off my guard, because I believe and hold for certain that Captain Francis is going to the coast of Nicaragua.' He had once heard him say that he would take in water at the island of Caño near Costa Rica, because his supplies were almost exhausted. It followed that he would probably careen there as well. 'Moreover this would be on the route by which Captain Francis told me he could return to his country.'

On 5 March, the fifth day of his captivity, San Juan de Anton was told that he was to be released. His ship was to be given back to him and all the Spaniards kept on board the *Golden Hind* for the sake of the local knowledge they might have were to be released also. So Nicolas Jorje, taken at Santiago near Valparaiso, and Custodio Rodriguez, captured at Payta, were free at last. It looked as if Drake wanted no more Spanish witnesses able to testify later as to the course he was taking.

The events of that last day were to be described by Fletcher, by the anonymous anti-Drake witness in the *Golden Hind*, and by San Juan de Anton. Although they do not contradict each other, there is hardly any point of contact between them. The English witnesses were suppressing a great deal, Anton indulging only in slight self-censorship. Fletcher adopted the jocular robbery-without-pain tone so familiar from past descriptions and after listing the enormous treasures removed from the prize and describing them as 'trifles', added:

'We gave the master a little linen and the like for these commodities, and at the end of six days we bade farewell and parted – he hastening somewhat lighter than before to Panama, we plying off to sea, that we might with more leisure consider what course henceforward were fittest to be taken.'

This would read well in wartime among patriotic Englishmen, particularly civilians.

The same audience would have rejoiced even more at the tale told by the anonymous witness, although Drake's actions might perhaps have seemed a trifle shabby. Remarking, wrongly, that San Juan de Anton's name was Don Francisco, Anon stated that he had two silver-cups among his belongings, and that Drake had said to him: 'Sir pilot, you have two cups and I must needs have one of them.' 'The pilot yielded willingly, because he could not choose,' added Anon. Nevertheless, as the pilot went back on board his own ship, he made a crude jest, according to Anon. He called out over the water to the silver-laden English galleon: 'Captain, our ship shall be called no more the *Cacafoga* but the *Cacaplata*, and your ship shall be called the *Cacafo*!'

'Whereat,' went on Anon, 'Drake and his men laughed heartily and so let the Spaniards depart.'

A similar tale, but with the ship's boy of Anton's vessel speaking the lines, and the Spanish crudities spelt not quite the same, was in fact to be published in a propaganda work for English exploration edited by the Hakluyts.

Anton did not mention this dialogue in his official deposition, understandably so. Nor did he speak of the theft of the silver-gilt cups. He did, however, report that he and the other prisoners were the recipients of gifts from Drake before they parted. 'He gave to me and to the passengers who came with me, many pick-axes and linen stuff and other things. Among the things that Captain Francis gave me was a gilt corselet and he also wanted to give me ammunition and powder and other things, but his soldiers told him not to.' This confirms Fletcher's mention of the gift of 'a little linen and the like'; but it is far from being a full and frank statement.

To Sarmiento, however, he made a much more detailed report:

'The Englishman made several gifts to those whom he had robbed. He gave thirty or forty pesos in cash to each. To some he gave pieces of stuff from Portugal [part of da Silva's cargo], and agricultural implements, such as hoes and pruning-knives; to others, two of his own cloaks adorned with trimmings. To a soldier named Victoria he gave some weapons. To me he presented a firelock, saying that it had been sent him from Germany and that he prized it highly. To the clerk [Domingo de Lizarza] he gave a steel shield and a sword, saying that he did this so that the clerk might appear to be a man-at-arms. To me he gave two casks of tar, six hundred-weights of iron from Germany, and a barrel of powder. To a merchant named Cuevas he gave some fans with mirrors, saying that they were for his lady. And to me he gave a silver gilt bowl, in the centre of which his name, *Francisco Draques*, was inscribed.'

A gift bowl at last (if not a gift cup) but the story surrounding it is not that told by Anon, in which Drake appears a mean robber; but rather that of a somewhat vain man aware of, and proud of, the reputation he was now in the process of making. Rather like an artist signing his own work and giving it away as a souvenir, hinting how valuable it would be in days to come. None of this apparent generosity to Spaniards would have gone down very well in England at a time of anti-Spanish feeling whipped up by propaganda.

However, Drake was probably more devious than he appeared. He gave Anton a letter of safe conduct in case he should encounter

G

Vice-Admiral Winter in the *Elizabeth*, saying that Winter was 'a very cruel man' and would have them all killed unless they showed him this passport. The letter contained in fact a further message to Winter: 'What we determined about the return to our country will be carried out if God so wills, although I greatly doubt that this letter will reach your hands . . . ' From Winter's eventual report, it seems that they had agreed to return home by the Moluccas, the Spice Islands.

The letter ended with the lines:

'I am in good hope, that we shall be in no more trouble, but that He will help us in adversity, desiring you for the Passion of Christ, if you fall into any danger, that you will not despair of God's mercy, for He will defend you and preserve you from all danger, and bring us to our desired haven, to whom be all honour, glory, and praise for ever and ever. Amen. Your sorrowful Captain, whose heart is heavy for you: Francis Drake.'

As he had written, the odds were against the letter being read by Winter. In fact, it never was. At that time the *Elizabeth* was just south of the Line (the *Golden Hind* being just north of the Line) but off Portuguese-held Brazil. On 17 March Winter would pass Cape St Augustine and set course away into the Atlantic towards the island of Fernando de Loronha and, eventually, England. By 30 May, Winter would sight St Ives in Cornwall. He was well on his way home.

Drake's letter arrived at an unexpected address, the Inquisition prison at Lima. It was given to John Butler, one of Oxenham's men, to translate into Castilian for the benefit of the Viceroy of Peru, Don Francisco de Toledo. The prisoners must have known, from their previous interrogations regarding gun manufacture, that an English warship had got into the Pacific and attacked Callao. Now they would know for certain that the raider was commanded by their old captain, Francis Drake, and that he was creating havoc on the Spanish shipping routes. That might be some solace for their defeat when they had almost won through with the treasure, and for the bitter realisation that they were beyond help, although an English ship had been no more than two gunshots' distance away.

It was July before that letter was brought to John Butler, and it was dated 6 March 1579. This was the date given by Fletcher as the day Anton was released and the two ships parted company. Da

Silva's log noted that it was 5 March at night, which could be a discrepancy of only a few hours, but Anton himself gave 7 March as the date. In his official deposition, made some ten days later, he described a final parting scene on board the *Golden Hind*. Although Drake was freeing all Spaniards, he was keeping with him the few negro sailors he had taken, including a man captured off Arica. Anton wrote:

'In my presence, the said negro knelt on his knees before Captain Francis and begged him to have mercy and let him come away with me, because his master was advanced in years. Captain Francis said to him: "Since thou wishest to go thou canst go with God's blessing, for I do not wish to take anyone with me against his will." He then asked me to send the negro back to his master, so I brought him with me. I do not know his name.'

When the two ships began to move apart there was little wind, and although the *Nuestra Señora de la Concepción* was heading northeast for Panama, while Drake was sailing north-west into the Pacific, Anton could see the sails of the *Golden Hind* in the distance for almost two days more. He watched carefully, but as long as the two ships were in view, Drake was unlikely to change course and give away his destination.

The news Anton brought in to Panama was not welcome: indeed, it was shocking. The Spaniards were used to piratical attacks on the Caribbean side of the Isthmus, which was open to any European seaman who cared to cross the Atlantic. But the Pacific was a peaceful Spanish enclave. To enter it, an enemy would have to pass through the forbidding Strait of Magellan, unbelievably distant, in the regions of snows and ice, or he would have to encompass the earth from the opposite direction. And that had never been done at all. And yet now a powerful commerce-raider was at large on their undefended coasts.

On the 16 March by the Spanish calendar, in the city of Panama, the president and judges of the Royal Court and Chancery resident there began their inquiry. The archives record that:

'The illustrious Doctor Alonso Criado de Castilla, who being the senior judge presides, ordered the appearance before him of San Juan de Anton, the master and owner of the ship named *Nuestra Señor de la Concepción*, which is at present anchored in Perico, the port of this City, so that he should declare what had happened and what he knows about having been robbed by Englishmen in this South Sea, who took from him the treasure that he was carrying, which belonged to His Majesty and private persons. After having from him the oath by God and Saint Mary and the sign of the cross in due form, he said "Yes, I swear" and "Amen", and said and declared as follows.'

Most of what he told them was in the past and could not be remedied. But he did say that in spite of attempts to spread false suggestions, the corsair was undoubtedly heading for Nicaragua to water and careen. A thing that made him more positive than ever about this, was that he had heard the corsair's Portuguese pilot asking about certain women of Sonsonate. This made it seem, as Custodio Rodriguez suspected, that he was the same pilot who had absconded with a great deal of gold and silver some fifteen or twenty years ago, for that man had been married in Sonsonate. Certainly, said Anton, this Portuguese pilot of Drake's was very skilled in the navigation of the South Sea. For instance, he knew that at one time ships had used the port of Panama instead of Perico. It followed that his knowledge of the best places to water and to careen would be equal to theirs and that he might therefore make the same choice as they would, in the same circumstances. Not in his formal deposition, but in conversation, Anton put his finger on the exact spot – the isle of Caño off the coast of Costa Rica on the way to Nicaragua. 'Everybody at Panama is of the same opinion,' he added.

That was on 16 March by Spanish reckoning. On 15 March, by da Silva's reckoning, land was sighted from the *Golden Hind* and next day they anchored to take in water. He did not mention where this sheltered spot was. Fletcher did, however, and for once, his date agreed with da Silva's:

'We set onward, March the 7, shaping our course towards the Island of Caines, with which we fell March 16, setting ourselves for certain days in a fresh river, between the main and it, for the finishing of our needful businesses. While we abode in this place, we felt a very terrible earthquake, the force whereof was such that our ship and pinnace, riding very near an English mile from the shore were shaken and did quiver as if it had been laid on dry land. We found there many good commodities which we wanted, as fish, fresh water, wood, etc., besides alligators, monkeys, and the like.'

What Fletcher called the Isle of Caines, the Spaniards called Caño. San Juan de Anton (and everyone alse in Panama) had guessed right.

On 18 March, according to da Silva, they moved a short distance to a careenage. The guns would have to be taken out of the *Golden Hind* and the vessel laid on her side to expose the bottom timbers for scraping, caulking and 'repainting', if that word can rightly be used of the horrible mixture to be laid on the planking to discourage the teredo and other marine borers. The process would take a week, and during that time the ship would be immobile and defenceless.

They could have done with the aid of Vice Admiral Winter and the *Elizabeth* at this juncture, but on the previous day Winter had set course out across the Atlantic past Fernando de Noronha for home. Like John Oxenham and his crew, they could so easily meet total disaster when flushed with success. Everything depended on whether the Spanish authorities could react as rapidly and efficiently against Drake's ship as they had against Oxenham's overland party, which had used the jungles and rivers and the help of the friendly natives, all in vain. Just a little carelessness, a trifling overconfidence, had brought their downfall.

Chapter 15

'THE WAY THAT HALF-DEAD MEN ACT'

Pursuit from Peru: 28 February–13 April 1579
Precautions at Cartagena: April–May 1579

THE raider's arrival had been inconveniently timed. The incoming fleets from Spain were expected on the Caribbean side of the continent; their routings were complex and they had to be escorted. On the Pacific side, as we have seen, a convoy system was not yet in operation. Because there had never been a threat in the South Sea the treasure was moved like any other commodity in individual ships; from the south to Panama, from the north to Acapulco. Eventually, it would be transferred overland to the Atlantic side and into the ships newly arrived from Spain. These would join together at Havana in one great strongly-escorted convoy for the return passage, and on their safe and timely return a good deal of Spanish power and policy depended.

Drake's blows struck at the weakest and most sensitive points of the whole vast operation. So the effects were felt from Chile in the south to Mexico in the north and over in the Caribbean also, in another ocean entirely. Like some drugged dragon, the Spanish colonies in the New World writhed in slow motion as the news came in and unhappy viceroys and governors wondered what action they should take. Not infrequently, the information given to them was false, and when it was true it might be as much as three months out of date. It was not much use to learn in Lima on 12 July that Drake had been seen off Nicaragua on the 4th of April.

A great responsibilty rested on the local officials, to react quickly and to pursue the corsair promptly and energetically. At the same time, there was not much use in pursuing him rapidly with inadequate forces. On the other hand, once the raider's sails had dwindled over the horizon he might next appear almost anywhere. The mere possibility could tie up great forces spread over a vast area. In this situation, a hundred men could pin down ten thousand in searching for them or guarding against them; in marching and counter-marching; in sailing here and speeding there; and, all the time, spending money on the wages of sailors and soldiers which other-wise would have gone to the royal revenues. The cardinal sin was committed by the pursuit force sent out immediately from Callao, with Drake still in full view from the port, in mid-February. When, from seasickness and a recognition of their own weaknesses, the Spaniards thought it best to turn back, contact was lost.

The Viceroy of Peru, Don Francisco de Toledo, sent a bark to Panama, which was to call in at every port on the way and alert everyone to the danger. Meanwhile he had two vessels fitted out as fighting ships and embarked in them 120 soldiers in addition to their crews. For their leaders, he chose a team containing some temperamentally incompatible elements. The senior post, that of Lieutenant-General, he gave to Don Luis de Toledo, and to an equally cautious man, Pedro de Arana, he gave the position of Camp Master. Diego de Frias Trejo, the general who had taken Oxenham, was given the subordinate position of Admiral, with Pedro Sarmiento de Gamboa as Sergeant-Major, Juan de Arrieta as Ensign-General and Miguel Angel as Chief Pilot. Diego de Frias Trejo was to have been both Camp Master and Admiral, but was in effect demoted by the appointment of de Arana to Camp Master at the last minute, on the actual day of sailing. This cannot have made for good command relationships. Their task was a difficult one in any case. Sarmiento wrote:

'All the men left with a great desire to fight the enemy but with little hope of being able to overtake him, for he already had a start of fifteen days. After going out to sea we began to parley with all ships we met and to run along the coast, exploring ports and points with a sailing launch we took with us for this purpose. When we arrived at Santa we learnt that the corsair had passed by there a fortnight previously and that, beyond the port of Trujillo, he had seized the bark of a certain Cataro and had taken from her what he wished.'

The transhipment of cargo or stores from a prize to the *Golden Hind* was certain to delay the raider. So, in a sense, the more fortunate Drake was in finding rich prizes the more likelihood there was that his pursuers might catch up with him.

'We therefore immediately started for the port of Trujillo,

having also heard that six days previously a great vessel with a sprit-sail, which was believed to be the pirate ship, was thereabouts. In that vicinity we saw a sail, and in view of this information, bore down upon her; but she turned out to be a merchant's bark.'

The pursuit from Peru reached Payta on 10 March by Spanish reckoning and learnt that they were still lagging fourteen days behind the raider. They were told that Drake had robbed a bark belonging to Custodio Rodriguez in that port, removing some wine, a native canoe and Custodio himself. Clearly, Drake had been in a very great hurry. 'He had not even cast anchor, for he had learnt that a pilot named San Juan de Anton had started ahead of him on the previous day from the same port, with many bars of silver,' wrote Sarmiento.

The Peru Force had been ordered to rendezvous with a galley at Guayaquil. An oared warship might be of great use in the light airs often found in the Gulf of Panama, but it seemed so urgent to press on that they did not enter the port, relying on a message sent overland from Payta ordering the galley to catch up with them.

On 13 March they were off Point Santa Elena and the launch was sent inshore. But the small port was empty.

On 17 March Peru Force entered the more important harbour of Manta, between Guayaquil and Cape San Francisco, and anchored. Two ships had arrived before them.

'One of these was that of Bravo who, on his way from Guayaquil to Panama, carrying gold, had been robbed by the Englishmen off the rivers of the Quiximies, five leagues from the Cape of San Francisco. They had taken from him fifteen thousand pesos in gold, belonging to private merchants, as well as all the clothing and food they wished ... The Corsair made experiments in sailing with the bark, but as she sailed faster on the wind than his own ship he wrapped her sails around her anchor and cast them into the sea so that she could not sail ahead and give warning. He released the men and the bark, permitting them to go back, and giving them a little coarse linen to make the small sail with which Bravo came to Manta. These men related that like a shameless robber who fears not God or man, the Corsair made many arrogant speeches, saying that San Juan de Anton could not escape him.'

Bravo had been captured near Cape San Francisco on 28 February and been released on 1 March, seventeen days previously. Although the Corsair's ship was not particularly fast, Peru Force was now more than seventeen days and a good many leagues behind: the pursuit was lagging, not gaining. There was only one way, now, to catch up, thought Sarmiento, and that was to cut across the half-circle represented by the vast bay which in turn enclosed two smaller bays, those of San Miguel and Panama. This vast expanse of water was known as the Gulf of Panama and it contained an infinite number of creeks which could conceal a ship, as well as a group of islands which might serve the same purpose. To comb this area would take weeks, perhaps months. It was a hopeless course to pursue. Far better to assume that, sooner or later, the corsair must escape from the trap via Nicaragua. If so, a pursuit which crossed over directly from Manta, avoiding the Gulf of Panama altogether, must either head him off (if he had strayed into the Gulf at all), or at least lose no more time in following after him (if he also had made direct for Nicaragua).

Sarmiento and his immediate superior, Diego de Frias Trejo, were both agreed about this and the latter put it to the General, His Excellency Don Luis de Toledo, when he met him ashore in Manta. All he got was an agreement to discuss the matter later in his flagship, the *Capitana*. Knowing the sort of man they had to deal with, Diego and Sarmiento studied the instructions which had been issued to His Excellency. At last they found what appeared to be the authority they needed, the phrase: 'As you are to pursue them by sea and by land.' That seemed to cover sailing off into the blue, out of sight of land, towards Nicaragua. And so they argued at the meeting in the *Capitana*. But His Excellency was unconvinced and said only that the matter required full discussion and that he would meet them formally next day in their ship, the *Almiranta*, bringing with him the Camp Master, Pedro de Arana.

Next day was 18 March. On this day Drake, having already crossed by the direct route, began to careen the *Golden Hind* at the island of Caño, off Costa Rica, between Panama and Nicaragua. In case of close pursuit, he had sailed well out to sea, out of sight of land, before unloading Anton's ship, a thoroughly professional move. He was extremely vulnerable while careening, but the *Golden Hind* was trailing weed and leaking badly. The risk had to be taken. Just how much of a risk it was would depend partly on the authorities in Panama, to whom San Juan de Anton had told his story on 16 March, and partly on the debate this day in the vice-flagship of the Peru Force.

An unseen factor in their arguments was John Oxenham, whose operations had been limited to the Gulf of Panama and thus served to concentrate some Spanish minds there. The thinking was false, because Oxenham had left his ship on the Caribbean side, had penetrated upriver in boats as far as possible, then marched down to the shores of the South Sea, where he had constructed pinnaces. His seaborne operations had been most successful. However, he had to return overland through an alerted province, and the Spaniards were very good soldiers. A force sent out from Panama found the English and their Cimarron allies, beat them and recovered most of the stolen treasure. Oxenham and a few others had escaped, but a force from Peru led by Diego de Frias Trejo had tracked most of them down, even in the wilderness of the rain forest. The problem offered them by Drake and his heavily-armed raider was utterly different, but Don Luis and Pedro de Arana were both timorous and incapable of original thought.

So they protested that they had no authority to cross the Gulf to Nicaragua. Diego de Frias Trejo and Sarmiento maintained that the words 'you are to pursue them by sea and by land' meant by sea as well as by land and constituted sufficient authority. The senior pair protested that the corsair would surely go to Panama or to the Bay of San Miguel, or would wait along the coast somewhere nearby in the hope of intercepting another silver ship like Anton's. It would not do to leave this coast unguarded.

Sarmiento stepped in to argue that the corsair could escape by one route only – past Nicaragua and New Spain (as Mexico was generally called). He demolished the idea that the Englishman might be found anywhere in the Gulf of Panama. The corsair would not go to the bay of San Miguel because he knew that troops under Pedro de Ortega were already there, besides being aware of the fate that had befallen Oxenham's expedition in the same area two years ago, in 1577. Further, if he was to escape that way, by crossing overland, he would have to destroy his ship with her valuable armament and ammunition stores, and his men would have to carry the silver on their shoulders over the Isthmus. The first he would be very reluctant to do and the second was impossible, even if he had a great deal of help from the natives.

Sarmiento went on to dismiss any idea that the corsair might turn back to Peru, for he had left the Peruvian coast in a tumult, with everyone up in arms. He must have seen also how quickly two ships had come out of Callao after him in pursuit (although, admittedly, they had soon turned back again), and must suspect that so powerful a country must be able to assemble a fleet. Having once escaped this danger, he was unlikely to risk it again; less so, because his booty has since grown so rich and he will be afraid to lose it.

Having put forward these very reasonable arguments to show where Drake would not go, Sarmiento reiterated his belief that the corsair had no alternative but to follow the coast northwards past Nicaragua and New Spain. The corsair himself had been heard to say so, and if there was any doubt about it the Portuguese pilot who was with him would confirm, because the man had been recognised as an experienced South Sea navigator who twenty-one years ago had run off with thirty thousand pesos in gold. The corsair would certainly have learnt from this man that the coast northwards had neither Spanish garrisons nor Indian encampments; nothing with which to resist and no ships with which to pursue. Further, the raider would be travelling ahead of the news of his own coming and would be able to surprise and rob the treasure ships bound for Sonsonate and perhaps even those which sailed from the Philippines with gold and many items of great value.

Sarmiento, an experienced explorer and navigator, was right in everything he said, except perhaps in taking for granted the accuracy of the identification of da Silva with the renegade Portuguese pilot of twenty-one years before. So his final prediction is extremely interesting, as it explores ground not made explicit in the surviving English documents and testimony.

'To these considerations must be added that about the safety of his voyage. From the present month of March onwards, until September, summer and the hot season prevail as far north as Cape Mendocino in forty-three degrees. That would be the shortest and quickest route for getting from this sea to his country, and while this route is not familiar to the pilots here, because they do not ordinarily navigate in that region, it is not unknown to the English who navigate to Iceland, Bacallaos, Labrador, Totilan and Norway. For them it is familiar and they are not afraid of navigating very far north. As this Corsair has, moreover, navigated in the aforesaid parts and is so well versed in all modes of navigation, it may be inferred and believed that he also must know all about this. A man who has had the spirit to do what he has done will not be lacking in courage to persevere in his attempt, especially as he can take advantage, at present, of its being summer in the polar regions.'

The Spanish navigator can only have been referring to the Strait of Anian, which some cosmographers supposed to lie between America and Asia and to afford a rapid return to Europe by going round the top of North America near the icy pole and so down past Norway to England. It seems as though Sarmiento believed in this Strait, the existence of which had never been proved, and assumed that the northern navigators, such as Drake, would know a great deal more about it than any Spaniard was likely to do. Judging by Drake's actual movements, Sarmiento may have been right once again; the corsair may well have intended to return by this route, provided that it existed and was navigable.

Sarmiento then gave detailed calculations of sailing times. Panama was distant twelve or thirteen days of slow sailing, whereas if they crossed over, twelve days would see them well on the way to Nicaragua. He worked out how far ahead of them Drake might be, in the case of his going for Panama and in the other case of his having crossed direct. His arguments convinced everyone in the *Almiranta* and many of those in the *Capitana*, but even after much discussion, His Excellency was still hesitant. He resolved that they would all sail as far as Cape San Francisco, and take a final decision there. He wrote to the Viceroy explaining this, and on 19 March the pursuit got under way again.

When the fleet arrived off Cape San Francisco, where Bravo had been released and (although they did not know it yet) Anton had been taken nineteen days previously, the *Almiranta* closed the *Capitana* for the conference. Then Miguel Angel, acting as chief pilot, told Sarmiento that the General's instructions were that the conference would be held when they reached Galera Point, two leagues further on. They were not off this headland until the following day, but His Excellency did not stop for a conference. A day later still, on 21 March, seventeen leagues beyond, off Manglares Point, the ships finally assembled for the senior officers to confer. However, no such thing happened. Instead, the General passed the word to the Admiral that he had decided to go to Panama and not attempt the direct crossing to Nicaragua. Presumably he hoped that his officers would all accept this without discussion. Miguel Angel signalled that he had known nothing about this abrupt decision and Sarmiento remarked, loudly: 'What's the good of proposing one thing and then not doing it; that's the way that half-dead men act.'

This sentiment, somewhat modified, was conveyed to His Excellency, who then agreed to hold a conference. He even sent his skiff over to the *Almiranta* to collect Diego de Frias Trejo and Pedro de Sarmiento. The arguments developed exactly as they had before between the two pairs of senior officers, but this time Miguel Angel was present, making a third, independent party. Sarmiento therefore stressed strongly the navigational side of his case, pointing out that the corsair had only certain exits available for his escape and that he certainly would not turn round and return by the Strait of Magellan. Therefore they were wasting their time by going along the coast towards Panama; the only course was to cross direct, and as for the navigation being difficult, he offered to do that himself and if he made a mistake, they were at liberty to chop his head off.

His Excellency picked on the one logical weak point in Sarmiento's case, that they had now dawdled so far into the Gulf of Panama that they could no longer have the full benefit in saved time of the direct crossing, which was from Cape San Francisco and not Manglares Point. Therefore they would go on to Panama but at the same time explore most thoroughly – most thoroughly – every port, creek, inlet and possible haven on the whole long coastline, not neglecting to search well inland. The only evidence of human use they found were a few traces of the natives, either local Indians or Cimarron negroes.

Sarmiento and Frias Trejo left His Excellency in the *Capitana* to his own devices and pressed on ahead to the Perlas Islands, where Oxenham had at one time taken refuge. They anchored off Del Rey, the largest island of the group, and sent ashore for news. It was definite, and the worst possible. The English corsair had met San Juan de Anton and taken all the silver he carried.

Next day, 31 March, the pursuit fleet reassembled and sailed to Perico, the port of Panama, without bothering any more to search all the small ports, creeks, havens and inlets where now, it was obvious, the corsair would not be found in hiding. When they came to anchor, one of the first men to go out to the Peru Force was San Juan de Anton himself, with his more firmly-based knowledge of the raider's movements, if nearly a month out of date, and his firm conviction that Drake would go to the Island of Caño to careen. His Excellency, however, displayed no great haste to press on after the pirate and Sarmiento had ample leisure time on board to write down San Juan de Anton's story and also to compose a brief history of the havoc the raider had created among the coastal shipping from as far south as Chile. This was firmly based on the testimony of the many witnesses released by Drake with Anton's ship, who were all present; and less firmly-based, inevitably, for earlier exploits to which there was no first-hand testimony at that moment in Panama.

Diego de Frias Trejo spent part of his time locating and then transporting into the fleet five pieces of ordnance which he had left at Panama after his last military expedition into Vallano. These might go some small way to countering the superior gun armament of the raider. While they were still at anchor, news was brought from the south that two other English ships had now appeared off the coast of Peru, possibly those which the corsair Drake was known to be expecting. This vital message had in fact reached Manta just after they had sailed from that port on 19 March. It had arrived, carried by a Spaniard travelling in an Indian canoe, just as the ship of Benito Diaz Bravo was about to sail for Panama, having completed the repairs made necessary by his encounter with the corsair on the last day of February.

The Spaniard in the canoe carried a letter addressed to one of Bravo's passengers, Juan Perez Medina, an inhabitant of Guayaquil. It had been forwarded as a matter of urgency by Pedro de Alva, the local Justice. The letter, dated from Yauco, near Guayaquil, on Saturday, 14 March, five days before, was from Fray Gaspar de Palma. The Peru Force had not put into Guayaquil, even to join with the galley which was being prepared for them there, in their haste to follow after the corsair, so any news might be welcome; but this was not. The friar had written:

'What has happened here is that a courier arrived, a fortnight ago, from Payta, to give warning to those of Guayaquil that two

ships of Lutherans were coming thither to seize the galley that
lay there. They had taken a pilot for this purpose but because
they started in pursuit of a vessel that is bound for Panama
carrying 200,000 pesos they have not yet entered Guayaquil.'

That, clearly, was Drake's raider and the accompanying pinnace
in their pursuit of San Juan de Anton's silver ship. The worrying,
new factor came in the next paragraph:

'Since then, further news has reached here from the spies in
the service of Don Francisco de la Puna. They say that four
ships (two very large and of a different pattern from those in
use here, and two launches) are off Saint Clara and from there
are on guard so that no one can pass out of nor enter the river
of Guayaquil.'

Soon after this, wrote the friar, these corsairs made clear what
manner of men they were.

'On last Tuesday, the tenth of March, another report reached
me while I was at Guayaquil. They say the Lutherans seized
Rivas, one of the Guayaquil residents, and demanded of him
that he was to take them up the river to the town of Guayaquil.
He told them that he did not know how to take large ships up
the river, having only had experience with small barks such as
his. Upon this they stabbed him with a dagger and killed him.
Two Indians from Payta told this news. They were in the bark
with Rivas and when they saw that he was being killed they
threw themselves into the sea and swam to Tunbes, where they
spread the news.'

The friar went on to describe his own plight:

'The people of this village are in great fear and although they
consist of not more than a hundred and are badly armed they are
all ready to lay down their lives. What causes us the greatest
anguish is that no help can come to us from Quito because the
Quiyos Indians have again rebelled and all are up in arms. It is
hoped that the Viceroy will send help from Lima . . . We are all
greatly perturbed, not knowing whether they will take San Juan
de Anton's ship, It is said that they wanted to take this port.'

Fray Gaspar de Palma specially asked that a warning be given to
a high ecclesiastic, the Reverend Vicar General, who was due to

have sailed from Panama for Manta on 15 February in Mondragon's ship:

> 'If they have arrived pray inform them of all this and tell them that not a bird can escape them [the Englishmen] if it gets within their reach and that they do not spare anyone's life. Give the same information to all ships that arrive there . . .'

Peru Force remained in Panama for two weeks, neither going north to Nicaragua in pursuit of Drake nor sailing south to succour the friar, but trying to obtain provisions from the local authorities. In this also they failed. The operations against Oxenham two years before had led to bad feeling between the Viceroy of Peru and the officials in Panama, largely because the latter felt that Don Francisco de Toledo was trying to assume powers over them to which he was not entitled. Perhaps they were not too displeased that his fleet had now performed less than brilliantly. The news of its first lamentable encounter with Drake when many of the crews had been worsted by seasickness without firing a shot, had spread even into the Caribbean. Some of the recipients were not above passing on the tale to the King, in their dispatches for Spain.

Don Miguel de Eraso y Aguilar, writing from Cartagena, was unlucky with his first letter, which was lost in the sea by shipwreck, but a later report reached Spain. Initially, he merely passed on the substance of news he had received from Panama of Drake's entry into the Pacific via the Strait of Magellan and his depredations up to the capture of San Juan de Anton's 'silver ship'. Some of his facts were shaky. He referred to the corsair as 'Captain Francis, a Frenchman who is married in England', but then went on to tell the King: 'It is a thing that terrifies one, this voyage and the boldness of this low man, the son of vile parents (for, it is said that his father was a shoe-maker). Yet it is a positive and accomplished fact that he undertook that navigation and came by that route . . .' It made him feel happier to be able to pass on the opinion of the Panama authorities, that the credit for the passage of the Strait was due to the presence on board of a skilful Portuguese pilot. The Don's contempt for anyone who combined the serious disadvantages of low birth and lack of education with a shameful non-military occupation on the part of his father was not a Spanish attitude only, but common enough in England too. Such beliefs had underlain the Doughty affair.

The military code in which Don Miguel de Eraso had been brought up did not allow him to spare Spanish deficiencies either, and particularly not when it was members of the hereditary military caste who had failed in what might be expected of them. His remarks to the King concerning Peru Force were not kind:

'It appears that the two vessels that were dispatched by the Viceroy to chase him, overtook him; but made no attempt to attack him, nor did they exert themselves in any way. This was because on board both ships there were neither sailors nor corsairs. If there had been either, even with the crew and forces they carried they would not have failed to attack, even if it had been "the carrack of Rhodes". I am confident that if these had been English ships they would not have turned back without seizing an opportunity to attack.'

To be compared unfavourably to pirates and Englishmen was a peculiarly cutting insult.

Also in Cartagena was a relative, Don Christobal de Eraso, General of the Guard of the Indies, the warships whose primary purpose was the protection and escorting of the treasure fleets. On 10 April he received two letters from Panama in the same post, one dated 4 March and the other 16 March. The latter contained the first news of Drake's arrival in the South Sea and of his capture of San Juan de Anton. Don Christobal also was 'filled with amazement at the boldness the corsair has displayed'. The President of Panama warned him that Drake might appear in the Atlantic, after abandoning his ship in the Pacific and making the overland crossing with the aid of his old allies, the negroes of Vallano. Don Christobal agreed that this was a possibility to be guarded against, as was the alternative crossing of the Isthmus by way of a trail across Nicaragua, and consequently he put on alert Spanish forces in the Caribbean:

'Within an hour of the time I received your Lordship's dispatch I made ready the man-of-war, the galleys and the galliot I had in the port of Cartagena. As quickly as I could I sent Don Pedro Bique with these two galleys and the galliot to search the creek of Acla. He was first to go to Tolu so as to take in whatever maize and cassava he might find there and was then to go along the whole of that coast and enter the river, searching all its tributaries and creeks. At whatever point he may think best he is to leave guards to protect that pass. I shall take with me the galleon *San Bartolomé* and shall send her to Islas de Agua or Cape Tiburon, to remain there as reinforcement to aid and succour the galliot.'

A month after leaving Cartagena, Don Christobal was lying anchored off Nombre de Dios, anxiously waiting for the galleys of Don Pedro Bique. At this port he had learned the latest news: that two of Drake's ships were reported to have been raiding on the coast of Chile on their way north, while Drake himself, having taken several other prizes, was headed for Nicaragua. 'This is an affair of great importance which requires serious consideration,' he wrote. 'If all three vessels should unite with their artillery and firearms they will constitute a force that could not possibly be vanquished by the ships sent by the Viceroy or those that have left there.' To prevent them from uniting, Don Christobal offered to cross over to Panama in person with his best officers and most experienced soldiers and embark in such vessels as they might have there. He offered also the use of some of his own ordnance, bronze guns of ten, twelve, fifteen and twenty hundredweight, if transport could be arranged for them. With these reinforcements, the force at Panama ought to go in search of the two ships reported off Chile and chastise them quickly, before they could join Drake. Meanwhile, Don Pedro Bique would be left on the Caribbean side of the Isthmus to guard those points where the two main passes met the sea, in case Drake came overland.

It was now 14 May and much could have happened in the meantime. 'The fleet of Tierra Firme had not arrived when I left Cartagena and its delay has caused me great anxiety. God grant that no misfortune had befallen it, as has been the case with the fleet of New Spain.' These were the incoming fleets, which on their return would carry the produce of the New World and also of the Far East back to Spain. Two specially strong ships specifically designated to pick up the treasure from Nombre de Dios and Veracruz had already reached Don Christobal at Nombre de Dios. They were the hired vessels of Chaves and Martin Monte Bernaldo; the latter's, the *Santa Isabel*, was soon to be wrecked, and although the gold and silver was saved the first reports to the King from Peru and from Panama of the depredations of the corsair Drake were lost.

A side effect of the wreck of the *Santa Isabel* between Nombre

de Dios and Cartagena was a law suit in Seville instigated by the
representative of the Viceroy of Peru against the shipowner, Martin
Monte Bernaldo. The basis of the charge of negligence was a
contention that the lost documents addressed to the King by the
Viceroy, Don Francisco de Toledo, 'were of greater importance
than the gold and silver, because at this particular juncture they
were greatly needed. For they contained accounts of what had
happened in connection with the Englishmen, of which His Majesty
has not received a complete and truthful relation.' In short, the
Viceroy was making out that, notwithstanding whatever the king
might hear from other sources (say, from Panama or Cartagena or
Nombre de Dios), he might rest assured that matters had been
handled at Lima with the utmost efficiency and dispatch. By then,
Don Francisco must have been aware that Peru Force had finally
demonstrated a degree of ineptitude shaming to most of those
concerned.

During the fortnight it had spent, doing nothing, in Panama,
the authorities there had fitted out a third ship to accompany
Peru Force. Although there was general agreement that Drake
would have gone north, this combined force was supposed to go
south to meet the two English ships reported off Guayaquil by
the friar. The English blockade of the river there, and the murder
– by stabbing or hanging – of the unfortunate Rivas, who had
refused to pilot them into the shallows upstream, had never been
more than an unsupported tale by two Indians told to a priest who
may well have been leading a dull life and so have welcomed the
opportunity of spreading a little drama. His mock heroics regarding
the 'badly armed' defenders of the settlement all ready to 'lay
down their lives' could not have inspired confidence in anyone
familiar with the oddities of behaviour which are produced by the
threat of war.

Now it became known that the corsair ships were phantoms and
that the murder was mythical, regardless of whether it had been
carried out by a knife or with a rope (some Spanish clerk, in making
a copy, wrote the one for the other). It had also become clear that
a second-hand story in San Juan de Anton's account, that Drake
had killed the entire crew of a prize taken at Lima, had no more
foundation than the fact that the ship had resisted and that one
Spaniard had been wounded, one Englishman killed, in an exchange
of fire. The actual losses, on both sides, at this moment stood at

two Englishmen killed by arquebus shot, Richard Minivy ashore at Coquimbo, a certain Thomas in the pinnace at Callao; and two Spanish captains wounded by arrows, Alonso Rodriguez Bautista Patagalana of the *San Christobal* at Callao, San Juan de Anton of *Nuestra Señora de la Concepción* off Cape San Francisco. Fray Gaspar de Palma's assertion that 'not a bird can escape them' represented merely the spreading of alarm and despondency without due cause, to say the least, quite apart from the fact that the Englishmen he was talking about did not exist, any more than did their ships.

Nevertheless, although this was now known, on 13 April 1579 the two ships of Peru Force and the single ship from Panama put out from Perico and sailed south, towards Peru. And 13 April was the precise day on which Drake, having carried out several more captures at sea, struck at a Spanish port to the north of Panama, and took it.

Chapter 16

THE LAST PRIZES

Costa Rica to Nicaragua:
18 March–6 April 1579

BEYOND Panama the Isthmus broadened out into Costa Rica, Nicaragua, Guatemala and the vast country of Mexico, governed by the Viceroy of New Spain, Don Martin Enriquez. Whereas in Peru the dominant native culture at the time of the coming of the Spaniards had been that of the Incas, here it was firstly that of the Mayas and then, further north, that of the Aztecs, although there were other cultures also, such as those of the Toltecs and Mixtecs. Mostly, the natives were pyramid-builders, but had not yet invented the wheel, and had no use for gold except in the manufacture of ornaments and works of art, at which they were adept. The Incas were an exception; for them gold had a religious significance – it was the 'sweat of the sun'.

When conquered, these regions had been storehouses of precious metals and jewels. The collected gold and gems amassed over thousands of years by the native civilisations, and by them turned into fabulous works of art, awaited the Spaniards. When the treasure of Montezuma, the Aztec emperor, went on display in Brussels during 1520, the artist Albrecht Dürer said that it appeared to him 'more beautiful than the things of which miracles are made'. The Spaniards melted it down, as they did with almost all the gold and silver objects they took or bargained for. Because Spain was a poor arid country with little manufacturing capacity, the gold and silver had to go into the coinage, which was almost immediately shipped abroad to pay for her imports and the wages of the soldiers of her distant garrisons. A cynical Spanish term for the treasures from the Indies was 'rain drops', because, like water falling on to parched soil, it vanished without visible effect.

This was an illusion, of course. What the treasure gave Spain was power. And that strength increased with each discovery, conquest and exploitation of rich regions in the New World. The earliest

Spanish penetrations had been into Panama and Costa Rica, and significant gold shipments had begun from there during 1511–15. The next wealthy area to fall into Spanish hands had been Mexico, conquered by Hernán Cortés in 1519–21. The third to be invaded was Peru, by Francisco Pizarro in 1532. In the perspectives of 1579, all this seemed to have followed rapidly on the first voyage of Columbus, begun in 1492. And Columbus himself had written: 'Gold is a metal most excellent above all others and of gold treasures are formed, and he who has it makes and accomplishes whatever he wishes in the world and finally uses it to send souls into Paradise.'

Ironically, the true wealth of the Indies proved to lie in the opening of new silver mines. In 1545 the fabulous Potosí mine had opened, followed in 1548 by the discovery of comparable deposits at Zacatecas in Mexico. The production of silver became so great that, in the long term, for every ton of registered gold which was shipped home to Spain ninety tons of silver were loaded. Francis Drake knew the proportions well enough – he had the proof with him in the hold of the *Golden Hind*. These silver bars and wedges represented consignments for Panama from Chile and Peru. What he intended to do now was to head for Acapulco and pick up some of the trade coming to Panama from the north, from Costa Rica, Nicaragua, Guatemala and even Mexico itself. It would be unwise to move into the Gulf of Panama, as he could easily be trapped there; best to cut directly across the mouth of the Gulf, find a quiet spot to careen, and then carry on northwards.

So, leaking and trailing long fronds of weed from her waterline, the *Golden Hind* came to anchor off Costa Rica at the island of Caño on 16 March. On the 18th Drake found a good place to careen and from then until the 24th the *Golden Hind* was vulnerable and defenceless, guarded only by the pinnace which patrolled outside. Peru Force, however, did not reach Manta until 17 March and was so delayed by dissensions and indecision that it was 19 March before they were off Cape San Francisco, where Drake had taken San Juan de Anton's ship on 1 March. They were thus nineteen days behind, so that even if the Spaniards had taken the same direct route as Drake and avoided Panama altogether, they could not have caught him careening; although an encounter later was always possible, theoretically, if the corsair was much delayed by any prizes he might take.

It was on 17 March that a small bark owned by Rodrigo Tello sailed from Rio de la Barranca, the port for Esparza in Costa Rica. She carried a cargo of maize, honey, sarsaparilla and planks for Panama. Crew and passengers together totalled fourteen men, of whom two were skilled ocean navigators ordered by Don Martin Enriquez, Viceroy of New Spain, to go to Panama as pilots for the season's voyage to China. The most experienced was Alonso Sanchez Colchero, aged fifty; the other was Martin de Aguirre. Of the remainder, ten were Spaniards, one a Negro, and one an Indian.

Three days later, on the afternoon of 20 March, the little vessel was idling along in light airs on a calm sea off the island of Caño when a launch, well-equipped with oars and sails, came out of a cove. The men in the bark at first thought that this must be the boat of some lost vessel, full of shipwrecked men. It came towards them, moving fast under oars, and they could see that it was packed, with probably thirty men in it. Then as the distance closed, the Spaniards realised that the men formed an armed party consisting of arque-busiers, archers and shieldmen. Their first thought was that these must be Englishmen from Oxenham's expedition who had not yet been rounded up.

The English began to blow trumpets, fire shots in the air, and shout out for the Spaniards to strike sail, which they refused to do. The English then fired in earnest, wounding one of the passengers, Giuscpe de Parraces, in the face and arm with arquebus shot. At that, Rodrigo Tello surrendered.

The bark was escorted for two or three leagues into a large cove where the corsair ship was anchored. It was a high-sided vessel of at least 200 tons, most of them thought, and had mounted twelve guns of cast iron and two of bronze, all heavy pieces of between sixteen and twenty hundredweight (that is, weighing up to a ton). Colchero, who was to stay in her longer than any of the others, put the raider at 300 tons and said she carried twenty-five 'great pieces' of artillery, which she may have done if some were down on the ballast, where for a time Colchero was imprisoned.

Six men whom the English judged to be important were taken out of the bark and lodged in the *Golden Hind*. They included the two navigators, Colchero and Aguirre. The former was carrying letters from the Viceroy addressed to the authorities at Panama, to Don Gonzalo Ronquillo, the Spanish General of China, and to Judge Sandia, the Spanish Governor of the Philippines; and in addition he had with him two maps for Pacific Ocean navigation and a collection of charts for inshore work on the China route. Drake was delighted to seize the entire collection, for much of it was exactly what he required if, as was probable, he had to return by way of the Spice Islands. Da Silva testified that 'he prized these greatly and rejoiced over them, saying that he was going to take them back to his native land.'

Da Silva made an odd impression on these prisoners, as on others taken by the raider earlier. Giusepe de Parraces, the young man who had been wounded, reported that he and his companions had spoken to the man, but that he did not answer or indeed ever speak to them. 'He only looked at us and laughed to himself, and therefore we did not learn his name.' Diego de Messa, another passenger, described da Silva as being dressed in black, with a long beard. And he recalled that Colchero claimed to recognise him, saying:

> 'that this man was a Portuguese and had been married in Moguer [Colchero's home town], and that he was a brother-in-law of Anton Manzera, a citizen of Triana, near Seville. He knew that the said man had run away from Moguer because he had been guilty of an unnatural crime.'

This was the second time that da Silva had been recognised as a Portuguese and a criminal. The previous accuser had been Custodio Rodriguez, taken a month before at Payta. The identification, however, was different, for the man Rodriguez remembered had stolen a treasure and his wife was living at Sonsonate in New Spain.

Now Drake himself began talking about Sonsonate. While looking for a local beach suitable for careening the *Golden Hind*, he fell into conversation with one of his captives, Cornieles Lambert, a Flemish merchant born in Leyden but long resident in Seville before coming to Nicaragua four years before. Drake appeared apologetic and said that he really wanted to return Rodrigo Tello's bark to him, but could not do so because he did not know in what necessity he might find himself out at sea, as his ship was leaking; even if the bark had belonged to his own father instead of Tello, he could not help taking her. 'Being thus in need of going to Acapulco or some other port of New Spain for the purpose of careening,' reported Lambert, 'he inquired many times what kind of ports were Acapulco, Sonsonate and the other ports of that coast'.

This seems to have been Drake's method of making mariners

talk. He would speak to one in the hearing of others on matters both of fact and of opinion. Human nature did the rest. Particularly if a question on Spanish seafaring was put to a Flemish merchant in the hearing of Spanish seamen. What he was seeking particularly was target information. The major overhaul really required by the *Golden Hind* before he dared undertake the immense journey back to England would take weeks, probably months. It would be madness to choose a port close to the centres of Spanish power. All he could do at the island of Caño was find a suitable beach for a limited careening to remove the weed growth and perhaps check attacks by marine borers.

He chose a place and then the guns were moved out of the *Golden Hind* and placed in the bark 'in disorder', according to Lambert. The raider rose higher in the water, exposing the weed growth to the air and sunlight. The locked and bonded treasure chests containing jewels and gold were also moved out into the bark, but there was too much silver for that small craft to carry, and so it was heaped carelessly on the beach. Colchero tried to make an account of the treasure. He estimated that there were 1800 bars of silver brought out of her; ten medium-sized boxes holding silver coins ('pieces of eight'); nine small gilded boxes, very well corded, said to contain gold; and a further medium-sized chest which certainly contained gold, because Drake opened it and showed him when he made his attempt to bribe Colchero a few days later. With the raider riding light and high, and using the rise and fall of the tide, the *Golden Hind* was first laid over on one side and then on the other for the bottom planks to be cleaned and caulked. During this time she was of course totally defenceless except for the patrolling pinnace.

The careening was hastily completed in about five days, then on the evening of 24 March they left the cove and steered north along the coast in the direction from which the bark had come originally. The wounded passenger, Giusepe de Parraces, still captive in the *Golden Hind*, had an opportunity to observe the religious customs of the crew:

'The Corsair, and all his company, the Portuguese pilot, and negroes were all Lutherans. I saw them perform their Lutheran ceremonies. There was a crucifix in Rodrigo Tello's bark which they broke to pieces, trod under foot and cast into the sea. They told me and my companions that if we did not want to witness their ceremonies we could withdraw to the prow or the poop, wherever we chose; which we did. The Lutherans allowed me and the others to tell our Christian beads, as we were accustomed to do before we were taken prisoners.'

Giusepe, like all the rest, failed to realise that da Silva was a prisoner too, making the best of a bad job after more than a year in captivity.

About 29 March they were nearing Esparza, the place from which Tello's bark had sailed. Because it was more suitable for an ocean crossing, Drake intended to retain the bark – which was of about fifteen tons, according to John Drake – and to give his own prefabricated pinnace in exchange to the prisoners. They would be released with enough provisions to enable them to make the port safely. Before they got into the boat, Drake handed out safe-conducts. Giusepe testified that his copy was in English and in Drake's own handwriting, and that when he folded it over, he wrote on the outside the names of the three English captains 'who commanded the ships of which he and all his men say he is the General'. Drake explained that one of the ships (Winter's) was large, the others quite small, that they were expecting to rendezvous in this region and would be glad to have news of their flagship.

This story, which the released prisoners were bound to report when interrogated, as they surely would be, might create further confusion in the lagging Spanish pursuit. It seems as though Drake had coached his crew to tell the same story in conversation with prisoners. Being close to the truth, it would be easy to remember.

Alonso Sanchez Colchero did not receive a safe-conduct. Instead, Drake tried to recruit him as his pilot for the Pacific. Drake said that he wanted first to go to Acapulco in New Spain and then across to China, where Colchero's knowledge of the coastlines would be important. After that, he would go on to Goa in India, but he could put Colchero ashore in China or the Philippines if he wished. Excuses came tumbling out of the unfortunate Spaniard. He was not familiar with the China route. He was a poor man, with a wife and children to support; they would starve if he was so long away. This would be a terrible thing to do to him. Anyway, he was not a pilot, but only a sailor.

Drake knew from the ship's documents who and what Colchero really was. He replied that the prisoner was not to plague him with such nonsense, that he would serve even if it was against his will, and that Drake would 'hang' him if he said another word. Anyway, all that was being asked of him was to reconnoitre coastlines. Drake would attend himself to everything that concerned latitude and knowledge of the stars.

Colchero said no, he would not do it.

Drake became persuasive. It was imperative that he should be accompanied by an experienced China pilot. He would be prepared to pay proper wages. More, Colchero could have a hundred pesos in pieces of eight immediately, to send to his wife in the next day or two, so that she would be provided for during the time he was away in the *Golden Hind*.

Since Drake seemed determined, Colchero gave in – but on conditions. He wanted permission to write two letters – the first to his employer, the Viceroy of New Spain, to explain that he was being taken away in the English ship by main force; and the second a note to his wife. Drake agreed – subject to a condition of his own, that he himself would read what Colchero had written and if there was anything disadvantageous to the English, he would have Colchero hanged.

Colchero dictated his letters to Giusepe de Parraces in the presence of several Englishmen who knew Spanish. In fact, there were three letters; one to Don Martin Enriquez, the Viceroy, in Mexico, one to Judge Palacios at the port of Realejo in Nicaragua, who was asked to forward the third letter, the one to his wife and children.

When the *Golden Hind* arrived off the mouth of the Rio de la Barranca, all the prisoners except Colchero got into Drake's pinnace. They were given a keg and a half of water, a bag of flour, a little maize, and were cast off. The river from which they had begun their voyage on 17 March was two leagues – about six miles – away. As they stood in towards the shore, they saw the raider sailing on towards the next port, Realejo, taking Rodrigo Tello's boat with her.

When they neared Realejo, Drake renewed his attempt to make Colchero serve him as navigator around the world, promising him a rich reward in gold and silver and a position in England if he became a Lutheran. When the Spaniard seemed unmoved by these prospects, Drake exclaimed: 'You! you must be a devoted subject of King Philip, and a great captain!' Then he pressed a minor but immediate path to his approval. It was only a little thing, just to pilot him through the intricacies of the channel leading into Realejo, where, so he had been informed, there lay a ship in process of being fitted out for the China trade. He wanted to burn that ship. He added (according to Colchero) that he wanted also to burn the town and to seize and hang its chief official, Judge Diego Garcia de Palacios, because he was a servant of King Philip and a friend of the Viceroy.

Colchero denied ever having been in the port of Realejo; therefore, from lack of knowledge, he dared not undertake to pilot Drake in.

Drake did not believe a word of this, considering Colchero's profession, and reacted characteristically. According to Colchero's own testimony (no independent account survives), he:

'uttered many threats and promises, and offered me bribes to pilot him into the port. When the captain saw that I would not do it he gave orders that I was to be hanged. Twice they placed a rope around my neck and raised me from the ground. When they saw I was exhausted, they left me alone. When this Englishman saw he could not carry out his evil design, he continued his voyage to the port of Sonsonate. When close to the volcanoes of Guatemala, we met a frigate in which came Don Francisco de Zarate . . . '

Don Francisco de Zarate was cousin to the Duke of Medina, head of one of the greatest families in Spain, and a member of the military order of St James. On 16 April, from Realejo in Nicaragua, he wrote to the Viceroy, Don Martin Enriquez, a concise and orderly report of his encounter with an English raider twelve days before:

'I sailed out of the port of Acapulco on the twenty-third of March and navigated until Saturday, the fourth of April, on which date, half an hour before dawn, we saw, by moonlight, a ship very close to ours. Our steersman shouted that she was to get out of the way and not come alongside us. To this they made no answer, pretending to be asleep. The steersman then shouted louder, asking them where their ship hailed from.

'They answered: "From Peru" and that she was the ship "of Miguel Angel", which is the name of a well-known captain of that route. The spokesman on the ship was a Spaniard.'

It was, in fact, Colchero, obeying Drake under duress. This time, as Don Francisco had no recent knowledge of the whereabouts of Miguel Angel, the deception worked.

'The ship of the adversary carried her bark at her prow as though she were being towed. Suddenly, in a moment, she crossed our poop, ordering us "to strike sail" and shooting seven or eight arquebus shots at us.

'We thought this as much of a joke as it afterwards turned out to be serious.

'On our part there was no resistance, nor had we more than six of our men awake in the whole boat, so they entered our ship with as little risk to themselves as though they were our friends. They did no personal harm to anyone, beyond seizing the swords and keys of the passengers. Having informed themselves as to who were on board ship, they ordered me to go in their boat to where their General was – a fact that I was glad of, as it appeared to me that it gave me more time in which to recommend myself to God. But in a very short time we arrived where he was, on a very good galleon, as well mounted with artillery as any I have seen in my life.

'I found him promenading on deck and, on approaching him, I kissed his hands. He received me with a show of kindness, and took me to his cabin where he bade me be seated.'

Don Francisco reported the conversation word for word, probably with more accuracy than one might expect, for Drake's technique for dealing with important prisoners is evident once again. He began with the familiar threatening note.

'I am a friend of those who tell me the truth, but with those who do not I get out of humour. Therefore, you must tell me (for this is the best road to my favour), how much silver and gold does your ship carry?'

'None,' said Zarate.

Drake repeated what he had just said. 'How much silver and gold does your ship carry?'

'None,' replied Zarate. 'Well, only some small plates that I use myself, and some cups – that's all there is in her.'

Drake pondered this for a few moments then, apparently accepting it, changed the subject.

'Do you know the Viceroy?'

'Don Martin Enriquez? Oh, yes.'

'Is there any relative of his in your ship? Or anything belonging to him?'

'No, sir.'

'Well, it would give me a greater joy to come across him than all the gold and silver of the Indies. You would see how the words of gentlemen should be kept.'

Don Francisco made no reply to this. Presumably he was unaware of the grudge Drake and many other English seamen had against Don Martin for his actions at San Juan de Ulloa.

Drake then stood up, beckoned to Don Francisco to follow him, and led him to a cabin situated in the poop below the main deck where there was a prison the English called 'the ballast' (presumably because it was literally situated on top of the ballast layer in the bottom of the hold). The prison already had one occupant, for there was an old man at the far end.

'Sit down,' said Drake to Don Francisco. 'Here is where you'll stay.' Then, as the Spaniard was about to sit down on the ballast, Drake checked him.

'I don't want you to try it just yet. Just tell me who that man is in there.'

Don Francisco said he did not know him.

'Well, know that it is a pilot named Colchero, whom the Viceroy was sending to Panama to convey Don Goncalo to China.'

Drake had Colchero released and then they all went up on deck together. During the conversation Don Francisco learnt that it was Colchero who had hailed his ship on Drake's order. Although there were a number of Spanish speakers on board the raider, including Drake, presumably their accents were those of obvious foreigners. Don Francisco had also had an oblique lesson in Drake's power to discomfort him if he chose. The prospect, for a splendidly-dressed nobleman, of having to sit on filthy ship's ballast in all his finery would be daunting; but for a Spaniard, any Spaniard at all, it would be intolerable. Whereas an Englishman liked to be proud of his dwelling, a Spaniard made more of his appearance.

After a long conversation on deck, it was time to dine. Don Francisco testified that Drake:

'ordered me to sit next to him and began to give me food from his own plate, telling me not to grieve, that my life and property were safe. I kissed his hands for this. He asked me if I knew where there was water to be had about here, adding that he needed nothing else, and that as soon as he found some, he would give me leave to continue my journey. I did not dare to ask aught of him at that moment. Awaiting an opportunity, I begged him not to oblige me to pass the gulf of Tehuantepec again. He answered that he would see and that he would dispatch me shortly.'

Colchero's testimony buttresses that of Don Francisco. In the hold there was an 'iron cage', a cell of some kind, and it was in this prison that he had spent the night, after hailing Don Francisco's ship. Drake had questioned him about Don Francisco de Zarate, offering money for correct information. What he particularly wanted to know was, if the nobleman was a relative, servant or magistrate of the Viceroy; if so he would hang him. When Colchero denied all knowledge of Don Francisco de Zarate Drake changed his tack slightly. He said that if Colchero himself ever came before the Viceroy he was to tell him to be on his guard, because he or other Englishmen were going to burn him alive for having broken his word with John Hawkins at San Juan de Ullao. No doubt this was primarily intended to establish the corsair as an intimidating figure of whom it would be well to be afraid, but real hatred underlay it. The Viceroy had been responsible for an English rout and the deaths of many friends; and so far they had done him no harm. They had not even encountered a rich ship from Mexico which they could rob.

The following day was Sunday, ceremonial day for the *Golden Hind*, according to Don Francisco, for Drake 'dressed and decked himself very finely and had his galleon decorated with all its flags and banners.' The corsair also had all the crew cleared out of de Zarate's ship and put into Rodrigo Tello's bark so that they would all be out of the way while it was looted. At nine that morning, Drake began his inspection of the new prize, which John Drake estimated at 60 tons. De Zarate had earnestly requested him not to touch his own wardrobe, which was very fine, and Drake agreed. Before leaving for the prize, he asked de Zarate to appoint a page to come with him and point out which was Don Francisco's apparel so that it would not be touched.

Drake spent much of the day inspecting the cargo. De Zarate recorded:

'He remained until towards dusk, examining everything contained in the bales and chests. Of that which belonged to me he took but

little. Indeed he was quite courteous about it. Certain trifles of
mine having taken his fancy, he had them brought to his ship and
gave me, in exchange for them, a falchion and a small brazier of
silver, and I can assure Your Excellency that he lost nothing by
the bargain. He asked me to pardon him for taking the trifles, but
they were for his wife. He said that I could depart the next
morning, when the breeze would rise, for which I gave him
thanks.'

According to the anonymous anti-Drake witness in the *Golden
Hind*:

'The owner of this ship having very costly apparel, earnestly
entreated Drake and besought him not to take away from him his
apparel, which he promised not to do, and the gentleman gave
him a falcon of gold with a great emerald in the breast thereof for
his favourable dealing with him.'

De Zarate assumed that Drake paid his men wages and had them
under strict control, 'for when our ship was sacked, no man dared
take anything without his orders. He shows them great favour, but
punishes the least fault.' Where the crew had shares in the voyage
instead of wages, naturally the loot was shared out at once, which was
often inconvenient; but even when wages were paid, men often
made private plunder from the personal possessions or clothing of
the men they had defeated (as distinct from ship's equipment and
cargo). It was very difficult to stop this. By some usages, the contents
of de Zarate's wardrobe, and indeed all his personal possessions,
would have gone to Drake, whereas the cargo would have been
shared.

This cargo proved to be largely the fruits of the China trade
carried on by the Manila galleons which plied across the Pacific
from Acapulco in Mexico. The anti-Drake witness recorded that
she was:

'laden with linen cloth and fine China silks, and there were also
in her divers chests full of fine earthen dishes, very finely wrought,
of fine white earth brought by the Spaniards from the country of
China, which dishes the Spaniards greatly esteem. Of these dishes
Drake took four chests full from them, as also packs of fine linen
cloth and good store of taffeta and other fine silks. Drake took out
of this ship a pilot to carry him into the haven of Guatalco and

also a negro wench called Maria, which was afterwards gotten
with child between the captain and his men pirates . . . '

On Monday morning, according to de Zarate, 'he gave back to
some of the passengers who were there, their boxes, and thus
occupied himself until the hour for dinner. He ordered this to be
served as the wind was rising.' At the same time, apparently, he sent
out a call for the pilot of de Zarate's ship, who was then detained in
Rodrigo Tello's bark. He was a man of twenty-six, named Juan
Pascual, a Portuguese like da Silva; he came from the Algarve. The
first intimation he had was when Pedro Hernandez, the captain of
de Zarate's ship, began to shout: 'Juan Pascual! The general is
calling you!'

'What General?' answered Pascual.

'He of the ship!' shouted Hernandez, meaning Drake.

On entering the *Golden Hind*, almost the first man Pascual saw
was Alonso Sanchez Colchero, the pilot of Rodrigo Tello's bark, who
came from Atlixco and was well known to him. 'He came and
embraced me,' testified Pascual, 'for we knew each other, and I
asked him how he came to be here and he related how he had been
robbed; and said that the Englishmen were laden with silver and
gold, but that they killed no one.' Colchero had obviously taken
Drake's measure accurately and was still firmly refusing to pilot
the *Golden Hind* to China. Now, however, he played a ruthless trick
of his own on his fellow pilot, Juan Pascual.

They were able to speak together for a while because at the
moment when Pascual went on board they were at prayers, the
English kneeling, the others seated, and just about to dine. After
the meal, Drake looked up at Pascual and pointed out at the coast.
In far from perfect, but understandable Spanish, he asked: 'Is there
water over in that direction?

Pascual replied that he didn't know, but that there was certainly
a heavy sea running on that coast.

Don Francisco de Zarate broke in impatiently, speaking directly
to Drake: 'For the love of God, let us go on our way!'

Drake said that he would see about it, which was a term he often
employed.

Then Colchero spoke, indicating Pascual: 'This youth will take
you to where there are water and fuel, for he knows very well
where they are.'

H

Pascual was indignant. 'It's true that this man knows me, but I know nothing of latitude or navigation, and could be but a poor guide to where there are water and fuel. I don't know why you want to take me with you, for I know nothing whatever of such things.'

Drake then appeared angry and said that if Pascual didn't shut up and do what he was told, he would have him first hanged and then beheaded. He repeated this twice more, so threateningly that Don Francisco de Zarate intervened with an offer which would spare Pascual. He was prepared, he said, if Drake would release his ship and crew, to remain behind personally in the *Golden Hind* with a single servant and would himself take the Englishmen into the port of Sonsonate, which lay behind them, but where they could certainly obtain water and fuel. The corsair was not impressed. He insisted that Pascual should come with him in the *Golden Hind*, and the negress, too. Colchero, however, he would release; the Spaniard would be set free along with Don Francisco de Zarate and his crew. Stubborn as a mule, Colchero had won his battle of wills with the corsair, although at the expense of his fellow pilot.

Getting up, Drake now made a grand gesture. He told Don Francisco de Zarate that he would personally escort him back to his ship and hand her over. Zarate described how:

'He ordered his sloop to be prepared and manned with two dozen archers. He had one of the artillery men called and ordered him to carry aboard half-a-dozen firearms. This done, he told me to embark with him, as all was in readiness. I did so, and on arriving at our vessel he boarded her first and having all our sailors called together, he gave each one a handful of reals. He also gave the same to some other men who appeared to him to be the most needy . . . With this he took leave of me, and his last words were to beseech me, earnestly, to tell certain Englishmen who were in Lima [Oxenham and his companions] that I had met him on April 6th and that he was well. From this it is to be inferred that he has spies in all this realm and in Peru. He has an intense desire to return to his own country.

'This General of the Englishmen is a nephew of John Hawkins, and is the same who, about five years ago, took the port of Nombre de Dios. He is called Francisco Drac, and is a man about 35 years of age, low of stature, with a fair beard, and is one of the greatest mariners that sails the seas, both as a navigator and as a commander. His vessel is a galleon of nearly 400 tons and is a perfect sailer. She is manned with a hundred men, all of service, and of an age for warfare, and all are as practised therein as old soldiers from Italy could be. Each one takes particular pains to keep his arquebus clean. He treats them with affection, and they treat him with respect. He carried with him nine or ten cavaliers, cadets of English noblemen. These form a part of his council which he calls together for even the most trivial matter, although he takes advice from no one. But he enjoys hearing what they say and afterwards issues his orders. He has no favourite.

'The aforesaid gentlemen sit at his table, as well as a Portuguese pilot, whom he brought from England, who spoke not a word during all the time I was on board. He is served on silver dishes with gold borders and gilded garlands, in which are his arms. He carries all possible dainties and perfumed waters. He said that many of these had been given him by the Queen. None of these gentlemen took a seat or covered his head before him, until he repeatedly urged him to do so. He dines and sups to the music of viols.

'He carries trained carpenters and artisans, so as to be able to careen the ship at any time. Besides being new, the ship has a double lining. He also carries painters who paint for him pictures of the coast in its exact colours. This I was most grieved to see, for each thing is so naturally depicted that no one who guides himself according to these paintings can possibly go astray.'

The ceremonial guards of archers and arquebusiers, the formalities at mealtimes, were all an intended display. They gave the impression to the visitor that the *Golden Hind* was a bigger ship than she really was, manned by many more men than Drake really had, all formidably alert and efficient. And that, far from being a pirate, her commander had royal sanction for his raiding.

Drake certainly managed to convince Don Francisco de Zarate of this. He told him that he had sailed with five ships originally and that half of them belonged to the Queen. 'I believe this to be so for the reason that I am about to relate to your Excellency,' wrote de Zarate to the Viceroy. The nobleman then repeated the story of the execution of Thomas Doughty, as told to him by Drake. According to Drake, Doughty had thought the enterprise of passing through the Strait of Magellan too dangerous, that they would do better to return to the North Atlantic where they would be certain of capturing prizes, and that they should 'give up seeking to make new discoveries.' De Zarate went on:

'All this he told me, speaking much good about the dead man, but adding that he had not been able to act otherwise, because this was what the Queen's service demanded. He showed me the commissions that he had received from her and carried.

'I tried to ascertain whether any relatives of the dead man had remained on board. They told me that there was only one, who was one of those who ate at his table. During all this time that I was on board, which was fifty-five hours, this youth never left the ship, although all the others did so, in turn. It was not that he was left to guard me. I think that they guarded him.'

Not unnaturally, the younger Doughty had conceived an undying hatred for Drake. Apart from him, de Zarate was able to report: 'I managed to ascertain whether the General was well liked, and all said that they adored him.' If unable to read English, the Spaniard would not have known if the terms of the Queen's Commission gave the Captain-General power to execute any gentleman or mariner, and thus whether or not the killing of Doughty had been legal. However, by examining the red seal which authenticated such documents, he would be able to judge whether Drake represented England or only Drake. It was for lack of such a document that Oxenham and his companions were being treated as brigands rather than prisoners of war.

Drake's last words, as he said goodbye to Don Francisco de Zarate, were of Oxenham and the other Englishmen lying in the Inquisition prison at Lima. The probable fate of his old friends and companions had been much on his mind during the past few months, and his inability to help them, except by the force of distant threats, must have been galling. Now that the *Golden Hind* was so far from Peru and heading still further away, even the threats would lose their power. Perhaps that is why Drake had asked the Spaniard to deliver for him, if he would, what seems to have been a farewell message. As for his crew, judging by what was shortly to occur, they would clearly have enjoyed getting their hands on the inquisitors of Lima.

So, on 6 April, the two forces drew apart. The *Golden Hind*, accompanied by the bark of Rodrigo Tello acting in place of the pinnace, stood away to the north for the ports of Mexico, while Don Francisco de Zarate's ship steered south towards the nearest harbour of importance, Realejo, in Nicaragua, to report the presence of the raider. That sail was to take her ten days and it was not until 16 April that de Zarate was able to send his letter to Don Martin Enriquez.

Possibly the only prisoner to have done well out of the affair, apart from a slight soreness of the neck, was Alonso Sanchez Colchero, the Viceroy's pilot for the China Seas. He had taken money from Drake (50 pesos' worth said some, 100 pesos' worth said others) to be sent to his wife for the maintenance of his family while he was away in the Pacific guiding the Englishmen; and that money had gone off with a letter in the pinnace a week ago and was already well on its way. But his stubborn refusals had had their effect on Drake, who had released him with Don Francisco. He had even got out of the chore of piloting the corsair to Acapulco or Guatalco, which was nearer, by nudging young Juan Pascual into prominence while Drake was still undecided. That was neat! He had got the better of both an English enemy and a Portuguese friend.

Chapter 17

THE 'ATROCITY' AT GUATALCO

Mexico:
13–17 April 1579

D AY after day the sea was empty. Uninterrupted, the long
swells heaved themselves against the shore. Drake kept
closer in to the coast than prudence dictated, for fear that
a ship might slip past him. Nevertheless, a vessel commanded by
Guillermo Hernandez and carrying a great deal of money left
Guatalco in early April and got away to the south unseen, perhaps
by going far out to sea or through being cloaked by night or fog at
the vital time.

The main ports on this coast were Tehuantepec, Guatalco and
Acapulco. Drake had been told by some of the crew of de Zarate's
ship that Acapulco held war vessels and many men. The captain,
Pedro Hernandez, and two others, Juan Daca and Juan Pascual,
had agreed beforehand that this would be their story, if asked.
Juan Pascual was later to claim that by this means they had saved
Acapulco from sack. Whatever the reason, but probably because
he had learnt that the settlement was small and defenceless, Drake
was making for Guatalco, which lay between the other two rival
ports. And because he also had Pascual, a mariner with local
knowledge of the harbour approaches, to lead him in.

Drake's fixed policy of always taking a local pilot to guide him
along the Pacific coasts, and never getting rid of one before he had
found another more suitable for his purposes, made excellent
sense. It meant also that there was at all times at least one foreign
witness, in addition to da Silva, to note what occurred and to give
testimony in writing or by dictation shortly afterwards. Historically
this was valuable, as was the fact that, being foreigners, they saw
and described or were asked to describe routine customs observed
in the *Golden Hind* which her own crew found so unremarkable
that they took them for granted.

Pascual for instance, unlike the majority of Drake's prisoners,

who were questioned openly by the local bureaucracy, was interrogated in secret by the Inquisition. On behalf of that body, Friar
Andres Aguirre asked the young sailor to elaborate on the religious
customs of the Lutheran heretics, with particular reference to
any believer who might have been compromised by them. Pascual
stated that church services preceded the two main meals of the day,
at noon and in the evening; that Drake customarily led but that
occasionally another man, certainly Francis Fletcher, preached.
The sailor told the reverend father:

'Every day before sitting down to eat at midday, and before
they supped, the said Francis Drake had a table brought out,
without a cloth or table cover. He, Drake, took out a very large
book and knelt down, bareheaded, and read from the book in
the English language. All the other Englishmen whom he had
brought with him were also seated without their hats, and made
responses. Some of them held books resembling Bibles in their
hands and read in these. The said Nuño da Silva was also seated,
next to the others, bareheaded, and read a book which was like
a Bible. I do not know what book nor in what language it was,
nor was I at any time present at the said ceremonies because, as
soon as the table was brought, I understood its purpose and went
to the prow of the ship. From there I saw what happened.

'I did not hear Nuño da Silva make responses at any particular
time, but I saw him bareheaded like the rest, whenever the
ceremonies were performed. Several times, when the ceremonies
were not being performed, I saw Nuño da Silva reading a book
which resembled a Book of Hours, but I don't know whether
it was the book he read during the ceremonies, or not. I did not
see or hear of any other prisoner taking part in the ceremonies.
On the contrary, all who could manage to do so withdrew
themselves, dissemblingly, so that the Englishmen should not
hear or see them doing so.

'Sometimes, one of the Englishmen, whom all appeared to
respect, preached to them in the English tongue, and was listened
to attentively; and I saw Nuño da Silva, with the others, at those
sermons.

'And I want to add, that during the whole time I was a prisoner
in the power of Francis Drake, it was Lent; and to say, that
Francis Drake and all the people from his country who

accompanied him, always ate meat; and that during the term of
my imprisonment, Francis Drake obliged me, and Nuño da Silva,
and all the other prisoners who were in his ship, to eat at his
table. And all ate meat for he gave us nothing to eat besides
biscuit, and meat, and wine.'

Questioned regarding any others, apart from Englishmen, who
might have been thought tainted by Lutheranism, Pascual could
think only of two negroes:

'One of the latter spoke Spanish, and also English, and everyone
said that the Englishman had brought him from England. The
other one also spoke Spanish, and told me so, and that he had
been seized at sea. I don't remember which of these two negroes
told me that he had made a contract with Francis Drake.'

This meant that the man had been freely enlisted for wages, on
the same basis as the native English in the crew.

Friar Andres Aguirre, who took this deposition, did so as a
passing duty; he was about to leave Mexico for China. Later,
Pascual was further examined by a most important person, the
Illustrious and Reverend Lord Don Alonso Garcia de Avalos,
Bishop of La Plata, of the Government of His Majesty, authorised
Inquisitor, to give his titles in full. Pascual volunteered that he had
forgotten some matters of importance when questioned by the
friar, and that these would have a bearing on the atrocities which
the English had committed in Guatalco.

Pascual's earlier deposition had shown the ship's routine of the
raider as being orderly, established, and religious (although here-
tically Lutheran in tone); even negroes, who might be thought of as
slaves, turned out to be under contract. The prisoners had been
served exactly the same food and drink as Drake himself; that it
happened to be Lent, and that the English may have had no fish,
was mere mischance, not a deliberate flouting of their religion. Nor
had the prisoners been forced to attend Lutheran services; they
were allowed to go to the prow to avoid any contamination.

For the Lord Bishop, however, after some prodding, Pascual
was able to produce evidence of a sacrilegious act:

'While we were out at sea I saw the boatswain of Francis Drake's
ship, whose name I don't know, take a small sacred image that
was on a tablet, and begin to strike blows with it. I begged him

not to break it, but to give it to me. The boatswain asked: "What do you want it for?" I answered: "Give it to me to give away to some boy." The boatswain said of the image: "This is no good!" and broke it into pieces against a beam of the ship.'

Having seen for himself what had been done in Guatalco, the Bishop cannot have been much impressed. Seeking something new, he questioned the Portuguese as to whether or not he had understood anything of the Lutheran rites: what were the prayers, for instance? what was preached in the sermons? by Drake especially?

Pascual was prepared to testify that Drake's favourite oath was: 'By God's faith.' That he sometimes said: 'If God wills, I will get out of this.' That he had heard him boast: 'There is no one in this sea that would dare to do me harm; I suffice for as many ships as there are in this sea.' And that he had predicted: 'Within eight months I will be in my own country.'

The Bishop then asked what sort of treatment, or physical force, was it that the Englishman used towards his prisoners? Pascual replied:

'I did not see Francis Drake do any harm to anyone. On the contrary, he made us eat at his table, and carried Nuño da Silva with him unconfined, and spoke to him in a friendly manner, although I did not understand what was said, for some of it was in English.'

When asked at once why he, Pascual, had helped Drake obtain water and fuel, if no force was used to make him give the information? the Portuguese was in a corner:

'It was because he said that he would cut our heads off, and that he had killed many others, and that it would be nothing to him to kill us all. On his ship, his men trembled before him and when he paced the deck they passed before him trembling, with their hats in hand, bowing to the ground.'

It was on 12 April that the *Golden Hind* had sighted a fire on land, Guatalco being nine leagues away, but as the wind was faint, Drake had anchored for the night. Pascual had pointed to the shore and said: 'There, I think, for certain, water can be had if one goes to fetch it.' Drake had replied merely that 'he would see'. Pascual said that he had intended to escape now, if he could, as he was familiar with this coast. But there had been no opportunity and next morning, when they arrived off the port, they could see the masts and spars of a ship lying inside the harbour. The prospect of another prize to rob had brought Drake in.

Guatalco was a Spanish corruption of the Chichimec Indian word *Coatolco*, signifying 'the Place of the Serpent'. It had been conquered more than half a century before by Pedro de Alvarado, a lieutenant of Hernán Cortés. The port, which was distant three leagues from the town, now handled all Spanish goods consigned to Honduras and Peru. The chief citizens of the district included the Governor, Bernardino Lopez; the Vicar, Simon de Miranda; the factor of the port, Francisco Gomez Rengifo; and the Alcalde Mayor, or chief executive, Gaspar de Vargas. The latter was the author already of a local history of the region and was shortly to record officially the events of Holy Week 1579. His letters were written within hours, sometimes minutes, of the events they described.

At eight o'clock on the morning of Holy Monday, 13 April, Gaspar de Vargas was told by some sailors from the ship of Juan de Madrid that two strange sails were approaching the harbour entrance. Their own ship was already loaded with a cargo for Sonsonate and was due to leave on Wednesday. The new arrivals would require supplies, no doubt, and in any case would have to be documented: that was his responsibility, Of the two vessels now approaching the headland, one appeared to be large, the other small. It looked as though the former was a ship from Peru which they were expecting. The small vessel was a bark of the type used on the coast for pearl-fishing. Vargas continued:

> 'Two hours later, at about ten o'clock, both ships began to enter the port abreast, and it became apparent that the larger one was, as everyone says, of more than 300 tons. The other one also appeared to be larger than first thought. They entered the port with great determination and the larger ship cast anchor.'

A number of people were now watching, including the crew and passengers of Juan de Madrid's ship, as well as the Governor, Lopez; the factor, Rengifo; and the Vicar, Simon de Miranda. Lopez heard some people suggest that this was the fleet of Don Gregorio Ronquillo, the Governor of the Islands of the West, who was expected from China.

The larger vessel lowered a boat, filled with men, who began to row for Juan de Madrid's ship. The bark also put out sweeps and accompanied it. After inspecting the freighter, both small craft headed for the shore, their oars rising and falling in the most determined way. Now why, in this heat, should anyone be as energetic as that? It was this strange behaviour which prompted feelings of alarm among a few of the watchers.

Seeing that de Vargas was innocently going down to the shore to meet the approaching craft, a Genoese sailor named Bartolomé Guerzo tried to stop him, shouting 'The English! The English!'

Alarmed, the Spaniards ran back to their houses along the waterfront to collect what weapons they could find. Then they began, under de Vargas, to rally on the square. There were not very many of them and they were ill-armed. The two English craft beached, and it could be seen that the occupants were fighting men equipped with arquebuses, bows and shields. Miranda, the Vicar, thought they numbered about thirty or forty; the Governor was to give an impossibly high estimate of sixty or seventy.

As the bowmen and shieldmen began to disembark, the arquebusiers in the ship's boat gave covering fire which kept the Spaniards from the beach at the critical moment. The assault force began to splash through the water for the shore. A gun fired from the bark behind them, and then another. With an appalling screech the shot howled over the heads of the Spaniards rallying round de Vargas at the square. The effect was remarkable. 'Not a person remained with me,' reported the Alcalde. 'Therefore I retired, little by little, until I reached the wood at about 50 or 100 paces from the church, and there I stayed for the space of three or four hours during which the Englishmen sacked the port.'

From the shelter of the wood, which covered a hillside, the Spaniards who had escaped fired a few arquebus shots at the English, but were unable to prevent them breaking into the houses and the church also, and carrying away prisoners. De Vargas saw three men hurried down the beach towards the boats and was close enough to recognise Vicar Miranda and factor Rengifo. The third man was a visitor, Judge Gutierrez de Miranda, a relative of the Vicar, Simon de Miranda.

Also sheltering in the wood was the Lieutenant-Governor, Bernardino Lopez, and he was close enough to see in detail the looting of the church. The most conspicuous figure among the English there was 'a tall hunchbacked Lutheran who was taking down the bell from the belfry'. Others were removing the vestments and the gold and silver vessels used for daily service. It was hot work in that climate and the English had taken the spare altarcloths and were using them as sweat rags to mop their streaming faces.

The factor, Francisco Gomez Rengifo, was seized in his own house, which included a store for valuable cargoes in transit. He deposed:

'From my home they robbed everything it contained belonging to me and to others, which amounted to about 7,000 pesos in reals, in silver and gold, and clothing.'

'The sacred images that were at the head of my bed and on my writing table were broken in pieces. The boatswain of the Englishman's ship took a crucifix which belonged to me, and seizing it by the feet struck its head against a table, breaking it to pieces, and saying:

"Here it is; here you go!"

'Seeing by my face that I was grieved, the boatswain said:

"You ought indeed to be grieved, for you are not Christians but idolaters, who adore sticks and stones."

'I do not know this boatswain's name. He was small, with a scant, fair beard and his face was pitted with pockmarks. He was the first to lay hands on me to take me to the ship, saying that I was "to come along" and that the Captain was "a good man".

'When on board the ship the boatswain approached Simon de Miranda, the Vicar of the port, and detached from the rosary he wore around his neck a gold image of Our Lady of the Rosary. On removing it from the rosary, the boatswain said:

"Why do you wear this? This is no good."

'And saying this, he placed the medal between his teeth and bit it, making a show of great anger. Then he took the medal in his hand, and made a gesture as though he were about to cast it into the sea. I don't know whether he threw it in or not.'

In his own deposition, Miranda did not mention this incident. He stated merely that the three Spaniards were guarded until Drake came out of his cabin where he had been sleeping or resting.

'When he came out, he told us we were not to be in fear of our lives, and that our lives would be protected as well as his own. He then had us taken below deck and placed four soldiers to guard us. After that, he went ashore with his men and plundered the whole port.'

The English versions of the affair, all brief, do not mesh very well with the Spanish accounts; both appear to be giving an incomplete story and there were some misapprehensions. The anonymous narrator in the *Golden Hind* tells how Drake, having carried out his routine ploy of pretending to be a Spaniard, entered the harbour without any alarm being given, and then at once 'hoisted out his boat and set about 20 men on land, for he knew by his pilot (Pascual) that there were not above seventeen Spaniards in the town'. Naturally, Pascual did not include this item in his deposition. As soon as the twenty well-armed men had landed, the anonymous narrator continued:

'They went to the town house, where they found a judge sitting in judgement, being associated with two other officers, upon three negroes who had conspired the burning of the town, and took the prisoners and the judges and brought them all on shipboard together.'

The capture of a court in session made a good story of course, and there is no corroboration from the Spanish side, On the other hand, they did capture Gutierrez de Miranda, who was a judge, plus two other officials, the Vicar and the factor. The Spaniards do not mention the three negro prisoners who were said to be before the court, whereas the English accounts are explicit: the negroes did not want to be handed back to the Spaniards; two asked to stay on board ship, the other wanted to go ashore and vanish into the woods. He was allowed to do this, and the others were allowed to stay on the *Golden Hind*. For the English, the story would be a good tale for the telling; for the Spanish authorities it would be humiliating, if true.

At one point only is there exact agreement. There is no doubt that the factor, as he said, lost a lot of money, his own and that of other people which had been entrusted to him. 'Drake's men rifled the town,' wrote the anonymous witness, 'and they found in one house a great pot, of the quantity of a bushell, full of royals of plate, which they brought away on board with them'. Some of this money belonged to merchants, one of whom was an Englishman, John Chilton, who had been in Mexico since 1568. He lost about 1000 ducats to his countrymen.

Apparently someone tried to escape from the factor's house and was caught. 'Here one of Drake's men, whose name was Tom

Moone, took a Spanish gentleman as he was flying out of town, and
rifling him he found a chain of gold about him, which Moone took
from him, and what else he had worth the taking, and so let him
go,' wrote the anonymous witness. Possibly Moone was the small,
pock-marked man with the fair beard who laid hands on the factor,
Rengifo, and smashed the crucifix in his bedroom. This incident,
and others like it, are not mentioned in the English accounts, not
even by the anonymous witness who regarded Drake and all his
crew as having acted like pirates in many of the ports they entered.
However, there is no reason to doubt the truth of Rengifo's narrative; and every reason to believe it.

With the benefit of an early start and scant resistance, it did
not take Drake long to plunder the few buildings in the little port.
He returned in time for an evening meal with his Spanish prisoners,
the two Mirandas and Rengifo, who found meat, pork and chicken
set before them. As it was Holy Week, the Vicar refused the meat
but ate the fish which was put before him instead. 'On this and the
following day,' the Vicar was to depose:

> 'the said Francis Drake had a large book brought to him and read
> it for some time. He said it was to them what the Bible is to us.
> It contained many illuminated pictures of the Lutherans who had
> been burnt in Spain. He spoke much evil of the Supreme Pontiff
> and said that he who would live six years longer would see what
> would happen, for not a friar was to remain alive. He also said:
> "How can it be tolerated that a prince or a monarch is to kiss the
> foot of the Pope? This is a swindle. Saint Peter did not act thus."
>
> 'He also expressed his abomination of the Pope in other words
> of great audacity. A certain Nuño da Silva, a Portuguese whom
> the said Francis Drake carried with him, held much intimate
> conversation with the said Englishman, who caressed him,
> treated him very well, and had him seated at his table. Both
> spoke in the English language and thus one could not understand
> what they were saying. When they prayed, the Portuguese
> prayed with them . . . there was no apparent difference between
> them, and he seemed to be one of them. The only difference was
> in his person and aspect, for he was small and the said Englishman
> were tall and ruddy complexioned.'

The factor, Rengifo, actually thought he knew one of the Englishmen; and that the man had been in Guatalco five or six years ago,

having previously been in service with the Viceroy himself as a pastry cook. There was a William Coke serving in the *Golden Hind*, and this could have been the same man as a William Cook who, confusingly, was a cook under John Hawkins and fell into Spanish hands in 1569, subsequently being employed by the Viceroy of New Spain.

There was also a group of three or four sailors who wore a different style of dress from that of the English, whom Rengifo felt could not be English. The Portuguese youth, Pascual, confirmed it, adding: 'How is it that you don't recognise them? Over there in the port of Guatalco they used to associate with our men.' At that, Rengifo remembered where he had seen them before. Recalling faces after a lapse of years is an uncertain business, but Drake might have recruited some of his crew from men who had experience of the parts of the world to which he was going.

The factor got into an argument with Drake about religion. This sprang from his curiosity about the Bible-like book which the corsair used at the mealtime services. It was probably *Actes and Monuments* by John Foxe, often spoken of as the *Book of Martyrs*. Three editions had already been published, approved by the Church. Drake and the author were friends, so the corsair may have been particularly touchy if he thought the work's authority was being questioned. The service began quietly, however. Rengifo deposed:

'Francis Drake had a table placed on deck at the poop of the vessel, and, at its head, on the floor, a small box and an embroidered cushion. He then sent for a book of the size of the *Lives of the Saints* and when all this was in place he struck the table twice with the palm of his hand. Then, immediately, nine Englishmen, with nine small books of the size of a breviary, joined him and seated themselves around him and the table. Then Francis Drake crossed his hands and, kneeling on the cushion and small box, lifted his eyes to heaven and remained in that attitude for about a quarter of an hour.

'He then said to me and to the other prisoners. that if we wanted to recite the psalms according to his mode, we could stay; but if not, that we could go to the prow. As we stood up to go to the prow, he spoke again, saying that we were to "keep quiet". He then began reading the psalms in the English language of which I understood nothing whatever.

'This act lasted about an hour. Then they brought four viols, and made lamentations and sang together, with the accompaniment of the stringed instruments. I could not understand what they sang. Immediately afterwards Drake ordered a boy, whom he had brought as a page, to come forward and dance in the English fashion.'

Drake then turned to Rengifo, whose attention had wandered during the service to the volume, resembling a Bible, which lay on the table, and asked him why he had been looking at it so long. The factor had actually been trying to read it to ascertain whether or not it contained heresy, but he could hardly tell Drake that.

'I was just looking at it to see if I could understand the meaning of the numerals at the front. Do they indicate the prayers you say?'

Drake looked angry and did not reply. Then, after a moment or two, he reached out for the book, which was lying shut on the table.

'That book is a very good book.'

He opened the volume at a page where a picture showed a man tied to a stake, praying, and being burnt alive.

'Look. Here you can see those who were martyred in Castile.'

He flicked the pages until he came to another picture, probably that captioned: 'Emperours kissing the Pope's Feete'. This picture, said Drake, depicted the astounding arrogance of the Supreme Pontiff. It seemed to Rengifo, or so he deposed, 'that Francis Drake did not think rightly about all this'.

The corsair then explained exactly what he thought, just as if he had caught some hint of scepticism in the reactions of his prisoner:

'You will be saying now, this man is a devil, who robs by day and prays at night in public. This is what I do. But it is just as when King Philip gives a very large written document to your Viceroy, Don Martin Enriquez, telling him what he is to do and how he is to govern. So the Queen, my Sovereign Lady, has ordered me to come to these parts. It is thus that I am acting, and if it is wrong it is she who knows best and I am not to be blamed for anything whatsoever. But I do regret to possess myself of anything that does not belong exclusively to King Philip or to Don Martin Enriquez, for it grieves me that their vassals should be paying for them. But I am not going to stop until I have collected the two millions that my cousin John Hawkins lost, at the least, at San Juan de Ulloa.'

Perhaps a gunner, hurling death into a town from a distance, might not feel the need to apologise to his victims or to differentiate nicely between the possessions of the State and those of private individuals. Robbing people directly was likely to make almost anyone (except a pirate) shamefaced; and even if it could all be thought of as rough justice for wrongs done to Englishmen in the past, the compensation was undoubtedly erratic.

As so often with a Drake set-speech, however, there was probably policy behind it. If they wished, the Spaniards in the port could show him where water was to be obtained and could allow him to refill his barrels unmolested. That was the prime need of the moment, and he wanted to negotiate, using one of the captured Spanish officials as go-between. Meanwhile they were led down to the cells and locked up for the night, with guards posted outside.

Gaspar de Vargas, the Alcalde Mayor, had spent the day more actively and was indeed probably the reason why Drake thought it necessary to negotiate rather than take. He had had the distinction of being probably the only Spaniard to leave the town at a slow walk, following behind the main body, which had run up the hill for the shelter of the trees, as soon as the first cannon shots had been fired in their direction. Once in comparative safety, he had set about mustering a small but reliable force of a few men only and with them had gone back into the town. The English had reacted very quickly, however, in an attempt to take more prisoners; so, for the second time that day, de Vargas retreated. At dusk he came down into the port again, mainly to get information, because he still had no idea who the corsairs were. Some sailors off Juan de Madrid's ship told him that they thought the name of the corsair's pilot was Morera. A sick Indian, who had remained in the port all the time, had recognised one or two of the corsairs as men who had been in Guatalco before, as sailors.

Gaspar de Vargas then made his way three leagues inland to the town of Guatalco, from where it would be possible to send off a dispatch to Mexico City, for the Viceroy, and a copy to Acapulco, a hundred leagues to the north, which might well be the next Spanish settlement to be attacked. He arrived at ten o'clock that night and as soon as he had completed the message dispatched a Spaniard to Acapulco: 'Even if he has to kill horses in doing so, he should reach that port before the ship, so that the necessary precautions can be taken.'

The message for the Viceroy would take longer, a week or more. De Vargas suggested that four hundred soldiers should be raised and embarked in two ships, with whatever ordnance was available. He had been told that the corsair's vessel had only eight or nine guns and that 'the ship is so low in the water that she appears as though she must be laden with gold, silver and merchandise.' For this reason, it was suspected that the corsair might have intercepted and plundered the ships of Don Francisco de Zarate and Sebastian Ruiz which had recently left Guatalco bound south. All the Alcalde's conjectures were reasonable, and some were accurate. Much fuller information became available to him next day, Tuesday, 14 April, because at five in the afternoon Drake released his prisoners, the watering operation having been completed.

The factor had been nagging at Drake all day. Whereas the average age of the Spanish officials in the port was about fifty (de Vargas at fifty-five was the oldest), Rengifo was only thirty-five and, as he kept reminding Drake, had a wife and children. The corsair had taken from him all he possessed. Could he not let him go ashore now? Drake only grunted that 'he would do so when he had taken in water'.

When the casks, refilled, were back on board, Rengifo tried again: 'Now that water has been obtained, do send me ashore.' Drake was using his prisoners as hostages in the negotiations, but he now said that they could all go ashore, if they promised to return. The boat was just about to come for them.

Rengifo took heart and made a last request.

'I beg your Lordship to return to me some of the biscuit and wine which were taken from my house. Give me a hundredweight of biscuit and one earthen jar of wine, so that we shan't die of hunger on land. For the Indians have all fled to the woods, and we won't find a maize-cake to eat.'

Francis Drake put on a 'merry countenance' and said:

'I like that!'

He considered a moment, and then went on:

'I can't give you a hundredweight of biscuit. Instead, I'll give you two bags of flour, two earthen jars of wine, one of oil, and two loaves of sugar. I'll have it all sent ashore for you.'

The three men got into the boat and later all the items which Drake had promised him were brought ashore separately by Nuño da Silva.

When they got ashore Rengifo contacted the Lieutenant-Governor of the region, Bernardino Lopez, who apparently was still hiding out on the wooded hill and had not ventured into town. According to Lopez, Rengifo said to him:

'Francis Drake is a man with whom one can talk without fear. He has given me his word not to harm anyone. It would be a good thing if you would go and speak to him. You could ask him not to burn the ship or the merchandise in her; also, not to burn the port, the church and the houses.'

A governor would make a better hostage than a factor, so, rightly, Lopez was cautious. Before making up his mind, he went to look at the looted church, which he had not yet seen. This did not convey a favourable impression of Drake and his men. Indeed, Rengifo, who had already looked inside, because the building and its contents were part of his official responsibilities, 'had been filled with sorrow' at the sight and had not gone further than the door.

Now Lopez went there, too:

'I saw the picture of the Mother of God, which was placed on the altar, broken into pieces and appearing to have been cut many times with a knife. The crosses that were there were also broken into pieces, and all the hosts from the box in which the unconsecrated wafers are kept were strewn on the floor and trampled on. With a bundle of twine I had on me I collected these wafers and put them back in the box.'

Then he went to look for the factor again and, after a long talk, they decided to take the risk of visiting the Lutheran heretic in his ship; but they would go after dining on Wednesday, so as not to have to eat with him. He ate meat, although it was Holy Week, when they were not supposed to, and that might lead to an undiplomatic incident.

Gaspar de Vargas quickly – rather too quickly – questioned the released prisoners for basic facts to include in a report for the Viceroy of New Spain, which he intended to write and dispatch this same day. On their evidence, Drake was described as a 'man of medium height, with a red beard shading into white, and aged 30 years'. The corsair claimed to have set out with six galleons and to have taken forty vessels, large and small; no more than four of those ships which he had met, had escaped him, he said. His own vessel was a 'strong, leaded ship, of two sheaths, of 300 tons, carrying a great quantity of bronze and iron artillery'. Did this mean, as it implied, a hull planked inside and out and with the outer skin being covered by a thin sheet of lead for protection against marine borers? Unfortunately, there are too many mistakes in the report, cheek-by-jowl with exact statements, to take this as more than being perhaps a possible indication of how the *Golden Hind* was prepared for the ravages of the Tropics.

De Vargas went on to state that the corsair's crew numbered 150 sailors and soldiers, much skilled in warfare, and very well armed, especially with incendiary devices for use against shipping; virtually all Drake's prisoners remarked on these and they seem to have been a novelty to Spaniards serving on the Pacific coasts. As usual, Drake personally had conducted his prisoners over the ship and pointed out the great variety of armament and ammunition. If he was hoping that these Spaniards would later spread the gospel that the raider was too formidable a craft to be engaged lightly, he succeeded. It was not in his interest to fight and thereby risk damage tens of thousands of miles from a friendly dockyard.

He also spread the story that he expected to meet the other five ships of his armada shortly, since it was not long before that they had been dispersed in a storm off Peru. On the other hand, he made no secret of how successful he had been:

'The ship is laden with bars of silver and a great quantity of gold, jewels and valuable ornaments, of silk and linens and other things of much value – all of which he displayed, in a grandiose way, to the prisoners. The plunder is worth more than a million. The General said so himself, to appear important.

'He carries with him a Portuguese pilot who is very skilful. It seems that it is he who governs and directs this Armada. This Portuguese speaks the English language as though it were his own and he is the General's all in all.

'Francis Drake is so boastful of himself as a mariner and man of learning that he told them that there was no one in the whole world who understood the art [of navigation] better than he. From what the prisoners saw of him during their two days' imprisonment, they judge that he must be a good mariner. He also told them that, since he had left his country he had navigated 7,000 leagues and that, to return thither, he would have to sail as many more.

'He told them that he had resolved to go to Acapulco and to burn and destroy that town and all ships there, for none could escape him. The English were resolved on this policy and would henceforth pursue it with all their might. With arrogance, he said that it was lucky for the prisoners that no soldier of his had been killed. If a single one had been killed he would not have left a man alive and would have destroyed the port. He states publicly that the warfare he is carrying on is a just one, for which he has a licence from his Queen; also other absurdities on this subject.

'Before releasing the prisoners he demanded from them that tomorrow Juan Gomez, the captain of Juan de Madrid's ship, which is laden and at anchor, is to give him all the wood he requires for fuel – if not, he threatened that he would burn the ship, laden as she was. He has kept guards in her. He ordered Juan Gomez to go and see him and gave him his word that he would not receive any harm. It is not known whether Juan Gomez will dare to go and see him because he suspects that Francis Drake needs him to serve as pilot. I have advised Gomez to supply Francis Drake with all the fuel that he can get, but not to go on Drake's ship.'

A Spanish negotiating party, led by Governor Lopez, went on board the *Golden Hind* on Wednesday, instead of Gomez. Rengifo was as good as his word, and came as well. They were accompanied by Juan Reyes, a tailor, and by a soldier and two sailors. As most of them had not been on board before, Drake gave them the usual grand tour of his ship, with emphasis on the armament, the ammunition, and the silver ballast. The Governor rather bitterly, noted that a tall Englishman was wearing a chasuble taken from the church and that the bell mounted by the ship's pump in the hold looked familiar; he was told that it now served the corsairs as a call to man the pump.

Drake was extremely affable, offering them dinner. On behalf of all the Spaniards, the Governor declined the invitation. 'We kiss your Lordship's hands, but we have already dined on shore.' Drake then had refreshments and drinks brought out and passed round; these they could hardly refuse. After a glass of wine, the Governor nerved himself for his task.

'What we have really come for is to entreat your Lordship to have mercy on us,' he told Drake. 'You have taken whatever you wished from our port and met with no opposition. The ship lying at anchor contains neither gold nor silver, but only local country goods belonging to poor men. I know this, because I saw it embarked myself. We beg your Lordship to think it over and content yourself with what you have already and not take more from poor men.'

Drake's answer was brief. 'The pilot of that ship is to present himself. If he comes and speaks to me, all will be well. If not . . .' The corsair said no more, but put a hand to his throat, apparently implying a hanging.

They were then ushered to the ship's side and Drake's last words were an invitation to dine with him next day, which was Holy Thursday. 16 April, when 'he would make it right with them all'.

The Spaniards were not lured by the corsair's offer to see them all right. They 'decided that they would not look upon his face again, and if he sent a boat for them, as agreed, he was to be told that the Port Alcalde had placed a severe penalty on those who went to his ship.'

On board the *Golden Hind* the guns were being dismounted and taken below, the gunport lids slammed down and caulked tight, as if a great ocean journey was in prospect. On Tuesday, Juan Pascual had been released along with the three captured Spaniards from Guatalco. Now, (not counting the negro refugees) no foreigners remained, except Nuño da Silva. On the morning of Thursday, 16 April, a boat took da Silva and a large sea chest containing his belongings from the *Golden Hind* over to the ship of Juan de Madrid, and left him there. Da Silva cried out continually to be taken off.

At three o'clock that afternoon, in light airs, the *Golden Hind* sailed from Guatalco. When the inhabitants of the port looked out of their windows at dawn on Friday, 17 April, the English ship was a speck far out on the sea.

Chapter 18

'BY FAIR OR FOUL MEANS'

In New Spain and Peru:
April–July 1579

IN an unsigned memorandum written by someone in the *Golden Hind*, occurs a line regarding da Silva: 'The poor man very unwilling to be left to the Spaniard for a prey.' Undoubtedly, this was true. His log entries end in a scrawl, indicating great distress. And no wonder. He was doubly in peril: from the Spanish civil authorities for having aided a corsair in his robberies; from the religious organisation for having assisted a heretic and having seemed to partake in Lutheran rites.

After being brought ashore, together with his belongings, from the crippled ship of Juan de Madrid (Drake had not left her in a fit state to pursue him), Nuño da Silva was questioned at length by Gaspar de Vargas for a report intended for the Viceroy in Mexico City. When he read it, about twelve days later, Don Martin Enriquez became extremely suspicious. Why had this expert navigator been left behind just when the corsair would have most need of him? Was it a plot by Drake? Was da Silva intended to be a spy in New Spain for the English? Eagerly, the Viceroy awaited the arrival of the man himself. 'By fair or foul means,' he confided to his colleague, the Viceroy of Peru, 'I shall manage to make a minute inquiry about this voyage and the Corsair's design in leaving him behind.'

By then, more boatloads of distressed seafarers had come ashore with their tales of an English raider being on the coast. On 29 March Captain Juan Solano wrote from Esparza in Costa Rica to the Licentiate Valverde of Guatemala that thirteen Spaniards had arrived that day in a launch given to them by the corsair; they had lost their own ship and nearly everything they owned, and were feeling very depressed. These were the crew and passengers of Rodrigo Tello's bark from which Colchero had been taken.

It was not until 6 April that the news reached Realejo in Guatemala, but by the following day the senior official, Licentiate Diego

Garcia de Palacios, was able to report to Valverde that he was building a small fort on the estuary and laying a chain-boom to block the river to ships. Even the main buildings of the port were of wood, and Palacios was afraid that he might be burnt out of his positions. 'My hopes are in God,' he wrote on 7 April, 'that I may be able to defend this building unto death, with the aid of the people of this province whom I am expecting, and with the men who are here.'

On 11 April Palacios received a parcel of letters from Panama containing the encouraging news that 'the Viceroy of Peru had promptly sent ships and men-of-war to punish the audacity of that Corsair'. Eager to join in the hunt, Palacios ordered a bark to be converted into a brigantine, so that she would be fast enough for scouting and reporting. Four days later, on 15 April, she was almost ready for her new role, when a shipload of newly-plucked Spaniards arrived. It was the vessel of Don Francisco de Zarate, which Drake had plundered and then released on 6 April. In her was the pilot Colchero, whom Drake had taken from Rodrigo Tello's bark in the hope that he would help him navigate the China route. There was no doubt that when last seen the corsair was heading north, and very probably he would eventually cross over to China.

Palacios closely questioned Colchero, an expert pilot for that route, and was even more encouraged by what he learnt. On 16 April he forwarded a copy of Colchero's deposition and other useful operational information to Peru Force at Panama:

> 'Through it you will be informed about the route this enemy has taken, and know that, if he be pursued, he cannot escape, even although he has the advantage of a long start. His vessel, on account of the long voyage, her great weight and the storms she has suffered, is in urgent need of careening.'

Palacios added that in the state that Colchero said she was, the raider could not risk an ocean crossing. She would be found eventually in some out-of-the-way haven north of New Spain, careened and helpless. One of the ocean-going ships from China had arrived at Acapulco, he heard; this was capacious enough to embark many soldiers, and could be used against the corsair also. 'With your valour and diligence,' he wrote, 'this enterprise will have so good a result that these enemies will get what they deserve'.

The matter was not quite so easy as Palacios thought, for in Drake the Spaniards were dealing with a a real professional, who was to act on the assumption that the pursuit would be conducted on equally efficient lines. Having entered Guatalco on 13 April, he had left on the 16th, the same day that Palacios sent news to Panama of where he had been on 6 April, ten days before. And then he vanished.

Although neither of them knew it, Peru Force also had moved on 13 April. As the *Golden Hind* was coming in to Guatalco, far to the south the *Capitana* and *Almiranta* of the Armada of Peru were coming out of Perico, the port of Panama. With them went a third vessel, the ship of San Juan de Anton, freed by Drake and now fitted out to fight under Canales, a relative of one of the royal officials at Panama. The five guns collected by Frias Trejo had been been put into them. Once they had cleared the harbour, all three ships turned away to the south, in exactly the opposite direction to that taken by Drake.

After less than five days the *Capitana*, in which Pedro Sarmiento was sailing, lost contact with her consorts. On 3 May the *Capitana* reached Point Santa Elena, where news was received that three English ships were pillaging the coast near Arica. Shortly after, the Spaniards sighted topsails, which they took to be the English fleet heading north; after preparing to fight, they discovered that these ships were the *Almiranta* and the ship of San Juan de Anton. Off Mancora they learned from a passing bark that the story about the English ships was as false as a similar tale they had heard while still in Panama.

On 12 June they put into the port of Santa, where they stayed until the 30th. While there, they received a letter from Panama dated 8 May which told them where Drake had been between 23 and 28 March – that is, careening at the isle of Caño, and quite helpless because the guns had been taken out of the *Golden Hind*. The letter contained a blistering reproof to General Don Luis de Toledo, Camp Master Pedro de Arana and Chief Pilot Miguel Angel – the trio who had preferred dawdling along in the Gulf of Panama to the policy of crossing direct from Manta towards Nicaragua, advocated by Pedro Sarmiento and Diego de Frias Trejo. Even they now understood what an error that had been, although the people at Panama were also in the wrong for letting the force go south to Peru instead of north for Nicaragua.

The Viceroy had to be contacted for his decision as to what the fleet should do now and the order was that, as the corsair must be at least 2000 leagues away from them, the two Peru ships should return to Lima and the Panama ship to Panama. The *Capitana* and the *Almiranta* left Santa on 1 July and arrived at Lima on 12 July. A few days later they received the latest news of Drake, which was that the corsair had robbed the ship of Don Francisco de Zarate off the volcanoes of Guatemala on 4 April and then made off north for Acapulco. The report was therefore more than three months out of date and partly misleading. True, Drake had told his prisoners that he was going to Acapulco, but he never actually went near that port.

More alarming perhaps than slow communications was evidence in the letter from Panama that the 'experts' there did not understand conditions on the coasts of Nicaragua, Guatemala and New Spain. They were convinced that Drake must winter somewhere on those coasts but they were mistaken as to which months were those of winter and which were summer, wrote Sarmiento. Summer was March to September up there, with westerly winds north of 43° at Cape Mendocino.

'A man like Francis, who knew all this, would not wish to lose time, nor risk his life and his booty. Therefore I have always openly declared that during the whole months of August and September this Corsair will be on his return voyage to England by the uppermost point of La Florida.'

By this, Sarmiento seemed to mean a return by the theoretical Strait of Anian. But if the route taken was that by China, he added, then the season for sailing to the west – within the Tropics – was twelve months long, although best in March or June.

Communications were so slow, however, that most Spanish documents recording the situations and decisions of the authorities were of historical interest only, even as they were being written. The enormous distances involved complicated the matter also. For instance, Drake had handed out a number of 'safe-conducts' to specially selected prisoners, such as Anton, Parraces and Zarate, before releasing them. San Juan de Anton had been given his copy on 6 March, the day he was released with his ship. It was written in English, being addressed to John Winter. In order to get a translation, the Spanish authorities sent it all the way to Lima, where it was hoped that one of the English prisoners held there by the

Inquisition might be able to translate it. The letter was handed to John Butler, one of Oxenham's men, on 7 July, more than four months after San Juan de Anton had been released, and nearly a thousand miles away.

Butler had first to be brought from prison to the court presided over by the inquisitors Cerezuela and Ulloa, shown the letter and required to take an oath to translate it truthfully into the Castilian tongue. He stated that the first two lines read: 'Safe-conduct. On board the ship named the *Golden Hind* on the sixth of March, 1579.'

The Spaniards were suspicious of everything Drake did or said. They scrutinised the translation of this document with special care. It appeared to be an instruction to treat the bearer well – the normal form taken by such papers – but contained a puzzling note that Winter (or four other named Englishmen) should pay the bearer double value for any cargo or supplies they felt they had to take from him to relieve their own wants. This seemed likely to make the bearer value the document more highly than usual and to produce it promptly if he met English ships. One sentence, however, contained an oblique message for Vice-Admiral John Winter: 'What we determined about the return to our country will be carried out if God wills.' Or, putting it in plainer language: 'The return route will be as we agreed.' What that route would be, was exactly what the Spaniards most wished to know, so as to cut off the corsair and recapture the treasure, but put in those terms, the document spoke only to Winter and perhaps one or two other senior officers with him.

The inquisitors asked Butler who this person Winter was, and were told that he knew four brothers of that name. They were very great people and never went forth except as captain-generals of the Queen's fleet. They owned many properties. The one mentioned had been a corsair for many years and was about thirty years of age. John Butler was then taken back to his prison to join John Oxenham, Thomas 'Xerores', and young Henry Butler. The three older men were all doomed, but perhaps Drake's threats of what he would do to Spaniards if they were executed, gave them an extra year or so of life. The Inquisition at length found them all guilty of heresy and condemned them to the auto-da-fé of 29 October 1580, held at Lima, and then handed them over to the civil authorities for hanging. Mercy was shown only to Henry Butler, on account of his youth; he was sentenced merely to perpetual imprisonment in the galleys.

Two other English prisoners, Miles Philips and Paul Horsewell, saw a little temporary freedom as a result of Drake's arrival on the coast of Mexico. They had been in Spanish hands for a long time, flotsam from the wreck of the Hawkins expedition at San Jaun de Ulloa in 1568, a dozen years earlier, and some 2500 miles to the north of Peru. Hawkins had lost all his fleet except the *Minion* and Drake's *Judith*; he had more men than he could feed, so had set 114 on shore. The Indians thought they were Spaniards and attacked them; later they fell into Spanish hands. On asking for their wounds to be dressed, they were told that they should have no surgeon but the hangman. Arms bound, they were marched towards Mexico City. One of their guards was kindly; the other urged them on with blows and shouts of: 'March! March, English dogs, Lutherans, enemies of God!'

They were made slaves with Spanish masters, until the Inquisition demanded them, whereupon they spent a year and half in solitary dungeons, being taken out only to be placed on the rack and questioned. A wrong answer, forced out by torture, meant the fire. Three of them, George Rively, Peter Momfrie and Cornelius the Irishman, were sentenced to be burnt; the rest to be lashed with whips two or three hundred strokes, and then slavery in the galleys or the monasteries. Only a few youngsters like Philips escaped. 'The whipping was cruelly executed on Good Friday,' he wrote. Two criers went before the sorry procession of condemned English prisoners, calling out: 'Behold these English Lutherans, dogs, enemies of God!' The inquisitors themselves, and their familiars, shouted also: 'Strike! Lay on those English heretics, Lutherans, God's enemies!' Then they were taken back to prison, 'all bloody and swollen, to perform the rest of their martyrdom'.

Miles Philips had served his sentence when, in late April or early May:

> 'there came news to Mexico, that there were certain Englishmen landed, with great power, at the port of Acapulco upon the South Sea; and that they were coming to Mexico City to take the spoil thereof: which wrought a marvellous great fear amongst them; and many of those that were rich began to shift for themselves, their wives and children. Then were Paul Horsewell and I sent for before the Viceroy.'

The Viceroy, Don Martin Enriquez, was the man Drake hated

above all others because of his conduct at San Juan de Ulloa, where he broke his word. He had also earned the enmity of Moya de Contreras, Inquisitor-General, because Don Martin did not want the Holy Office operating in his territory of Mexico, and took every opportunity to humiliate the Chief Inquisitor.

Don Martin's knowledge of Drake, however, was minimal. At San Juan de Ulloa the corsair had played only a minor role, as the young inexperienced captain of the tiny bark *Judith*. The early letters from Gaspar de Vargas, which reached Mexico City in the last week of April, were based only on reports from the Guatalco authorities, who knew little. Nuño da Silva, who was much better informed from his long stay on board the corsair's ship, had not yet arrived (although he was on his way), and the Viceroy was eagerly awaiting the chance to interrogate him under pressure. Letters sent by the fastest means were taking ten or twelve days to reach the city from the coast and whoever was bringing the Portuguese pilot must be travelling at a much slower rate.

Consequently, when Philips and Horsewell were brought before the Viceroy, the first question was an unusual one, oddly phrased:

'Do you know of an Englishman named Francis Drake, who is brother to Captain Hawkins?'

The prisoners replied that they knew Captain Hawkins. But he only had one brother, who was the Governor of Plymouth in England.

'Do you know Francis Drake?' was the next question.

They did, of course, although it was a dozen years since they had seen him, but they both promptly answered: 'No!'

Miles Philips was told to remain as interpreter, to serve with one of the fighting columns which were to be sent out against Drake, (the Viceroy had to seek permission from the Inquisition for this), so he had the opportunity to observe the Spanish preparations as a reasonably unbiased witness. He thought they were quite futile (a view with which some Spaniards agreed), but the tone of the official correspondence suggests as prime motive a desire to impress the King with the zeal and efficiency of his servants in New Spain.

There was a clash of opinion – and perhaps of personality – at the top, between the Viceroy and one of his officials, Don Luis de Velasco, who himself became Viceroy eleven years later. The latter was one of those who stressed the need for haste because, to him, Drake appeared to be 'so expert and astute a Corsair'. He suggested that the main force should search north along the coast towards California, while a ship should be sent across the South Sea to the Moluccas carrying the warning there, in case he should return by that route instead. This was a good appreciation of Drake's most likely moves. Don Luis was extremely critical of the time it took to bring da Silva to Mexico City – in excess of thirty days – as his information might have been vital. He offered to serve against Drake in any capacity, even as an ordinary soldier, but the Viceroy disregarded his offer of personal assistance as well as his advice, which seemed to anger him.

The military action taken by Don Martin Enriquez was to divide his force into four equal parts and set them marching off in four different directions, after such a delay that Drake was virtually certain not to be found lingering at any of the four eventual destinations, but if he was encountered was almost bound to be the victor in any engagement as he would be facing only a quarter of the available Spanish force. Miles Philips wrote:

'There came news that all the Englishmen were gone. Yet there were 800 men made out, under the leading of several Captains. Whereof 200 were sent to the port of San Juan de Ulloa upon the North Sea, under the conduct of Don Luis Suarez; 200 were sent to Guatemala in the South Sea, who had for their Captain, Juan Cortes; 200 more were sent to Guatalco, a port in the South Sea, over whom went for Captain, Don Pedro de Robles; and 200 more were sent to Acapulco, the port where it was said Captain Drake had been, and they had for Captain, Doctor Robles, Alcalde de Corte; with whom I went as Interpreter, having licence given by the Inquisitors.'

Doctor Hernando Robles, who was the captain-general of the whole expedition, wrote direct to the King about what he had done:

'Within three days I had raised and enlisted 300 very splendid men, the majority of them experienced in warfare in Your Majesty's service. These were organised into a body of somewhat less than 200 picked and chosen soldiers, whom I dispatched within eight days from the City, all paid and very well armed. My son, Don Felix de Robles, by appointment of the Viceroy, went as their captain-general and I followed them within three days with a company of more than 30 gentlemen, men of position and experts, many of them well-known cavaliers. I arrived at the port [of Acapulco] within fifteen days with all my company but one soldier who had fallen ill. There I found a very fine ship of Your Majesty's and another belonging to a private individual which, through the foresight of the Viceroy, had been prepared, armed and victualled with utmost and incredible activity. As it appeared that it would be advisable to build a launch that could act as a guide to the two vessels, by reason of the inlets and shallows on that coast, I had one made in a very short time.'

This bright, efficient picture was not how matters appeared to Miles Philips, who accompanied Doctor Robles to assist him in interrogating captured corsairs:

'When we came to Acapulco we found Captain Drake was departed from thence, more than a month before we came thither. But yet our Captain Alcalde de Corte there presently embarked himself, in a small ship of 60 tons or thereabouts, having also in company with him, two other small barks; and not past 200 men in all. With whom I went as Interpreter in his own ship; which, God knoweth, was but weak and ill appointed; so that, for certain, if we had met with Captain Drake, he might easily have taken us all.'

At the last moment, Doctor Robles was ordered to return to Mexico City because there was a lack of judges there. Appointed in his place was Don Juan de Guzman, chief justice and purveyor of Acapulco. 'After I had given them public and secret instructions about the route they were to take, according to the information the Viceroy had received, they set sail with a very favourable wind; greatly regretting that I had been forced to leave them,' the Doctor wrote.

However, Miles Philips was with them, to give a different picture :

'We being embarked, kept our course and ran southward towards Panama, keeping still as nigh the shore as we could, and having the land upon our left hand. Having coasted thus, for the space of eighteen or twenty days, and having reached more to the south than Guatemala, we met at last with other ships which came from Panama. Of whom we were certainly informed that Captain Drake was clean gone off the coast, more than a month before; and so we returned back to Acapulco again, and there landed; our

Captain being forced thereunto because his men were very sore seasick.

'All the while that I was at sea with them, I was a glad man. For I hoped that if we met with Master Drake, we should all be taken: so that when I should have been freed out of that danger and misery wherein I lived, and should return to my own country of England again . . . But when I saw that we must needs come on land again, little doth any man know the sorrow and grief that inwardly I felt; although outwardly I was constrained to make fair weather of it.'

Afterwards, Miles Philips escaped to Spain and from there at last got back to England in 1582, having embarked, aged fourteen, in 1567 and then served fourteen years of imprisonment or slavery. He was lucky. A fellow survivor, Job Hartob, served twenty-two years until he was able to escape and get back to Portsmouth, where he landed in December 1590, having been captured in October 1568.

What 'secret' information Don Martin Enriquez had, that sent the 'armada' of Acapulco south towards Panama, is as conjectural as the reasons for the southward sweep a month earlier by Peru Force from Panama. One man, however, sent his ships northwards during this period and possibly it was these vessels which Miles Philips says they met with the news that Drake had been gone a month. This official was the Licentiate Valverde, who in May wrote from Guatemala to the King in order to justify his decision. He had, he said, given his captains the order to go north beyond the furthest region of Mexico (New Galicia), as far as the Californias and the Vermilion Gulf, and beyond there even, if necessary. Valverde pointed out that Drake had only four alternatives for his return voyage: the strait the Spaniards called 'de los Bacallaos' ('of the stockfish', but known to the English as the Strait of Anian); by the route of China; by the pass of Vallano across the Isthmus of Panama; by the Strait of Magellan. Valverde analysed them all in turn:

'The return by the strait "de los bacallaos" is held to be impossible because this is a strait which has never been navigated and is not known to exist. Although it is painted in some maps, it is always designated as "unknown and undiscovered strait".

'The navigation by China would be so difficult for the Corsair, that it may be considered impossible, for there are many things that would dissuade him from undertaking it:

(1) The navigation is so long and troublesome, that he would have to pilot and coast the entire world in order to return to his country, England.

(2) He cannot convey, in one ship only, the provisions sufficient for the 80 men he carries, during such a long voyage, even if his ship were to carry no other cargo but victuals.

(3) He would have to touch at, or pass in sight of, Portuguese ports, where he would certainly run the risk of being seized and severely chastised by the armadas that are there. On reaching Asia, he would also run the risk of the Turks.'

Apart from a consideration of the difficulties and dangers, which were real enough, Valverde thought he detected several clues in Drake's behaviour which tended to exclude the China route as Drake's way of escape:

'As he has been proclaiming that he intended to return by the route of China, we must believe the contrary. For soldiers, in order to put their enemy off their guard, are apt to proclaim what they do not intend doing. Then, he put ashore at Guatalco Nuño da Silva, a most experienced Portuguese pilot, most skilful in the art of navigation and the knowledge of the heavens, whom he had brought with him for 15 months. He would need his counsel and ingenuity in so long a navigation, so much that he never would have left him behind had he intended to return by China. On account of these debatable points and also of the resolution that was taken by the Councils of Pilots which were held in Lima by order of Your Viceroy, and in Panama by Your order, all have come to the conclusion that the said pilot would not dare to attempt to return by China.'

With equally logical arguments, the Licentiate was able to support a definite conclusion:

'From the aforesaid, it must be held as most certain that the said Corsair entered the South Sea with the design of going out by Vallano, if possible, or by the same Strait of Magellan, which is the most likely.'

Valverde got much nearer the mark when he asked himself why no one had seen Drake's ship for some time:

'The great probability is, therefore, that the Corsair has wintered

on the coast, in the region of the Californias, in those small bays
or deep coves that are there or off one of the adjacent islands. He
may be there with the design of returning in the month of November when the following winds would assist him . . . His sole
consideration will be to allow time to pass, so that the coasts will
be as unwatched and unprepared as when he came. An indication
of this is his having carried off from Guatalco the entire supply
of Indian women's petticoats, and also taken other articles of
clothing used by the Indians, disregarding a great quantity of
valuable silk clothing which he could have taken from the ships
he had seized on his way. It would seem that the taking of these
articles of clothing used by the natives was done so that he could
take harbour where there were Indians, and exchange them for
victuals . . . for he was not going to wear the said Indian clothing,
nor would it be of utility in England . . . '

Like Don Martin Enriquez, Valverde thought there was something highly suspicious in Drake's action of landing Nuño da Silva
at Guatalco:

'He was in actual need of his services, and yet he landed him
without giving him anything, although the Corsair was usually
so liberal with others whom he made prisoners on the voyage.
He gave them money and silver and left them their clothing and
properties. For this reason I, and many others, have the strongest
suspicions that he left the pilot as a spy so that he should proclaim
and persuade people, as he has, in fact, tried to do, that the
Corsair was going to return by China or the Strait "de los
Bacallaos", and that the negro was not of those from Vallano but
that he had been taken from a ship near Panama.'

Here, as so often, the lawyer's views were based on insufficient
evidence, for there were two negroes, one from Vallano (who might
conceivably have helped Drake return by that way, overland), and
one taken at sea. Nevertheless Valverde concluded, ominously for
the Portuguese navigator: 'All this is done so that . . . when the
Corsair returns to fetch Nuño da Silva the latter can warn him of
the preparations that have been made against him, so that he can
protect himself from them.'

Valverde stated in the most diplomatic way that the sentinals
posted by the Viceroy all along the coast to watch seawards for the

corsair's vessel had been stationed so late that Drake might already have passed; and in any case, by keeping six or eight leagues out to sea, the corsair's vessel might be out of sight even of watchers on high ground, let alone low. He gave all these reasons as justification for sending his ships north to search the Californias for the corsair's winter hideout, and concluded: 'May it please God to make my design hit the mark in accordance with my zeal and desire that Your Majesty be well served and the Corsair punished.'

Nuño da Silva was brought into Mexico City on 20 May at eight o'clock in the morning, thirty-four days after Drake had abandoned him, protesting, at Guatalco. Don Martin Enriquez reported to his fellow Viceroy in Peru:

'I awaited this Portuguese for hours so as to ascertain from him all particulars concerning the voyage he had made and, above all, to gain information and learn about the return voyage of the Corsair. I spent the whole day of yesterday, and this day (21 May) until noon, with him, examining him as minutely as I could about the entire voyage . . . Although I made every possible effort to ascertain the Corsair's intended course and the route he intended to get out of the South Sea, he remained firm in his denial, saying that he could give no light nor knew anything concerning this. I handed him over to the judges so that they should obtain the information from him by other means.'

The torture did not bring a breakdown or a confession, as Don Enriquez had hoped, nor did sympathetic questioning:

'But neither the one way nor the other sufficed to make him declare anything more than that he had heard, at different times, that Drake was bound to go to look for the strait "de los Bacallaos" and that this was not to be done by keeping close to the coast . . . The pilot says he used all his artillery as ballast and placed the water-casks on the top of it. This would appear to indicate . . . that he intended to take to the open sea, although this is a course that I have hitherto never heard of anyone having taken.'

The Viceroy was becoming convinced that Nuño da Silva had not, as they had at first assumed, been signed on as navigator for the voyage from the beginning, but had been captured at sea and carried off to help the Englishmen find water on the Brazilian coast, which the Portuguese knew well. However, he still suspected him of the unforgivable sin (in Spanish eyes) of having piloted Drake through the Strait of Magellan. The Viceroy considered da Silva's explanation of why he had been kept for fifteen months in the English ship as an evasion of the truth:

> 'He says that the Corsair brought him along because, after reaching the Strait of Magellan, they had not been in any country where he could have been left, and he did not want to land him near Lima, lest he give information about the Corsair to the Viceroy of Peru.'

This could well have been true, so far as it went, And if da Silva wanted to return home as quickly as possible, then – providing he had no trouble with the authorities – New Spain was a good place to be landed because shipping routes to the Iberian peninsula were well established there. Or from there he could go to Brazil, which was under Portuguese control. But the English evidence is that da Silva did not want to be left in New Spain. Drake must have had a strong reason for leaving him, but this could have been perhaps as trivial as vanity, for Drake was very proud of his supremacy as mariner and navigator. Had it come to his notice that most of his prisoners unthinkingly gave all the credit for his passage through the Strait of Magellan to the Portuguese pilot? Some even assumed that da Silva was the real power on board! The Guatalco prisoners, for instance, told Gaspar de Vargas of da Silva: 'It seems that it is he who governs and directs this Armada.' Drake's habit of leading scouting and fighting forays from the pinnace, leaving da Silva behind to navigate the big ship, may have contributed to this impression. The simplest and most conclusive way of disproving this idea was getting rid of da Silva and completing the second half of the voyage without him, otherwise the Portuguese might obtain the whole popular credit for what would be, if successful, only the second circumnavigation of the globe. One may recall the fate of Thomas Doughty, who challenged Drake's supremacy.

One who knew him well was to testify that Drake was ambitious to a fault, exceeding John Hawkins in this, that he had 'an insatiable desire of honour indeed beyond reason'. Such a temperament was capable of the act, provided that da Silva would not obviously come to harm; and being landed immediately in a Catholic country rather than a Lutheran one much later might prove after all in the best interests of his Portuguese friend. Of course he was bound to be

questioned as to Drake's movements, and after he had been interrogated the Spaniards would know more about the *Golden Hind*,
her armament and crew; but by then Drake would be far away. The
information would be merely history.

What he may not have divined was that his other prisoners would
be questioned, one after the other, as to whether or not da Silva had
appeared to take part in the Lutheran services. He certainly could
not have imagined that da Silva had been 'recognised' as being two
different criminals, one of them a 'wanted man' for twenty years.
Nor that Don Martin Enriquez would, within three days, hand the
Portuguese to the Holy Office for expert questioning. There was no
immediate charge of heresy, just a skilled interrogation by inquisitor
Bonilla to establish the chronology of events, followed by detailed
probing of matters of pressing interest to the lay authorities, particularly the route by which the corsair intended to return.

Da Silva's reply was preserved:

'The Englishman proclaimed that he was bound to return by the
Strait of the Stockfish which he had also come to explore, and
that, by August 1579, he must be back in his country.

'While in the port of Guatalco, he produced a map and pointed
out a strait situated in 66 degrees latitude north, saying that he
had to go there, and that if he did not find an opening he would
have to go back by China.

'He proclaimed that he came by order of his Queen, and carried
written orders from her, according to which he governed himself;
that he had come for something more than for the seizing of
vessels. On a bronze cannon he had the sculptured figure of a
globe crossed by the north star and he said that these were the
coat-of-arms that the Queen had given him, sending him to sail
round the world.'

PART THREE

Chapter 19

A NEW ENGLAND

The Pacific and 'Nova Albion':
17 April–25 July 1579

WHAT would the corsair do now? There were some bad guesses. A few good guesses. What Drake did was designed to baffle the best. He vanished.

Some Spaniards had been so shaken by the incursion of the English into the South Sea that they suggested fortifying the Strait of Magellan and stationing ships there. That was to prove costly; losses were to be high, purely from reasons of climate and geography, without enemy action at all. Others, considering earlier precedents, feared the crossing of the Isthmus by the upriver and overland routes. So the Caribbean fleet was put on the alert, to buttress military measures already taken to block the pass of Vallano.

Pedro Sarmiento de Gamboa, the navigator, believed Drake would go north for a possible passage round North America; but if there was no practical way, then by China. He personally was to be ordered by his superiors to go south, to guard the Strait of Magellan with ships. That was exactly where he thought the corsair would not go, exactly the opposite direction to the raider's most probable course; and also he was sent much too late – on 11 October 1579, six months after Drake had last been seen, sailing away from Guatalco.

Don Luis de Velasco thought Drake would attempt to 'search for the new strait of which they say he spoke so much', but if he missed it would return by China, the route of the Portuguese; never by the Strait of Magellan. He had therefore proposed that a swift vessel be sent halfway across the Pacific as far as the Philippines, from where a warning could in turn be carried further west to the Moluccas. That way, the corsair might find himself sailing into a trap. But Don Luis was too junior at this time for his advice to be taken: the Viceroy turned it down.

The Licentiate Valverde believed that the corsair would hide away north of California, both in order to careen and to let the alarm die

265

down; only then would he return by the Strait of Magellan. So he proposed that a force be prepared to search the Vermilion Gulf and further north also. There were, he pointed out, two 120-ton vessels which normally carried timber and other shipbuilding materials for the two large freighters being constructed in Nicaragua for the China trade; and there was one small ship at Sonsonate. They could be armed with four bronze guns to be made from church bells to be contributed by the Bishop of Guatemala. About forty or fifty days would be needed to gather and equip this force from the time he suggested it, on 14 April. So the search could begin during early June, if Valverde's estimate was right and if his suggestion was authorised.

Drake acted as if pursued by professionals. He moved fast, far, and in an unexpected direction. Even if he had kept in sight of the shore, he would have been gone before the Spanish coast watchers had even been posted. But he did not keep close in, where the searchers would travel. Instead, he drove straight out to sea for 500 leagues, an immense distance, in order to pick up a wind and at the same time lose himself in the vast wastes of the Pacific. Then he turned north and, covering about 1400 leagues in all, sighted land for the first time in seven weeks on 5 June, having vanished on 17 April.

It was in 48° north latitude, according to Fletcher's published narrative, and Drake had not expected to find land there. Evidently, the coast of North America trended much further to the west than they had suspected; and if there was a way back, it would be a longer journey than they had planned for. The climate was also very much colder than they had expected, even allowing for the fact, as they did, that having just come from the Tropics, they might feel the cold more. As Fletcher pointed out, there were objective tests to show that what they felt was real.

In 42°, on 3 June, it had been warm still, but:

'In the night following we found such alteration of heat into extreme and nipping cold that our men did grievously complain thereof, some of them feeling their healths much impaired thereby. Neither was it that this chanced in the night alone, but the day following carried with it not only the marks, but the stings and force of the night going before, to the great admiration of us all. For besides that the pinching and biting air was nothing altered, the very ropes of our ship were stiff, and the rain which fell was an unnatural congealed and frozen substance, so that we seemed to be in the Frozen Zone . . . '

As they sailed even a few degrees further north, the hands of the men became so numbed that they put them inside their clothes for warmth and were loath to take them out even to feed.

'Our meat, as soon as it was removed from the fire, would immediately in a manner be frozen up, and our ropes and tackling in a few days were grown to that stiffness, that what 3 men afore were able with them to perform, now 6 men, with their best strength and uttermost endeavour, were hardly able to accomplish . . . The 5 day of June, we were forced by contrary winds to run in with the shore, and to cast anchor in a bad bay. We were not without some danger by reason of the many extreme gusts and flaws that beat upon us. If they ceased, immediately upon their intermission there followed most vile, thick, and stinking fogs . . .'

If this was 48°, what would 66° be like? According to what da Silva was now telling the Inquisition, that was the latitude of the Strait of Stockfish, and that was where Drake, showing him a map, had said that he must go in search of a short route for his return. Fletcher said the same, without actually specifying 66°, which is the latitude of northern Norway, Iceland and southern Greenland.

'The time of the year now drew on wherein we must attempt, or of necessity wholly give over that action, which chiefly our General had determined, namely, the discovery of what passage there was to be found about the Northern parts of America, from the South Sea, into our own Ocean. Which being once discovered and made known to be navigable, we should not only do our country a good and notable service, but we ourselves should have a nearer cut and passage home. Otherwise, we were to make a very long and tedious voyage of it . . . We therefore all of us willingly harkened and consented to our General's advice, which was, first to seek out some convenient place wherein to trim our ship, and store ourselves with wood and water and other provisions as we could get, and thenceforward to hasten on our intended journey for the discovery of the said passage, through which we might with joy return to our longed homes.'

Most cosmographers supposed the Strait of Anian to lie in something under 50 degrees, which is exactly where Fletcher says Drake sighted land, found an untenable anchorage, and then turned south to discover a careenage in $38\frac{1}{2}°$. But Drake's map, according to da Silva (in a testimony given under torture), showed the Strait in 66°; where, many years later, an actual strait was to be found (although the route it led to was not practical). It may be that Fletcher's published narrative was subject to censorship (and perhaps some misleading rewriting) regarding this sensitive matter. The impassability of this route was not to be shown for many years, and until that time any information which might lead to such a revolutionary short-cut to the Spice Islands was highly secret. Drake may have gone much further north than Fletcher says he did before deciding that time was running out and the *Golden Hind* in no state to combat the hazards of the Arctic icecap. Or the story may be literally true; perhaps a freak Polar airstream caught the *Golden Hind* and forced Drake to run south for California, where the Spaniards might be cruising for him. Southward he most certainly went, searching for a protected haven, shielded from the winds and from the view of any passing ship; and defensible, in case the worst occurred. Fletcher wrote:

'We found the land, by coasting along it, to be but low and reasonable plain. Every hill (whereof we saw many, but none very high), though it were in June, and the sun in his nearest approach unto them, being covered with snow. In 38 degrees 30 minutes we fell with a convenient and fit harbour and June 17 came to anchor therein, where we continued till the 23 day of July following. During all which time, notwithstanding it was in the height of summer, yet were we continually visited with like nipping colds as we had felt before.'

They were warm only in winter clothing or in bed, but there was too much hard and filthy labour to allow them to swaddle themselves in heavy coverings. To the penetrating chill was added the damp depression of long-lasting fogs; for a fortnight, during this time, they never saw the sun or the stars.

There was an Indian village three quarters of a mile from the shore of the bay in which they had anchored; and on their second day there a native emissary came out in a canoe with gifts, including a basket of tobacco. He was very shy and would not come aboard, contenting himself mostly with making speeches at a distance.

The *Golden Hind* had sustained a leak at sea and was therefore to be brought as close to shore as possible, and the bulk of her contents unloaded, prior to careening. But as Drake had twice suffered losses from hostile natives and here might additionally have to meet a Spanish force, he proceeded in due order as for a military operation. First, the armed soldiers went ashore to guard the beachhead – low-lying ground at the foot of a small hill. Then an entrenchment was dug, the excavated soil built up into a bulwark, faced with stone; and tents and workships erected within the encircling walls.

This landing of armed men in force brought an instant reaction from the natives. In numbers, and with such weapons as they had (mostly weak bows), they rushed down the hill towards the English. But when they came close to these white strangers, they stopped, said Fletcher, 'as men ravished in their minds, with the sight of such things as they never had seen or heard of before that time: their errand being rather with submission and fear to worship us as Gods, than to have any war with us as with mortal men.' It may be so. The two communities had not a single word in common (except *Tabah*, the Indian word for the herb which the English called tobacco); all communication was by improvised signs. The English signed for the Indians to put down their bows and arrows and to advance, and they did so. The native men went almost entirely naked, the women largely topless, and this so embarrassed the English that the first gifts they pressed on the Indians were items of clothing. The gambit did not succeed, for some of the Indians, including the women, promptly took off the animal skins they were wearing and gave them to the strangers in exchange.

This was merely a preliminary visit by the locals. Its peaceful nature argued that the Spaniards had not been here before them, to stir up a deadly hatred of pale-skinned Europeans. All the same, they had had a savage lesson at Mocha and some bore the scars still, including Drake. The English did not feel really happy until their improvised fort had its walls faced with stone.

When it was finished, two days later, a much greater gathering of Indians approached. Apparently, the locals had been joined by tribes from the interior. They brought gifts and an orator came forward to deliver a speech in the native tongue, very loudly and rapidly, with violent gestures. When he had completed his discourse, of which the English understood no word, all the Indians bowed and uttered an *Oh* (long drawn out and in a dreamy manner, according to Fletcher). Then the men only, putting down their bows, came forward, leaving their women and children behind. The women simultaneously began to shriek and lacerate themselves with their fingernails, so violently that the blood came; tearing at their faces, at their breasts, at their nipples, and then flinging themselves down on the ground. They had discarded even the loose furs they wore flung over their shoulders, so that they were all naked to the waist and acting as if they were desperate.

The English thought this an act of homage or adoration, that the Indians had mistaken them for Gods. Drake tried to mime the idea that he was not a God, for God was in heaven (looking up into the sky, talking and pointing). In case the idea had not completely taken root, he then called for a prayer, followed by the singing of certain psalms and a reading from the Bible. The psalms were well received, the natives crying out *Gnaáh*, which appeared to be Indian for encore.

On 26 June an important Indian chief, with a bodyguard of one hundred tall and warlike men, paid the encamped English a visit. The ceremony was long and impressive, recorded by Fletcher in detail. Drake had to organise a reception which while seeming friendly, would prevent the badly outnumbered Europeans from being overwhelmed at close quarters if the chief and his fine warriors should prove hostile. There was never a sign of this. Indeed, part of the ceremony appeared to the English to be an act of submission, of the giving of the land to them; of asking Francis Drake to be their King. It might well have been the reverse, telling them merely that they were welcome as long as they did not intend to settle there.

As soon as the ceremony was over, however, a strange thing occurred. The women, and some of the old men, too, began to shriek and tear at their faces with their fingernails, as before. Then they closed in on the English and looking very hard at each man, chose the ones they wanted (which, wrote Fletcher, 'were commonly the youngest of us'). These they carried away to their tents and only then did they cease to cry and groan and tear their flesh.

This intimacy broke some barriers and the Indians began to ask the Englishmen for medical help, believing that if an Englishman just touched a wound or blew upon a limb which ached, or upon an open sore, the thing would be cured. Again, embarrassingly, the sailors had to try to explain in sign language what they conceived to be the difference between a man and a god; using the physical nature of their remedies to help make the point, applying lotions, plasters and unguents to aching limbs, shrunk sinews, old sores, cancered ulcers, and freshly-inflicted nail wounds.

So fascinated with these strangers were the Indians, that they forgot to hunt and soon lacked meat. Drake gave them some of the sea-lions and mussels which his men had been collecting in the bay as part of their own food supplies for the long voyage home. 'They are a people of a tractable, free, and loving nature, without guile or or treachery,' wrote Fletcher. Soon, Drake felt confident enough to venture inland to see the real nature of the country, for the locality of the bay was barren and desolate. Fletcher reported:

'The inland we found to be far different from the shore, a goodly country, and fruitful soil, stored with many blessings for the use of man. Infinite was the company of very large and fat deer which there we saw by thousands, in a herd; besides a multitude of a strange kind of conies, by far exceeding them in number . . . the people eat their bodies, and make great account of their skins, for their king's holiday coat was made of them.

'This country our General named *Albion*, and that for two causes: the one in respect of the white banks and cliffs, which lie towards the sea; the other, that it might have some affinity, even in name also, with our own country, which was sometime so called.

'Before we went from thence, our General caused to be set up a monument of our being there, as also of her majesty's and successors' right and title to that kingdom: namely, a plate of brass, fast nailed to a great and firm post; whereon is engraven her grace's name, and the day and year of our arrival there, and of the free giving up of the province and kingdom, both by the king and people, into her majesty's hands; together with her highness's picture and arms, in a piece of sixpence current English money, shewing itself by a hole made of purpose through the plate; underneath was likewise engraven the name of our General, etc. The Spaniards never had any dealing, or so much as set foot in this country, the utmost of their discoveries reaching only to many degrees Southward of this place.'

The anonymous witness in the *Golden Hind* put the whole thing into a paragraph, with some divergence from Fletcher:

'Drake sailed northwards till he came to 48 degrees, still finding a very large sea trending toward the north, but being afraid to spend long time in seeking for the strait, he turned back again, still keeping along the coast as near land as he might, until he came to 44 degrees, and there he found a harbour for his ship, where he grounded his ship to trim her, and here came down unto them many of ye country people while they were graving of their ship and had conference with them by signs. In this place Drake set up a great post and nailed thereon a sixpence, which the country people worshipped as if it had been God; also he nailed upon this post a plate of lead, and scratched therein the Queen's name.'

John Drake, under interrogation, said that Drake sailed north on a wind all the time until he reached 44°, when it changed; whereupon 'he went to the Californias where he discovered land in 48°. Here he caulked his large ship and left the ship he had taken in Nicaragua. He departed, leaving the Indians, to all appearance, sad.'

Fletcher's account is so detailed that it must have been based on notes. His published testimony was that they ran north until 3 June, when they were in 42°; then the wind and the weather changed; they first saw land in 48° on 5 June and went south to 38½° where they found the harbour and country Drake claimed for England, and which, because of its 'white banks and cliffs', actually looked like England (or, at least, like part of the English Channel coast). Unless the published narrative was intended to mislead rivals, Fletcher's detail is likely to be more reliable than recollection, both as regards the place of careenage and the type of plate put up to mark it.

A plaque was more likely to be made of lead than of brass, because sheet lead was readily available on shipboard, being carried as raw material for making the shot for swivel guns and handguns in small stone moulds. And it would be easy to fit a sixpence securely into a lead sheet. However, as the annexation of such a fertile country well to the north (they thought) of the sphere of Spanish influence would be important, perhaps Drake felt the use of brass justified. Probably Fletcher is right and the plaque was brass and inscribed as he says. And no doubt the English really were the first there.

Spanish ships may have passed this place, far out to sea, for part of their route from China lay north of Cape Mendocino, following the wind pattern; but that any deliberate landings had been made seems unlikely. From Colchero and his charts, the English had learned something about wind circulation in the Pacific, and the China route appeared to be the best, although now that the *Golden Hind*'s leak had been repaired and the hull thoroughly trimmed it was physically possible to make a second attempt to discover the Strait of Anian. Psychologically, it was not. The 'general squalidness and barrenness' of the shore they were on, the unmelted snows of winter still lying patchily, the shivering fogs that so often cloaked everything – all these made the thought of going still further north into the unknown a nightmare. For this was the height of summer!

Some of the men, on other voyages, had been as far north as 72°, at summer's end, and still felt nothing like the chill that they did now. Even if there was a passage round North America, it would surely be blocked by ice. Fletcher wrote:

'From these reasons we conjecture that either there is no passage at all through these Northern coasts (which is most likely), or if there be, that yet it is unnavigable. Add that, though we searched the coast diligently, even unto 48 degrees, yet found we not the land to trend so much as one point in any place towards the East, but rather running on continually North-West, as if it went directly to Asia. And even in that height, when we had a frank wind to have carried us through, had there been a passage, yet we had a smooth and calm sea, with ordinary flowing and reflowing, which could not have been had there been a fret; of which we rather infallibly concluded, then conjectured, that there was none.'

These were very good guesses; and practical. If there was a strait at all, and even if it was navigable round the top of the world, it was of no use to them if it was to be found a further thousand miles or so over to the west; in that case, they might just as well go home by China anyway. A North-West Passage, to be of use to them, and to English navigation generally, had to be a short-cut between the Pacific and the Atlantic. And that might well depend on the answer to the question: how wide was the north part of North America?

It was not possible to know; only that, as they had seen, the continent appeared to spread out wider and wider to the west the further north one went. This was more than a bad omen, it was a plain hint, the sort of evidence which, although hardly conclusive, was not to be ignored by any commander balancing his instructions against the practicalities of carrying them out.

Drake's decision was to return by the Moluccas, the Spice Islands, which were on the Equator. They would be sailing south-west into the sunshine and the warmth. As the final preparations were made, the *Golden Hind* refloated, ballasted and armed, the natives realised that the strangers were about to leave. Fletcher described their response:

> 'That exceeding great joy wherewith they received us at our first arrival, was clean drowned in their excessive sorrow for our departing. For they did not only lose on a sudden all mirth, joy, glad countenance, pleasant speeches, agility of body, familiar rejoicing one with another, and all pleasure what ever flesh and blood might be delighted in, but with sighs and sorrowings . . . with bitter tears and wringing of their hands, tormenting themselves.
>
> 'The 23 of July they took a sorrowful farewell of us, but being loath to leave us, they immediately ran to the top of the hills to keep us in their sight as long as they could . . . '

An exceedingly long voyage lay ahead of them. Magellan's men had suffered dire starvation while crossing the Pacific. Knowing this, when Drake sighted some islands well stocked with seals and birds, he anchored and collected the fresh food. They stayed there two days, leaving on 25 July, having named them the Islands of St James. This was the last land they were to see for more than two months. Ahead of them were sixty-eight days of empty sea and sky – the last week of July, all of August, all of September.

Exactly as Sarmeinto had predicted. Except that they were going by the China route, having tried and failed to find a North-West Passage around the top of the globe.

Chapter 20

THE SHOALS OF CELEBES

The Pacific: 25 July–30 September 1579
The Islands: 30 September 1579–26 March 1580
Africa: 21 May–24 July 1580
Plymouth: 26 September 1580

THE *Golden Hind* was without sight of land for sixty-eight days in crossing the North Pacific, passing south of the Ladrones Islands, where Magellan and the surviving members of his crews had made their desperate landfall some sixty years before. When on 30 September 1579 the English sighted land it consisted of a string of atolls in 8° latitude, to the south-west of the Ladrones. Their reception by the natives, however, was identical. Roundly, they dubbed the place 'Island of Thieves'. The natives, 'with browes of brasse', come on board to steal, not to trade, European goods being as fascinating to them as gold and silver was to the sailors.

On being ejected from the ship, they returned to their dugout canoes and began a vicious hail of stone-throwing at the *Golden Hind*. Drake retorted by having a warning shot from a heavy gun fired over their heads. The thunder of the discharge cleared the canoes; every man leapt overboard and hid under the water, while the English ship sailed slowly away from them. That is what Fletcher said, and it would be typical of Francis Drake's policy – 'not to hurt them, but to affright them'.

John Drake gave what seems a different version when first under interrogation: 'The Indians in these islands are very warlike Indians, of whom we killed twenty because a hundred canoes full came out against us.' But he identified the islands where this took place as the Ladrones, where indeed Magellan and his men had been forced (by their own weakness) to open fire and kill many natives, back in March 1521. The Spanish interrogators (or their translator) may have confused a reference by John Drake to Magellan's very similar experience in much the same area. When forced to tell his story a second time, John Drake made no mention of this 'massacre', saying merely that the Indians quarrelled among themselves over the beads

275

and other European trade goods offered them in exchange for fish.

He stated also that, before reaching the Philippines, they met and chased a European ship (probably Portuguese) which would not trade provisions because they were Lutherans. The vessel escaped them in the shallows. On 16 October they were coasting the Philippines and on the 21st put in to Mindanao for water. Magellan had got no further than the nearby island of Mactan where, having involved himself in local politics, he was killed in a native war.

Drake now became similarly enmeshed. After more than two months of sailing across empty ocean, the *Golden Hind* was badly in need of provisioning, and Drake had intended to take the risk of heading for the island of Tidore in the Moluccas and trying to trade with the Portuguese who held it. He now learned, however, that he could expect a better reception by making an ally of the King of the neighbouring Spice Island of Ternate, who was an enemy of the Portuguese. He had recently led a rebellion and driven them out of the island.

The King sent out war canoes to greet the Englishmen and to tow their ship to an inner harbour commanded by what had been a Portuguese fort. These craft were not simple dugouts but elaborate and powerful vessels seating eighty rowers on superimposed galleries and mounting at least one small gun. As they took the *Golden Hind* in tow, the King himself came out in the royal canoe and bowed to the visitors. Drake honoured his host with a salute, 'Our ordnance thundered, which we mixed with great store of small shot, among which sounding our trumpets and other instruments of music, both of still and loud noise,' wrote Fletcher. The King was delighted and the progress of the corsair ship began to closely resemble a naval review.

Nevertheless, Drake was cautious and found a diplomatic excuse for not going ashore in person during the week they spent in Ternate. But he entertained a number of important visitors on board, including a young Chinese nobleman who was interested in Western things. He pleaded with Drake to visit China before returning home, because of the richness and power of Chinese civilisation:

'In particular, touching ordnance and great gunnes (the late invention of a scab-shind Friar amongst us in Europe), he related that in Suntien, which is the chiefest city of all China, they had brass ordnance of all sorts (much easier to be traversed than ours were, and so perfectly made that they would hit a shilling) above 2000 years ago.'

Among the provisions loaded by the *Golden Hind* was a large quantity of rice, together with chickens, bananas, sugar and sugar canes, and an item new to them, sago. As cargo, they loaded ten tons of spices, cloves, ginger and pepper; they could have had much more of these immensely rare and valuable commodities, 'but our care was, that the ship should not be too much pestered or annoyed therewith'. According to John Drake, they also 'lightened their ship by reducing their company to sixty men'.

Nicolas Jorje, the Flemish prisoner, had counted seventy-one or seventy-two men when the *Golden Hind* was at the height of her raiding career, so as many as a dozen may have been put ashore. There is no mention of anyone actually dying during the crossing of the Pacific (although such deaths were not uncommon), but Fletcher does say that on arrival at Ternate many were 'sickly, weak, and decayed'. The Spice Islands, where the population included a number of Europeans, would be a suitable place to leave behind any man who was seriously ill or any fit man either, for employment as soldier or sailor might not be too difficult to obtain and ships not infrequently sailed for Europe. Mostly, these were giant carracks of up to 2000 tons and great cargo capacity which could carry sufficient provisions for such a voyage.

The *Golden Hind* on the other hand had a very limited capacity for storing food and water; she was deep-laden with the richest treasure any ship in memory had ever taken, was heavily armed and had expended hardly any ammunition. In addition, she was foul with weed after three and a half months without careening, and a number of the iron-hooped water casks required immediate repair at a blacksmith's forge. The crew were in dire need of a lazy convalescence if not an outright holiday. So, leaving Ternate in light winds on 9 November 1579, they sailed southward of the Celebes until on 14 November they came to a quiet and uninhibited island a degree and forty minutes south of the Equator. Here they anchored and set up a fortified camp in tents ashore, where they were to live for twenty-six days.

The island was small and wooded. At night it was alive with bats and fireflies. By day, food was there for the taking, including crustaceans such as crabs and lobsters which at this season came to the land. A particular delicacy was 'the huge multitude of a certain kind of Crayfish, of such a size, that one was sufficient to satisfy four hungry men at a dinner, being very good and restorative meat; the especial means (as we conceived it) of our increase of health.' So they called it Crab Island.

Officially, however, the place was to be named Francisca Island, after one of the negro refugees who was to be left there. They numbered three in all, including 'the negro wench Maria, she being gotten with child in the ship, and now being very great', as the anonymous witness put it, tartly. Maria had been taken out of the ship of Don Francisco de Zarate, probably at her own request. The two males likewise had never been enlisted as part of the original ship's company, unlike poor Diego the blackamoor, died of wounds at Mocha, and another man who had been with Drake for many years. According to the anonymous narrator, these were the pair who had sought sanctuary with the English when Drake had raided Guatalco and broken up a court in full session; but according to John Drake, one only was an escaper from Guatalco, the other was an ex-Cimarron taken from the bark of Gonzalo Alvarez off Payta. They were given a store of 'rice, seeds and means of making fire', so that they could found a settlement. There was an inhabited island in full view to the west, so they were not exactly being marooned. However, there was no doubt that Drake was discarding all 'passengers' before attempting the great ocean voyage which still lay ahead; and it was a measure of the seriousness with which he viewed its hazards.

The *Golden Hind* was careened and trimmed, so that the hull would be sound. A forge was set up and because all the smith's coals were now exhausted, charcoal was burnt instead, to produce new ironwork for the ship and for the repairing of the hoops of the watercasks. The men were not driven, but allowed to refresh themselves with peace and good food, so that 'in a short space grew all of us to be strong, lusty, and healthfull persons', as Fletcher expressed it.

Anon, however, recorded a quarrel Drake had with Will Legge. He suggested that Drake used this as an excuse to take from him a gold wedge, 'but because he would make some show of honest dealing, he called for a chisel, and gave the gold a mark, and said he would restore it to him again at his arrival in England, or else he would give to Legge's wife the value thereof'. Without knowing the terms of the contract signed with Drake by Legge it is hazardous to attempt a judgement; except to note that Spaniards had observed that Drake was paying wages and that no man was allowed to take anything for himself from the prizes.

On 12 December 1579 the wind was strong enough for them to leave; they weighed anchor and stood out to the west in an attempt to break through into the Indian Ocean. On the 16th, however, the wind – what there was of it – turned against them. They were drifted among a tangle of islands and sudden reefs which rose from the depths without warning; for three days they were trapped inside a deep bay, unable to beat their way clear of the encircling headlands; and eventually they were forced to sail south, in the hope of finding a way and a good wind to blow them through.

But, wrote Fletcher, they found

'that course also to be both difficult and very dangerous by reason of many shoals, which lay far off, here and there among the islands. In all our passages from England hitherto, we had never more care to keep ourselves afloat, and from sticking on them. Thus were we forced to beat up and down with extraordinary care and circumspection till January 9, at which time we supposed that we had at last attained a free passage, the land turning evidently in our sight to Westward, and the wind being enlarged, following as we desired with a reasonable gale.'

That night, at eight o'clock in the first watch of the ninth day of the New Year, it happened. Under full sail, with no danger in sight, no trace of shallowing water anywhere, the deeply-laden ship touched. There was the appalling hollow boom of a timber and iron structure encountering rock. The *Golden Hind* reared up and came to rest, firmly lodged on whatever obstruction it was that she had struck. It was a disaster as complete as it was sudden. They were more than 15,000 miles from the nearest English port from which assistance might be had. The Portuguese, who had bases much nearer, would destroy them if they could. Probably that would be unnecessary. The physical circumstances of shipwreck in such a place would suffice within a short time. There were fifty-eight of them, by Fletcher's reckoning, and the ship's boat would take no more than twenty in safety.

'Nothing now presented itself to our minds, but the ghastly

appearance of instant death,' wrote Fletcher. They all got down on their knees while Fletcher led the prayer, 'humbly beseeching Almighty God to extend His mercy unto us in his son Christ Jesus. And so preparing as it were our necks unto the block, we every minute expected the final stroke to be given unto us.'

Having partaken in the prayers, Drake now made a 'comfortable speech' of his own. If they were going to die, he said, it was only to enter the joys of another life. And now, they should bestir themselves and see how bad their situation really was. Fletcher wrote:

> 'Showing us the way by his own example, first of all the pump was well plied, and the ship freed of water. We found our leakes to be nothing increased. Though it gave us no hope of deliverance, yet it gave us some hope of respite, as it assured us that the hulke was sound. Which truly we acknowledged to be an immediate providence of God alone, as no strength of wood and iron could have possibly borne so hard and violent a shock as our ship did, dashing herself under full sail against the rocks, except the extraordinary hand of God had supported the same.'

Apparently, they had ridden up on to a rock ledge along which perhaps the keel had skidded to bring the ship unnaturally high out of the water. And the ledge must be the crest of a submerged mountain, a drowned pinnacle rising almost vertically from immense depths. Almost the first thing that was done, after the pump had quickly dried the hold and so proved that the hull was still tight, was to take a sounding from the poop, which raked aft, out over the water. And what they got was no bottom with a 300-fathom line, according to John Drake. There was absolutely no possiblity of winching the ship off by first taking out anchors to a distance and then hauling in on the cables. That method of refloating stranded ships worked only in shallow waters, and even then only when a rising tide or a lightened hull made the task easy.

Luckily, the sea was calm. But the first spell of heavy weather with high waves must inevitably fracture the hull and collapse the very deck beneath their feet. The nearest land was six leagues away, and upwind. To set everyone ashore, the ship's boat would have to make three trips with some twenty men each time, largely under sail, and with the wind in that direction, it was impossible. And even if the wind changed, so that they could all reach land, they must then either starve or fall into the hands of the natives as helpless castaways. It was with these prospects before them that they spent the night.

High water was soon after dawn on 10 January 1580, and with the coming of the light renewed attempts were made to find some shallows in which the anchors might be laid. These attempts were as fruitless as their previous endeavours had been – they could find no bottom at all; an enormous trench in the seabed must lie below them. 'This second attempt left us nothing to trust to but prayers and tears,' wrote Fletcher, 'seeing it appeared impossible that ever the forecast, council, policy, or power of man could ever effect the delivery of our ship, except the Lord only miraculously should do the same.' He then staged a full church service to pray for deliverance. Although his own expectation was 'now turned into the awaiting for a lingering death . . . one thing fell out happily for us, that the most of our men did not conceive this thing.'

The anonymous witness shared with what Fletcher considered to be the wiser men among his comrades the same feeling of imminent extinction. But that was all he shared with them. His recollections even of this solemn moment held a bitter hatred long suppressed:

'While we stuck fast on this rock, thinking there to have all perished, Mr Fletcher, our minister, made us a sermon, and we received the communion all together, and then every thief reconciled himself to his fellow thief and so yielded themselves to death, thinking it an impossible thing to escape the present danger.'

Having carried out the soundings in person, Drake was convinced that by no means could the *Golden Hind* be hauled off; therefore the only move remaining was to jettison enough heavy weights between this high tide and the next to allow the ship to float off. But the *Golden Hind* was ballasted with silver, not pig iron or stones or shingle; she was in enemy waters and would continue to be until she reached the Channel, if she ever did; and the provisions she carried might not be enough to carry her crew home, even so. It must have been a hard choice.

Anon wrote that Drake threw overboard two pieces of ordnance, three tons of cloves, and some provisions – meal and beans. John Drake recalled later (or so he told his Spanish interrogators) that eight pieces of ordnance were cast overboard, one half of the ten tons of spices, cloves, ginger and pepper obtained in the Moluccas, two pipes of flour and a quantity of clothing. On this evidence, no treasure was jettisoned, and some battleworthiness was retained together with most of the foodstuffs – for the spices, although extremely precious and valuable, were of little use to a hungry man. It seems a judicious choice. But would it work? Would the *Golden Hind* slide off the rock before a rising wind smashed her to pieces and sent the treasure cascading down the unfathomable abyss that lay under her stern?

It seemed as if there could be no answer until the next high water, in the evening of 10 January. In fact, something very startling happened soon after low water, when the new tide had only just begun to make. There was then only six or seven feet of water on their starboard side, and less to larboard, where the rock rose up from a cleft. The *Golden Hind* was unnaturally high in the air, for in her heavily laden state she required thirteen feet of water in order to float. Nevertheless, she remained upright because the wind had blown all day long on her starboard side, helping to jam her side-ways against the higher part of the rock. But at about four o'clock in the afternoon the wind died away, swung round completely and rising, began to blow hard against the larboard side. Now totally unsupported to starboard, the *Golden Hind* heeled over drastically, her keel came free of the rock so that she floated on her side, and the pressure of wind on her raised sails drifted her out over the deeper water. When they pumped again, the crew found only a slight leak in the hull, one that could easily be contained. It seemed a miracle, in which good management had played a part. 'Of all the dangers that in our whole voyage we met with, this was the greatest,' wrote Fletcher, 'but it was not the last.'

In all, they had spent twenty hours grounded on the rock. During that time the main part of the company, taking their cue from Drake's bustling and confident example, looked to survival in some form or other, even if it came to the worst and the ship was lost (which it would have been if it had stayed there another two days, for a gale blew up). Fletcher wrote that Drake was one of 'those few others that would judge of the event wisely', but hid his forebodings and made 'cheerful speeches and good encouragements into the rest'.

Perhaps Fletcher exaggerated the depths of Drake's pessimism, or showed his own bad presentiment too much. He may even have forgotten himself so far as to express for once his real feelings over the killing of Thomas Doughty and to suggest that the rock was perhaps divine retribution for their sins. The anonymous witness certainly had not forgotten; his bitterness was as corrosive as ever. Perhaps a number of people felt like this. With death certain to result anyway from their shipwreck, no need to dissemble any longer. Whatever the reason may have been, Drake moved against Fletcher with calculation as well as rage, almost as soon as they were off the rock and no longer faced with imminent death.

He ordered a staple knocked into the hatch in the forecastle, had Fletcher taken there, and assembled all the company. He then had Fletcher shackled by the legs to the staple, so that he could not move far. He himself locked it and then, sitting cross-legged on a chest in front of the minister, and waving a pair of slippers declaimed: 'Francis Fletcher, I do here excommunicate thee out of ye Church of God, and from all the benefits and graces thereof, and I denounce thee to the devil and all his angels.'

Then, more roundly, he warned: 'I charge you on pain of death not once to come before the mast, for if you do, I swear I shall have you hanged!'

That was Drake's normal style of address when admonishing, not to be taken too literally. Being translated, it meant: I'm not standing any more nonsense from you!'

Drake next introduced an element of humiliation, mockery even. An inscribed armband was put on the shackled minister. It read: 'Francis Fletcher, ye falsest knave that liveth.'

'Take off that poesy,' shouted Drake, 'and you shall be hanged!'

This was a more degrading form of the tether-and-humiliate technique which Drake used sparingly. Thomas Doughty had been tied to the mast; Colchero had been confined in a cage because he would not help Drake with his navigation in this very area.

The reason, in Fletcher's case, is still mysterious. The minister himself, for obvious reasons, did not mention the incident; but neither did the anonymous witness who so hated Drake and most of the company. It was not anyway written in his style or with his spellings, although the author of it is equally unknown. The story occurs merely among some memoranda* relating to the voyage, most of which are lists of mundane facts. Further, the incident is noted twice: once in great detail (not always legible), and once in a single sentence which seems to hint at a future inquiry and to suggest that the dates of confinement and release (which we do not know) are significant.

* Harleian MSS No. 280 folio 8.

It took two months for the *Golden Hind* to break out from behind the barrier presented by the maze of uncounted islands and uncharted shoals by the Celebes. The oily calms they had experienced before now gave way to wilder weather. On 12 January they had to anchor under bare poles. On the 20th, having sent the ship's boat ahead to search for an anchorage, a violent squall screamed up out of the south-west, separated the boat from the ship, and seemed likely to repeat the loss so long before of the pinnace manned by Peter Carder and seven others. This time they were more fortunate and the boat found them again; but both vessels had been close to destruction on hidden shoals.

On 8 February they were fortunate enough to be hailed by the native occupants of two canoes, who wanted the English ship to visit their settlement, which was called Baratiua. These people were as unlike the natives from the 'Island of Thieves' as could be imagined. They were 'of handsome body and comely stature, of civil demeanour, very just in dealing, and courteous to strangers'. The men wore only loincloths, headdress and ear-rings; the women were covered from their middles to their feet and wore many bracelets upon their naked arms. The two days the English spent with them they counted the happiest of the whole voyage, exceeded perhaps only by their stay at Ternate.

On 11 March, having sailed past many islands on their way south, they came to anchor close to a town on a substantial island which proved to be Java. With Sumatra and the Sunda chain of islands, this was indeed the final frontier before the Indian Ocean, where they must rest, reprovision and replenish their water supplies before striking out far to the south in order to round the tip of Africa, the Cape of Good Hope, or Bon Esperance, Bona Speranza, as many called it. It was the last stop also for souvenirs. Most of the men chose to buy examples of the distinctive and well-made Java daggers.

They spent more than a fortnight in Java, longer than was necessary to careen and trim the ship – 'which was so overgrown with a kind of shell-fish sticking fast unto her, that it hindered her exceedingly, and was a great trouble to her sailing.' But it was hard to resist native hospitality. Drake, with his officers and many of his company, went ashore to visit the local king and his rajahs, for whom he laid on a display of arms drill and as much English music as his small band could manage. The rajahs professed appreciation and when they in turn boarded the *Golden Hind* for an official visit gave a recital of local music 'which though it were of a very strange kind, yet the sound was pleasant and delightful'. The trading was more than satisfactory to both sides. The English exchanged wools and linens as well as silks for chickens, goats, tons of rice, coconuts and an ox.

On 26 March they stood away from Java and steered west-south-west direct for the Cape of Good Hope. Ever since the Moluccas, they had been in Portuguese territory, or at least in an area awarded to Portugal by papal decree, and any sail they sighted would almost certainly be potentially hostile almost up to the Isles of Scilly and the entrance to the Channel. Drake may have deliberately avoided the route taken by the Portuguese carracks; in any event they sighted no strange ship at all and no land even until 21 May. This was part of the mainland of Africa, but they did not double the Cape of Good Hope, the Portuguese *Boa Esperanca*, until 15 June, when they were critically short of water. John Drake said they were down to three pipes of water and one pipe of wine for fifty-nine men, one having died out of the sixty with whom they had left Ternate. He seems to have excluded the three negroes from his calculations, probably because they were refugees, not full members of the ship's company. Drake's policy of reducing the number of the crew and of putting the negroes ashore was now being vindicated. They had to find water or die.

West of the Cape they found a great bay and entering it in search of water became trapped by adverse winds without being able to find any convenient and safe supply. The ration was down to one pint between three men, and death a matter of days away, when a heavy rainstorm saved their lives by allowing them to collect six or seven tons of fresh water. With this on board, Drake took the direct route across the Gulf of Guinea, avoiding the slave coast which he knew from his days under Hawkins, and made directly for Sierra Leone, where they put into a river mouth for two days to collect water and fresh fruit. They found lemons in plenty, nutritious and refreshing, and oysters. And they sensed Africa. 'Here we saw three elephants and heard the noise of divers other beasts, but saw them not,' noted Anon.

By 15 August the returning raider was fifty leagues out from the coast of Africa north of Cape Blanco and on the Tropic of Cancer, the wind at north-east. By 22 August they had reached, by estimation, the latitude of the Canaries, still far from land and without sighting a single ship. No doubt this was by design. Drake was deliberately avoiding the known Portuguese routes to and from their staging post in the Cape Verdes and also the Spanish routes to and from their bases in the Canary Islands. With so rich a treasure aboard one lone ship, it was wisest to be discreet in the final approach to home waters.

Caution had been Drake's watchword since the friendly rajahs of Java had warned him of the presence of large European vessels. The best asset of a raider is invisibility. When the *Golden Hind* appeared off Plymouth on 26 September 1580, the only vessels she had seen since 26 March had been some native fishing boats off the coast of West Africa on 15 July – and these Drake had been careful to avoid. The most those natives could have told anyone was that they had seen a distant sail. Size, type, nationality, mission – unknown.

Drake and his company had 'shot the globe' in a voyage which ranked with that of Magellan; an almost unbelievable achievement. Indeed, in a few years more, English historians were to maintain that Drake's circumnavigation could be matched by no single foreigner; only by amalgamating the greatest voyages of the four greatest foreign seamen could one find anything comparable. Honour apart, every man of that company was potentially rich; Drake himself was likely to become a great landowner. There was enough wealth in the hold to run a kingdom like England for a year.

But the *Golden Hind* did not sight Land's End and then coast along the Cornish cliffs to Devon, advertising her arrival to all. On the contrary, Drake suddenly appeared off Plymouth from out of the Channel haze nearly three years after he had left his home port at the head of a little fleet. Homes and wives were only a few miles away now, but the *Golden Hind* did not enter the harbour. Instead, she sailed up to a group of fishing boats working outside the port and Drake hailed them.

'How is the Queen?' was the question he shouted across the water.

'In health! but there's much pestilence in Plymouth,' was the reply that came back.

That was a good excuse, if Drake wanted one, for not entering harbour. He anchored behind St Nicholas's Island in Plymouth Sound and instead of going ashore to see his wife and the town officials, his wife came out to the ship, as did the Mayor of Plymouth. The fact that the Queen was alive and well and still on the throne was encouraging. She could have been in her grave, of sickness or by assassination, and perhaps a Spanish sympathiser might have succeeded her. Drake was lamentably out of touch with affairs in England, and that lack of news could be fatal in times such as these. Also, he feared, although he had had no news of England for more than a year, it did not follow that in England they had no news of him. And further, now that they were home, John Doughty would have to be released. He had influential friends and the legality of the trial and execution of the second-in-command might come into question.

Compared to what lay ahead in England, negotiating the shoals of the Celebes might come to seem safe and easy.

Chapter 21

'MASTER THIEF OF THE UNKNOWN WORLD'

Homecoming and its Aftermath:
1580–1662

DRAKE had been away nearly three years. The expedition had made a false start on 15 November 1577, being driven back to Plymouth by storm damage. Finally they had left on 13 December 1577. And now it was Monday, 26 September 1580, by the reckoning of those ashore in Plymouth; but by their own log it was still only Sunday. Somehow they had lost a day! The same thing had happened to Magellan's expedition also. They thought the mistake must be theirs, but on rechecking could not discover how the error had occurred.

The expedition had sailed as a fleet of five ships: *Pelican*, 100 tons; *Elizabeth*, 80 tons; *Marigold*, 30 tons; *Swan*, 50 tons; *Christopher* (or *Bark Benedict*), 15 tons. And in those ships a total of 164 men and boys. And now Drake was returning alone with some fifty-seven or fifty-nine men (but having left a dozen or so ashore in the Spice Islands).

The *Christopher*'s successor, together with the storeship *Swan*, had been stripped and abandoned on the coast of South America in June 1578; the prize *Santa Maria*, taken from Nuño da Silva, had been similarly left behind at Port St Julian, with the bones of Thomas Doughty. With the force reduced to three ships and a pinnace, it had been scattered. The *Marigold* had sunk with all hands in the terrible storms south of Magellan's Strait; the *Golden Hind*'s pinnace with Peter Carder and seven other men aboard had vanished; the *Elizabeth* had parted company, and although they had looked for her at the appointed rendezvous, had failed to sight the Vice-Flagship.

Apart from the crews of the missing vessels, known casualties were small, amazingly so for such a voyage. A boy had been lost overboard from the *Christopher* when they were outward-bound off Portugal. John Fry had been seized by natives at Mogador and they

288

had been forced to abandon him (in fact he was able to return to England soon after). At Port St Julian Robert Winterhey and Oliver the master gunner had been killed by Giants; Thomas Doughty executed. At Mocha Tom Brewer and Tom Flood had been killed by natives; Great Neil the Dane and Diego, Drake's Cimarron servant, had died of their wounds soon after. Richard Minivy and a man named Thomas had been shot by Spaniards. And one man had died off the Cape of Good Hope. Normally, seamen died by scores from scurvy and other shipboard diseases resulting from poor diet or insanitary conditions. Drake had spent a high proportion of time during the cruise in looking for fresh food and fresh water for his men, and he had careened and cleaned the ship often. These were undoubtedly major factors in ensuring the success of the voyage. Sick or dying men sail no ships. The single vessel which returned from the Magellan expedition came back as a floating graveyard, in much the same state as John Hawkins had returned from San Juan de Ulloa.

Clearly Drake had learned this dire lesson thoroughly and had taken great care to put his knowledge into effect. He must also have ensured as firm a discipline among his men as he had over himself, for the casualties the raider had inflicted in the space of nearly three years amounted to one native killed in a fight begun by the natives (under a misapprehension that the English were Spaniards), and three Spaniards wounded – Alonso Rodriguez Bautista Patagalana, San Juan de Anton and Giusepe de Parraces. Although many ships had been plundered, little harm had been done to shipping beyond minor damage to ensure that a particularly fast vessel was in no state to pursue. This was perhaps appropriate to a state of undeclared war. It would have been too lenient in a commerce-destroyer proper.

As Captain-General, Drake could be faulted for his initial dealings with natives; his lack of caution had cost six of his men their lives, while others had been wounded, including himself. Only in California had he learned this lesson and been wary from the first. Technically, he was responsible for the loss of Peter Carder's crew in the pinnace; but the safety of the flagship did require a shallow-draught vessel in attendance and, since the *Marigold* had been lost, there was no other option available. He was responsible for stranding the *Golden Hind* on a rock pinnacle (and also for getting her off again without damage). Equally, he was the

K

first captain to sail his ship right round the globe (for Magellan had never come home, having died as a result of poor diplomacy). And Drake had done this with, at the best, poor charts, and often with no charts at all.

As a result, new features could be drawn on the charts, except that for reasons of state it would be wise to keep the information secret. Especially the new fact that south of Magellan's Strait was no mainland but only a few islands and then open sea. Potentially, this was a new and better route into the South Sea. The theoretical way by the Strait of Anian had not been proved or disproved, but appeared now to be hardly practical because of the steady trend of the continent far to the north-west and the biting cold experienced there even in summer. And, of course, the Captain-General had been able to claim for his Queen a new land north of the existing sphere of Spanish influence. He had besides, under his feet, perhaps the richest treasure any ship ever carried. So much that it could make a poor nation powerful.

Until now, Drake could have had no certain knowledge of what had become of John Winter and his vice-flagship the *Elizabeth*. They had in fact reached England sixteen months before, on 2 June 1579, when the *Golden Hind* was nearing 'Nova Albion'. Winter also had lost a pinnace with its eight-man crew off the coast of South America, in much the same circumstances as had Drake; and he had had one man killed and a number badly hurt in an accident with a capstan. Additionally, two men had deserted from the *Elizabeth* off Brazil. Some members at least of Winter's crew foresaw failure and death for Drake and their comrades in the flagship. For his part, John Drake made clear even to his Spanish interrogators that he regarded Winter's action as meriting the hangman.

In England, up to now, they had been given only Winter's version. The Vice-Admiral had covered himself most adroitly, first by claiming that it was his crew who would not go on with the voyage and had forced him to turn back against his will, and then that Drake had committed unlawful acts and had forced Winter to take part in them.

Shortly after his return in 1579, Winter reported having in his ship some stolen goods. The document was headed:

'A declaration made by me John Winter of a ship taken by Francis Drake, Captain and General of five ships and a bark bound for the part of America for discovery and other causes of trade of merchandizes necessary and requisite.'

The Declaration began:

'First the said John Winter sayeth that upon the coast of Africa near unto a certain island of Cabo Verde the said Francis Drake by himself and others by his power and forceable commandments did take a certain Portugal Ship wherein were certain wines and what other goods he knoweth not.

'And after the taking of the said Ship he, the said Drake, did put the men aland in a pinnace and carried away the wines with the Ship for the relief and maintenance of himself and company, being bent upon a long voyage of two years, as he said, and as it was then supposed, the taking of which ship I protest was utterly contrary to my good will which I could not let nor gainsay, for that I had no authority there, but such as pleased the said Drake, to give and take away from me at his will and pleasure, and being in great fear of my life if I should have contraried him or gone about to practise to withstand him in any part of his doings. He would have punished me by death, for that his words and threatenings many times tended there unto by open speeches, as by example a gentleman who he executed afterwards. And for that I was there with the said Drake where no Justice would be heard, was enforced to content myself with silence . . . I do here notify unto this court and you the Judge thereof, that I did never give my consent or allowance any way to the taking of any ships or goods unlawfully . . .'

Winter claimed not to know where the goods had originated or from whom Drake had stolen them, or how much there had been in the first place. He explained that some items had been put to good use in the *Elizabeth*, sails being made out of the canvas, shoes out of the leather, and so on; while other items still, 'being rotten', were cast overboard. But he was adamant that their presence aboard his ship was through no fault of his, and headed the list with the words: 'A note of such things by estimation as were put into the *Elizabeth* at Port St Julian by the commandments of Francis Drake, the which was received of the Company without inventory or any other remembrance in writing.' No doubt he had consulted a good lawyer.

An inventory was then taken by two Justices of the Peace, Sir

Arthur Bassett and Sir Richard Grenville, of exactly what now remained in the *Elizabeth*. The answer was: hardly anything. All the Justices could find were thirty-three pieces of linen cloth, ten dozen Cordovan skins, and eight or nine pieces of Portuguese canvas. And this was all Drake's fault, according to Winter. The Justices may have agreed with him. Grenville at least regarded Drake as an upstart, both socially and as a seaman. His own father had been a battleship captain when he had been drowned in the sinking of the *Mary Rose* in 1545, whereas Drake's father had been only a chaplain in the Navy, and then but for a short time. The Drakes were a mean and poverty-stricken family, by the standards of the Grenvilles.

By June 1580, the matter was before the Court of Admiralty. with the Portuguese ambassador, Don Antonio de Castillo, pressing urgently for the recovery of the goods from Winter. Apparently, the Vice-Admiral's plea of ignorance as to their original ownership had not in the end prevented them from being recognised as being cargo from Nuño da Silva's *Santa Maria*. Edward, Earl of Lincoln, Baron of Clinton and Say, Lord High Admiral of England, Ireland and Wales, ruled on 17 June 1590 that the goods concerned had been 'at some previous time piratically taken on the seas by Francis Drake and his accomplices and thereafter convoyed by John Winter to this realm . . .' And he ordered that they be delivered to the Portuguese ambassador.

Within two months, everything was in flux. The throne of Portugal becoming vacant, King Philip II of Spain put forward a claim well grounded in fact and, seconded by the strongest and most formidable army in Europe, joined the two nations and their navies. Theoretically, the ocean trade of the entire globe was now the sole monopoly of Spain and in robbing da Silva Drake had further offended Spanish power. Da Silva himself would now come legally under Spanish jurisdiction (he was already in an Inquisition prison) and any claim for restitution should now be made by the Spanish ambassador.

In Madrid they had been in possession of the facts of Drake's raid on the coasts from Peru to Mexico for a year, the news having arrived some time in August 1579. Don Antonio de Padilla, President of the Council of the Indies, sent the reports to the King with a covering letter. Philip II gave his decision in a marginal note: 'Before the Corsair reaches England, it is not expedient to speak to the Queen. When he arrives, yes.'

Don Antonio ordered a letter to be drafted in these terms for the information of Don Bernadino de Mendoza, the distinguished and outspoken soldier who was Spanish ambassador in London, adding:

> 'It would be advisable to enclose in the same letter what Don Bernadino is to say to the Queen on the Corsair's arrival. It would be so much better if he were never to arrive! It would also be fitting that Don Bernadino should know, and this is to be written to him in the same letter, that at the time when this Francis Drake departed from England with those five ships he left behind given securities that he would not seize or rob any persons of that kingdom or any other with whose sovereign his Queen was on peaceful terms.'

John Drake testified that the Captain-General did not himself venture ashore, but 'dispatched a messenger to the Queen who was in London which was sixty leagues distant, apprising her of his arrival'. This messenger was John Brewer, the trumpeter.

> 'And he wrote to other persons at Court who informed him that he was in Her Majesty's bad graces because she had already heard, by way of Peru and Spain, of the robberies he had committed. They also told him that the Spanish Ambassador was there at Court, and it was said that he was making a claim for what Francis Drake had taken.'

He was indeed, and with plenty of documentation to back it, but nevertheless the Queen sent word to Francis Drake:

> 'that he was to go to Court and take her some samples of his labours and that he was to fear nothing. With this he went to Court by land, taking certain horses laden with gold and silver. All the rest he left in Plymouth in the custody of one of the principal men there.'

The treasure must have been a great argument in Drake's favour, whereas pleas of illegality and robberies and hostile actions towards friendly states can have had but small effect. There had been changes since Drake had sailed from Plymouth in 1577. In 1579 Spanish troops had taken part in a landing in Ireland designed to assist the Irish rebels to drive out the English. In return, but secretly, Elizabeth was subsidising German mercenaries in an attempt to aid the Netherlanders who had rebelled against Spain. Negotiations were taking place to bring about an alliance with France against Spain, and the Portuguese pretender to the throne Philip II had just occupied was to be supported by English arms and money. Perhaps more important was that the Protestant cause had dangerously lost ground and that of the three seaborne expeditions Elizabeth had dispatched lately, only one had succeeded. Sir Humphrey Gilbert had failed in the West Indies and Martin Frobisher had been unsuccessful in his search for the North-West Passage and the Strait of Anian from the Atlantic side. Whereas the exploits of Captain-General Francis Drake were the talk of Europe. For the first time an Englishman was numbered among the legendary figures of global exploration.

Don Bernadino was not able to put the Spanish case directly to the Queen, for she would not see him. Instead, she received Francis Drake and spent six hours with him in her palace at Richmond, while he described the voyage and showed her some of the charts he had used and the jewels he had taken. And no doubt they discussed how the treasure, which had not yet been inventoried, was in principle to be divided. The Queen herself, and some of her ministers, had supported the voyage in cash or kind; others had opposed it, and some of these were talking about piracy.

On 22 October, from Richmond, she directed Edmund Tremayne in writing to give Drake personally £10,000, keeping the transaction most secret:

'We are pleased that for certain good considerations that there should be left in the hands of the said Drake so much of the said bullion by him brought home as may amount unto the sum of ten thousand pounds which we require you to see performed accordingly.'

There were other instructions which she did not care to commit to paper, but subsequently Tremayne mentioned them to Mr Secretary Walsingham (who had been a supporter of the voyage):

'Now to give you some understanding how I in particular, proceeded with Mr Drake, I have at no time entered in to the account to know more of the very value of the treasure than he made me acquainted with. And to say truly I persuaded him to impart no more to me than needed. For I saw him commanded

in her Majesty's behalf that he should not reveal the certainty
to no man living . . .'

Not only was the sum total of the treasure to be kept secret but
the amount actually taken by Drake was to be equally unknown.
Drake was left alone with the treasure 'before my son Harry and I
should come to the weighing and registering of that which was left',
so that he could remove £10,000 or as much more as he wanted.
'And so it is done accordingly, no creature by me made privy unto
it but myself and myself no privier to it than as you may perceive by
this,' wrote Tremayne. Whatever sum it was, Drake had earned
every ducat, as had his crew, who were also well rewarded. The
total cannot be known, even from the Spanish records and claims,
because of the Spanish habit of defeating their bureaucracy by
declaring for customs only about half the value of what they were
actually carrying. But certainly it would have been enough to make
the Queen and her ministers easy in their minds, knowing that they
could afford defiance, afford to fight, afford to finance further
expeditions for exploration and trade.

The Spanish ambassador was reduced to showing his documentary evidence to two junior officials, although the papers eventually
reached Lord Burghley, a minister more sympathetic to Spain than
Sir Francis Walsingham. The lists of robberies committed began
with the *Capitana* (or *Great Captain of the South Sea*) of Licentiate
Torres at Valparaiso and ended with the taking of San Juan de
Anton's treasure ship off Cape San Francisco. The treasure taken,
together with damages sustained, was estimated by the witnesses
as 'a million of pesos of gold, every peso worth 450 maravedis'.
The lists, probably of fair accuracy, were not up to date and did
not include, for instance, the sack of Guatalco nor the 'atrocities'
committed in the church there. Indeed, the desecrated church had
only been inspected on 15 May 1580, after the lapse of a year, by
an important churchman, Alonso Granero de Avalos, Bishop of
La Plata in Peru, who reported on 'the havoc made by the English,
which is indeed grievous'.

However, Bernadino de Mendoza more than made up for this
when on 29 October he declared that: 'In fight, Drake has cut off
the hands of some of his Majesty's subjects . . .' This day, in
far-off Lima, Oxenham and his two companions were led out to
execution. The law could not protect them because they had been

acting outside the law, having no commission from Elizabeth; Drake's threats of revenge if they were killed had not sufficed either. These lacked credibility anyway because, as the Spanish authorities had long ago discovered, most of Drake's captives testified to good treatment (with the exception of those few who would not cooperate).

Drake could not very well deny the robberies alleged against him by the Spanish ambassador (although the value of the goods taken, on the Queen's direct orders, was not to be admitted). But he was concerned to stamp out any suggestions of maiming or murder, whether in fight or otherwise. Drake therefore approached Edmund Tremayne and asked for an official inquiry to be carried out at once, while most of his company were still with the ship and could conveniently be examined. Forty-nine men, gentlemen and mariners, gave answers to three points:

'Firstly, Whether Mr Drake and his company had taken from the King of Spain and his subjects in gold and silver to the value of one million and a half or not.

'Secondly, Whether they have in their voyage taken any ships or vessels of the said King or his subjects and after sunken them with their men or mariners, or not.

'Thirdly, Whether they had at any time in any fight killed any of the said King's subjects or had cut off their hands or arms or otherwise with any cruelty mangled any of them.'

The first to answer these questions was Lawrence Eliot, who declared:

'To the first I say that to the value I can say nothing, the thing being unknown unto me; only silver and some gold there was taken, but how much I know not; but a very small sum in respect of that that is reported.

'To the second, I confess there were ships taken; but that any were sunken with their men and mariners, it is altogether untrue.

'To the third that to my knowledge there was no Spaniards slain by any of us, or had their arms or hands cut off, or otherwise by any cruelty mangled or maimed. Only one man I remember was hurt in the face, which our General caused to be sent for, and lodged him in his own ship, set him at his own table, and would not suffer him to depart before he was recovered, and so sent him safe away.'

This latter was San Juan de Anton. Presumably, Eliot had forgotten Giusepe de Parraces, also slightly wounded; but neither of these men bothered to report their wounds officially to their own authorities. Alonso Rodriguez, captain of the ship which resisted at Callao, may have been more seriously hurt, although the English would know only that they had lost one man themselves.

John Chester, Gregory Cary and George Fortesque signed individual documents to the same effect. The rest of the ship's company, headed by Francis Fletcher, put all their names on one document. William Hawkins and John Doughty either did not sign or were unable to because they had left the ship by this date, 8 November 1580. Probably John Doughty had left because he planned to bring an action against Drake in the Earl Marshal's court for the murder of his brother, Thomas Doughty, at Port St Julian. So this charge also was to hang over Drake's head after his homecoming.

The impact of the voyage on public opinion, as far as it could be judged by the popular broadsheets and in the pulpits, was immense. The annalist John Stow recorded: 'The people generally applauded his wonderful adventures and rich prizes. His name and fame became admirable in all places, the people swarming daily in the streets to behold him, swearing hatred to all that misliked him.'

On New Year's Day, 1581, Queen Elizabeth appeared wearing a new crown, presented to her by Master Francis Drake. It held five large emeralds, 'three of them almost as long as a little finger', reported Don Bernadino. There is small doubt where they came from. The anonymous witness recorded that, from the 'Friar's Bark' off Payta, Drake had taken 'a great crucifix of gold and certain emeralds near as long as a man's finger'. Drake's New Year's gift to the Queen was a valuable diamond cross; this could have come from any one of several ships, including the Friar's and the *Capitana*.

In some quarters, the proceedings were regarded as scandalous; in others, as downright unwise. The government was dangerously split. On one side were the Queen, the Earl of Leicester, Sir Francis Walsingham, and Sir Christopher Hatton – all of them investors in the voyage and, as was later calculated, likely to receive £47 for every £1 with which they had backed Drake in 1577. Naturally they did not want to see the treasure returned. On the other side were some of the most experienced and formidable of

Elizabeth's councillors, including Lord Burghley, the Lord High Admiral, the Earl of Sussex, Sir James Crofts and Secretary Wilson. These men foresaw crippling Spanish reprisals against English trade if the plunder was not returned, and they actually drafted an order to that effect, stipulating that in the meantime the treasure should be stored in the Tower for safety. Attempts were made to bribe them – Burghley was offered ten bars of gold, Sussex was to be given silver vases and salvers. Both men refused. Cruel jokes were going the rounds. The Queen, it was said, was going to knight Francis Drake 'Master thief of the unknown world'.

The Spanish ambassador learnt that it was indeed Elizabeth's intention to confer a knighthood on the corsair, and that she was so proud of his exploits that his ship was to be brought round from Plymouth into the Thames and docked for public display at Deptford. In some fashion, behind the scenes, the divisions among Elizabeth and her ministers had healed. The decision to take the bolder course probably owed much to outside events. Towards the end of the year 1580 the Irish resistance movement led by James Fitzmaurice Fitzgerald and the Earl of Desmond, accompanied by a papal legate and a force of Spanish soldiers, was dispersed or destroyed by the English; and the Spaniards were massacred. Temporarily, that removed a dagger from England's back.

On the positive, offensive side, a French delegation was due to arrive in a few months' time to discuss terms for the possible marriage of Elizabeth to the Duke of Alençon. For as long as anyone could remember, the traditional English alliance was with Spain and against France. Indeed, in the time of Elizabeth's father, Henry VIII, a great French armada of 235 ships and some thirty thousand men had sailed for England and actually invaded. French seaborne landings, because France had harbours close to England, often did succeed even if, as in this case, the troops had not been able to hold their lodgements ashore for more than a few days. Throughout most of Henry's reign, Spain had been the ally, not always very effective, of the English Crown. Now, with such a momentous change, and remembering how comparatively far away were her harbours from England, perhaps she might prove a not very effective enemy.

John Drake was one of those who helped bring the *Golden Hind* into the Thames, where she secured at Tower Wharf for the unloading of her cargo of silver. Then she went down river to Deptford, near the royal palace of Greenwich, which was to be her final resting place, one of unparalleled honour. 'The Queen said that they were to make a house wherein the ship could be preserved as a memorial,' reported John Drake. On 4 April 1581, he was there to take part in the ceremony when Elizabeth and her Court came on board the *Golden Hind* and were shown over the ship, which it was now intended to preserve for all time. There was such a crowd assembled that a hundred of them swarmed on to a plank bridge built for the Queen to walk on, and it collapsed under their weight, fortunately without seriously hurting anyone.

Don Bernadino de Mendoza was not there, the only ambassador not to have been invited. However, the Seigneur de Marchamont, the personal representative of the Duke of Alençon, was prominent among the guests; and his master, as it happened, was not merely brother to the King of France but laid claim to the Spanish-occupied Netherlands. This gave the ceremony its point. As Drake knelt before Elizabeth on the deck of the ship he had taken round the world, she told him that the King of Spain had asked her for his head. Now she had a gilded sword ready to strike it off. At that she handed the sword to Alençon's representative and asked him to knight Drake for her. The Seigneur de Marchamont, and not Elizabeth, performed the ceremony.

The Queen also presented Sir Francis Drake with two gifts – a miniature of herself by Nicholas Hilliard and a green silk scarf with a motto worked in gold letters: 'The Almighty be your Guide and your Protector to the End.' The message would hardly be lost on Don Bernadino; nor, for that matter, could it escape the notice of those Englishmen for whom Drake was a pirate.

John Doughty reacted violently and wrote: 'When the Queen did Knight Drake she did then Knight the arrantest Knave, the vilest villain, the falsest thief and the cruelest murderer that ever was born.' He was prosecuting for murder in the Earl Marshal's court, and although Drake's lawyers applied for a writ to stay proceedings, the Lord Chief Justice ruled that the case lay within the jurisdiction of the Marshal and that Doughty might proceed. This threat must have spoiled much of the flavour of Drake's triumph, although in the end it never came to trial, as Doughty was eventually arrested for combining with Spaniards in a plan to either kill or kidnap Drake.

Sir Francis Drake, Knight, required a more imposing base than a town house in Plymouth; he needed a country estate. What he desired to own was Buckland Abbey, a former religious building which had been converted by the Grenvilles into a pleasantly mature manor house. It was now owned by Sir Richard Grenville, the most direct rival to Drake in the business of seaborne exploration of the globe, who, although more nobly born, had been passed over in favour of Drake for the voyage into the South Sea. The Grenvilles resented Drake very much and would, he suspected, not knowingly sell to a man they considered an upstart, even if he had lately joined the select band of three hundred or so knights who, together with about sixty peers, formed the aristocracy of England. So he arranged with two friends to buy it for him in their names, for £3400, and then convey it to him; which they did. When his wife Mary died in 1583, Sir Francis waited only a year or so before marrying again; he chose Elizabeth, the twenty-year-old and exquisitely beautiful only daughter of Sir George Sydenham.

John Drake had gone to sea again in 1582, sailing with the Fenton expedition. However, his ship was wrecked off the River Plate, he was captured by Indians and later handed over to the Spaniards. He was interrogated in March 1584, regarding the circumnavigation, while his memory was still fresh; and again in January 1587. He took part in the auto-da-fé of 30 November 1589, but although his life was spared, he never got back to England.

In the year John Drake had set out, 1582, Miles Philips had escaped from captivity in Spain and managed to reach England; and Nuño da Silva had been released by the Inquisition in Mexico and sent to Spain. In 1583 he was set free.

In 1585 an expedition organised by Sir Walter Raleigh and led by Sir Richard Grenville sailed from Plymouth to found a colony in America to be known as 'Virginia' (after the Queen). Unlike Drake, they antagonised the Indians and the project was a failure. The English could not match the care and attention which the Spaniards paid to nourishing their colonies from home, without which aid they almost invariably collapsed. John Dee's dreams of a 'British Impire' were premature.

The last member of Drake's expedition to return home was the long-lost Peter Carder. The only survivor from the *Golden Hind*'s pinnace which had parted company in a storm south of Magellan's Strait, he had been away nine years and fourteen days when at the end of November 1586 he arrived at Chichester Harbour in an English ship. Carder had managed to get on board one of five Portuguese ships bound home from Brazil; then, when off the Azores, they were intercepted by two English warships commanded by Captain Raymond and Captain George Drake. The Portuguese surrendered and Carder was free.

The revelation of who he was must have fascinated his liberators. Carder wrote:

'My strange adventures, and long living among cruel savages being known to the right honourable the Lord Charles Howard, Lord High Admiral of England, he certified the Queen's Majesty thereof with speed, and brought me to her presence at Whitehall, where it pleased her to talk with me a long hours space of my travels and wonderful escape, and among other things of the manner of Master Doughty's execution; and afterward bestowed 22 angels on me, willing my Lord to have consideration of me. With many gracious words I was dismissed; humbly thanking the Almighty for my miraculous preservation, and safe return into my native country.'

The proposal to build a 'house' for the *Golden Hind* as a permanent memorial and perhaps museum got as far as the preliminary plans and estimates stage. A brick wall 15 feet high and 180 feet long in circuit was to be built for the cost of £130. There was to be a space of 24 feet between interior walls, so that there would be room for visitors to walk round the ship under cover. A further £90 was allowed for the construction of a timber-and tile roof. The total of £220 was modest enough, for what would be in effect a covered dock with, presumably, a good many openings in the surrounding wall for light and ventilation. Given such protection, the hull might have lasted for many centuries.

With events moving slowly but inexorably towards openly declared war and the possible arrival of a Spanish Armada in the mouth of the Thames, it appears that the proposal was never carried into effect. Even so, the neglected hulk had considerable drawing power for visitors, especially foreigners. Thomas Platter, a Swiss, went to see her in 1599 and thought her fabric so rotten that he was tempted to take a piece home to Basle as a souvenir. A Dutch chart of about 1601–1606, *Wagher's Thresoor der Zeerart* published by Benjamin Wright, included a sketch of a vessel lying ashore at Deptford with the note 'Captain Dracke's Schip'. In 1618, nearly forty years after she had been laid up, the Secretary to the Venetian Ambassador wrote: 'We likewise passed along the banks of the Thames in sight of some relics of the ship of the famous Captain Drake, which looked exactly like the bleached ribs and bare skull of a dead horse.' In about 1662, after more than eighty years of neglect, by breaking or by burning, or both, the site was tidied up.

It is difficult to dispose entirely of ship timbers lying in mud, and it is possible that some portions of Drake's vessel may have survived, buried perhaps under a quay or some later construction. Even if found and exhumed, however, this would not be at all the same as if the ship and her furniture had come down to us complete, as had been first intended. All that remains directly of the fabric of the *Golden Hind* are some relics made from her timbers – such as a chair at the Bodleian Library, Oxford, and a table at Middle Temple Hall, London. The Bodleian also possess what may be a model of her, but crudely made as if built to serve as a child's toy. There are no shipbuilder's models and no shipbuilder's plans, and even the estimates for the building which was to house her give only a rough idea of her dimensions. As a ship, the *Golden Hind* has vanished without trace; only the achievement remains.

AFTERWORD

In order to see the achievement for what it was I have excluded the twentieth century in the writing of this book as much as I could, and attempted to think about the world in sixteenth-century terms. Even the appearance of hindsight might ruin the illusion. After all, anyone can circumnavigate the globe nowadays, provided that they can pay for it. Matters have gone so far that yachtsmen can even challenge each other to a race round the world.

More than many, I was uneasily conscious of this. From Spithead, off Portsmouth, I watched the start of two Whitbread Round-the-World Races, those of 1973 and 1977, and suspected irritably that the competitors were publicly demeaning the achievements of the sixteenth-century explorers. This feeling was heightened by the fact that I was not at Spithead in order to watch the start of the races, but to carry on excavations of a Tudor ship older than the *Golden Hind*. This was the 700-ton carrack *Mary Rose*, which was captained by Sir Richard Grenville's father and sank in battle in 1545, perhaps a year or two after Francis Drake was born.

While on the one hand I knew all the modern answers to the problems of geography which so many of the pioneer explorers died to solve, on the other hand I was acquainted not merely with an actual Tudor ship but also with a mass of shipboard items, from wrought-iron guns to brass block-sheaves, from pewter drinking tankards to wooden eating bowls, which were all practical reminders of the actual technology of the distant world I was researching and writing about.

Perhaps this was why I found myself unable to give any glib account of shipboard life in Drake's time: I was aware, better than most, how little we actually know about it. Although I was trying to show how matters may have appeared to men living at the time the *Golden Hind* circumnavigated the globe, I was forced to rely mainly on documents, and could not go beyond them. On many interesting questions, I must plead ignorance because, as so often for the Tudor period, the surviving authentic information tends to be patchy or confused; and some of it is much less than objective.

On the other hand, I was prevented from thrusting forward too obviously the facts of modern geography, which were either unknown or unsure in Drake's time, but which any reader can verify for himself from a globe (not, please, a map or a chart, these being inaccurate in one respect or another).

Drake was certainly right not to try too hard for the supposed Strait of Anian, because an actual Strait, far to the west, was not discovered until 1728 by Vitus Bering. The North-West Passage which Frobisher and others sought from the Atlantic was non-existent in terms of sixteenth-century shipping and barely practical even to twentieth-century vessels. The North-East Passage was to prove a better proposition, although only at certain times of the year and aided by icebreakers. But somebody has to go in and find out, and these sixteenth-century explorers were not wrong in making the attempt; they simply had the odds loaded heavily against them.

In comparison, a modern space age explorer hardly merits even the name, being directed all the way to his objective by organisations in possession of very complete information long in advance of actual arrival. The qualities required might seem to be those of a most superior test pilot.

Sixteenth-century seaborne exploration required a very different type of man. Unlike his twentieth-century equivalent, he commanded a force which was 'teeth' rather than 'tail'. Not one rocket from an enormous base and control complex, but five vessels with several hundred men which were beyond their own limited dockyard resources within a few days of sailing. There is the time factor, too – three years instead of three weeks. Questions of crew morale and command became critical, and it is no accident that 'mutinies' and executions were commonplace on the really long and hazardous voyages into the unknown, although the notorious sixteenth-century practice of divided command certainly did not help. All went well as long as the pair at the top were compatible and, by sharing their knowledge, more effective than a single brain; but as soon as there arose stress or doubt as to who was to direct, then the matter could be resolved only by the death of the one or the other. As a later comrade of Drake wrote: 'He never attempted any action, wherein he was absolute Commander, but he performed the same with great reputation, and did easily dispatch great matters.'

The voyage of circumnavigation was the greatest of these, carried out almost without flaw, and lasting three years. All too often, Drake was doubtfully linked with someone else, because authority did not wholly trust him: Hawkins often enough and, during the Armada campaign, Howard. Unlike many at that time, who either did not know their business completely or, more often, were insufficiently thorough and left too much to chance, Drake was a true professional. He 'was the first Englishman that did compass the world; wherein, as also in his deep judgement in sea causes, he did far exceed not Sir John Hawkins alone, but all others whomsoever.' The justice of this statement by a contemporary can be realised only by considering in detail the fortunes of those who came after; what seemed deceptively easy when performed by Drake resulted often enough in ruin and disaster when attempted by anyone else.

In modern times Drake has either become unreal or been simplified in schoolboy fashion because most of us first read about him as schoolboys, in simple English primers, and he is therefore not an adult figure. His career is all excitement, bravado, buccaneering and swashbuckling as conceived by a fifteen-year-old.

The centuries, equally with the generations, raise another absolute bar. In Drake's time, the only people with the chance to become widely travelled and see strange, exotic and warmer places were a few thousand seamen. The feeling of superior experience which this imparted is unconsciously hinted at by Fletcher, who often lambasts the academically-knowing stay-at-home ignoramuses of England. But eliminating sinful pride altogether, it is possible to underrate, as a lure to sixteenth-century exploration, both the risks (to predominantly youthful optimists) and the astounding experiences and sensations of being among the very fortunate few able to explore the globe.

Nowadays it is all too easy to leave Gatwick two hours late (because a March snowstorm has caught the English unprepared) and four hours later, having followed the old maritime explorers' route (but at 33,000 feet and 600 mph), to arrive at Tenerife in brilliant sunshine and satisfactorily boiling heat. And to be among friendly Spaniards who have long since forgotten the visits of Hawkins and Drake but do remember Nelson (because they shot his arm off here).

The only way to go back in time for an accurate appraisal of the circumnavigation is to see how the return of the *Golden Hind* appeared to a Tudor schoolboy, then at Winchester, who wrote:

> 'The Stars above will make thee known
> If men here silent were
> The Sun himself cannot forget
> His fellow-traveller.'

NOTES ON USE OF QUOTATIONS

In the interests of clarity and easy understanding, I have 'edited' some of the quotations from original sixteenth century sources, most often by changing one long and involved sentence into two, or even three, shorter sentences. This was achieved by the liberal use of the full stop; but some of the semi-colons are mine also.

In the text I have modernised and standardised the spelling which in Tudor times varied much; some writers cared so little for rules that they would employ two different spellings of the same word in the same sentence. Their ghosts are therefore in no position to complain. In any case, the spellings which seem strangest to us appear phonetic, perhaps a representation of local dialect.

Very occasionally, where a word has now changed its meaning, I have substituted the modern for the old. The most common word so altered is 'presently', which ought to mean 'at once' or 'immediately', and in Tudor times actually did so, but nowadays lazily implies some short time in the future.

For the convenience of the student of language I have listed all the sources, but it should be remembered that many of these are actually translations from original Spanish. A point which has been made before is that error is likely where a Spanish civil servant was trying to translate an English maritime phrase into a Spanish equivalent of which he was ignorant. Further error may occur when this is translated back into English during the 19th century by an English scholar without nautical background.

These errors will be of minor importance. The greatest defect of the sources is that Drake's illustrated journal of the voyage is not among them. Presumably it was kept secret and then lost or destroyed.

SOURCES

Much of the basic source material is still in print, thanks largely to the Hakluyt Society, London, and the Kraus Reprint Corporation, Liechtenstein.

Spanish Documents Concerning English Voyages to the Caribbean, 1527–1568. Ed. I. A. Wright (Hakluyt, 1929; Kraus, 1967). Includes the defeat of Hawkins and Drake at San Juan de Ulloa (Vera Cruz) as seen through Spanish eyes.

Documents Concerning English Voyages to the Spanish Main, 1569–1580. Ed. I. A. Wright (Hakluyt, 1932; Kraus, 1967). Part I consists of Spanish documents from the Archives of the Indies at Seville and includes those concerning the defeat and capture of John Oxenham. Part II consists of English accounts including *Sir Francis Drake Revived*, published by his nephew in 1628 and said to be compiled from eye-witness narratives edited by Drake himself. The story of Nombre de Dios and the assault on the mule trains from Panama is here told from the English side and may be compared with the Spanish versions printed in Part I.

English Privateering Voyages to the West Indies, 1888–95. Ed. Kenneth R. Andrews (Hakluyt, C.U.P., 1959). Background.

The Last Voyage of Drake and Hawkins. Ed. Kenneth R. Andrews (Hakluyt, C.U.P., 1972). Contemporary remarks on the methods and characters of Drake and Hawkins.

New Light on Drake: A Collection of Documents relating to His Voyage of Circumnavigation, 1577–1580. Ed. Zelia Nuttall (Hakluyt, 1914; Kraus, 1967). The bulk consists of Spanish documents, including the depositions of witnesses who were prisoners of Drake and the interrogations of Nino da Silva and John Drake. The translations are also by Zelia Nuttall.

The World Encompassed. Ed. W. S. W. Vaux (Hakluyt, 1854; Burt Franklin, New York). Originally published 1628 by the Drake family and stated to have been 'Carefully collected out of the Notes of Master Francis Fletcher, Preacher in this employment, and divers others his followers in the same.' The Appendix by Vaux includes the narratives of John Cooke, Edward Cliffe and the Anonymous Pacific witness.

The World Encompassed and Analogous Contemporary Documents. Ed. N. M. Penzer (Argonaut Press, 1926). This transcription and arrangement is generally regarded as being better and more accurate than that of Vaux; the latter, however, is still in print in New York.

An Elizabethan in 1582: The Diary of Richard Madox, Fellow of All Souls. Ed. Elizabeth Story Donno (Hakluyt, 1976). This story of a failed voyage to the Spice Islands is interesting for comparisons and parallels, including shipboard intrigues and bad feeling, diary writing in code (Latin and Greek). The author suspects Francis Drake either falsified his charts of Magellan Strait or stole them from the Portuguese, but confirms he reached 48 degrees North. This was the Fenton expedition on which John Drake's ship was wrecked.

The Observations of Sir Richard Hawkins, Kt. on His Voyage into the South Sea, A.D. 1593. Ed. Sir Clements Markham (Hakluyt). A failed attempt to emulate Drake. The English are beaten and taken by Spanish ships commanded by, among others, Miguel Angel who had harder luck with Drake. Nevertheless, very detailed account of shipboard life and practices not to be found elsewhere. Some contemporary comments on Drake.

Hakluytus Posthumus or Purchas His Pilgrimes, Vol. XVI. Ed. Samuel Purchas, London, 1625 (MacLehose, 1906). Includes the narratives of Miles Philips and Peter Carder and gives career and character information on Drake and Hawkins.

The Principal Navigations, Voiages, Traffiques and Discoveries of the English Nation. In three vols (1589, 1598, 1599). Ed. Richard Hakluyt. An account of Drake's circumnavigation arrived so late it was not included in the title page, being inserted during the binding stage. It is innocuous. Later editions included the narrative of Edward Cliffe and the second interrogation of Nuno da Silva, plus a discourse by Lopez Vaz based on what da Silva told him. This material has been republished lately as *Hakluyt: Voyages*, Vol. 8 (Everyman, 1962).

The Hakluyt Handbook, Vols. I and II. Ed. D. B. Quinn (Hakluyt, 1974). Contains a good deal of valuable commentary as well as indicating the nature and scope of the literature of exploration.

The Family and Heirs of Sir Francis Drake by Lady Eliott-Drake (Smith, Elder, 1911). Prints the two interrogations of John Drake in full, both in Spanish and in English, plus much biographical detail. (Wright gives an abbreviated version of the interrogations and in English only.)

The Naval Tracts of Sir William Monson. Ed. M. Oppenheim (Navy Records Society, 1902). Background information and some adverse comments on Drake by a contemporary, born 1569.

A Regiment for the Sea and other writings on navigation by William Bourne (*c.* 1535–1582). Ed. E. G. R. Taylor (Hakluyt, 1963). This treatise on navigation, with tables, was published in various editions between 1571 and 1580.

A Sea Grammar by Captain John Smith (*c.* 1580–1631). Ed. Kermit Goell (Michael Joseph, 1970). Smith was born in 1580, the year Drake's voyage ended, rose to be Governor of Virginia and Admiral of New England, and published his guide to War at Sea in 1627. He describes the structure of a ship, naming the parts, and the ropes and the sails; and how it is handled in storm and in battle. He describes the guns and ammunition and shows how important the rations were. His work may in part have been based on *The Seaman's Dictionary* by Sir Henry Mainwaring.

Explorer's Maps by R. A. Skelton (Spring Books, 1970). Many 16th century maps and charts illustrated and described.

Discovering the New World. Ed. Michael Alexander (London Editions, 1977). Selection of American pictures from Theodore de Bry's contemporary engravings illustrating *Great Voyages*. De Bry was born in 1528, died 1598.

Articles in the *Mariner's Mirror* concerning the backing and planning of the circumnavigation:

Vol. XV 1929:   *Master John Dee, Drake and the Straits of Anian*
                   by E. G. R. Taylor.
Vol. XVI 1930:   *More Light on Drake: 1577–80* by E. G. R.
                   Taylor.

Contains the Draft Plan and Winter's Report.

Articles in the *Mariner's Mirror* regarding the *Golden Hind*:
Vol. XXIV 1938:   *The Little Ship of the Ashmolean* by R. Morton
                   Nance.
Vol. XXXIV 1948:   *The Mystery of the Tonnage and Dimensions of
                   Pelican–Golden Hind* by F. C. Prideaux Naish.
Vol. XXXV 1949:   *The Evidence about the Golden Hind* by Gregory
                   Robinson.
Vol. XXXVI 1950:   *The Identification of the Ashmolean Model* by
                   F. C. Prideaux Naish.

The Elizabethan Ship by Gregory Robinson (Longmans, 1956).
A simple guide which tells a good deal without going beyond the
evidence.

English Merchant Shipping 1460–1540 by Dorothy Burwash
(David & Charles, 1969). Deals with wages and contracts, conditions
of work, the Laws of Oleron, etc.

The First Ships round the World by Walter Brownlee (C.U.P.,
1974) Magellan's ships and the general problems of sailing round the
world in them, written by a master mariner.

GENERAL READING, MOSTLY RECENT & EASILY AVAILABLE

Imperial Spain 1469–1716 by J. H. Elliott (Pelican, 1970)
The Portuguese Seaborne Empire 1415–1825 by C. R. Boxer (Pelican,
1973)
Portugal and the Quest for the Indies by Christopher Bell (PBS)
Magellan by Ian Cameron (Weidenfeld & Nicolson, 1974)
The Voyages of Columbus by Rex & Thea Rienits (Hamlyn, 1970)
The Four Voyages of Christopher Columbus: documents ed. J. M.
Cohen, (Penguin, 1969)
Christopher Columbus, Mariner by Samuel Eliot Morison (Mentor,
1955)
Columbus by Marianne Mahn-Lot (Evergreen, 1961)

The Life and Times of Cortes by Roberto Bosi (Hamlyn, 1969)
History of the Conquest of Mexico by William H. Prescott (Swan Sonnenschien, Le Bas & Lowry, 1886)
The Aztecs of Mexico by G. C. Vaillant (BCA, 1975)
European Culture and Overseas Expansion by Carlo M. Cipolla (Pelican, 1970)
The Opening of the World by David Divine (Collins, 1973)
The World Atlas of Exploration by Eric Newby (Beazley, 1975)
The European Discovery of America: The Northern Voyages by Samuel Eliot Morison (OUP, 1971)
The European Discovery of America: The Southern Voyages by Samuel Eliot Morison (OUP, 1974)
Sir Francis Drake's Voyage Around the World, Its Aims and Achievements by Henry R. Wagner (San Francisco, 1926)
The Silver Circle by Lewis Gibbs (Dent, 1963)
Drake's Voyages by K. R. Andrews (Panther, 1970)
The Defeat of John Hawkins by Rayner Unwin (Hamlyn, 1962)
Undreamed Shores: England's wasted Empire in America by Michael Foss (BCA, 1974)
Francis Drake by Neville Williams (Weidenfeld & Nicolson, 1973)
Elizabethan England by A. H. Dodd (BCA. 1974)
All the Queen's Men: Elizabeth I and Her Courtiers by Neville Williams (Cardinal, 1974)
The England of Elizabeth by A. L. Rowse (Macmillan, 1959)
Elizabethan Life in Town and Country by M. St. Clare Byrne (Methuen pb, 1961)
The Tudors by Christopher Morris (Fontana, 1970)
The House of Tudor by Alison Plowden (Weidenfeld & Nicolson, 1976)
Renaissance Europe 1480–1520 by J. R. Hale (Fontana, 1971)
Europe Divided 1559–1598 by J. H. Elliott (Fontana, 1971)

INDEX

Acapulco, 152–3, 198, 214, 216, 218, 220, 224, 230, 241, 248, 250, 252, 254–6
Acla, 209
Aguilar, Don Miguel de Eraso y, 208 9
Aguirre, Friar Andres, 231 2
Aguirre, Martin de, 215
Alençon, Duke of, 298–9
Alexandria, 22–3, 29, 139
Alvarado, Pedro de, 234
Alvarez, Gonzalo, 174
Angel, Miguel, 157, 161, 182, 199, 204–5, 220, 249
Anian, Straits of, 27, 171, 190, 204, 250, 256, 267–8, 273, 290, 294, 303
Anonymous Narrative, 128, 131, 146, 192–3, 272, 278, 281, 285
Anton, San Juan de, 157, 166, 173, 182–95, 197, 200–1, 204–8, 211–212, 250, 289, 296 7
Anthony, Nicolas, 21, 84, 100
Arana, Pedro de, 163, 199, 201–2, 249
Arequipa, 155
Arica, 142, 146, 154–5, 249
Atlantic, 10
Audley, John, 100
Avalos, Rev. Lord Don Alonso Garcia de, 232–3, 295
Azores, 8, 33
Aztecs, 213

'Bacallaos' (Strait of Stockfish'), 203, 256, 258–9, 261, 267
Bahia Salada, 133–5

Baratiua, 284
Barbas, Cape, 35
Bassett, Sir Arthur, 292
Bering, Vitus, 303
Bernaldo, Martin Monte, 210–11
Bique, Don Pedro, 209–10
Blanc, Cape, 34–8, 285
Bodleian Library, 302
Bojador, Cape, 8
Bon Esperance (Bona Speranza, Boa Esperanca), 284–5
Book of Martyrs, 239–40
Brava Island, 44
Bravo, Benito Diaz, 175–9, 200–1, 204, 206
Brazil, 8, 33, 42, 57, 141, 187, 194, 259, 301
Brewer, John, 48–9; quarrel with Doughty, 52, battle with Giants, 75, 79, 89, 114; overboard, 118–9; Mocha, 124–5, 183
Brewer, Tom, 124–6
Bright, Edward, 48, 79, 84, 86–8, 92, 95–7, 104–5, 114, 119
Buckland Abbey, 300
Burghley, Lord, 87, 101–2, 113, 295, 298
Butler, Henry, 159, 251
Butler, John, 159, 166–8, 194, 251, 295

Cabot, Sebastian, 171
Callao, 107, 151, 159–65, 179, 182–3
California, 256, 268–9, 265, 268, 272
Camargo expedition, 107
Camões, Luis de, 11
Canary Islands, 10–11, 32–3, 286

Caño Island, 191, 196–7, 201, 206, 214–17, 249
Cano, Sebastian del, 79
Canters (fishing boats), 35–6
Cantin, Cape, 33
Caravels, 35–6
Careening, Trimming, Fouling, Anti-Fouling, 31; *at Cape Blanc*, 37; *at P.S. Julian*, 103, 134, 150, 191, 197; *at Caño*, 217; *California*, 269; *Crab Is.*, 277–8; *Java*, 284
Carder, Peter, 117, 141–2, 158, 284, 289, 300–1
Carracks, 277, 285
Cartagena, Juan dem 74–5
Cartagena, port of, 208–11
Cary, Gregory, 84–5, 297
Casualties (Killed), *Boy overboard*, 33; *Oliver & Winterhey*, 76–7; *Great Neil the Dane and Diego the Moor*, 124–5; *Tom Brewer & Tom Hood* (*Flood?*), 126; *Minivy*, 133, 212; *1 man in the Elizabeth*, 141; *Thomas at Callao*, 162, 212; *1 man died after Ternate*, 285; *Summary*, 288–9
(Wounded), *8 men at Mocha*, 124–6; *some men in Elizabeth*, 141; *Alonso Rodriguez*, 162; *S. J. de Anton*, 184, 212; *Giusepe de Paraces*, 215–16
Cataro, 199
Celebes, 277, 284
Chester, John, 21, 52–6, 68, 84, 297
Chichester Harbour, 301
Chilton, John, 237
Chule, 155
Cimarrons, 15–18, 174–6, 189, 205, 278
Cliffe, Edward, 39, 56, 58, 65–6, 108, 112, 119, 136–9, 146
Clinton, Lord Edward, 292, 298
Colchero, Alonso Sanchez, 215–23, 225–6, 229, 247–8, 273, 283
Columbus, Christopher, 7, 9–10, 16–17, 32, 37, 214
Contreras, Moya de, 253
Cook (or Coke), William, 239

Cooke, John, 22, 30–1, 34, 36, 39, 45, 47–9, 51–2, 54–5, 58; *re pro-Drake & anti-Drake factions*, 54–5, 68, 84, 91; 61, 65–6, 68–71, 75; *condemns Drake*, 78–80; *re Doughty trial*, 84–94, 96–8, 104–5, 139–40, 146
Copiapo, 142
Cortés, Hernán, 11, 214, 234
Costa Rica, 191, 196, 201, 213–14
Crab Island (Francesca Is.), 277–9
Crofts, Sir James, 298
Cusco, 145
Cyppo (Coquimbo), 132

Da Silva, Nuño, *attacked by Drake*, 41; *biography*, 42; *taken by Drake*, 43; *assesses Pelican & Drake*, 45, 49; *into Pelican*, 53, 58–61, 64, 73–4; *re Drake–Doughty*, 80; *re Magellan Strait*, 109–10, 112, 117, 119, 150, 173; '*recognised*', 173–4, 176, 196, 202, 216, 241, 261; *description of*, 173, 238; *speaks Spanish*, 191, 178; *at Church services*, 231–2; *friendly with Drake*, 233, 238, 244; *put into ship of Juan de Madrid*, 246–7, *taken to Mexico City*, 253–6, 258–61, 265, 267–8, 292; *released Spain*, 300
Dee, Doctor John, 24–8, 300
Deptford, 298–9, 301–2
Díaz, Bartholemew, 8
Diego, negro, 43; *killed Mocha*, 124–5, 278
Diet (crew health), 30–1, 67, 108, 110, 118, 121, 123, 138, 141–2, 173, 233, 277–8, 289
Doughty, John, 53, 71, 96–7, 228, 287, 297, 299
Doughty, Thomas, *powers & part in venture*, 22, 31–2, 53; *drills soldiers*, 36; *attacks Mayo*, 39; *made captain of* Santa Maria, 45–8; *captain of* Pelican, 49–50; *put into* Swan, 52–6; *supernatural powers*, 53–4, 71; *returns to* Pelican, 64, 69; *put into* Elizabeth,

70–1; *accused*, 78–82; *trial &
execution*, 83–94; *burial*, 95–6,
117, 136, 140, 227–8, 260, 282–3,
301
Drake, Edmund (father of Francis), 46
Drake, Francis, *birth*, 46; *early career*,
9, 46; *San Juan de Ulloa*, 9, 20,
153–4, 187, 252–3; *Caribbean
raids*, 15–21, 43, 170; *character*,
19–21, 146, 169, 185, 193, 208–9,
224–8, 243–4, 253, 260, 280,
282–3, 304
descriptions of: by da Silva, 43–4;
by Johnny Greek, 147; *by de
Zarate*, 226, *by Miranda*, 238, *by
Vargas*, 243; *tactical methods*,
60–2, 148, 157, 183–4, 215, 221,
230, 234–5, 260; *native diplomacy*,
129, 142, 174; *collects charts*, 73,
132, 216, 268, 273; *criticism of*,
19–21, 54, 78–9, 225, 281, 292,
294–5; *Command Powers &
Commission*, 22–4, 31–2, 46, 56,
85, 87, 89–90, 261
quarrels with James Lyde, 30–2,
with Thomas Cuttill, 68–9, *with
Thomas Doughty*, 46–50, 52–3,
71, 78–82, *with Ned Bright?*, 104,
with Will Legge, 278–9; *Interrogation techniques*, 175–9, 190–1.
216–17, 220–6, 241, 245–6, 296
treatment of prisoners, 175–9, 185,
191–4, 216, 218–29, 231–3, 236,
238–43, 245–7, 296; *threats re
Oxenham*, 188–9; *in danger in
boat*, 62–3; *his cap stolen*, 64,
66–7; *fights Giants*, 75–9; *sermon
at Port St. Julian*, 98–103;
wounded Nombre de Dios, 43;
wounded Mocha, 124–5; '*painting*',
150, 226; *Drake Strait*, 118–21,
290; *which way home?*, 171,
189–91, 194–5, 202–5, 248, 250–1,
254, 256–61, 265; *gives gift,
cup/bowl*, 192–4; *letters to Winter*,
194; *Spanish pursuit*, 163–6,
198–212, 248–50, 253–6, 266;
Boasts to Spaniards, 200, 233,

243–4; *claims 40 ships*, 243;
names 'Nova Albion', 271; *achievements & losses*, 288–90; *sees the
Queen*, 294; *Spanish accusations*,
295–7; *knighted*, 299
Drake, Captain George, 301
Drake, John (cousin), 58, 66, 73, 75–6,
80, 116, 118, 125, 130, 146, 150,
160, 178, 180, 182, 218, 223, 272,
275, 277–8, 280–1, 285, 290, 293
Drake, Thomas (brother), 44–5, 47–8,
53, 63, 75, 79
Dürer, Albrecht, 213

Eliot, Lawrence, 296
Elizabeth I, 25–8, 32, 87, 89, 94, 101,
117, 167–70, 240, 286–7, 293–4,
297–9, 301
Enriquez, Don Martin, 153, 213, 215,
219–23, 229, 239–40, 247, 253–6,
258–61, 265
Eraso, Don Christobal de, 209–10
Esparza, 215, 218
Espinosa, Fray Alonso de, 10–11
Essex, Earl of, 32, 86, 89, 101

Falmouth, 29–30
Fenton, Edward, 300
Fletcher, Francis, *re Cape Blanc
natives*, 36; *Cape Verdes*, 39–40,
44; *attacks academics*, 40, 50,
108–9, 120, 123, 305; *attacks
Pope*, 40, 158; 47–9; *re tropics*,
50–1; 59; *re Drake's methods*,
60–2; *seal oil*, 60; *Seal Bay
natives*, 65–7; *graves at P. S.
Julian*, 74; *giants*, 76–8; *re
Doughty–Drake*, 79–80; *trial of
Doughty*, 84, 92–8, 104; *Strait of
Magellan*, 108–12; *storms*, 113–16
Mocha, 123–7; *Spanish colonial
rule*, 129; *sees treasure*, 185, 192;
Caño Is., 197; *preaches*, 231,
266–8; *California*, 269–74, 275,
277, 279–83, 297, 305; *his MSS*,
79–80, 127–8, 146
Flood, Thomas (*see* 'Hood')

Food (see 'Diet')
Fortesque, George, 297
Fouling of Ships, 31, 103, 134, 150
    (see also 'Careening')
Foxe, John, 239
France, 7, 298–9
Frobisher, Martin, 25, 27, 294, 303
Fry, John, 34–5
Fuego Island, 44

Gamboa, Pedro Sarmiento de, 129–32,
    142, 147, 154–5, 159, 163–6, 171,
    188–90, 199–206, 249–50, 265,
    274
Gatwick, 305
Galleys, 200, 209
Geography (see 'Navigation')
'Giants', 64–6, 75–8
Gibraltar, 29
Gilbert, Sir Humphrey, 25, 27, 294
Gold & Silver, 10, 11, 16, 24, 131–2,
    145, 154, 156, 162–3, 166, 172,
    178, 185, 213–14, 217 (see also
    'Mining')
Gomera, 32
Gomez, Juan, 245
Good Hope, Cape of, 61, 284–5
Greek, John the, 130–2, 147, 154, 164
Grenville, Sir Richard, expedition
    plans, 167–70, 292, 300, 303
Grenville, Roger, 292, 303
Guaras, Antonio de, 22
Guatalco, 224, 229–46, 249, 253–4,
    258–61, 265–6, 278, 295
Guatemala, 214, 220, 250, 254–5
Guayaquil, 200, 206–7
Guerre, Cape de, 35
Guerzo, Bartolomé, 235
Guns, invention of?, 276–7

Hakluyt, Richard, 193
Hall, 27
Hartob, Job, 256
Hatton, Sir Christopher, 21, 25, 32,
    63, 87, 89, 101–2, 105, 297
Havana, 198
Hawkins, Sir John, 9, 20–1, 32, 43,
    101, 117, 153, 187, 223, 226,

239–40, 252–3, 260, 285, 289,
    304–5
Hawkins, Sir Richard, 121
Hawkins, William, 297
Health of crews (see 'Diet')
Hernandez, Pedro, 225
Henry VIII, 7, 9, 15, 298
Hilliard, Nicolas, 299
Hispaniola, 9
Hood (or Flood), Thomas, 75, 85,
    100, 124, 126
Horsewell, Paul, 252–3
Howard, Lord Charles, 301, 304

Incas, 172, 213
Inquisition, 130, 153, 159, 166–70,
    188, 228, 232, 251–3, 261
Ireland, Spanish troops in, 293, 298

Jacome, Francisco, 175–9
Java, 284, 286
Jorje, Nicolas, 154–7, 173–6, 187,
    190, 192, 277
Joy, Cape, 60
Julian, Port St., 72–8; departure from,
    104–5

Ladrillero expedition, 107
Ladrone Islands, 275
Lambert, Cornieles, 216–17
Laws of Rhodes, Oleron, 29
Legge, Will, 278–9
Leicester, Earl of, 297
Lima, 107, 151, 153, 156–9, 163,
    166–70, 172, 194, 207, 228, 250,
    257
Lizarza, Domingo de, 186, 188–90
Loaysia expedition, 107, 112
Lok, Michael, 25
Lopez, Bernadino, 234–6, 243, 245–6

Mactan, 276
Madeira Islands, 8
Madrid, 292
Madrid, Juan de, 234, 241, 245–7
Magellan, Ferdinand, 9–10, 16–17,
    37–8, 78, 139, 275–6, 286,
    289–90; executes captains, 17, 23,
    56, 73–5, 93, 120

Magellan, Strait of, 17, 23, 29; *Drake*, 105-12, 119, 137, 167-70, 190, 260, 265
Manila galleons, 25, 151-2
Manta, 179, 200-1, 206
Marchmont, Seigneur de, 299
Marcks, Tom, 155
Maria, negress, 225, 278
Markham, William, 18, 100
Martin, Domingo, 173
Martin, Gaspar, 157, 160, 164
Mayas, 213
Mayo, 39-40
Medina, Juan Perez, 206
Mendana expedition, 129-30
Mendochino, Cape, 203, 273
Mendoza, Don Bernadino de, 293-5, 297-9
Mercury (in mining), 16
Messa, Diego, 216
Mexico (New Spain), 10, 213 14
Mexico City, 241, 252-3, 259
Mindanao, 276
Mines, Mining, 10, 145, 151, 213-14
Minivy, Richard, 137, 212
Miranda, Judge Gutierrez de, 235, 237-8
Miranda, Simon de, 234-8
Mocha Island, 123-7, 147, 269, 278
Mogador, 32-5
Moluccas, 274, 276, 285
Montalvo, Gaspar de, 174
More, Sir Thomas, 94
Morro Moreno, 142

Navigation & Cosmography, 25-7, 37-8, 40, 122-3, 150
Neil the Dane, 125
Nelson, Horatio, 305
Netherlands, 9, 10
Nicaragua, 191, 196, 201-2, 209-10, 266
Nombre de Dios, 15-16, 19, 170, 210-11, 226
North-East Passage, 9, 27, 189-90, 203-4, 303
North-West Passage, 9, 27, 190, 203-4, 267-8, 273-4, 294, 303

Norway, 189, 190, 203-4, 267

Oliver, master-gunner, 75-8, 140
Oxenham, John, 17-19, 153, 159-60, 163, 166-70, 188-9, 197, 202, 205, 215, 226, 228, 251, 295

Pacific, hazards of, 10, 16, 112, 139, 152, 273-4
Padilla, Don Antonio de, 292-3
Palacios, Judge Diego Garcia de, 219-20, 247-8
Palma, Fray Gaspar de, 206-8, 212
Panama, 15-20, 151-2, 157, 175, 182, 195-9, 201-2, 204-6, 208-15, 248-9, 255-7
Paraces, Giusepe de, 215-19, 250, 289, 297
Pascual, Juan, 225 6, 229-33, 237, 239, 246
Patagalana, Alonso Rodriguez, 162, 212, 289, 297
Payta, 173-4, 191, 200, 206
Peru, 10, 15, 172
Philip II, 7, 101, 167-70, 240, 292, 294
Philippines, 25, 151-2, 215, 218, 265, 276
Philips, Miles, 252-6, 300
Pigafetta, Antonio Francesco, 75, 79
Pinnaces, 18-19, 21, 34-7, 45, 53, 117, 134, 140, 157 (*see also* 'Ships')
Pizarro, Francisco, 172, 214
Plans ('Plots'), 22-8, 32, 87, 100 3, 167-71, 291
Plate Fleets, 151-3, 198, 209-10
Plate, River, 59-60, 140, 300
Plates, Plaques, Monuments, *at Cape Desire*, 112; '*uttermost Cape*', 121; *St. of Magellan*, 137; *California*, 271-2
Platter, Thomas, 301
Plymouth, 21, 30-1, 86, 88, 286, 288, 298
Pope Alexander, VI, 8
Porto Bello, 151
Portsmouth, 256, 302
Port St. Julian, 72-8, 104-5

Portugal, expansion overseas, 8–9, 11, 33, 38; Spanish occupation, 292
Potosí, 10, 145, 151, 154, 214
Provisions (see 'Diet')

Quesada, Gaspar de, 74
Quilca, 157
Quito, 207

Raleigh, Sir Walter, 300
Realejo, 219–20, 229, 247
Reinea, Sanchez de, 75
Religion, 10, 40, 128, 131, 158–9, 174, 187–8, 217–8, 232–3, 236, 238–40, 243, 245, 252
Rengifo, Francisco Gomez, 234–40, 242–3, 245
Robles, Dr. Hernando, 254–5
Rock, on the, 279–83, 289
Rodriguez, Alonzo Bautista Patagalana, 161–2, 212, 289, 297
Rodriguez, Custodio, 173–4, 185, 191–2, 196, 200, 216
Ronquillo, Don Gregorio, 215, 234

San Francisco, Cape, 175, 180, 182, 204
San Juan de Ullao (Veracruz), 9, 20, 153–4, 187, 222–3, 240, 252–4, 289
Santiago, 40–1, 129, 131
Saracold, John, 52–3, 55–6, 84
Sarmiento (see 'Gamboa')
Seal Bay, 63–9
Ships of Henry VIII:
    Jesus of Lubeck, 153
    Mary Rose, 29, 292, 303
Ships of the Hawkins expedition:
    Judith, 20, 252–3
    Minion, 20, 252
Ships of Magellan:
    Concepción, 74
    San Antonio, 74
    Victoria, 74, 107
Ship of Camargo preserved at Callao, 107
Ships of the Drake expedition:
    Pelican/Golden Hind: size & arma-
    ment, 21, 31, 42–3, 100, 104, 148–50, 164, 166–7, 176–7, 186, 188, 215, 221, 227, 242–4; incendiaries, 166–7; crew numbers, 147–8, 156, 164, 177, 186–7, 235, 244, 277–9, 285, 288; crew nationalities, 150, 239; renamed Golden Hind, 105, storm damage, 30; on the Rock, 279–83, 289; pretends to be ship of Miguel Angel, 161, 182, 220; put on show, 299, 301–2
    Elizabeth: size & armament, 18, 31, 43, 62–4, 70–2, 99–100, 103, 116–17, 121, 134, 136–42, 194, 197, 277, 282, 288
    Swan: 21, 52; missing, 60–1, 63; found, 64; to be broken up; burnt Seal Bay, 68, 71, 288
    Marigold: 21, 30, 35, 43, 63, 99–100, 104; sinks, 114, 117, 121, 288
    Bark Benedict (Christopher): 18–19, 21–2; boy lost, 33; exchanged for Canter, 36; missing, 59–60; rejoins, 63; missing again & found, 69; abandoned, 70–1, 288
Prefabricated Pinnaces:
    Pinnace assembled Mogador, 34, 45
    Pinnace exchanged for Santa Maria, 45
    Pinnace lost (Peter Carder), 117
    Pinnace assembled Bahia Saluda, 134, 141
    Pinnace assembled by Winter, 140; and lost, 141
    Pinnace exchanged for Tello's bark, 218–19
    Tello's bark burnt California, 272
Santa Maria (prize name Mary): 43–9; exchanged for pinnace, 45; missing, 53; missing again, 63–4, 71–2; sighted, 72; stripped & abandoned Port St. Julian, 103, 288; cargo found in Elizabeth, 290–2
Drake's temporary prizes off Africa: Canters & Caravels, 35–6

Drake's temporary prizes off America:
Capitana (Grand Captain of the South): of Licentiate Torres, 129–30, 132, 134–5, 154; cast off, 156; spoils, 188, 297
Ship of Felipe Corco, 154; cast off, 156
Ship of Jorje Diaz, 154; burnt, 155
Ship of Bernal Bueno, 155–6; cast off, 156
Ship of Francisco Truxillo, 157
Ship of Miguel Angel (Nuestra Señora de Valle), 157, 161, 163
Ship of Andres Murielo, (Nao de Muriles?), 157, 163
Ship of Sebastian Perez, 166
Ship of San Juan de Anton (Nuestra Señora de la Concepción: Cacafuego), 158, 166, 175, 177, 179; sighted, 180–2; taken, 183–95, 249
Ship from Panama (San Cristobal) of Alonso Rodriguez Bautista Patagalana, 161–4
Bark bound for Lima, 172–3
Ship of Custodio Rodriguez, 173, 200
Bark of Benito Diaz Bravo, 175–9, 200, 206, 297
Bark of Cataro, 199
Ship of Mondragon, 208
Ship of Chaves, 210
Bark of Rodrigo Tello, 215, 217–19, 223, 247–8
Ship of D. S. de Zarate, 220–30, 242, 248, 278
Ship of Juan de Madrid, 234, 241, 245–7
Shipworm (see 'Careening' & 'Fouling of Ships')
Silver (see 'Gold & Silver')
Sierra Leone, 285
Silva, Nuño da (see 'Da Silva')
Smith, Hugh, 94
Solano, Captain Juan, 247
Solomon Islands, 129
Sonsonate, 174, 196, 203, 216, 220, 226, 234, 266

Sotomayor, Simon de Alcazaba, 107
Southampton, 182
Spain: expansion overseas, 7–11, 32–3; colonial policy, 10–11, 40, 129
Drake rumours & defiance, 207–8, 210–12, 248–9
Pursuit of Drake, 163–6, 198–212, 248–50, 254–6, 266
Spice Islands, 8, 24, 216, 268, 274, 276–7
Spindelay, Henry, 54
'Stockfish', Strait of (see 'Bacallaos')
Stores, 30–1
Sumatra, 284
Sunda, 284
Sussex, Earl of, 298
Sydenham, Elizabeth, 300

Tarapaca, 145
Tehuantepec, 223, 230
Tello, Rodrigo, 215
Tenerife, 11, 32–3, 305
Ternate, 276–7, 284–5
Terra australis incognita, 108–9, 113, 115, 120
Thomas, John, 21, 35, 63, 75, 85–6, 89, 100, 105, 114, 162, 212
Tidore, 276
Tierra del Fuego, 111
Toledo, Don Francisco, 159, 163, 165–6, 179, 188, 194, 199, 204, 208, 211, 247–50
Toledo, Don Luis, 199, 201–2, 205–6, 249
Tordesillas, Treaty of, 8, 187
Torres, Licentiate, 130
Treasure (Drake's), 293–8
Trejo, General Diego de Frias, 163, 165, 199, 201–2, 205–6, 249
Tremayne, Edmund, 26

Valdivia, 129
Vallano, Pass of, 189, 206, 209, 257–8, 265
Valle, 157
Valparaiso, 129
Valverde, Licentiate, 247, 256–8, 265

Vargas, Gaspar de, 234–5, 241–2, 244, 247, 253, 260
Vas, Lopez, 81
Velasco, Don Luis de, 253–4, 265
Veracruz, 153
Verde, Cape Islands, 8, 33, 38–46, 286
Vermilion Gulf, 256, 266
Vicary, Leonard, 28–9, 84, 88
Virginia, 300

Walsingham, Sir Francis, 32, 87, 89, 101, 294–5, 297
Watkins, Emanuel, 84
Whitbread's Round-the-World Races (1973 & 1977), 302
Willoughby, 25
Winter, George, 18, 137

Winter, John, 18, 21–2; takes canters, 35; attacks Mayo, 39; blames Drake at Santiago, 41, 44–7, 58, 61–5, 84, 86, 91, 94, 98–100, 103–5, 115–16; turns back, 136–42, 194, 197, 218, 250–1, 290–2
Winter, Sir William, 18, 101, 137
Winterhey, Robert, 75–8, 140
Worrall, 100, 104
Wright, Benjamin, 301

'Xerores', Thomas, 159, 163, 166, 170, 251, 295

Zacatecas, 214
Zarate, Don Francisco de, 81, 83, 220–30, 242, 250